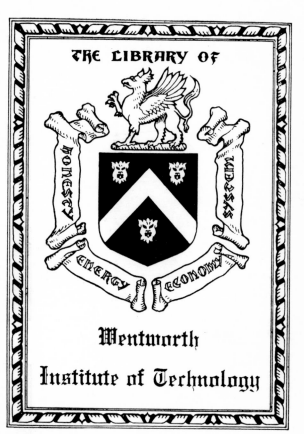

THE LIBRARY OF

HONESTY

SYSTEM

ENERGY ECONOMY

Wentworth

Institute of Technology

To student learning
May it forever bloom in
David D'Agostino's memory

The Electronic Design Studio

The Electronic Design Studio

Architectural Knowledge and Media
in the Computer Era

edited by Malcolm McCullough,
William J. Mitchell, and Patrick Purcell

The MIT Press
Cambridge, Massachusetts
London, England

This book was set in Palatino and printed and bound in the United States of America.

Library of Congress Cataloging-in-Publication Data

The Electronic design studio: architectural knowledge and media in the computer era
/ edited by Malcolm McCullough, William J. Mitchell, and Patrick Purcell.
    p. cm.
   Includes bibliographical references.
   ISBN 0-262-13254-0
    1. Architectural design—Data processing.   2. Computer-aided design.
  3. Architectural design—Study and teaching.
  I. McCullough, Malcolm.   II. Mitchell, William J. (William John). 1944–
  III. Purcell, Patrick.
  NA2728.E44   1990
  720'.285—dc20   89-48106
                                                                      CIP

Contents

Information Delivery Systems for Design

Preface

Design is the computation of shape information that is needed to guide fabrication or construction of artifacts. But it is not so straightforward as, say, the computation of numerical information required to balance a checkbook. This is partly because algebras of shapes are not as well understood and precisely formalized as algebras of numbers, partly because the rules for carrying out shape computations tend to be fluid and ill defined and partly because the predicates that must be satisfied to achieve successful termination are often complex and difficult to specify.

For centuries architects have carried out shape computations by hand, using informal procedures and the simplest of tools. Over the last two decades, though, they have made increasing use of more formal procedures executed by computers. It is still too early to be sure of the gains and losses that follow from this development, but there is no doubt that it raises some challenging questions of architectural theory and some perplexing issues for those concerned with the future of architectural education. This book frames those issues and provides a diversity of perspectives on them. Its contents were initially presented at the CAAD Futures 89 Conference—an international gathering of researchers and teachers in the field of computer-aided architectural design which was jointly sponsored by the Harvard Graduate School of Design and the MIT Department of Architecture and held in Cambridge, Massachusetts, in July 1989.

There are four major sections: Theoretical Foundations, Knowledge-Based Design Tools, Information Delivery Systems, and Case Studies: Electronic Media in the Design Studio. In a representatative collection of current views, over thirty extensively illustrated papers discuss the experiences of universities in the USA, Europe, Japan, Israel, Canada, and Australia, articulate present theoretical and practical concerns, provide criticism of media and methods, and suggest directions for the future. Architectural educators and architects concerned with the effect of computer technology on the design process will find here an indispensable reference and a rich source of ideas.

This book was itself prepared in an electronic design studio. Composition and typography, most image collection and placement, and such editing as was practical within this publishing format, were all performed digitally using Macintosh computers at the Harvard Graduate School of Design during a period of a few weeks in 1989.

Introduction:
A New Agenda for Computer-Aided Design

William J. Mitchell

Harvard University Graduate School of Design

Design is the computation of shape information that is needed to guide fabrication or construction of an artifact. This information normally specifies artifact topology (connections of vertices, edges, surfaces, and closed volumes), dimensions, angles, and tolerances on dimensions and angles. There may also be associations of symbols with subshapes to specify material and other such properties.

The process of design takes different forms in different contexts, but the most usual computational operations are transformations (unary operations) and combinations (binary operations) of shapes in a two-dimensional drawing or a three-dimensional geometric model. An initial vocabulary of shapes, together with a repertoire of shape transformation and combination operators, establishes the shape algebra within which the computation takes place.

The computation terminates successfully when it can be shown that certain predicates are satisfied by a shape produced by recursively applying the transformation and combination operators to the initial vocabulary. These predicates are usually stated in symbolic (verbal or numerical) form. Thus determination of whether a predicate is satisfied usually involves producing a numerical or verbal interpretation of a drawing, then deriving inferences from this interpretation by applying rules or formulae.

This definition may seem provocatively reductionist and to leave little room for creativity. But I shall argue, in this paper, that taking a computational view of design can reveal precisely where creativity enters and why we intuitively take it to be characteristic of all but the most trivial design processes. In particular, I shall focus on the roles of ambiguity and discontinuity in shape interpretation, instability in the rules for carrying out shape computations, and nonmonotinicity in critical reasoning to determine whether or not a design proposal is complete and satisfactory. My examples will be taken from the sphere of architecture, but I shall provide a general theoretical treatment that applies to many other areas of design as well.

Describing and Manipulating Shape

A computer drafting system (or three-dimensional modeling system) models a shape algebra in essentially the same way that a four-function electronic calculator models the familiar algebra of real numbers. The calculator's display shows a number in the set of numbers that carries the number algebra, and the drafting system's display shows a shape in the set of shapes that carry the shape algebra. The calculator's keyboard provides a set of operators (addition, subtraction, multiplication, division) for manipulating numbers, and the drafting system's menu provides a set of operators for manipulating shapes (insertion, deletion, translation, rotation, and so on). The calculator is useful because we can employ numbers to represent balances in bank accounts, or areas of rooms, and we can then employ operations on numbers to represent operations on bank accounts or rooms. The drafting system is useful because we can use shapes to represent spaces and construction components, and we can then employ operations on shapes to represent operations on those entities. For this to work, however, it is essential that the formal properties of the algebra that is modeled correspond appropriately to the structure of the situation that we wish to represent. Let us, then, consider the formal properties of shape algebras.

One very common approach to formalization and computer implementation of a shape algebra emerged in the earliest days of computer-aided design. It is founded on the idea that a straight line segment can be described by the coordinates of its endpoints. A shape can thus be described as a set of lines, or equivalently as a set of vertex coordinate pairs or triples together with a relation of connection in that set. Basic editing operations follow directly: lines can be added by specifying and associating endpoints, and deleted by disassociating endpoints. It also follows that translation, rotation, reflection, scaling, shearing, and perspective transformations can be performed by multiplication of coordinate vectors by transformation matrices. This idea provided a foundation for Ivan Sutherland's pioneering Sketchpad system, and a quarter of a century later it is still the basis of popular computer drafting systems such as Autocad.

The idea of describing a geometric element by specifying its boundaries can be generalized. Just as a zero-dimensional points bound one-dimensional lines, so one-dimensional lines bound two-dimensional surfaces, and two-dimensional surfaces bound three-dimensional solids. This insight provides the basis for the data structures of surface modeling systems and solid modeling systems, with their extended sets of editing operations—sweeping to create surfaces, and the spatial set operations on closed solids.

In a retrospective article, Sutherland (1975) suggested that "the usefulness of computer drawings is precisely their structured nature." The behavior of such drawings, he noted, "is critically dependent upon the topological and geometric structure built up in the computer memory as a result of drawing operations." Traditional drawings, by contrast, have no inherent structure, and are merely "dirty marks on paper."

It is a short step from recognition that structure is important to the idea that a CAD system should automatically *maintain* structure as a designer manipulates a geometric model. If a designer shifts an element, for example, neighboring elements should be adjusted to maintain specified alignments and attachments. Sutherland introduced the idea of constraints that could be specified by a designer and thereafter maintained by a CAD system. Eastman (1978) later explored it in the context of three-dimensional solid modelers. More recently the idea of generalized constraint programming languages has emerged (Leler, 1988), and has found some application in computer-aided design. Gross (1989) has implemented an interesting prototype CAD system built around concepts of constraint maintenance.

The idea of modeling in terms of geometric elements, combined with maintenance of relationships between elements, proved to be a useful and durable one. But its inherent limitations began to show up when attempts were made to use CAD systems for design exploration, rather than just representation of completed designs.

First, the structure that a designer puts into a drawing or geometric model by virtue of input operations is a limiting one. The only subshapes that it allows the designer to indicate or manipulate are subsets of the elements. Emergent subshapes are, from the computer's viewpoint, unrecognizable. Designers, however, frequently recognize emergent subshapes, and subsequently structure their understanding of the design and their reasoning about it in terms of emergent entities and relationships—ones that they never explicitly input. When this happens there is a mismatch between the way that a CAD system is explicitly structuring the design and the way that the designer is implicitly structuring it, so the explicit structure becomes a hindrance rather than a help.

The problem is compounded by the propensity of designers to see the same shapes as different things in different contexts and on different occasions. This is most dramatic in the case of so-called ambiguous figures, such as the famous one that can be seen either as a rabbit or as a duck (but not both at once). More "creatively" it can also be seen as a front elevation of an asymmetrical Cyclops. Which structure should be maintained—that of a rabbit, that of a duck, or that of a Cyclops?

Ambiguous figures might be dismissed as bizarre anomalies but, in fact, any figure has competing readings. The following, for example, can be seen as two large triangles, or as four small triangles, or as two parallelograms, or as a pair of vertical bowties, or as a diamond bracketed by an epsilon and a reflected epsilon, or in many other ways as well (Reed 1974, Stiny 1989). There is, in fact, a substantial psychological literature on alternative structural descriptions of figures and the roles that these play in cognition (Hinton 1979, Palmer 1977).

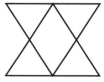

Seeing a shape as different things, I must emphasize, is not just an idle game. The act of assigning it to a class is an act of defining which of its properties are to be taken as essential and therefore maintained during design manipulations (if the shape is not unintentionally to become a thing of another kind), and which of its properties are to be taken as accidental and therefore subject to variation. If you see the following object as a square you can translate, rotate, reflect, and scale it, but you cannot change its proportions since its particular proportions are characteristic of squares. If you see it as an instance of a rectangle you *can* change its proportions but not its vertex angles. If you just see it as four lines you can shift and resize these lines in any way that you want.

Conversely, if you translate, rotate, reflect or scale this object you are tacitly treating it as a square. If you scale it unequally you are treating it as a rectangle. If you shear it you are treating it as a parallelogram, and if you otherwise shift and resize the lines you are just treating it as a line figure. You may want to treat it in different ways at different moments.

Different readings of shapes also induce development and refinement in different directions. What further operations are suggested by the rabbit/duck? If you see it as a duck you may (like Robert Venturi) want to substitute a decorated shed. If you see it as a rabbit you may (like Elmer Fudd) want to perform some violent transformation on the rascal. What can you make out of the "two-triangle" figure by displacing its parts?

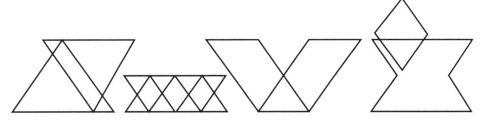

A further twist is given to the problem if different designers operate on the same representation—a possibility that is often claimed as an important advantage of CAD systems. What if they all see a shape as different things? What if some of them are "aspect-blind", and cannot see the shape as others see it? (Wittgenstein raised the question of aspect-blindness in *Philosophical Investigations* (1968), and suggested that the aspect-blind would have "an altogether different relationship to pictures from ours.") What if, by virtue of the particular structure that it imposes, the CAD system itself is significantly aspect-blind?

An impatient practical man might reply that this is all very well, but ambiguity is just a bad thing—precisely the sort of sloppiness that a CAD system, built on sound engineering principles, should root out. You should just take the commonsense course of deciding what a thing is, assigning it an appropriate structure, and sticking with that. But design is not description of what *is*, it is exploration of what *might be*. Drawings are valuable precisely because they are rich in suggestions of what might be. To blind oneself to these suggestions by imposing a rigid, Procrustean structure on a drawing is to impoverish the creative imagination.

Thus the meaning of a drawing is not adequately captured by imposing *one* structure on it. The last thing that I want, as a designer, is a clanking mechanism doggedly maintaining some structure that is, for me, irrelevant and forgotten. Perhaps an analogy with word processing will make this clear. It would be absurd if your word processor allowed you to change *Time flies like an arrow* into *Time flies like a boomerang* but not (because of the syntax that you had assigned to the sentence by virtue of your input actions) into *Australian flies like a sheep.* Maintenance of structure is useless, and perhaps actively detrimental, unless a system also provides for convenient, fluid restructuring, and for parallel maintenance of alternative structures.

To my knowledge, no such systems yet exist in industrial strength—although there has been some experimentation with small-scale prototypes—and it will be a formidable task to build them. But some theoretical foundations have been laid, particularly by George Stiny (1989). If we really want CAD systems to support creative design exploration (not just representation and analysis of completed designs) we will need to break away from simplistic, rigid notions of structure, and face up to the difficult problems of building systems that are sufficiently flexible and pluralistic in their handling of it.

Formalizing Design Rules

The earliest idea about computational treatment of design rules was that they could be expressed as procedures which would accept design requirements as input and produce appropriate shape information as output. Such a procedure might, for example, accept a list of rooms together with area and adjacency requirements and produce a plan that satisfied those requirements. This was consistent with the dogma of early modernism that architectural design was a matter of satisfying an established set of requirements as closely and efficiently as possible, and it was also consistent with early, procedurally-oriented approaches to programming in languages like Fortran.

Much useful research was done within this paradigm, and sometimes this resulted in programs that actually worked. In the mid-1970s, for example, Philip Steadman, Robin Liggett and I published an efficient, rigorous procedure for producing small rectangular floor plans that satisfied adjacency, area, and dimensional constraints, and that minimized total floor area (Mitchell, Steadman, and Liggett 1976, Steadman 1983).

A fundamental limitation of this approach, however, is that it requires design rules to be expressed in a very cumbersome and artificial way—strictly in terms of the constructs provided by procedural programming languages. A clever programmer can certainly do this, but the architectural content of the resulting code is very difficult to comprehend, and this makes it difficult to subject the rule system to critical scrutiny. Furthermore, the rules are inextricably intertwined with information that specifies a strategy for applying them, so it is usually very difficult to isolate and modify them.

But human designers learn. They see the work of others, become sensitive to new issues, become aware of new possibilities, respond to criticism, and constantly modify the rules that they apply. We usually call this stylistic evolution. It may take the form of sweeping stylistic change, or that of refinement and elaboration of an established style. In any case it is an essential component of creative design, and we must provide for it in CAD systems that are seriously intended to support creative design. Further evidence for this need is provided by the experience of those who have attempted to implement rule-based design systems, and have typically found that they must spend a great deal of time tinkering with the rules to get them to produce the right sorts of results.

Adoption of a more modular and declarative style of programming is an important step in the right direction. If rules are expressed as productions, for example, they are decoupled from control information, and it becomes convenient to add rules, delete rules, and modify rules. It is possible to adapt and tune a rule system in incremental, experimental fashion. Some sort of general inference engine can be used to apply the rule system in whatever form it currently exists.

There are now many ways to set up production systems that encode design rules. You can build them in Lisp, or you can take advantage of Prolog's high-level facilities for processing rules expressed in the format of first-order logic. Numerous shells for knowledge-based systems provide facilities for expression of rules in *if . . . then* format. A shape grammar is also a production system, with the additional advantage that it expresses rules directly in terms of shapes rather than in terms of some symbolic calculus. The following rule, for example, shows one thing you can do with a square—one possible compositional move.

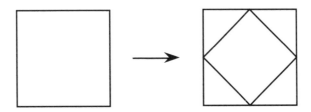

By sketching you can rapidly discover other things to do with squares—some of them interesting and some of them not. By remembering the interesting ones you can establish a grammar for composing squares, then you can go on to explore the language specified by that grammar. If you think of some more interesting things you can add corresponding rules to the grammar, and thus structure a new terrain for design exploration. (See Knight (1986) for a detailed discussion of the way that changing the rules changes a designer's output.)

Shape rules can be thought of as stereotyped responses to stereotyped situations, and therefore as constraints on the free play of the imagination. This was certainly the position of the romantics, who opposed the hegemony of classical rules. But the imagination needs something to play *with*. Though the consequence of applying a given rule to a given shape is plain to see, the consequences of *recursively* applying a rule *system* to that shape can be very surprising. The rules of a grammar are not limiting prescriptions, but tools for constructing a path from the known to the unknown—tools that can be changed if they do not seem to get you to the right place.

What sorts of shape rules *should* a designer use to structure paths into the unknown? Useful and interesting sets of shape rules are, I think, those that yield a lot for a little. Any set of designs can be generated in an uninteresting way by a grammar that has a rule to produce each of the designs in the set, but it is no advantage to a designer to know this sort of grammar. It *is* advantageous, however, to know a concise grammar, with few but powerful rules, that specifies an extensive and interesting set of designs. It has been shown that such concise yet powerful grammars can be provided for interesting and important bodies of architectural design work (Stiny and Mitchell 1978, Mitchell 1989).

Graphically-expressed shape rules are much easier for a designer to understand and criticize than, say, pages of Prolog, so there is good reason to suggest that shells for building knowledge-based design systems should take the form of shape grammar interpreters that can be programmed graphically, and that allow quick and easy modification of rules. Some interesting prototype systems of this sort have been developed (Mitchell, Liggett, and Tan 1989, Nagakura 1989, Tan 1989).

The interface details of systems for building and applying sets of design rules are less important, however, than the general point that we should focus on the expression of design rules in declarative, modular, easily-understood, and easily modifiable format. In other words, we should think of design systems as open, flexible, constantly-evolving knowledge-capture devices rather than static collections of familiar tools and dispensers of established wisdom. When we can do this I think we will see the emergence of design systems that do not just mechanically assemble banalities, but that have real style and flair.

Control Strategies for Design Processes
The earliest (and still the most basic) idea here was that designing could be understood as a process of state-space search. Herbert Simon gave classic expression to this in *The Sciences of the Artificial* (1981)—suggesting that possession of effective heuristics for searching was an important aspect of design competence, and I emphasized it strongly in my *Computer-Aided Architectural Design* (1977). In his essay "Style in Design" Simon (1975) went on to ask, "Why do we think the architect is synthesizing, or even 'creating'

when he makes the layout?" His reply was, "Because he solves his problem by moving through a large combinatorial space in which he adds one element after another to his design . . . The richness of the combinatorial space in which the problem solver moves . . . is the hallmark of design creativity."

The theory of search has been investigated extensively. Basic distinctions have been made between breadth-first and depth-first search, and between top-down and bottom-up strategies. The idea has been elaborated by introduction of ideas of abstraction and planning in search spaces. Some successful architectural CAD software has been based on the idea of sophisticated searching within very large state-spaces. Some floor plan layout programs, for example, use statistical estimates of the probability of finding a good solution to choose between alternative placements (Liggett and Mitchell, 1981).

But searching is not the answer to everything. We know now that many of the most interesting design problems, when formulated for solution by search, turn out not to be amenable to rigorous solution with a feasible amount of computation (Garey and Johnson, 1978). The attitude has grown, in the artificial intelligence community, that extensive searching is usually a bad idea—something to be attempted only when you can think of nothing better to do. Instead of doing a lot of searching guided by relatively little knowledge about a problem domain, we should emphasize limited searching guided by a lot of specialized knowledge about the particular domain of interest.

What, specifically, does this general principle (now almost a platitude) mean in the context of design? My speculation is that a designer needs to know where to direct attention in an evolving design, and needs some mechanism for indexing knowledge by shape so that it can be evoked by paying attention to a particular conditions in a design. The left-sides of shape rules in a shape grammar can be thought of as definitions of the conditions that a designer should watch out for and possibly pay attention to as a design develops, and the right-sides specify responses that can be evoked for consideration by the occurrence of particular conditions. Typically (as in the example below), left-sides will consist of patterns of abstractions and construction lines, while right-sides tell how to develop these, in various different directions, into more detailed and explicit depictions of elements and subsystems.

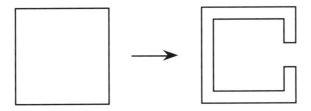

Alternative right-sides associated with a given left side specify the different things that an abstraction might be developed into. By adding the following rule to a grammar, for example, we record the suggestion that a square *parti* might be developed either into a room (by the rule above) or into a pyramid.

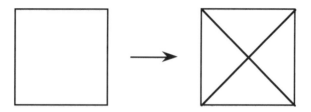

My experience of teaching design studios has provided me with a good deal of anecdotal evidence that designers use weak and general rules for combining fairly abstract and ambiguous shapes at early stages in design processes, then use stronger and more specific rules for combining shapes with unambiguous meaning at later stages. At an early stage, for example, it might be unclear whether a given line is to be taken as a construction line or a wall of a room, and lines might be combined according to very general rules of rhythm, proportion, and symmetry. At a later stage, shapes unambiguously stand for doors, windows, walls, columns, beams, and so on, and their combination is guided by rules that encode knowledge of how these components function and how they must be interfaced to each other. The following rule, for example, tells how to relate an entry step appropriately to a door.

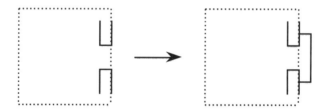

At early stages visual metaphors seem to play an important role. A designer might pursue the thought that a building could be like a tree, or like an elemental primitive hut, or like a human body. These metaphors provide abstract structures that can be developed towards proposals for buildings by applying rules that substitute shapes with more precise architectural reference for construction lines that have been extracted from another context.

The lesson to be learned from this is, I suggest, that skilled architectural designers use sophisticated, domain-specific control strategies when they develop rough sketches into detailed, finished designs. These strategies can be expressed, in a direct and natural way, by means of shape rules that have patterns of abstractions and construction lines on their left-sides. We will, I think, make faster progress towards the development of truly creative computer-aided design systems if we shift our focus from ideas about search, control, and planning imported from theorem-proving and game-playing to consideration of what designers actually do when they draw.

Knowing When a Design is Finished

There is a famous paradox in Plato's *Meno* which seems to suggest the impossibility of truly creative thought. The protagonist asks Socrates how it is ever possible to attain new knowledge. If you know what you are looking for, he suggests, it will not really be new to you when you find it. But if you don't know what you are looking for, if you can't put forth something definite as the subject of inquiry, you will have absolutely no way of ever knowing that you have found it, and the search will never terminate. Turing provided us with a modern resolution. We can establish a process for generating information to consider (propositions, or numbers, or shapes), and we can specify a test which determines whether a given piece of information is that for which we are looking—the solution to our problem. When we have generated some information that passes the test we have solved the problem, and the process terminates. More specifically, in the context of design, we can set forth the requirements that a shape must satisfy, then attempt to instantiate a shape that does so. The design is successfully completed when we can show that we have a shape which satisfies the requirements. We may never have seen this shape before we make it explicit for consideration: it may be genuinely new and surprising to us.

In the early days of CAD this was seen as a matter of stating programmatic and technical requirements, then applying analysis procedures to a database to determine whether or not these requirements were satisfied (Maver, 1988). A floor plan layout program, for example, might incorporate procedures to test a proposed plan for compliance with given room adjacency and area requirements. This approach was a very direct extension of the traditions of engineering analysis that had begun with Galileo's analysis of designs for a cantilever beam to determine whether they would prove strong enough.

Clearly this approach was, and continues to be, very useful. But analysis procedures certainly have not supplanted human critics. Why?

One reason is that architectural designs (as opposed to some sorts of engineering designs) often have extraordinarily complex entailments. Buildings perform subtle economic, social, and cultural roles, and these can only be understood adequately by reasoning about them in the light of extensive economic, social, and cultural knowledge. It might be possible, in principle, to build artificial critics that could apply such broad-based knowledge to produce detailed, useful evaluations of design proposals, but no such systems have emerged so far. The evaluations and appraisals that CAD systems *do* successfully produce are extremely narrowly focused.

A second problem may be thought of as a special case of the well-known "frame problem" in artificial intelligence (Dennett 1984). How do you know what possible consequences of a design proposal should be given attention and explored? There are indefinitely many ways that a design does *not* fail, but most of these are irrelevant. Why doesn't a critic spend time carefully demonstrating, to everybody's satisfaction, that painting the walls yellow won't cause the bathtub to explode? This is a perfectly valid line of inference, but not one that is worthwhile to pursue. Clearly the critic has some way of knowing which parts of the indefinitely extensive entailment of a design are worth attention and which are not, but precisely *how* the critic knows this is a very difficult (and I think unsolved) problem.

It might seem that the issue could be settled by setting forth an *a priori* agenda of relevant issues for consideration. In well-defined problems, such as chess problems and theorem-proving problems, it is fairly straightforward to provide a complete specification of what is required. But in creative design, characteristically, this is impossible: issues and solution criteria are evoked contextually as the design takes shape (Reitman 1965, Akin 1986). You do not necessarily know what you want until you see what you can have. Nor do you know what to avoid until you have seen some failures. So the critical agenda may evolve and change as the design possibilities structured by shape rules are made explicit, and may not, in fact, stabilize until the point of termination has almost been reached. The most original and incisive criticism is often so because it departs from established agendas, establishes new issues for consideration, and reshapes the discourse.

Furthermore, different presumptions about what a thing is meant to be, or needs to be, or just might be, lead to different diagnoses of what it lacks. If you see that a shape might be a duck you can, from the rule *All ducks have feathers*, derive the criticism that the proposal lacks feathers, and suggest that feathers must be added to yield a complete and satisfactory design. But if you are more interested in its potential rabbithood you can, from the rule *No rabbits have feathers* derive the critical conclusion that addition of feathers would *not* be an appropriate way to complete the design. In general, a designer's sketch is an incomplete, ambiguous, and possibly inconsistent depiction of a possible artifact. Thus it allows contradictory observations to be made and contradictory critical inferences to be drawn from these. Design development is, in large part, a matter of identifying and resolving these inconsistencies: hence the frequent critical comment that a design in its early stages is still "unresolved". It is only in the endgame of design, when the final details are being worked out within a well-established overall framework, that there is value in the mechanisms for automatically maintaining semantic integrity of designs that have so frequently been proposed for CAD systems (Borkin 1986, Eastman 1987, Kalay 1989).

A final problem, and perhaps the most important one, is that analysis programs work within a framework of strictly monotonic reasoning. They draw critical conclusions from observations of the design together with some fairly stable, consistent body of facts and rules about the world. Adding facts and rules, or new observations about the design, should never invalidate critical conclusions that have already been drawn. But interesting critical discussion, as heard at architectural juries for example, is not really much like that. In fact, it exhibits the classic hallmarks of *nonmonotonic* discourse (Ginsberg, 1987). Conclusions are frequently modified or retracted when critics notice things about the design that they had not noticed before, or evoke knowledge of the world that had not previously seemed relevant, or revise their beliefs in the face of argument. From the observation that a room has no windows a critic might, for example, conclude that it would be intolerably stuffy. A second critic might challenge this conclusion by observing that the room could easily be served by airconditioning. A third critic might respond that airconditioning would be too expensive, and so on. All these critical conclusions hold in the absence of information to the contrary—but such information might be on the tip of another critic's tongue.

In sum, it is unrealistic to assume that a definitive, consistent set of design requirements can always be established ahead of time in order to provide an ironclad test for a solution. A creative design proposal may, in fact, provide a challenge to established beliefs and critical agendas. We should recognize that architectural designs are tested against a rich and complex interpretational discourse that develops in parallel with the processes of establishing design rules and making design possibilities explicit.

Conclusion

Ivan Sutherland's idea of structured design representation in computer memory, the Galilean tradition of design validation by analysis for compliance with predefined criteria, and faith in stable, universal design rules, provided the foundation on which computer-aided architectural design was initially built. But we should not remain prisoners of these ideas. Close consideration of the phenomenology of design exploration and the epistemology of criticism suggests that we must embrace the possibilities of designs that have ambiguous and unstable structural descriptions, of constructive rule systems that are provisional, fluid, and mutable as we discover what they can produce, and of critical reasoning that is not bound by assumptions of monotonicity. These issues are not, I suggest, ones that arise under anomalous conditions that can safely be ignored in mainstream, "practical" CAD systems. On the contrary, their centrality is *characteristic* of creative design processes.

I do not see the emergence of these complexities as cause for pessimism. The great achievement of pioneering work in CAD has been to construct a sufficiently rigorous and comprehensive theoretical framework to allow clear identification of these issues and appreciation of their importance. The challenge now is to build a new generation of CAD systems that responds to them in sophisticated ways. The language games that architects play are subtle, and require commensurately subtle instruments.

References

Akin, Omer. 1986. *Psychology of Architectural Design*. London: Pion.

Borkin, Harold. 1986. "Spatial and Nonspatial Consistency in Design Systems." *Environment and Planning B* 13: 207-222.

Dennett, Daniel. 1984. "Cognitive Wheels: The Frame Problem in AI." In Christopher Hookway (ed.), *Minds, Machines and Evolution*. Cambridge: Cambridge University Press.

Eastman, Charles M. 1978. "The Representation of Design Problems and Maintenance of their Structure." In Jean-Claude Latombe (ed.), *Artificial Intelligence and Pattern Recognition in Computer-Aided Design*. Amsterdam: North-Holland.

Eastman, Charles M. 1987. "Fundamental Problems in the Development of Computer-Based Architectural Design Models." In Yehuda E. Kalay (ed.), *Computability of Design*. New York: John Wiley.

Garey, M. R., and D. S. Johnson. 1978. "Strong NP-Completeness Results: Motivation, Examples, and Applications." *Journal of the Association of Computing Machinery* 25, no. 3: 499-508.

Ginsberg, Mathew L. 1987. *Readings in Nonmonotonic Reasoning*. Los Altos, California: Morgan Kaufmann.

Gross, Mark. 1989. "Relational Modeling--A Basis for Computer-Assisted Design." This volume.

Hinton, G. E. 1979. "Some Demonstrations of the Effects of Structural Descriptions in Mental Imagery." *Cognitive Science* 3: 231-250.

Kalay, Yehuda E. 1989. *Modeling Objects and Environments*. New York: John Wiley.

Knight, Terry Weissman. 1986. *Transformations of Languages of Designs*. Ph. D. dissertation, Graduate School of Architecture and Urban Planning, University of California, Los Angeles.

Leler, William. 1988. *Constraint Programming Languages*. Reading, Mass.: Addison-Wesley.

Liggett, Robin S., and William J. Mitchell. 1981. "Optimal Space Planning in Practice." *Computer-Aided Design* 13, no. 5: 277-288.

Liggett, Robin S., and William J. Mitchell. 1981. "Interactive Graphic Floor Plan Layout Method." *Computer-Aided Design* 13, no. 5: 289-298.

Maver, Thomas W. 1988. "Software Tools for the Technical Evaluation of Design Alternatives." In Thomas W. Maver and Harry Wagter (eds.), *CAAD Futures 87*. Amsterdam: Elsevier.

Mitchell, William J. 1977. *Computer-Aided Architectural Design*. New York: Van Nostrand Reinhold.

Mitchell, William J. 1989. *The Logic of Architecture*. Cambridge Mass.: MIT Press.

Mitchell, William J., Robin S. Liggett, and Milton Tan. 1989. "Top-Down Knowledge-Based Design." This volume.

Mitchell, William J., Philip Steadman, and Robin S. Liggett. 1976. "Synthesis and Optimization of Small Rectangular Floor Plans." *Environment and Planning B* 3, no. 1: 37-70.

Nagakura, Takehiko. 1989. "Shape Recognition and Transformation--A Script-Based Approach." This volume.

Palmer, S. E. 1977. "Hierarchical Structure in Perceptual Representation." *Cognitive Psychology* 9: 441-474.

Reed, S. K. 1974. "Structural Descriptions and the Limitations of Visual Images." *Memory and Cognition* 2: 329-336.

Reitman, Walter R. 1965. "Creative Problem Solving: Notes from the Autobiography of a Fugue." In *Cognition and Thought*. New York: John Wiley.

Simon, Herbert A. 1981. *The Sciences of the Artificial*. (Second edition.) Cambridge Mass.: MIT Press.

Simon, Herbert A. 1975. "Style in Design." In Charles M. Eastman (ed.), *Spatial Synthesis in Computer-Aided Building Design*. New York: John Wiley.

Steadman, Philip. 1983. *Architectural Morphology*. London: Pion.

Stiny, George. 1989. "What Designers Do that Computers Should." This volume.

Stiny, George, and William J. Mitchell. 1978. "The Palladian Grammar." *Environment and Planning B* 5, no. 1: 5-18.

Stiny, George, and William J. Mitchell. 1978. "Counting Palladian Plans." *Environment and Planning B* 5, no. 2: 189-98.

Sutherland, Ivan E. 1975. "Structure in Drawings and the Hidden-Surface Problem", in N. Negroponte (ed.), *Reflections on Computer Aids to Design and Architecture.* New York: Petrocelli/Charter.

Tan, Milton. 1989. "Saying What it Is by What it Is Like." This volume.

Wittgenstein, Ludwig. 1968. *Philosophical Investigations.* Oxford: Basil Blackwell.

Theoretical Foundations

1
What Designers Do That Computers Should

George Stiny

Graduate School of Architecture and Urban Planning
University of California, Los Angeles

Designers do many things that computers don't. Some of these are bad habits that the stringencies of computation will correct. But others are basic to design, and cannot be ignored if computation is to serve creation and invention. Two of these provide the correlative themes of this paper. Both are concerned with description, and its variability and multiplicity in design.

Ambiguity
In 1786 Charles Percier won the 1er Grand Prix . His design for "A Building for Assembling the Academies" was exceptional in many ways, but especially for

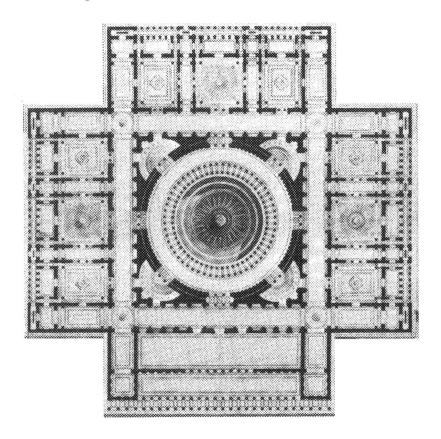

its ambiguity within a fixed grid. David Van Zanten (1977) describes this in his history of *Beaux-Arts* composition.

By bringing all of his spaces to rectangles, and forming them into rectangle-within-rectangle figures, Percier permitted his spaces to link together smoothly, to interpenetrate. The outer rectangle of the figure is always shared with the neighboring figure. When three such figures are set side by side, as they are laterally and longitudinally in Percier's plan, it is unclear whether one should read the resulting configuration as two interlocking rectangles, as four rectangles overlapping at the center square, or as four rectangles set around the sides of the central square. Percier thus bound his plan together and introduced a play of ambiguity through the use of the modular grid, of consistently rectangular spaces, and of the rectangle-within-rectangle figure.

From the designer's point of view, this description merely states the facts, and does so without recourse to special devices of any kind. Percier's design is a variation of the standard Greek cross

that can be decomposed into parts in many ways. If transformations are used to change the rectangles in this list

into similar ones that may be combined for this purpose, then the decompositions suggested by Van Zanten follow immediately.

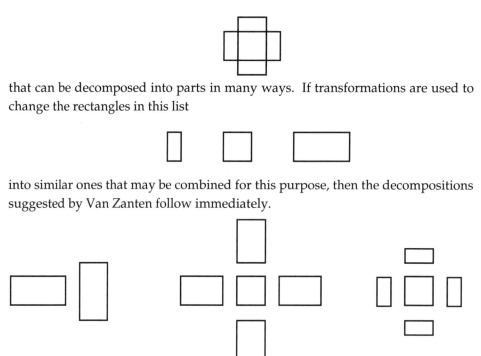

And other decompositions are possible, too, in terms of rectangles

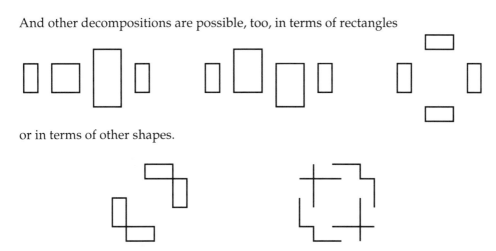

or in terms of other shapes.

Ambiguity has important uses in design where it fosters imagination and creativity, and encourages multilayered expression and response. But ambiguity is conspicuously absent from design when it is computer aided, even in the basic case where designs are given in line drawings. The reason for this is the structured nature of computer drawings, as described by Ivan Sutherland (1975).

> *To a large extent it has turned out that the usefulness of computer drawings is precisely their structured nature. . . An ordinary [designer] is unconcerned with the structure of his drawing material. Pen and ink or pencil and paper have no inherent structure. They only make dirty marks on paper. The [designer] is concerned principally with the drawings as a representation of the evolving design. The behavior of the computer-produced drawing, on the other hand, is critically dependent upon the topological and geometric structure built up in the computer memory as a result of drawing operations. The drawing itself has properties quite independent of the properties of the object it is describing.*

Sutherland's enthusiasm for computer drawing is well known, and is shared widely in the CAD community. But enthusiasm alone is not enough to sustain design. It would appear that the *uselessness* of computer drawings in design is precisely their structured nature. Because the pencil and paper drawing has no inherent structure, it can be decomposed and manipulated in any manner of interest to the designer. An evolving design may thus have alternative descriptions that may change from time to time in unanticipated ways; it may be decomposed and manipulated in this way now and in another way later without difficulty. The structure of the computer drawing, however, makes all of this impossible. This structure is fixed in definite drawing operations. If the following cross

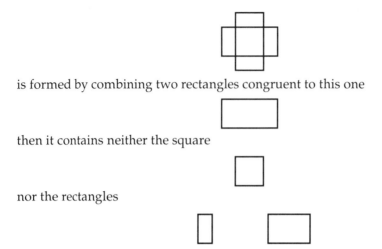

is formed by combining two rectangles congruent to this one

then it contains neither the square

nor the rectangles

In felicitous circumstances, the two rectangles that describe the cross may coincide with a decomposition or a manipulation of interest to the designer, so that the computer may truly aid him. Otherwise, the computer will obstruct his progress. The designer cannot modify his approach or have a new idea unless his changing insights conform to the structure in the computer.

From the computer's point of view, there is no ambiguity. Every line drawing has many descriptions. Of these, the computer only recognizes the one determined as the structure of the drawing is "built up in the computer memory as a result of drawing operations". This description may or may not be of use. In the unlikely event that it is for *all* designs at *all* times, there is no reason to worry. The computer has grasped the essence of design. But if it isn't, then a change is required in CAD, from the "A" in *aided* to the "O" in *obstructed* . CAD is impossible.

This conclusion is premature. Neither the computer nor the imposed identification of a line drawing with one of its many descriptions need preclude ambiguity or obstruct design. The real problem lies elsewhere in the steadfast reliance on inappropriate topological and geometric structures in the computer to describe drawings and their parts, and to carry out drawing operations on these descriptions. Ambiguity can play its full role in CAD once the lines used by ordinary designers in drawings made with dirty marks on paper are taken seriously. Success in this effort depends on a simple relation on lines.

Every *line* is given by endpoints that are always distinct. Lines defined in this way are related according to whether one is *embedded* in another. This relation holds whenever one line is part of another, when it is a segment of it. One line can be embedded in another line in any of three basic ways

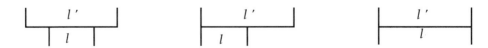

In each of these cases, the line l is embedded in the line l' In the third case, the line l' is also embedded in the line l, but in neither the first nor the second case is this so. If three lines l, l', and l'' are embedded in this way

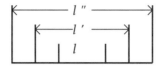

so that l is embedded in l', and l' in l'', then l is also embedded in l''. As these examples show, embedding is a partial order on lines: it is transitive, and two lines are identical whenever each is embedded in the other. With lines ordered in this way, every line has a common structure given by the lines embedded in it that, with the addition of a zero assumed here only, forms a complete lattice.

Once the embedding relation is defined, shapes (drawings, and their counterparts in space) are easy to describe, so that each is identified with a definite structure in the computer that allows for arbitrary decompositions and manipulations by the designer. Every *shape* is determined by a finite but possibly empty set of maximal lines. *Maximal* lines are such that no two combine to form a line. When maximal lines are colinear, they are separated by a gap; otherwise, maximal lines may touch or intersect. Alone, every line is maximal. And so are the two longest lines that form these shapes

and the three longest lines that form these shapes

Of all of the different sets of lines that might be given to describe a shape, the set of maximal lines has the fewest lines in it.

This approach to shapes departs from the more customary, atomic view of things as sets of primitive components that are themselves without structure. Every shape is described uniquely by the smallest number of longest lines that combine to make it, rather than in terms of the greatest number of shortest ones—however these might be conceived—that do.

The lines given to describe a shape are maximal, but they may still have other lines embedded in them. When these lines are maximal in combination, they describe the shapes that are parts of the shape and that can be used to decompose it. The subshape relation fixes this idea formally: one shape is a *subshape* of another shape whenever every maximal line in the first shape is embedded in some maximal

line in the second shape. The cross

is determined by a set of eight maximal lines. It has eleven different rectangles as subshapes. Two of these are formed by combining maximal lines in the cross, and are described by subsets of the set that describes it. The other nine, though, have maximal lines that are not in the cross but that are embedded in maximal lines that are. The cross has other subshapes, too, that may be used to decompose it. Some of these are distinguished by line weight in these illustrations

The complete structure of a shape is given by all of its subshapes. These are partially ordered by the subshape relation, and form a Boolean algebra. Similar shapes have the same structure.

The subshape relation allows for shapes to be decomposed in any way whatsoever. Manipulating shapes goes forward reciprocally with two operations to combine shapes, in addition to the transformations. These operations are *sum* and *difference* . They correspond, respectively, to drawing and erasing lines, and are readily defined in terms of the subshape relation. A constructive approach, however, is needed for the computer; it is to be had with *reduction rules*.

The shape produced by drawing two shapes together is their sum. The shape

is the sum of a rectangle and a square

its subshapes are subshapes of the rectangle or the square, say, the three shapes

or combine subshapes of the rectangle and the square, as does the shape

Every pair of shapes A and B has a unique sum $A + B$ given by the set of maximal lines determined according to the following three reduction rules. These rules are applied recursively in any order, first to the union of the sets of maximal lines that describe the shapes A and B, and then until no rule can be applied.

(1) If l and l' are lines in the current set, and l is embedded in l', then remove l.

(2) If l and l' are lines in the current set related to each other in this way

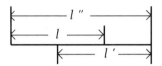

so that neither is embedded in the other, but a line determined by an endpoint of one and an endpoint of the other is embedded in both, then replace l and l' with the line l'' determined by the remaining endpoints of each.

(3) If l and l' are lines in the current set related to each other in this way

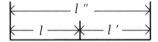

so that neither is embedded in the other, but they share an endpoint and can both be embedded in the line l'' determined by the remaining endpoints of each, then replace l and l' with this line.

It is interesting to notice here that the reduction rules for sum allow for shapes to be defined in schemata. This establishes families of shapes that share special features, and the basis for parametric variation in design. A shape *schema A (x)* is a set of variables. Lines are assigned to these by a function g , and may be required to satisfy certain conditions. Of course, the set $g(A(x))$ produced in this way may not describe a shape, as the lines in it may not be maximal. However, once the reduction rules for sum are applied to the set, the shape $R(g(A(x)))$ is determined.

Difference is characterized in the same fashion as sum. The shape produced by erasing every subshape of one shape that is shared by another shape is the difference between these two shapes. The difference of the rectangle

and the square

with the same centers is the shape

as the two shapes have subshapes of the shape

as their common subshapes. Conversely, the difference of the square

and the rectangle

is the shape

Every pair of shapes A and B, taken in this order, has a unique difference A - B. The set of maximal lines for this shape is determined by three reduction rules that apply recursively in any order, beginning with the set of maximal lines for the shape A, until no rule can be applied.

(1) If l is a line in the current set embedded in a maximal line in the shape B, then remove l.

(2) Conversely, if l is a line in the current set related to a maximal line l' in the shape B in this way

so that l' is embedded in l without sharing an endpoint of l, then replace l with the lines l'' and l''', where these lines are each determined by an endpoint of l and an endpoint of l', and do not have l' embedded in them. Alternatively, if l and l' are related in this way

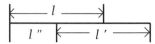

so that l' is embedded in l and shares exactly one endpoint of l, then replace l with the line l'' determined by the remaining endpoints of l and l'.

(3) If l is a line in the current set related to a maximal line l' in the shape B in this way

so that neither line is embedded in the other, but a line determined by an endpoint of one and an endpoint of the other is embedded in both, then replace l with the line l'', where this line is determined by an endpoint of l and an endpoint of l', and is embedded in l but not in l'.

Shapes and the operations on them form an algebra with a well known structure. The set of all shapes, and sum and difference are equivalent to a Boolean ring with a zero but no unit. If the transformations are used in this algebra, then they distribute over sum and difference. And in this case, with the trivial exception of the set containing the zero only, the algebra has no proper subset with exactly the same properties.

The algebra of shapes provides a medium for design that is equivalent in every important respect to pencil and paper. In the algebra, a shape has no inherent structure; it can be decomposed and manipulated in any way desired. But even more than this, the algebra provides for computations with shapes to be carried out by following rules, and so to define subsets of the algebra that contain shapes of certain kinds. Rules are comprised of shapes, and apply to shapes to make shapes.

With pencil and paper, one shape is changed into another shape by drawing and erasing lines. In the algebra of shapes, a sequence of these operations is defined in a *rule*

$$A \rightarrow B$$

that replaces an occurrence of the shape A with the corresponding occurrence of the shape B. The rule applies to a shape C to produce a new shape according to the formula

$$(C - t(A)) + t(B)$$

if there is a transformation t that makes A a subshape of C. The rule exploits the full resources of the algebra in a replacement operation that is the basis of every computation with shapes. These computations are of all sorts. In fact, every computation defined in a Turing machine can be carried out equivalently by following rules in the algebra of shapes.

Like shapes, rules may be defined in schemata. This is an important generalization that combines replacement and parametric variation, and so greatly facilitates writing rules that are of broad use in design. A rule schema

$$A(x) \rightarrow B(x)$$

is a pair of shape schemata $A(x)$ and $B(x)$ that may share variables. If g is a function that assigns lines to all of the variables in both of these schemata, then the rule

$$R(g(A(x))) \rightarrow R(g(B(x)))$$

is defined.

A computation is a series of shapes that is produced when rules are applied recursively. In this sense, computations with shapes are the same as computer computations with symbols. And both, too, allow for an important type of ambiguity that arises whenever there are multiple computations for the same thing, each with equal claim to describe it. But in another sense, computations with shapes differ from symbolic computations in a very fundamental way. Every object in a symbolic computation can be resolved into its primitive components. This description is unique and is independent of the rules that may apply to the object. In contrast, no shape in a computation need correspond to any single decomposition. Its descriptions may vary discontinuously according to context, being determined by different rules and transformations. This does not mean that computations with shapes cannot be carried out by the computer, but only that special symbolic devices —the embedding relation, maximal lines, and reduction rules— are needed for this purpose.

Computations with shapes produce some surprising results that follow from discontinuities in description. The rule

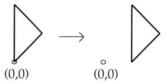

simply translates an isosceles right triangle, so that its hypotenuse is moved to its right-angled corner. Intuition suggests that nothing remarkable will happen when the rule is applied. As anyone knows who has ever moved a shape from here to there, changing positions is harmless. The shape stays the same. Intuition, however, is sometimes incomplete. The rule applies first to the hourglass

and then two more times to produce the shape

But neither of the triangles in the hourglass is congruent to any subshape of this shape. Where have the triangles gone? The answer is easy to see in the shape

that is produced in the first applicaton of the rule. This shape has competing descriptions. In one, the triangles from the hourglass are recognized but in the other, smaller, emergent hourglasses that are made up of subshapes of these triangles are distinguished.

If the rule is applied to translate triangles in the emergent hourglasses, then the triangles from the original hourglass disappear. More accurately, they do not exist: they are not recognized in the description of the shape

invoked when the rule is used in this way.

The usual response to this example and to a host of other ones is to dismiss them. They are frivolous and of theoretical interest only. CAD is a practical business concerned with real objects like floors, stairs, roofs, columns, walls, windows, doors, and sundry other devices that are combined in designs because they mean something. Even here, though, the present approach to computation with shapes can be recommended. Good reasons make it ineluctable.

First, discontinuities in description may arise when objects share functions and have multiple uses. This is not unknown in architecture where designs are regularly decomposed and manipulated according to unrelated categories established in different points of view, and buildings sometimes outlast their intended purposes, being adapted to new programmes. Another reason, however, addresses CAD more directly in terms of a persistent difficulty with this endeavor. There is no way to anticipate *all* of the devices and methods of composition that will be used in practice. What form a door takes and how it is placed in a wall in every case is the kind of question that many approaches to CAD find themselves asking. But answers to such questions are always incomplete. Practice changes, and so do ideas of doors and walls. What is needed is an approach to design that can circumscribe practice as desired and accommodate changing interests and goals within a common computational framework, so that past efforts and present enthusiasms connect. This is only possible if descriptions can vary, as in the algebra of shapes. New devices and methods of composition can be given in rules that are defined in drawings and in schemata, and that apply to all shapes in the same way, independently of how they were described originally or at any other time.

Parallel Descriptions

Ambiguity is basic to design with shapes, but does not thereby preclude descriptions of shapes or diminish their importance. Nor does it imply that all such descriptions are of equal value. In design, shapes are descriptions that may themselves be described for definite purposes, and that may serve with descriptions of other kinds. A more complete account of design thus requires that the algebra of shapes be combined with other algebras, so that shapes and useful descriptions in different domains of interest can be computed in parallel. In this way, a *design* may be viewed as an element in an n -ary relation among shapes, other descriptions, and correlative material as needed. These relations are at the root of design, providing descriptions of things for making and accounts of how they work.

This approach is already familiar to designers. It is standard practice to combine drawings and symbols to describe form and aspects of function, material, construction, and so on. Multiple drawings are used together to establish three dimensional relationships in plans, sections, and elevations. Assemblies are broken up into smaller components that have interrelated descriptions, with details being described in ancillary documents. And analyses of one sort or another are performed on shapes and with other descriptions. In practice, drawings, symbols, documents, and analyses of many kinds connect to make a design.

Designs are complicated and multifaceted, but they are well within the realm of the computer. This is illustrated nicely with labeled shapes that allow for drawings and symbols to be combined in an integrated computational process. For this purpose, a new algebra is formed in the Cartesian product of the algebra of shapes and the algebra of sets of labeled points.

A *labeled point* is defined when a label from a specified set, say, the alphabet $a, b, c \ldots$, is associated with a point. Labels may be just that, in which case, they are used simply to identify and classify particular points, or they may have a semantics allowing them to carry important information. A labeled point may be transformed to produce a new one in which the same label is associated with another point. Finite sets of labeled points are partially ordered by the subset relation, and are combined by union and relative complement to form the algebra of sets of labeled points. Like the algebra of shapes, it is equivalent to a Boolean ring with a zero but no unit. And if the transformations are used in this algebra, then they distribute over both of its operations.

Sometimes, it is convenient to define sets of labeled points in schemata. Each *schema* $P(y)$ is a set of variables. Labeled points are assigned to these by a function g, and may be required to satisfy certain conditions. Further, pairs of schemata $P(y) \rightarrow Q(y)$ define *rules* that apply to carry out computations in the algebra of sets of labeled points according to the formula given above, where A, B, and C now stand for sets of labeled points, and subshape, sum, and difference correspond to subset, union, and relative complement, respectively. And notice that these rules, too, are enough to carry out any computation defined in a Turing machine.

In a Cartesian product, the algebra of shapes and the algebra of sets of labeled points form another Boolean ring. The relation and operations of this algebra combine subshape with subset, sum with union, and difference with relative complement. If these combinations are named by the shape relation or operation involved, then the labeled shape $<A, P>$ is a subshape of the labeled shape $<B, Q>$ if the shape A is a subshape of the shape B, and the set of labeled points P is a subset of the set of labeled points Q. And, for example, the sum of these labeled shapes has as components the sum of A and B, and the union of P and Q. Further, a transformation t of the labeled shape $<A, P>$ is the labeled shape $<t(A), t(P)>$.

Computations in the algebra of labeled shapes are defined in *shape grammars*. These use schemata of the form $<A(x), P(y)> \rightarrow <B(x), Q(y)>$ to obtain rules that apply according to the formula given above, this time interpreted for labeled shapes. Values are assigned to variables in both sides of a schema by a single function, and conditions on values may relate lines and labeled points.

In a shape grammar, a computation with shapes and a computation with sets of labeled points are carried out in parallel, each influencing the other in terms of how rules in the algebra of shapes and rules in the algebra of sets of labeled points are paired in schemata in the grammar, and in terms of how conditions on values assigned to variables in these schemata relate lines and labeled points. As a result, dependencies between shapes and labeled points are established and vary as this combined computation proceeds. And conditions placed on shapes or on labeled points can be propagated between these components of the computation as the conditions are met. Labeled shapes produced in computations in the grammar define a *language* of designs that follow from a confluence of considerations, some dealing with form as described by shape, and others dealing with aspects of function, material, construction, and so on as described by sets of labeled points. The impetus for design comes from multiple perspectives that may each be dominant at different times but that are connected in computation.

It is easy to imagine different extensions of this approach in which languages of designs are defined in computations carried out by following rules in Cartesian products of appropriate algebras. For example, the algebra of labeled shapes may be combined in repeated products to define relations among plans, sections, and elevations for buildings in certain styles, or among components in assemblies of certain types. Or this algebra may be combined with an algebra of sets of labeled shapes to provide relations between labeled shapes and decompositions of them needed in different analyses. And further elaborations are also possible if labeled shapes in sets are ordered hierarchically and assigned to particular categories. Opportunities for languages of designs are vast, and can always be multiplied in yet another Cartesian product.

Designers work with descriptions involving drawings and symbols in many different ways. To do this with the computer, so that original designs can be produced in computations, requires at the very least an approach something like the one outlined in this paper. This approach is neither novel nor radical. At root, it allows for variability and multiplicity in description as they are exploited in creative practice to be used as successfully in the computer by following rules. The approach continues a tradition in design that extends from Vitruvius to this day in which descriptive devices are invented, tried, and extended to provide an increasingly better account of past and present experience, and a more confident grasp of future possibilities. It does so without making design a science, or appealing to the computer to remake designers and what they do. Designers do just fine with pencil, paper, and imagination. The computer can do as well with shapes and symbols, their algebras, and rules.

Background

This approach to design was considered originally in Stiny (1975). More recent discussions include Stiny (1981; 1986; 1989; in preparation).

References

Stiny, G., 1975, *Pictorial and Formal Aspects of Shape and Shape Grammars*, Birkhauser, Basel.

Stiny, G., 1981, "A Note on the Description of Designs", *Environment and Planning B*, 8, 257-267.

Stiny, G., 1986, "A New Line on Drafting Systems", *Design Computing,*, 1, 5-19.

Stiny, G., 1989, "Formal Devices for Design", in S. L. Newsome, et al (eds.), *Design Theory '88*, Springer, New York.

Stiny, G., in preparation, *Shape: A Primer in Algebra, Grammar, and Description*.

Sutherland, I., 1975, "Structure in Drawings and the Hidden-Surface Problem", in N. Negroponte (ed.), *Reflections on Computer Aids To Design and Architecture*, Petrocelli/Charter, New York.

Van Zanten, D., 1977, "Architectural Composition at the Ecole des Beaux-Arts from Charles Percier to Charles Garnier", in A. Drexler (ed.), *The Architecture of the Ecole des Beaux-Arts*, The Museum of Modern Art, New York.

2
Syntactic Structures in Architecture: Teaching Composition with Computer Assistance

Ulrich Flemming

Department of Architecture
Carnegie-Mellon University

The present paper outlines a plan for the teaching of architectural composition with computer assistance. The approach is to introduce students to a series of architectural languages characterized by a vocabulary *of elements and a* grammar *whose rules indicate how these elements can be placed in space. Exercises with each language include the analysis of precedents; the generation of forms using a given rule set; and follow-up studies with an expanded rule set. The paper introduces languages and exercises through illustrative examples. This architectural content can be taught in the traditional way. The use of computers is motivated by expectations which are stated, and some basic requirements for the needed software are listed. Work to develop this software has started.*

Introduction

The present paper expands on ideas that I have presented before (together with Gerhard Schmitt) [3]. A portion of the earlier paper dealt with principles of architectural composition and how they could be introduced to students with the help of computer programs. The underlying assumption was that compositional skills are an important ingredient of an architect's expertise and deserve to be taught explicitly. The increasing number of texts dealing with this topic that have appeared over the past few years seem to support this contention. I have found in my own teaching that composition and formal aspects of design are not always easy to teach, at least if one does not adhere to a rigid school or subscribe to a particular 'party line'.

I believe that computer programs can be of great help in this matter. This belief is ultimately based on the notion that the process of architectural design can be viewed as a form of computation, that is, as a sequence of operations performed on a symbolic representation of the object being designed. The predominant representation used by architects to develop and describe a design for the last 400 years has been the line drawing. A design starts with an initial idea, which is sketched and then subjected, again through sketches, to a series of modifications and expansions. Some of these attempts might lead to dead ends, which are abandoned, and the process returns to an earlier stage, or a new idea is introduced. That this process can be viewed as computation manifests itself most clearly through the way in which designers use transparent paper to trace features of the evolving design that are to remain unaltered (for the time being) and to redraw only those portions they wish to change. Especially in its earlier stages, this process is highly exploratory in nature and can be propelled by ideas that it itself created; the simultaneous appearance of certain shapes on the same sheet in a particular configuration might suggest possibilities that otherwise would not have occurred to the designer.

The notion of design as computation is also supported by sequences of sketches architects frequently produce to explain the form of a design after it has been generated. In such a sequence, an initial configuration is typically subjected to a series of modifications that follow a certain logic and lead to a form with the basic properties of the design under consideration. The sequence might be a distillation of the exploratory process that produced the design or an *a-posteriori* rationalization. This mode of thinking also applies when designs of others are discussed and analyzed.

These observations suggest to me that architects think constructively; that is, the principles they apply are conceived in generative terms. The notion of design as computation captures this constructive attitude and indicates, at the same time, basic possibilities for utilizing the generative power of computers in design education (or design in general, an issue I will not address in the present paper). It will come as no surprise that my suggestions are particularly influenced by the theory of formal grammars and its application in various forms, particularly the shape grammar formalism [11] [12].

In the technical sense, an architectural language is given by a collection of rules that embody the compositional principles or conventions that underlie a certain piece of architecture (or a collection of such pieces) and make it *recognizable* (e.g. as belonging to a certain period, or as the work of a particular architect). These rules form the *grammar* of the language. They manipulate the shape and placement of a distinct set of elements, which constitute the *vocabulary* of the language.

I use the term 'architectural language' primarily in this technical sense. No 'linguistic analogy', or analogy to natural languages, is implied at the outset. A particular inspiration to me were attempts to explain the conventions underlying classical architecture in linguistic terms, from popular introductions [13] to more detailed accounts [14]. Space limitations prevent me from introducing the notions of language [1] and formal grammar here in greater detail. Readers not familiar with these concepts are referred to [3] and the literature cited there.

I shall outline in the following a plan for the teaching of compositional principles and the acquisition of compositional skills based on exercises with selected languages that I have used in the past for this purpose (albeit without computer aids). The intention is to make students familiar with the languages themselves and to develop their compositional skills in general. In this plan, each language will be presented through (1) buildings or unbuilt projects that clearly demonstrate the underlying principles or rules and the possibilities inherent in the language; (2) an explicit statement of some basic rules of the language and exercises in which students are asked to apply these rules to generate designs; (3) follow-up exercises in which students are asked to modify or expand the given rule set and work with it.

Basic computational techniques available today suggest that computers can play an important role in such an enterprise. Of particular interest are the shape operators (union, intersection and difference) provided by any decent solids modeler, and the capabilities of a shape grammar interpreter able to accept rule definitions, to determine the applicability of rules, and to apply rules to generate new shapes [4]. The plan does, however, pose demands on the robustness of the software used and especially on the user interface that are not met by any program known to me. I will specify some of these demands in a concluding section.

The following sections will introduce a selection of languages that has emerged in connection with my own teaching over the past years. Some of these languages are elementary and can be found in various vernaculars. Others are restricted to the high-style tradition. In each case, I will briefly characterize the language followed, in most cases, by diagrams representing the constructive analysis of a prime instance. For selected languages I will then show more formalized versions of the underlying rules and examples of their application. I will also indicate how this basic material can be expanded and enriched. My own understanding of the languages presented and my attempts to develop the content of the plan are far from complete. But I hope that I will be able to provide enough examples to give readers a concrete impression of my intentions.

Wall Architecture

I like to start my introduction to architectural languages with what I call *elementary wall architecture*. The basic element in its vocabulary is a wall, a cuboid whose depth is small compared to its length and height. The basic use of walls is to enclose space, and a basic rule to accomplish this is to demand that the end of each wall touches another wall. Openings appear as punched-out holes or as cut-outs from the bottom or top; these openings form essentially two-dimensional, graphical patterns that animate the wall surfaces in which they occur; no other treatment of these surfaces is allowed in the elementary version of this language.

Elementary wall architecture is the language of numerous vernaculars. In high-style architecture, Palladio, Ledoux or Soane produced almost pure instances. Among more recent practitioners, Irving Gill and Adolf Loos used this language with particular success.

Figure 1 shows perspective views of one of Loos's unbuilt projects. Figure 2 shows different constructive readings of the project, together with elevation diagrams that relate the placement of windows in a wall to the distribution of rooms behind that wall.

Figure 3a specifies basic rules that make the intuitive notion how walls relate to each other in the present language operational.[2] Rule 0 creates a single wall both ends of which are unattached to other walls and labeled 'h' (which stands for 'hot'). Rule 1 places a wall at a right angle to the hot end of another wall (and removes label 'h' from that end). Rules 0 and 1 can be used to generate endlessly folding walls like configuration 1 shown in figure 3b. They also generate spiral labyrinths.

Rule 2 connects the hot ends of two walls and thus completes an enclosure. Together with the previous rules it generates simple boxes and other forms of enclosures (configurations 2 and 3). It can also be used to create stacked boxes (configuration 4). Rule 3 can be used sequentially to dissect a given enclosure into an arbitrary number of compartments (configuration 5). This rule expresses clearly the basic attitude towards space making that underlies the present language. It is able to generate a great variety of spatial divisions most with the exception of pinwheel configurations. To generate these, rules 4 and 5 must be used (configuration 6). This set of rules can be augmented by a second set that generates roofs and places walls on top of other walls under the same restrictions. With this expanded set, catalogues of archetypical buildings (such as the ideal designs of Ledoux) can be generated.

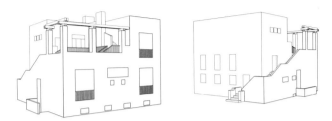

Figure 1   Project for a house at the Lido (A. Loos)

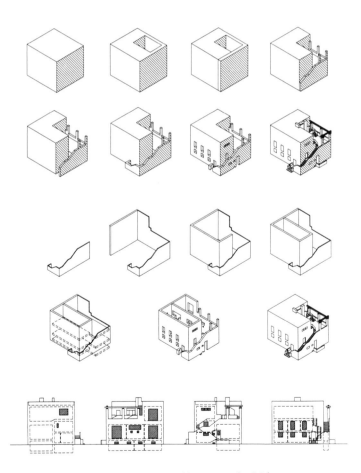

Figure 2   Constructive analysis of house at the Lido

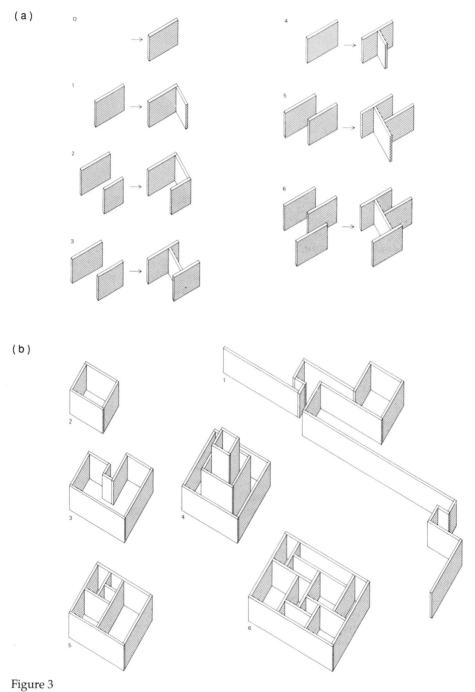

Figure 3
a) Generation rules for wall architecture
b) Configurations generated by these rules

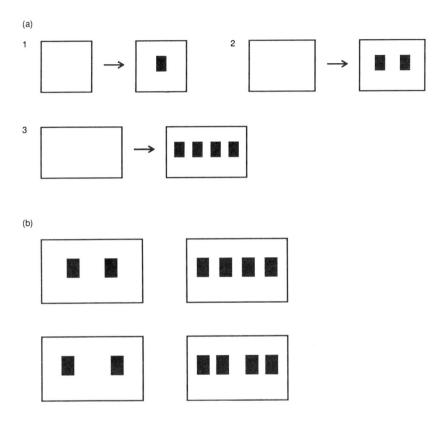

Figure 4
a) Rules to create openings in a wall
b) Patterns generated by these rules

A distinct class of rules needed in elementary wall architecture deals with openings in walls; examples are shown in figure 4a. It is important to note that these rules apply from both the inside and the outside; an interesting exercise is to study the effects of both types of application on the exterior elevations and on the ways in which light is introduced into spaces. Figure 4b shows, for example, different window patterns generated for an exterior wall covering two rooms of equal width. The patterns in the top row are generated by applying rules 2 and 3 from the outside, while the patterns below result from applying rules 1 and 2 from the inside.

No application of any of the rules shown demands an underlying grid. It would be interesting to contrast the above grammar with a second one that depends on such a grid which, in turn, enforces the placements of certain elements (including openings; see [10]).

In both vernacular and high-style architecture, elementary wall architecture is enriched not only by the contrast between walls and openings, but also by the introduction of linear, stick-type elements that contrast with the former two: posts, beams or tubes used to form lattices and other types of stick patterns (railings, trellises, pergolas, window frames etc.). Students might be asked to define rules under which such elements are introduced and to experiment with them.

Mass Architecture

From elementary wall architecture, I like to take the discussion of languages into two directions. The first of these is indicated by what I call *mass architecture*. In the prior language, the two major surfaces of a wall are parallel, while in the present language, they are less closely related. This makes the interior of a building more independent of its exterior form. Spaces appear to be 'carved' out of the building's mass. Notable vernacular forms of this language are the cave dwellings known from various regions of the globe, where this happens literally.

Mass architecture gives architects great freedom in the definition of interior spaces, which become *figurative*; that is, they have a distinct and complete three-dimensional form, which can be displayed and studied as a positive solid, for example, with the aid of a solids modeler [7]. These figurative spaces can be inserted into a fabric with irregular boundaries and have been used to generate remarkable interiors and courts in dense urban situations. This process can be applied hierarchically, where at each level, the mass remaining from operations at the previous level is further eroded [2]; the shape difference operator provided by solids modelers is uniquely appropriate to display and study this process (see figure 5a.) The result is, of course, *poché*, as both a rendering technique and a compositional device.

The approach that I am currently taking to formulate rules for the generation of architectural poché creates figurative spaces as *positive solids* and arranges them axially in the Beaux-Arts tradition.

Substractive operations can also be used to carve into the surfaces of the remaining walls, creating profiles, reveals etc. and finally windows and doors. This often results in a layered facade as shown in figure 5b.

Panel Architecture

A second direction that the study of walls can take is to treat them as independent elements. This move can be motivated by an interest in abstraction that strips an element from its overt purpose and considers it as pure form; this leads to Neo-Plasticism as exemplified by the programmatic composition shown in figure 6, in which rectangular panels are placed in the three major directions to form an abstract composition that follows Picturesque ordering

(a)

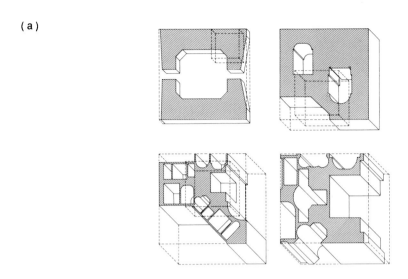

(b)

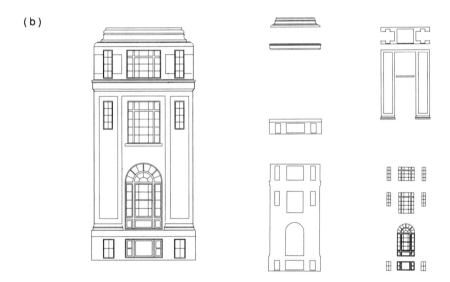

Figure 5
a) Hierarchical poché (after Dennis [1]);
b) Mass wall: Baker Hall on the CMU Campus (H. Hornbostel)

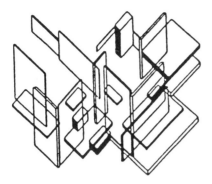

Figure 6   Architectural composition
by Th. van Doesburg and C. van Eesteren

principles. But the 'destruction of the box' achieved in this way can also result from a very concrete interest in eliminating the strict separation between inside and outside implied by the former languages and in a more open plan; this was the stated purpose behind F. L. Wright's moves in this direction.

I call such compositions panel architecture. The basic element manipulated is a rectangular panel placed vertically or horizontally to form vertical enclosures or roofs. Windows and other openings are given by the gaps between panels; in pure versions of the language, openings cannot be punched out of a panel. To close these gaps, a second, transparent panel is needed. I know of no vernacular versions of this language; it clearly belongs to the high-style tradition and stands at the end of a line of development leading from the aesthetic of the Picturesque to the Queen Anne revival, F. L. Wright, Neo-Plasticism and the Modern Movement. The most famous examples are perhaps Rietveld's Schroder House and the Barcelona Pavilion (and related projects by Mies, such as his court house projects).

Irregular patterns are, of course, sometimes difficult to interpret, and I know of no concentrated effort to understand the principles underlying the placement, for example, of the solid panels in Mies's projects. My own preliminary attempts are illustrated in figure 8a, which specifies rules to locate solid panels as indicated in the Mies projects. In all of these instances, panels seem to engage each other in deliberate ways; in fact, a very plausible explanation emerges when one views panels as placed sequentially as shown in figure 7. Each new panel is close to the previously placed panel. Its direction seems to be governed by attempts to direct the visitor in a particular direction or to frame a particular view. The rules shown accomplish this directly. Rule 0 again creates an initial panel with a hot end. The next three rules show the three ways in which a new panel can be added to an existing panel. Figure 8b shows some configurations generated by these rules.

Panels placed by rules 1-3 do not touch; but this is clearly allowed in the projects under review. Rule 4 can be used to this end, and Rule 5 allows a panel to be thickened and turned into a more three-dimensional element. The insertion of transparent panels is straightforward once the solid panels have been placed.

Posts, columns and other linear elements play an intricate role in both Mies's and Rietveld's work. This might be a fruitful topic for follow-up exercises. Students might also explore the effects of loosening the rules of engagement between panels, for example, by allowing panels to form solid corners (as in the outer panels of the Barcelona Pavilion). A particularly interesting extension of the rules set would allow for the generation of truly three-dimensional compositions. A student project that explores this possibility is shown in figure 9.

Layered Architecture

A different form of abstraction occurs when a wall is not isolated as a physical object, but used to define a plane or layer that provides a datum or reference for organizing a composition. Rowe and Slutzky, in their famous article [7], claim that parallel layers organize buildings such as LeCorbusier's Villa Stein or his project for the Palace of Nations. They establish links with principles of Cubist paintings, and the 3-dimensional analysis of such paintings in terms of spatial layers has been popular in introductory design courses ever since B. Hoesli published his precedent in his commentary on the article [8]. Layers occur horizontally, where they establish a basic division into floors, and vertically, where they establish planes perpendicular to the main direction of access through which the visitor progresses. To establish connections between layers and to create the transparencies Rowe and Slutzky were so interested in, layers exist physically (as a piece of floor or wall) only in portions of their plane. When vertical layers are involved, the cut-outs generate spaces of various heights and visual connections between floors; for horizontal layers, they create, for example, contrasts between 'deep' and 'shallow' space as analyzed in [9].

My understanding of layered architecture has not progressed to the point where I can give precise rules (although I would very much like to achieve this). It is clear that Rowe and Slutzky's explanations are insufficient to explain the buildings under consideration. Layers are related in intricate ways that want to be discovered. I also believe that the more three-dimensional, sculptural elements that populate the designs of Le Corbusier and his followers play a more important role than has been attributed to them.

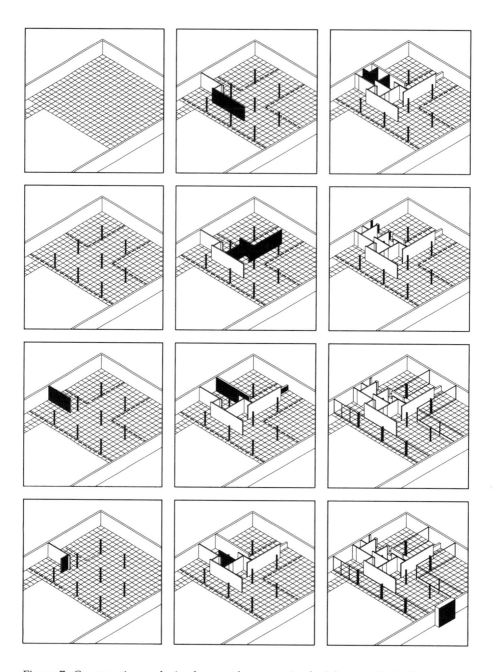

Figure 7   Constructive analysis of a court house project by Mies van der Rohe

11

(a)

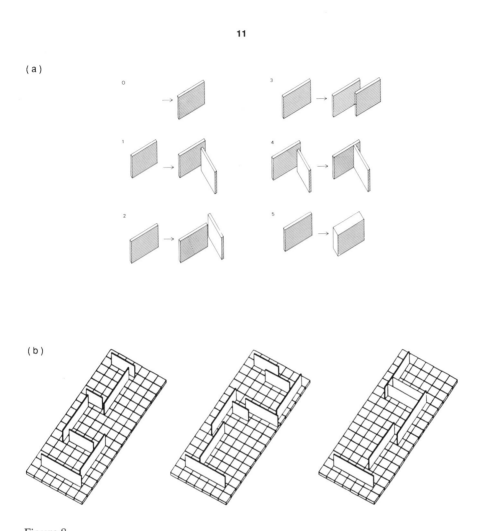

Figure 8
a) Generation rules for panel architecture
b) Configurations generated by these rules

Structure/Infill Architecture

The vocabulary of this language contains two basic types of elements: posts (or columns) and beams out of which a structural frame can be constructed, and infill elements that generate enclosures and spatial divisions. The frame establishes the whole and divides it into clearly related parts; it is always exposed at the outside. In high-style versions, the frame is also often exposed at the inside, which affirms its overall ordering function, establishes continuity with the outside and might provide a logic for the placement of spatial divisions.

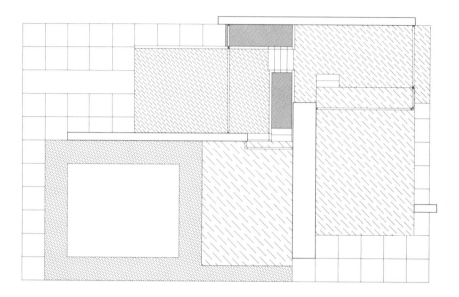

Figure 9 Panel architecture (student project)

The infill responds more closely to local conditions (both inside and outside) and introduces variety that contrasts with the rigidity of the frame. Vernacular versions are given by the half-frame timber structures of Central and Western Europe. Modern textbook examples are the Eames house or Kahn's Center for British Art at Yale.

A basic grammar of structure-infill architecture needs two sets of rules to create, respectively, the frame and the infill. The latter should reflect the fact that infill supports only itself, not the building; in particular, it should not look like a punched-out wall that happens to be placed between structural elements (see [5] for a related discussion). The formulation of rules to accomplish this is straight-forward. Experiments with different types of infill seem particularly promising as the topic for exercises.

Skin Architecture
I believe that the present review of basic languages should conclude with skin architecture, in which the non-structural elements become more independent of the structural frame. C. Pelli talks eloquently about this architecture; but so far, I have done very little work on it.

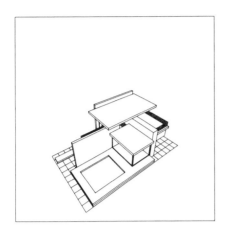
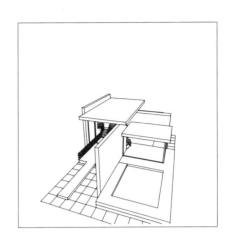

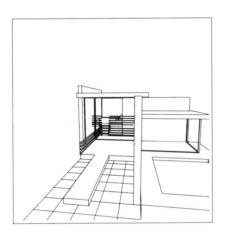
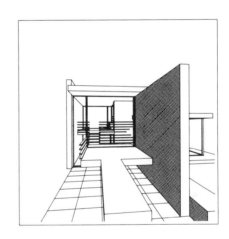

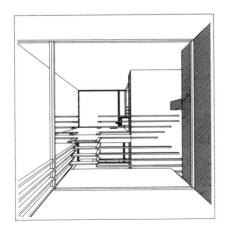
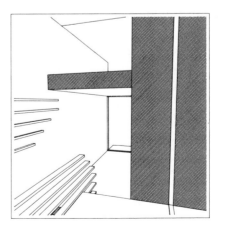

Figure 9   (continued)

Discussion

I divide the discussion of the plan presented here into two parts, its *content* and the particular *means* suggested for introducing this content to students. The languages presented in the preceding sections are intended to provide students with a basic repertoire upon which they can built their own vocabularies and strategies. I was interested in some breadth so as to avoid bias, and I believe that my selection covers a broad range of architectures, from various vernaculars to strands in the high-style tradition. Links to the Modern Movement were inserted deliberately. An open question is if the entire enterprise should start with a treatment of classical architecture itself.

It is also important to me that students start working immediately with three-dimensional elements and their placement in space. I hope that this will alleviate difficulties I have observed when students always start with plans. The material presented here is meant to complement such work, not to replace it. In fact, I do not plan to implement the program outlined above in a design studio. I envisage a lecture course parallel to or preceding a studio emphasizing language and composition, with shorter, focused exercises that have a higher probability of success because they avoid the agonies often connected with studio projects.

All of this material can be presented in the traditional way (I have done this myself). But I have particular hopes for a more determined and substantive use of computer programs. I have already indicated that solids modelers offer some basic capabilities that seem particularly suitable for the constructive analysis of given designs. Their advantage over the usual drawings or physical models could be efficiency and, more importantly, directness: they provide a means to execute a sequence of modifications directly on a model and—and this is important—to save intermediate states. Computer graphics provide opportunities to document and display the results in various ways.

More exciting to me are the possibilities that open up when the rules of a language are specified explicitly and precisely enough so that they can be applied by a rule interpreter. This requires, first of all, that instructors do their homework. It allows them, in turn, to focus their exercises; to instill them with a discipline; and to set some standards that are difficult to achieve by other means. I consider it important, however, that students gain experience not only with a pre-determined set of rules, but also with extensions or modifications of this set that are under their control.

The notion of a rule or grammar as used in the present paper is often misunderstood. It does not represent some form of unwanted and unnecessary restriction. Rather, it represents a means to capture and express the identity or recognizability of a piece of architecture in a constructive way. If viewed in this manner, it becomes absolutely natural to the study of composition and language in architecture. As a side benefit, a concentration on basic rules (as opposed to the 'style' of a particular architect) might avoid the pure mimicking that occurs sometimes when students are asked to design 'in the style' of that architect.

The software to be used in the way indicated here must satisfy some minimal requirements. Aside from meeting obvious demands for robustness and ease of learning, it should first of all allow rules to be defined interactively and graphically. Some interesting technical problems arise in this connection, specifically when these rules are in some way 'parametric', that is, allow for variations in their application with respect to the coordinates of crucial points. Furthermore, the selection of rule applications must be under user control. This eliminates many problems that are likely to occur due to the combinatorics of the search space set up by even a simple grammar. More importantly, it forces users to stay involved in the process of form generation and to continuously reflect on it. Theirs is a dual task: they must direct the process of rule application into desired directions, while keeping an open mind about the surprises and unanticipated results produced by the interpreter.

The rule interpreter should probably be built on top of solids modeler with good display capabilities. This facilitates the generation of graphic output. Furthermore, it makes it possible to edit shapes generated by the application of generation rules to create dimensional variations. It would be extremely inefficient, if not impossible, to generate all of these variations by generation rules. The standard set of operations provided by the modeler will probably have to be extended to include higher level operations (e. g. alignment). The picking and pointing capabilities provided by interactive graphics should be used naturally and extensively to this end.

Work towards developing this type of software has started at my institution. I plan to test the plan outlined here in an experimental course during the academic year 90/91.

References

[1] Dennis, Michael. 1983. *Court and Garden: from the French Hotel to the City of Modern Architecture.* Cambridge, Mass.: MIT Press.

[2] Flemming, Ulrich. 1987. "The Role of Shape Grammars in the Analysis and Creation of Designs". pp 245-272. In Y. Kalay (ed.) *The Computability of Design* New York: Wiley Interscience.

[3] Flemming, Ulrich and Gerhard Schmitt. 1986. "The Computer in the Design Studio: Ideas and Exercises that Go Beyond Automated Drafting". pp 55-78. In J. A. Turner, (ed.) *ACADIA Proceedings '86* .

[4] Krishnamurti, R. 1981. "The Construction of Shapes". pp 5-40. *Environment and Planning B* . Vol. 8.

[5] Macsai, John and Paul Doukas. 1987. "Expressed Frame and the Classical Order in the Transitional Period of Italy 1918-1939". pp 10-17. *Journal of Architectural Education* number 4 .

[6] Mitchell, William J. 1986. "Solid Modeling and Volumetric Composition in Architecture". pp 123-135. *Design Computing.* Vol 1.

[7] Rowe, Colin and Slutzky, Robert. 1963. "Transparency: Literal and Phenomenal". *Perspecta 8* .

[8] Rowe, Colin and Robert Slutzky, (with commentary by Bernhard Hoesli). 1968. *Transparenz.* Basel, Switzerland: Birkhauser.

[9] Schumacher, Thomas L. 1987. "Deep Space/Shallow Space". pp 37-42. T*he Architectural Review* (January 1987)

[10] Summerson, John. 1963. *The Classical Language of Architecture.* Cambridge, Mass.: MIT Press.

[11] Stiny, G. and William J. Mitchell. 1978. "The Palladian Grammar". pp 5-18. *Environment and Planning B* .Vol 5.

[12] Stiny, G. "Kindergarten Grammars: Designing with Froebel's Building Gifts". pp 409-462. *Environment and Planning B* . Vol 7.

[13] Stiny, G. 1981. "Introduction to Shape and Shape Grammars". pp 343-351. *Environment and Planning B* . Vol 8.

[14] Tzonis, Alexander and Lefaivre, Liane. 1986. *Classical Architecture. The Poetics of Order.* Cambridge, Mass.: MIT Press.

---

[1] In the remainder of the present paper, the term *language* will denote an architectural language

[2] I present these rules through the usual diagrams omitting technical details; readers unfamiliar with such specifications are again referred to [2].

3
A Locus for Knowledge-Based Systems in CAAD Education

John S. Gero

Department of Architectural and Design Science
University of Sydney

This paper outlines a possible locus for knowledge-based systems in computer-aided architectural design education. It commences with a review of computer-aided architectural design and knowledge-based systems. It then proposes their use at various stages in CAAD education.

Introduction

There are a number of paradigms to consider in computer-aided architectural design education. We could think of CAAD education as a means to equip student architects with the ideas and skills needed to use CAAD systems in their work after they graduate. We could think of CAAD education as a means of specialising architecture students to control the development of CAAD systems and even to contribute to the development of such systems themselves. We could think of CAAD education as a means of providing architecture students with commercial-quality facilities to expedite the production aspects of their design processes. We could think of CAAD education as a means of providing a laboratory for architecture students to explore a new design medium. We could think of other paradigms but these four cover the major issues. In this paper, we briefly examine the potential role of knowledge-based systems in each of these paradigms.

The next section provides an overview of computer-aided architectural design. The following reviews knowledge-based systems. The final section examines the locus of knowledge-based systems in CAAD education.

Computer-Aided Architectural Design

Computer-aided architectural design has passed through a number of distinct phases. It commenced in the 1960s with a concern for graphical representation of objects being designed. This graphical genesis still manifests itself in today's computer-aided architectural design systems. In the 1970s there was a concern for object modeling to support graphical representation. The aspect being modeled was geometry and topology. It is often simply called geometric modeling. There was the recognition that aspects other than geometric were also needed, so many systems allowed the inclusion of non-geometric attributes by attaching them to geometric entities.

By the end of the 1970s and the early 1980s geometric modeling had reached sophisticated levels. At the same time analysis tools were finding their way into computer-aided architectural design systems. However, with some exceptions, computer-aided architectural design systems were not concerned with providing direct assistance to designers in their design decision-making processes. The exceptions derived their impetus from operations research techniques but did not find widespread acceptance. Recently, there has been renewed interest in using computer-based methods as direct aids to design decision making.

Designing, whether with the aid of computers or not, involves transforming a description expressed in function terms to a fixed description expressed in structure terms. *Functions* are the requirements, specifications or goals. Part of designing involves determining the functions. *Structure* is the set of elements and their relationships that go to make up an artifact. When looking at the description of structure there is no explicit function evident. Similarly, function contains no structure. Since these two classes have no descriptors in common how can one be transformed into the other.

A designer's experience allows him to map function onto structure. This is how the abductive rules in expert systems encode this knowledge. However, such a direct mapping does not allow for any reasoning about the transformation process since it is a direct mapping. How does a designer incorporate new structures? It is suggested that both function and structure are translated into a homogeneous concept, namely, behaviour. Function is decomposed into expected *behaviour*. If this behaviour is exhibited by the structure then the function is produced. From the structure the actual behaviour can be deduced. In engineering the deductive process of producing the actual behaviour is called "analysis". Further it is suggested that function, structure, and behaviour are bound together into a single conceptual schema through experience (Gero, 1989).

What are Knowledge-Based Systems ?

Knowledge Engineering

Knowledge-based systems are computer programs in which the knowledge is explicitly coded rather than implicitly encoded. They make use of knowledge engineering. *Knowledge engineering* is a subfield of artificial intelligence. It is concerned with the acquisition, representation and manipulation of human knowledge in symbolic form. Human knowledge is thought of as being reasoning (rather than the simple ability to acquire facts as you might find in an encyclopedia). Just as the industrial revolution can be considered to have automated mechanical power, and the computer revolution to have automated calculation, so knowledge engineering automates reasoning.

Feigenbaum (1977) defines the activity of knowledge engineering as follows:

The knowledge engineer practices the art of bringing the principles and tools of artificial intelligence research to bear on difficult application problems requiring experts' knowledge for their solution. The technical issues of acquiring this knowledge, representing it, and using it appropriately to construct and explain lines of reasoning are important in the design of knowledge-based systems. . .The art of constructing intelligent agents is both part of and an extension of the programming art. It is the art of building complex computer programs that represent and reason with knowledge of the world.

The fundamental structure used to represent reasoning and, hence, knowledge, is symbolic inference. Inference is based on well established logic principles and has been extended to operate on symbols. The obvious advantage of inferencing is that it does not require an a priori mathematical theory such as is found in, say, hydraulics or structures. It can be used to manipulate concepts. Barr and Feigenbaum (1981), talking about the applicability of knowledge engineering in conceptual areas, state:

Since there are no mathematical cores to structure the calculational use of the computer, such areas will inevitably be served by symbolic models and symbolic inference techniques.

Expert Systems

Expert systems have been defined as knowledge-based computer programs which use symbolic inference procedures to deal with problems that are difficult enough to require significant human expertise for their solution. Human experts can be compared with conventional computer programs in the following respects (Lansdown, 1982):

• Human expertise arises from the possession of structured experience and knowledge in a specific subject area. These skills grow as more and more experience is gained.

• Human experts can explain and, if necessary, defend the advice they give and are aware of its wider implication.

• Human experts determine which knowledge is applicable rather than proceeding algorithmically.

• Human experts can, and frequently have to, act with partial information. In order to supplement this, they ask only sufficient and pertinent questions to allow them to arrive at a conclusion.

Conventional computer programs differ markedly from programs which act as experts.

• They are usually complex and difficult for anyone other than their designers to understand.

• They embody their knowledge of the subject area in terms designed for computational efficiency such that this knowledge is intertwined with the control parts of the program. Thus, the knowledge is implicit in the program in such a way which makes it difficult to alter or change.

• They cannot suggest to their users why they need a particular fact nor justify their results.

Thus, expert systems aim to capture the ability of human experts to ask pertinent questions, to explain why they are asking them, and to defend their conclusions. These aspects are unrelated to a specific domain of knowledge and apply to all experts. Expert systems are computer programs which attempt to behave in a manner similar to rational human experts. They all share a common fundamental architecture even if the knowledge encoding mechanisms differ. An expert system will have the following components:

• an inference engine — this carries out the reasoning tasks and makes the system act like an expert

• a knowledge base — this contains the expert's domain specific knowledge and is quite separate from the inference engine

• an explanation facility — this interacts with both the knowledge base and the inference engine to explain why an answer is needed at a particular point or how a question can be answered; further it is used to explain how a conclusion was reached or to explain why a specific conclusion could not be reached

• a state description or working memory — this contains the facts which have been inferred to be true and those which have been found to be false during a particular session, as well as the facts provided by the user or another system.

- a knowledge acquisition facility —this allows the knowledge base to be modified and extended.
- a natural language interface — few expert systems have this yet.

Knowledge-Based Design Systems

Expert systems were originally developed to carry out diagnosis using classification concepts. They readily lend themselves to engineering analysis and evaluations, i.e. design analysis. Design analysis may be considered as the interpretation of a design description. The facts which describe an object and the knowledge by which properties of the object can be derived can be modelled as formal axiomatic systems. The advantage is that knowledge becomes amenable to formal proof procedures and the mechanism of logical inference (Kowalski, 1983).

Workable systems can be devised which operate on the basis of formal reasoning. This is particularly so in the case of interpreting the properties and performances of buildings where the theory by which interpretations can be made is well understood. This is generally the case, for example, when evaluating the performance of buildings for compliance with the requirements of building codes.

Expert systems of this type are also applicable to the synthesis of designs, particularly for those classes of design problem which can be subdivided into independent subproblems. But expert systems which are applicable to the more general class of design problem can also be devised.

Expert systems for design analysis are well-described in the literature (Sriram and Adey, 1986a; Sriram and Adey, 1986b; Sriram and Adey, 1987a; Sriram and Adey, 1987b; Sriram and Adey, 1987c; Gero, 1988a; Gero, 1988b; Gero, 1988c; Dym, 1985; Maher, 1987; Pham, 1988). Expert systems for design synthesis can also be found in the above references as well as in Rychener (1988), Gero (1985), and Gero (1987). The foundations of the use of expert systems and knowledge-based systems for design analysis and design synthesis are presented in Coyne et al. (1989).

Locus of Knowledge-Based Systems in CAAD Education

Learning How to Use CAAD Systems

Current CAAD systems involve constructing geometric and topological models of buildings. Often the manuals for these systems are many hundreds of pages long. Some are even over a thousand pages long. The typical student learning curve to develop facility with such a system looks like that shown in figure 1.

The complexity of these systems, their lack of standardisation and their lack of an intuitive approach and interface means that the development of skills to use them in a productive fashion is enormously time-consuming. Further, it takes considerable teaching staff time to provide the necessary tutorial effort to support this skill development.

Much of the knowledge in the manuals could be translated into the knowledge base of an expert system. This expert system could sit alongside the CAAD system as a desktop accessory and provide both information and guidance to the CAAD system user. It could be used by both novices and experienced users, each of whom would utilise different knowledge. Bennett et al. (1978) developed an expert system to guide users in the proper use of a large computer-aided analysis package. The approach is presented graphically in figure 2. The expert system is considerably more than an on-line manual. It can be interrogated by the user and extensive dialogue between the user and the expert system is likely to occur. A further sophistication would be to have a generic expert system for this task which semi-automatically acquired the knowledge about the CAAD system directly from the users manual. Such an expert system would have a model of CAAD systems as its foundation.

Learning About Developing CAAD Systems
CAD systems used to be considered general purpose, i.e. the same system was used by engineers and by architects. It was soon realised that specialisation was needed for each professional group. Thus, we see CAAD systems being developed which share elements with systems designed for other professionals but having approaches built into them that make them unique to architecture. We are beginning to see *expectation-driven systems* that contain domain-specific knowledge being developed. Such CAAD systems embody considerably more architectural ideas than before. A small percentage of architecture students will end up developing the next generation of CAAD systems and it is to these students that such an approach is addressed.

An expert system that contained knowledge about the design ideas behind current CAAD systems and about CAAD system principles could be used to assist students to learn about developing CAAD systems. This approach is presented graphically in figure 3. The expert system would sit between the user and a variety of CAAD systems. it would draw specific instance examples from the CAAD systems to demonstrate system design principles.

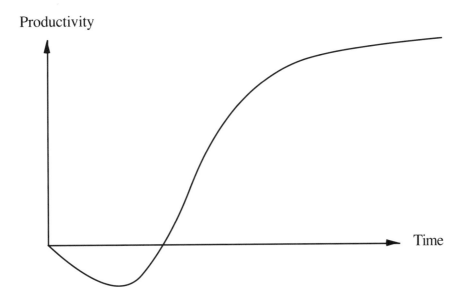

Figure 1 Typical time-productivity learning curve

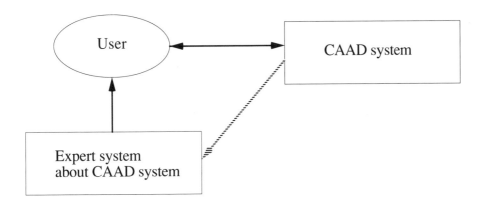

Figure 2   Using an expert system to inform and guide users of the CAAD system.

Learning About Production

It takes experience to develop an intuitive understanding of what needs to be presented at the various stages in developing a design. The information presented to the client at the concept stage is quite different to that needed by the city planning department. This in turn is quite different to that needed by the contractor. This professional practice knowledge could be encapsulated in the knowledge base of an expert system. This expert system would interact with the user to determine the stage of the project and then control the CAAD system to produce the appropriate documentation. This is shown graphically in figure 4.

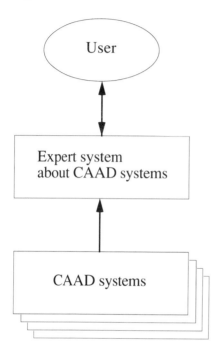

Figure 3 Using an expert system to teach about CAAD systems design and development.

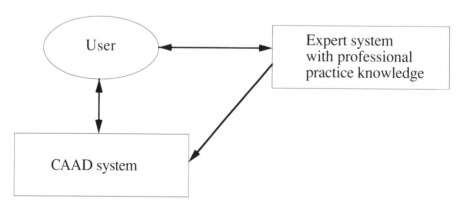

Figure 4 Using an expert system to teach about and to control the documentation produced at various stages of a project.

Since there are no legal consequences if the documentation is incomplete, it would be sufficient if the expert system controlled the CAAD system to produce indicative documentation in some areas.

Learning About Design Using a Novel Medium
Probably the most interesting approach is to consider the use of artificial intelligence in computer-aided architectural design systems as presenting a novel design medium. It is only now that research into knowledge-based design is beginning to show results. The inclusion of symbolic reasoning, one of the bases of artificial intelligence, is changing our expectations of CAAD systems. Further, it is re-awakening the interest in design theory and methods as we develop more powerful representation tools (Coyne et al., 1989; Gero and Maher, 1988).

We are beginning to see the emergence of knowledge-based CAAD systems (figure 5). It is still very early but the promise is there. New ideas about how design experience can be acquired, represented, and manipulated offer the potential that we can produce systems closer to our expectations than existing systems (Gero and Rosenman, 1989).

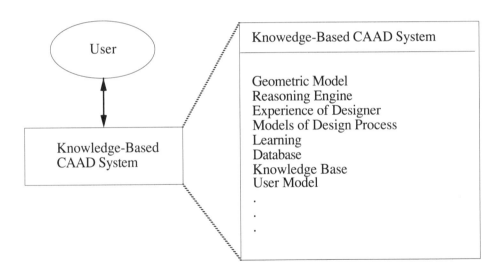

Figure 5 Knowledge-based CAAD systems

Conclusion

The first three paradigms of the use of knowledge-based systems are founded on the body of research into tutoring using artificial intelligence (Woolf, 1988). Intelligent tutoring systems are concerned with how to guide a student to learn new concepts. Intelligent tutoring systems have been successfully constructed.

The fourth paradigm draws ideas but not systems from other domains. It is here that we, as educators and researchers, will have to carry out both the research and development.

References

Barr, A. and Feigenbaum, E. (eds). 1981. *Handbook of Artificial Intelligence*, Vol.1. Los Altos: William Kaufmann.

Bennett, J. S., Creary, L. A., Engelmore, R. M., and Melosh, R. E. 1978. *SACON: A knowledge-based consultant in structural analysis, Heuristic Programming Project Rep. No. HPP-78-23*. Stanford: Computer Science Department, Stanford University.

Coyne, R. C., Rosenman, M. A., Radford, A. D., Balachandran, M. and Gero, J. S. 1989. *Knowledge-Based Design Systems*. Reading, MA: Addison-Wesley.

Dym, C. L. (ed.). 1985. *Applications of Knowledge-Based Systems to Engineering Analysis and Design*. New York: American Society of Mechanical Engineers.

Feigenbaum, E. A. 1977. "The art of artificial intelligence: themes and case studies in knowledge engineering". pp.1014–1029. *IJCAI-77*. Los Altos: William Kaufmann.

Gero, J. S. (ed.). 1985a. *Knowledge Engineering in Computer-Aided Design*. Amsterdam: North-Holland.

Gero, J. S. (ed.). 1987a. *Expert Systems in Computer-Aided Design*. Amsterdam: North-Holland.

Gero, J. S. (ed.). 1988a. *Artificial Intelligence in Engineering: Design*. Amsterdam: Elsevier/CMP.

Gero, J. S. (ed.). 1988b. *Artificial Intelligence in Engineering: Diagnosis and Learning*. Amsterdam: Elsevier/CMP.

Gero, J. S. (ed.) 1988c . *Artificial Intelligence in Engineering: Robotics and Processes*. Amsterdam: Elsevier/CMP.

Gero, J. S. 1989 . "Prototypes: a basis for knowledge-based design". pp.11-17. In J. S. Gero and T. Oksala (eds), *Knowledge-Based Systems in Architecture*. Helsinki: Acta Polytechnica Scandinavica.

Gero, J. S. and Maher, M. L. 1988. "A future role of knowledge-based systems in the design process". pp.81–90. In T. Maver and H. Wagter (eds). *CAAD Futures '87*. Amsterdam: Elsevier.

Gero, J. S. and Rosenman, M. A. (1989). "A conceptual framework for knowledge-based design research at Sydney University's Design Computing Unit", in J. S. Gero (ed.), *Artificial Intelligence in Engineering: Design—II, CMP*, Southampton, pp.361–380.

Kowalski, R. 1983 . *Logic for Problem Solving*. Amsterdam: Elsevier-North Holland.

Lansdown, J. 1982. *Expert systems: their impact on the construction industry*. London: RIBA Conference Fund.

Maher, M. L. (ed.) 1987. *Expert Systems for Civil Engineers: Technology and Application*. New York: American Soc. Civ. Eng.

Pham, D. T. (ed.) 1988. *Expert Systems in Engineering*. Berlin: IFS Publications/Springer- Verlag.

Rychener, M. (ed.) 1988. *Expert Systems for Engineering Design*. New York: Academic Press.

Sriram, D., and Adey, R. (eds.) 1986a. *Applications of Artificial Intelligence in Engineering Problems*—Volume I. Berlin: Springer-Verlag.

Sriram, D., and Adey, R. (eds.) 1986b. *Applications of Artificial Intelligence in Engineering Problems*—Volume II, Berlin: Springer-Verlag.

Sriram, D., and Adey, R. (eds.) 1987a. *Artificial Intelligence in Engineering: Tools and Technique*. Southampton: Computational Mechanics Publications.

Sriram, D., and Adey, R. (eds.) (1987b). *Knowledge-Based Expert Systems in Engineering: Planning and Design*. Southampton: Computational Mechanics Publications.

Sriram, D., and Adey, R. (eds.) (1987c). *Knowledge-Based Expert Systems in Engineering: Classification, Education and Control*. Southampton: Computational Mechanics Publications.

Woolf, B. (1981). "Intelligent tutoring systems: a survey". pp.1–43. In H. E. Shrobe and AAAI (eds), *Exploring Artificial Intelligence*. San Mateo: Morgan Kaufmann.

4
Computer Modeling:
A First Course in Design Computing

Bharat Dave
Robert Woodbury

Department of Architecture
Carnegie-Mellon University

Introduction

Computation in design has long been a focus in our department. In recent years our faculty has paid particular attention to the use of computation in professional architectural education. The result is a shared vision of computers in the curriculum [Woodbury 1985] and a set of courses, some with considerable history[1] and others just now being initiated[2]. We (Dave and Woodbury)[3] have jointly developed and at various times over the last seven years have taught Computer Modeling, the most introductory of these courses. This is a required course for all the incoming freshmen students in the department. In this paper we describe Computer Modeling: its context, the issues and topics it addresses, the tasks it requires of students, and the questions and opportunities that it raises.

Computer Modeling is a course about concepts, about ways of explicitly understanding design and its relation to computation. Procedural skills and algorithmic problem solving techniques are given only secondary emphasis. In essential terms, the course is about models, of design processes, of designed objects, of computation and of computational design. Its lessons are intended to communicate a structure of such models to students and through this structure to demonstrate a relationship between computation and design. It is hoped that this structure can be used as a framework, around which students can continue to develop an understanding of computers in design.

Intellectual Underpinnings

Underlying the course is the notion of a model, which Echenique [Echenique 1972, p.164] aptly characterizes:

"...a representation of a reality, in which the representation is made by the expression of certain relevant characteristics of the observed reality and where reality consists of objects or systems that exist, have existed, or may exist."

We present the entire course as a conscious exercise in model building (modeling) and explanation. We feel that it is important to present a single coherent view, and we thus have to embrace a single overall model. We find that the notion of rational decision making (RDM) has much to commend itself. According to this notion, design is an iterative, or cyclical, activity with distinct types of actions occurring in a fixed order in each cycle. These actions are: the generation of alternatives, performance prediction, the simultaneous evaluation of predictions, and the selection of alternatives. Further the process is purposeful, it has goals, and these are captured in the evaluation and selection steps. Stepping outside of this local view of an individual decision cycle, the basic model can be seen to accommodate a wide variety of global processes, from strictly linear ones in which only one alternative is generated at each step and no changes are ever made to decisions already made, to very complex processes, with multiple agents, with compound branching and significant retraction of decisions.

All of the activities involved in rational decision making must be carried out by some agent and further structure is introduced when that agent is human. To describe this structure we introduce as the second of our models an abstract model of human cognition [Newell 1972]. According to this model, the structure of the human mind itself necessitates a certain way of conducting design. Humans design by searching in a state space; they move from one representation (or model) of a designed object to another, at each step applying the last three actions of the RDM cycle to some degree. Further, humans have a very limited capacity for immediate storage and access of information, and this implies that they will virtually always use some form of externally stored information to assist them in designing. This information may represent the object being designed, the process of design, the goals of design or general knowledge about objects or designing.

Humans code, and understand, all of this information as symbol structures, that is, sets of discrete objects and relations between them. This way of representing objects works well in many contexts but encounters difficulties in architectural design. Space, a continuous phenomenon, is at the center of everything in architecture and its discrete representation has always been problematic. Over the centuries a number of ways of representing things spatial, none entirely satisfactory, have evolved in architecture, and the current intellectual struggles in building computer based spatial representations continue this pattern. We explain the relation between representation (in the form of symbol structures) and space as the third model of the course. To demonstrate this idea, and to introduce them in their own right, we use examples of spatial representations as the basis for sections of the course.

The three models above, rational decision making, human cognition, and spatial representation, describe design as done by humans. Our course is about computation in design and two additional models must be brought to the table. The first is a model of computation, that describes single processor serial machines, operating on dual memory. The second is an augmentation of the basic model of human cognition to include these computational agents. This last model is the only normative and speculative model in the course. In its presentation we take the position that the goal of using computation in design is to be supportive of humans in areas of strength and to provide new capabilities in areas of human weakness.

Computer Modeling thus consists of explaining five models. Taken together we believe that these constitute a framework on which a broad understanding of design computation can be built. Through explanation, demonstration, and a set of structured exercises we hope to help students learn and apply these models. Since our goal is communication of the ideas, we stress a conceptual approach in the course. Students are given the concepts in lectures and a minimal amount of procedural instruction in labs. The assignments are designed to stress the concepts and to exercise the students use of the models. By and large, the procedural parts of the assignments are left in the students' hands.

Course Content

We structure the course around examples of spatial representations (or models); introducing and explaining the other four models in the context of specific representations. Each of these—*graphic pictures, graphic 2-dimensional, graphic 3-dimensional, databases,* and *parametric models*—represents and supports manipulation of design information in a different fashion, thus providing ample grist for our pedagogical mill. For each spatial type, we provide a set of lectures and computer based exercises using existing commercial software.

Graphic Pictures

Graphic pictures (our name in this course for bitmaps) are collections of point marks; these are perceived by humans to possess some properties like pattern, orientation, and so on. Our tendency to see some organizing pattern (or lack thereof) lets us associate representations of points with larger conceptual elements like lines, surfaces, texture, and others. Thus graphic pictures as models make use of points as basic building blocks, and patterns of points to represent semantic concepts. A set of fundamental and most often-used operations on picture-based models are the similarity transformations: translation, rotation, scaling, and reflection. An exercise to introduce these notions is to alter (by subdivision, line editing, introduction of elements, etc.) a polygon in such a way that when many such polygons are packed together using the similarity transformations, an aesthetically pleasing and complex composition is obtained (figure 1).

Within this exercise, some of the other course models are easy to introduce. The exercise is stated in terms of an initial state (the polygon), and a suggested set of operators upon that state (subdivision, line editing, introduction of new elements, etc.). We have observed that successful students naturally use a state space approach in this context. We elaborate on state space search here to introduce the notion of a rule, a semantically meaningful operation, and show that rule discovery and search are two inseparable aspects of state space search. Further, each alteration to a polygon has often unexpected effects on a composition of many polygons; at the end of a set of operator applications students usually find it necessary to stop and compose a few polygons together to

Figure 1   Paint system exercise (Michael Choung)

evaluate the overall effect. This provides a natural opportunity to discuss the RDM model.

We use paint programs as computational tools to develop graphic pictures. The painting paradigm operates directly on a bitmap, and input from the bitmap to any operators must be stated in terms of pixels and (possibly ordered) sets of pixels only. The operations may appear to output higher level entities such as lines and polygons, but these are laid into the bitmap representations, and their meaning is immediately lost in the representation, though often not in perception of that representation by humans. We demonstrate to students that painting thus supports only a small part of the operations required for the task, and that with painting, rule creation and application must reside entirely on their side of human computer interaction. At this point, we also introduce the notion of a procedure, or an ordered series of operations, by showing that many of the operations required in the exercise occur in repetitive groups. As manually executing these repetitive groups is the most oppressive part of the task, a strong motivation for understanding and using procedures is created.

Graphic 2D Models

If we model and operate upon representations of objects as collections of points only, the amount of information to be represented and processed becomes unwieldy. By adding certain structure to graphic pictures, we obtain graphic 2D models. A set of graphic 2D elements like lines, curves, etc. and a set of operations upon them are defined in graphic 2D models. A point represents a location in space and a certain order of distribution of points is used as a basis for construction of graphic 2D elements. For example, given a center and a radius, a circle represents locations of all points such that all points are equidistant from the center by an amount equal to the radius. A set of points are coalesced into a small number of parameters to completely define all points in that set. Graphic 2D models thus make use of geometric concepts and when applied in a domain like architectural design gain further semantic structure by concepts and conventions of that domain.

These notions are introduced in an exercise in which students design an interior layout for a given site and develop a set of scaled drawings. This exercise is an elaboration of some ideas presented in the earlier section. The goal is to develop a spatial composition using a set of familiar objects and their relationships. Unlike developing a graphic composition as an end in itself as in the earlier exercise, students have to take into account architectural requirements of the spatial composition. The iterative process of design development as RDM and state space search can be made more explicit by requiring students to record intermediate design layouts and sketches.

In this exercise, scaled drawings are used as the means to represent and conduct design inquiry. In particular, the role of representations and inferences they support are emphasized. For example, a square may be represented once at least the length of its side is known. Even if we do not know where it is located, we can infer its area since it is defined in terms of parameters we already know. On the other hand, if we require a square of certain area, we can infer the length of its sides. This process of translating known information into other desired forms enables us to represent and communicate our ideas, and this very process also allows us to translate design purposes into realizable products.

By using 2D drawing programs in this context, we introduce additional computational notions. While working on a traditional medium like paper, articulation of design intentions and their realization as a design solution are the primary responsibility of human agents. In contrast, while working on computers, students have to not only articulate their intentions but also explicitly select and communicate such operations to a drawing program. This observation leads to further discussion of structured data representation, i.e. from pixels to graphic 2D elements and attributes, and representation of actions as procedures or parametric operations, e.g. creation of a square by specification of two opposite vertices. By seeing and realizing that interpretation and execution of purposeful actions as procedures can be encoded in computer programs, students are exposed to further possibilities of computers augmenting the design process.

Figure 2   2D Drawing Systems (Yi-Ren Wang)

Graphic 3D Models

Two dimensional graphical representations like plans, sections, etc., are but partial views of spatial environments. To make these views as informationally consistent and complete with real spatial environments as possible, we introduce graphic 3D models. Like the way in which point-based graphic pictures were extended to define higher level graphic 2D models, we extend graphic 2D elements into the third dimension by introducing the notion of volumes that can be solids or voids. Based on certain parameters, volumes can be categorized into classes, e.g. cubes, cylinders, spheres, and others. By using these parameters, a small number of parametric definitions can be used to generate and represent a large number of instances of volumes.

Application of graphic 3D models in a domain like architectural design requires introduction of additional parameters—domain specific attributes and relations—to these models. For example, an instance of a cube may represent a wall made out of concrete blocks of certain strength and color. Another instance of a cube may represent void space with qualitative attributes like acoustic and lighting properties.

We introduce these ideas using an exercise in which students develop a graphic 3D model (at a certain level of detail) of an existing design project. In this exercise, the emphasis is not on the generation of a new design but rather on its representation in terms of design elements. By taking apart and modeling a design project, students are expected to understand design projects as assemblies of physical and qualitative elements brought together in order to satisfy some design context. The underlying model of design as a set of purposes and their realization in the form of volumetric compositions becomes more articulated in this exercise. Further, parametric relations in graphic 3D models can be used to infer new information—both geometric and architectural. Thus, given a cube with its length, width and height, we can infer its volume; and conversely, given a volume and some constraints on any two other parameters, the third can be inferred. Similarly, architectural concepts like adjacency, spatial continuity, rhythm, etc. are realized as well as evaluated using volumetric parameters and relations between them.

The role of 3D drawing programs in this exercise is to make obvious the issues discussed above. Further, students also realize that the underlying volumetric model in a modeling program affects the level of detail and consistency of information that can be represented. Thus, a 3D drawing program based on constructive solid geometry exhibits different capabilities than the one based on sweep representation or octrees. Additionally, data representation

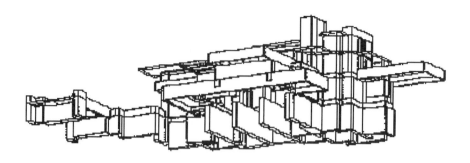

Figure 3   3D Drawing system exercise (Glenn Cottrell and Matt Wittmer)

and operations supported in such programs are organized as one large set of structured information—a database. Various views like plans, elevations, perspectives, are results of operations that retrieve and transform selected information from that database. What we understand and represent about a phenomenon is affected by the model we use and the vantage point we choose. On a secondary level, computer programs that support 3D representation, hidden-line removal, and specification of attributes like color, texture, light sources, etc., also enable accurate visualization of three dimensional spaces. This has a subtle impact on students in that they become more attuned to thinking in three dimensions since such programs also offer fast generation of realistic 3D views.

Databases

The graphic models introduced earlier are sufficient to model a number of phases in architectural design. These models are made more complete by introducing the notion of databases that integrate graphic and nongraphic representations. Architectural design projects start with a statement of needs or a design brief. Based on a programmatic description, a design is developed using various kinds of graphic and nongraphic representations, e.g. architectural and engineering drawings, specifications, bills of quantities, and others. Once a project is constructed, another set of descriptions may be developed to record the design project as built. Taken together, all such project descriptions constitute a project database in which each description is derived based on another description and augments or selectively transforms information.

An exercise introduces these notions. The task is to develop a database of project information for interior layout for a given site.   Some of the notions about the model of design as the RDM and state space search,

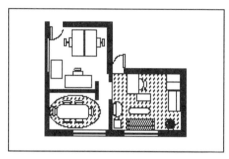
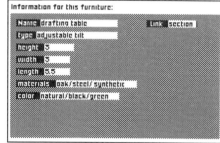
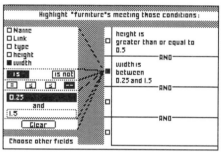
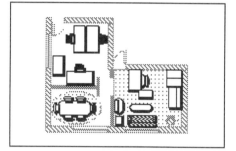

Figure 4   Database exercise   (Jeff Goldstone)

introduced earlier remain the same in this exercise. Additionally, students
learn to select a complete set of parameters—both the graphic and nongraphic,
that are necessary to develop a model of spatial entities.

Design databases offer two significant advantages: generation of new
descriptions as needed and reduction of effort in representing those aspects of
design that are repetitive within a project and across a number of projects. In
the former case, that is generation of a new description, we take a given
description, define a format for new description and extract information from
what is available. For example, given a plan, a schedule of doors and windows
for each opening represented in drawings can be generated. This is an example
of using information that is implicit in a graphic representation to derive a
nongraphic representation based on some selection criteria. In addition, the
newly derived description may be used with other graphic or nongraphic
information to generate yet another description. To illustrate, a drawing may
explicitly describe only a tiling pattern and material specifications for some
floor area. Based on this, a total required number of tiles may be derived. Using
this quantitative description and construction costs, a new description, e.g. cost
estimate, can be derived. In other words, a design database consists of a number
of graphic and nongraphic descriptions that are related, and using some
operations, a given description can be transformed into another description.

The second advantage, that is reduction in effort, derives from the fact that certain design information may be used quite often in a design project, (e.g. window details), or a number of projects may use similar details, (e.g. elevator cores). Such information that does not change and is used repetitively can be stored in a standard details database, and can be referenced from that database when needed.

These notions are made more explicit by using a computer-based database program. In order to develop a project database, students have to define, represent and associate a sufficient number of parameters in both graphic and nongraphic descriptions. Further, operations of sorting and searching on the information represented give students an opportunity to selectively generate new descriptions. This also leads to the discussion of some parallels between database concepts and design experience. A database is a collection of structured information, and such information can be collated in various ways to generate new information relative to design goals. Similarly, design expertise can be viewed as a large collection of design rules that are applied in varying contexts, and their combined processing brings forth new design descriptions.

Parametric Variations

According to the model of design as RDM and state space search, design development goes through a number of stages; at each stage, some information is asserted in keeping with given design purposes. Each stage in the design process supplements and transforms information from the preceding stage. Throughout this process, design representations are externalized in the form of drawings, sketches, and others. Externalization of representations consists of asserting relevant information about design elements and some techniques or procedures to manipulate and transform such data.

In the process of generation and searching for appropriate representations, the critical issues are selection of operators and statement of a final goal that controls and directs the sequence of design information processing. But in most design tasks, information states and operators are not so clear cut. Information available at the start of design process may be only loosely or partially defined. At any given stage in the design process, more than one operator may be available to manipulate and transform a current design state. Out of a huge amount of information, a designer has to select appropriate transformations and an order in which they are to be carried out. This situation in design leads to a large number of possible alternatives which are but variations derived by changing some design parameters. This process of design exploration can be viewed as generating various design scenarios.

These concepts are introduced using an exercise in which students build a parametric model for calculating illumination levels in a space given some artificial light source. Once a parametric model is defined, students generate various design alternatives by either changing the location of light source, its intensity, or both. The results are graphically displayed using graphs and contour charts.

This exercise, in a limited fashion, brings together a number of issues as they pertain to modeling in architecture and computation. By explicitly developing a parametric model of a design task and generating a number of alternatives, students learn to articulate dependencies among design parameters. Design scenarios may involve parameters that are independent of each other, e.g. placement of a stairwell and floor finishes are relatively independent of each other. On the other hand, both the number and size of steps are dependent on floor height and linear distance available in a given design. The latter kinds of decisions involve relational information involving dependent parameters. If the significant parameter is tweaked, its effect will propagate to parameters that are dependent on it. Such relational information can be modeled as algebraic equations, e.g. computing number and size of steps given other relevant information.

Secondly, this exercise also gives students a chance to explicitly define a state space, and search for feasible states for a given design task. By using spreadsheet programs, the ideas of computation as representation of data, relations between them, and procedures by which possibilities inherent in a model can be explored, are made obvious. This, in turn, leads to the discussion of parallels between architectural design process and computation, and how the experience accumulated by designers over a number of years might be represented and used in a computer. The most significant impact of experience manifests itself in the selectivity exercised in design development. The kinds and ways in which experienced designers generate and manipulate design information evolves into a consistent pattern. This consistency of design development or information processing in design is what gives rise to identifiable design styles. These ideas become evident once we explain a paradigm like shape grammars and their application to the works of some noted architects.

Course Summary

The ideas introduced in the course exhibit a tight hierarchy in that each exercise is an enhanced and more structured version of the one preceding it. Once students have completed these exercises, we present a taxonomy of computer-assisted design paradigms [Galle 1981] and representative examples for each of the following categories:

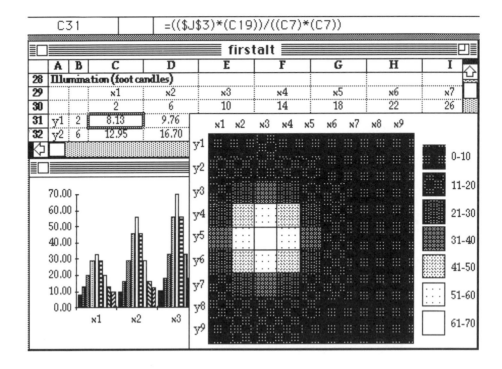

Figure 5   Spreadsheet exercise   (Christine Kochinski)

1. Automated evaluation of designs generated by traditional means
2. Stepwise interactive generation
3. Non-exhaustive generation of feasible solutions
4. Exhaustive generation of feasible solutions
5. Generation of (sub)optimal designs

By taking a structured approach to the introduction of these ideas, we hope that students acquire a conceptual understanding of the role of models and their representations. By emphasizing a conceptual over a procedural approach, we also hope that students articulate the knowledge they gain in this course in a fashion that is independent of particular tasks, domains, and software or hardware considerations.

Course Materials and Facilities
The course is organized as a combination of lecture sessions, alternating with hands-on demonstration in the use of computers and various applications. Lecture sessions are scheduled for about 50 minutes, once every week. These sessions are used to introduce concepts, and are supplemented with a set of recommended readings. Two texts that we have found useful in this regard are [Mitchell 1977] and [Radford 1987]. We have also developed an extensive set of

lecture notes that closely follows the course structure, and that is made available to students.

Lab sessions meet for about 80 minutes, once every week. Currently, we use MacPaint[4], MacDraw[5], FileVision[6], and Excel[7] running on the Apple Macintosh[8]machines to introduce paint systems, two-dimensional drawing systems, databases, and spreadsheets. For three-dimensional drawing systems, we use AutoCad[9] running on the IBM AT [10] machines. All these machines, software applications, and printing facilities are maintained in public clusters on campus and are accessible to students on an extended basis including weekends.

Reflections

An informal evaluation of the course through student feedback, both written and oral, and course assignments, gives us a general feeling of satisfaction with both format and content. We are particularly pleased with our choice to use representation as a common thread throughout the course and to explain the other four models within this context. When we designed the course, we saw this format as the one that provided the most concrete basis from which to build—a view we still hold today. We have found that students are increasingly interested in learning about computers and their architectural applications. The course seems to provide a good beginning for these interests; indeed, some students, after taking the course, have spontaneously used their experience in other courses.

These preenings aside, we see several areas that can be improved. Each of our course components could build more structured links to the five basic models we communicate, and to other courses in the departmental sequence. The graphic picture (bitmap) component could more formally introduce geometric operations and could be more explicit about state space search. In the 2D model component, we get relatively small intellectual content from a large amount of student drawing effort. Neither the particular topic (interior layout) nor the drawings required (plan, section, and perspective) provide any especially stimulating content to the exercise. In the 3D model component, we are somewhat frustrated by the lack of appropriate solid modeling systems on inexpensive hardware. The content of the database component has improved recently, but it remains at too trivial a level to really motivate student interest. Finally, the spreadsheet module is very interesting, but we have just begun to explore the possibilities for architecturally relevant exercises.

On a larger scale, we feel a need to more tightly integrate Computer Modeling with the rest of our course sequence and with the departmental curriculum as a whole, while maintaining its emphasis on concepts independent of particular applications and tasks. A stronger treatment of procedural ideas would assist our introductory and advanced programming courses. More rigorous consideration of geometry could motivate our course on geometry and computation. If search were treated more seriously, students could be better prepared for the material in our advanced course on rules and representations.

References

[Echenique 1972]   M. Echenique. "Models: A discussion." Chapter 7, pages 164-174. In L. Martin and L. March (eds.), *Urban Space and Structures*, Cambridge: Cambridge University Press.

[Galle 1981]   P. Galle. "An algorithm for exhaustive generation of building floor plans." Pages 813-825. *Communications of the ACM*, 24, 1981.

[Mitchell 1977]   W. Mitchell. *Computer-Aided Architectural Design*. New York: Van Nostrand Reinhold.

[Newell 1972]   A. Newell and H. Simon. *Human Problem Solving*. Englewood Cliffs, NJ.: Prentice-Hall.

[Radford 1987]   A. Radford and G. Stevens. *CAAD Made Easy*. New York: McGraw Hill.

[Woodbury 1985]   U. Flemming, O. Akin, R. Woodbury. "A Comprehensive Computing System for Architectural Education". pp 637-642. In K. Duncan and D. Harris (eds.), *Computers in Education, First World Conference on Computers in Education*. Amsterdam: Elsevier Science Publishers B.V. (North-Holland).

Notes

[1] Introduction to Programming, Introduction to CAD, Rules and Representations, CAD Laboratory

[2] Geometry and Computation, Rational Decision Making

[3] Roy McKelvey, faculty in the Department of Design, has also played a significant role in teaching Computer Modeling.

[4] MacPaint is a product of Claris Software.

[5] MacDraw is a product of Claris Software.

[6] FileVision is a product of Telos Software.

[7] Excel is a product of Microsoft Coropration.

[8] Macintosh is a product of Apple Computers.

[9] AutoCad is a product of Autodesk.

[10] Personal computer AT is a product of IBM Corporation.

Knowledge-Based Design Tools

5
Classes of Design—Classes of Tools

Gerhard Schmitt

Architekturabteilung
ETH Zürich

It is unrealistic to expect one computer-aided design tool to sufficiently support any one given design process. Yet it is necessary to define new CAD programs that give semantic support in design. To this end, the paper first differentiates phases and classes of design and then attempts to establish relations between the defined classes and appropriate computer-aided design tools. In three main sections it describes (i) routine, innovative and creative design, (ii) a set of corresponding prototype design tools, and (iii) two examples of routine and innovative design which use these tools. The purpose of the paper is to make a contribution to the definition of domain specific aspects of CAD and to propose a mapping between processes and tools.

Introduction

Architects employing computers in teaching design have encountered a number of severe conceptual problems in applying the new tool to established design methods and theories. The reasons are two-fold: obvious weaknesses of current CAD systems in representing qualitative and functional aspects of design and the lack of appropriate teaching and design methods which will be fundamentally different with the new tools. The object representation and manipulation capabilities of state-of-the-art CAD systems are far more advanced than functional modeling capabilities or the necessary accompanying design methodology [Schmitt 88].

There seem to exist two alternatives to solve this problem. The first would be to adjust design teaching to the capabilities of hardware and software thus, creating a constant dependency on commercial developments. The second alternative would be to attempt a classification of the design process itself and to search and define a set of conceptual tools each of which support a particular class of design. This approach will guarantee some independence from commercial developments and has the potential to create a general body of design knowledge which is comparable to summaries of methods and experiences in other disciplines, such as medicine.

Most often the design process is broken down into several *stages* [Laseau 80], reaching from program development to construction. Beyond this however, there are obviously different *types* of design which Gero has appropriately coined as routine, innovative and creative [Gero 88]. A *class of design*, then, is defined as the intersection of design *types* and design *stages* that share common characteristics, such as routine program development. A *class of tools*, accordingly, is a set of programs that share common characteristics, such as 3D solids modelers. Upon closer examination of existing and planned tools for design, a certain mapping between classes of design and classes of tools begins to emerge. This paper claims that general CAD tools are best suited for the general production of drawings and that the few emerging parametric programs are well suited for routine design. There seems to be very few support tools for creative and innovative design which in part explains the absence of any new architecture which involves the use of computers in design process.

Classes of Design

The architectural design process includes several stages, as proposed by Laseau: program development, schematic design, preliminary design, design development, contract documents, shop drawings, and construction [Laseau 80]. While this differentiation is useful for understanding and possibly formalizing stages of design, for the development of a new design methodology a classification of different design types is necessary.

It seems appropriate to differentiate at least three types of design, as proposed by Gero, Maher, and Zhang: routine design, innovative design, and creative design [Gero 88]. While this is a useful classification for research purposes, it does not quite reflect architectural reality and must therefore, be seen as a means of abstraction. From the intersection of types and stages we derive design classes. For lack of a better alternative, design classes are represented using prototypes which at the moment do not well express important factors necessary for successful real-world design such as the socio-economic environment, existing context, and client profiles.

The challenge is to describe the "roots" or qualitative and functional aspects of the prototype and not the external representations. The roots are almost always functional whereas the external representation is a well described object. We are experimenting presently with a different representation of design, treating existing architecture as cases and new design as a combination of case-based reasoning and rule-based inferencing, but an in-depth description of this approach would be beyond the scope of this paper.

Parametric Design

Parametric design, also often called routine design [Gero 88], is the major focus for commercial programs in defining and supporting the design process. Routine design assumes that:

- The design problem is well defined and client requirements are well understood.
- There exists a parameterized prototype for the type of design that is to be developed and a data base of parameter variations.
- The final design may be derived by refining, but not fundamentally changing the prototype.

This type of design is characterized by *"prototype refinement"*, a goal-directed activity. Beginning with a given prototype of, for example, a piece of furniture or equipment, the designer adjusts a number of parameters to the specifications of the design program. The parameters, typically geometric properties or materials, are normally well understood and are manipulated either in the designer's memory or with advanced modeling systems. The functional requirements of the design are known and the semantics or the teleology (the purpose of each element) of the design are not changed but accepted from previous examples. This type of design and design process rely heavily on instantiation of designs from a *catalogue* of parameterized examples [Kramer 88].

Innovative Design

Innovative design, also referred to as prototype adaptation [Gero 88] and prototype combination [Faltings 88] is used when the refinement of a known prototype will most likely not lead to a satisfactory solution. Prototype adaptation and prototype combination can potentially lead to creative design. The designer has a general idea of the desired object and the design process is still a goal-directed activity. It cannot be completed with routine design because either the functional description or the object properties are not achievable utilizing a given prototype. Therefore, combination of two or more prototypes which each have some of the desired properties is necessary. In some cases, innovative design is achievable with prototype modification. An example would be the development of an advanced type of intelligent office building for which some information infrastructure needs, such as new requirements for communication are still unknown. *Case-based reasoning* (the entire building being the case) and *explanation-based learning* systems (functions or building parts being the examples) are of particular interest in innovative design. Once a prototype is adapted or several prototypes have been combined, the design process becomes routine design.

Creative Design

Creative design is rare and defined by the development of new solutions that may only be partially defined at the outset. Both functional requirements and the object's properties are not necessarily and completely known and the final design may in fact influence the original problem definition or even render it partially irrelevant. It is possible that a unique solution (Ronchamps, Sydney Opera House) may be found to a problem in which case the result would be an "archetype." In most cases, "prototype creation" is necessary, which later can be combined and modified (innovative design) and instantiated (routine design). An example is the invention of a new machine, such as the personal computer. Although creative design must be mentioned as the perhaps most important design class, the attempt to formalize creative design is outside the scope of this paper.

Classes of Tools

Different tools support different types of design. As a general rule, object presentation and manipulation tools such as word processing, drafting and three-dimensional modeling programs—in the following referred to as generic tools—have a larger application base and a more robust and commonly understandable user interface than experimental programs for parametric modeling or grammar generators. The following classes of tools are to be considered:

• Generic tools. Those include word processing (e.g., WORD, Emacs), spreadsheets (i.e., EXCEL), painting (e.g., MacPaint), drafting (i.e., AutoCAD), three-dimensional modeling (e.g., Personal Architect), hypermedia (e.g., Hypercard). Generic tools are particularly strong in representing objects, rather than qualitative or functional properties and requirements.
• Parametric tools. Those include two-dimensional parametric design tools (Synthesis) and teaching programs (Topdown) [Mitchell 89] which make use of formalized design knowledge about machine parts, classical orders, and trees, as respective application examples.
• Prototype editors. Those include tools to interactively establish, manipulate, and combine prototypes through interactive input or forms of machine learning.

The GPC and TARTAN prototypes described below are examples with particular emphasis on supporting conceptual design development.

• Grammar editors. Those include tools to interactively define and edit shape, structure, or later possibly knowledge grammar generators, to manipulate their control structure, and to add domain-specific knowledge. The FROEBEL and GRC programs described below are examples for programs intended to support experimental design development.

There is no simple mapping between generic tools and routine design, for example, or between complex tools and creative design. In some cases, the opposite holds true. Graphic, symbolic, and alpha-numeric information are not readily made compatible at the moment. The following table attempts an overview of a mapping between phases of the design process, types of design, and design tools.

	Routine	Innovative	Creative
Program development	G	G	G
Schematic design	P	P E S	S
Preliminary design	P E	P E S	P E S
Design development	P E	P E S	P E S
Contract documents	G	G P	G E P
Shop drawings	G	G	G E P
Construction	G	G	G

G   Generic tools
P   Parametric modeling tools
E   Prototype editors
S   Shape grammar generators

The following two sections present examples from two tool classes: prototype editors and grammar editors. Seen in isolation, the programs described are rather simplistic. They become interesting if used in combination and through their strong visual feedback and real time evaluation capabilities.

Prototype Editors
Prototype editors primarily support tasks that relate to the category of routine design. The prototype to be manipulated is either built into the program as it is in the case of ARCHPLAN [Schmitt 88], or it is defined by the designer, a possibility offered by the Edisyn program [Maher 87]. The manipulation of

parameters of the prototype can be performed manually, in which case the visual feedback and some information from attached attributes determines the value of each new object variation, or it may occur automatically through local optimization of parameters and the necessary local and global conflict resolution. The following examples represent partial approaches for prototype definition and manipulation.

GPC: a graphical prototype constructor

As a simplification, a prototype for standard or routine design tasks may be defined as an object of non-trivial complexity in the sense of object-oriented programming. As such, GPC allows the graphical construction of objects which in isolation or as combinations of instances describe the prototype for design. To build the prototype of a conference room, for example, GPC needs different types of knowledge, all of which may be input graphically:

• Geometric knowledge. This includes the position of the object in three-dimensional space, and its dimensions.
• Hierarchical knowledge. It includes the knowledge of belonging to a named assembly or a *part_of* relation.
• Relational knowledge. It includes relations between parts of the design that are established (and, if desired, enforced) graphically by pointing. Examples are *on_top_of, north_of, south_of*, etc.
• Functional knowledge. This includes the definition of the main function of the object, which could describe static (fixed location for a certain part or activity), as well as *dynamic* (move along a certain path) functions.
• Constraint knowledge. Constraints can be defined graphically or numerically and include, for example, *less_than, greater_than*, or geometric constraints.

The program could be seen as a graphical shell that allows the construction of the basic units of a prototype and their combination. Figure 1 shows examples of the user interface. GPC has at the moment very limited inferencing techniques. It is possible, however, to produce OPS5 rules with the program so that more complex inferencing may be executed externally in OPS5. GPC is programmed in C, using frames and the graPHIGS [IBM 86] package, on the IBM RT 5080 graphics workstation operating under AIX.

Tartan: a three-dimensional grid editor

A tartan grid is a representation of three-dimensional objects which uniquely defines each corner, edge, intersection, plane, and plane orientation or direction of objects in the grid. The TARTAN grid editor allows a designer to

- define the tartan grid in three dimensions.
- insert into and delete three-dimensional building blocks from the tartan grid.
- inquire about attributes of building blocks.
- write to and read from an input file.
- display and manipulate the building in real time in sections, elevations and perspectives.

The designer manipulates the primary building elements and the grid with a set of function keys and direct keyboard input. A digitizer supports the selection of objects; analog dials allow real time view and scaling operations. Examples from a typical session are shown in figure 2. The design begins with the presentation of a default three-dimensional grid which is the average of grids from previous sessions. The grid itself may be manipulated by sets of integers which represent the distance between horizontal and vertical grid lines. Subsequently, building blocks are filled in by specifying areas and heights with digitizer and numerical input. Although the described sequence corresponds to an additive method, a subtractive approach is available as well in which individual or groups of building blocks are selected, moved, or deleted. The ultimate effect is one of carving or direct modeling of a large block.

The tartan grid editor is most appropriate for the development of massing models with an underlying three-dimensional grid structure. Object manipulation feedback is instantaneous and encourages direct visual judgement.

Alternatives that appear satisfactory are written to a data base and can be retrieved for comparison. A disadvantage is the restriction of the grid. The program employs

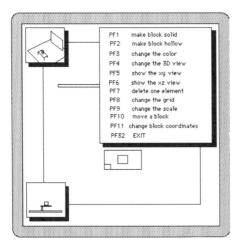 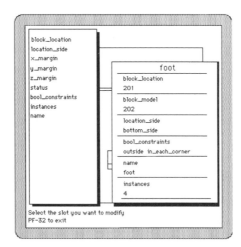

Figure 1   User interface of GPC, the Graphical Prototype Constructor. Object definition and frame assembly.

direct object manipulation, that is, by modifying the screen object, the data structure is manipulated as well.

Shape Grammar Editors

Shape grammars are a subclass of production systems and consist of graphical rules with a left hand side (the condition) and the graphical results of a transformation as the right hand side (the action). Shape grammars in design have been popularized mainly by the work of Stiny, Mitchell and Flemming [Flemming 86]. Chinese gardens, Gothic church windows, and Victorian residences name a few of numerous successful implementations. In most cases, shape rules are defined manually or in source code and cannot be easily edited. The following two examples provide a real time graphical user interface for the application of pre-defined graphical rules, and an interface for the construction and application of graphical rules. In both cases the construction of graphical "sentences" (3D objects) consisting of simple "words" (shapes) is possible. Prototypes are either the rules themselves or the "sentences" formed with the macro language.

Froebel: a graphical production system

FROEBEL generates three-dimensional objects from a set of twelve three-dimensional shape grammar rules. The production system was inspired by Stiny's work on Froebel's Kindergarten grammars [Stiny 80]. A three-dimensional object can be defined either by applying shape rules step by step or input of a simple "sentence", using the program's macro parser. The "sentences", constructed by a

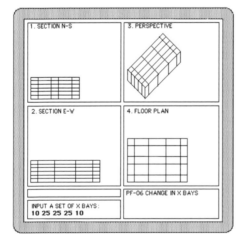 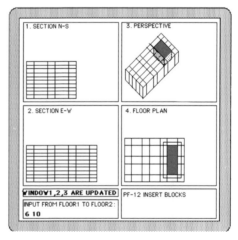

Figure 2   TARTAN, the three-dimensional shape editor. Two interactive screens

combination of a string of rule names, recursion levels, and geometric constraints, may be seen as the actual prototypes. The rules can be executed within the tartan grid described in the previous section.

A typical working session begins with the display divided into six windows as shown in figure 3. Window 1 contains twelve three-dimensional rules, window 2 shows the initial shape. Window 3 displays error messages and current information, window 4 prompts the user and accepts answers. Window 5 lists pre-defined function keys, and window 6 presents the generated results in three dimensions.

The designer may choose an initial shape from window 2 and any rule with the digitizer from window 1. The result of applying the rule to the initial shape appears in window 6. Any rule in any order may be applied to the object in window 6. The dials allow real time transformations such as rotation, translation, and scaling in all axes.

A simple macro language allows the formation of objects by combining individual rules (words) into complex sequences (sentences). Constraints in each orthogonal direction guide and terminate the execution of rules and "sentences."

A typical application is the construction of a stair. The user selects the appropriate rule (one step with its lower left edge on the upper right edge of the previous step), inputs the floor to floor height as a constraint, and requests the system to begin executing this rule. Once the stair reaches the next floor, it will automatically stop. In other words, each rule becomes an object in the sense of object-oriented programming and is therefore, able to handle simple constraints. The program is most useful

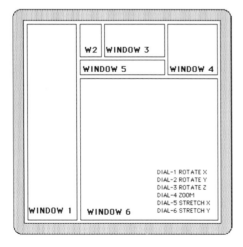
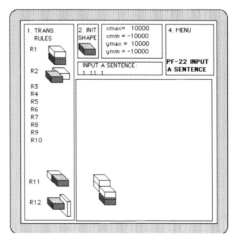

Figure 3 FROEBEL: a graphical production system. Snapshots from the interactive screens.

for the exploration of rule combination and constraint application. Its strengths are the convenient interface and the direct object manipulation capabilities. Disadvantages at the moment are the restrictions of rectangular shapes and the limitations in the "intelligence" of objects.

GRC: a graphical rule constructor

The graphical rule constructor is a program for the graphical definition and execution of two-dimensional production rules. It supports the routine and to a degree the innovative design process as it enables the designer to define own rules, produce simple shape "words", and produce graphical "sentences" by combining these words into "sentences" manually or with the built-in macro parser. "Sentences" and combinations of "sentences" may be stored as a new prototype, or existing "sentences" may be edited.

The screen is divided into six windows as shown in figure 4: window 1 stores and displays user defined rules, window 2 displays the result of rule application, window 3 is the rule definition window, window 5 shows error messages and current information, window 6 contains dialogue, and window 7 presents user options. Keyboard, function keys and dials are used in the same way as in the previous examples.

A typical session begins when the user defines a new shape rule in window 2. The initial shape (left hand side) is specified. Then the first rule (right hand side) may be input graphically. The result appears immediately in window 1 and is available for application. Following the input of one or more rules, the interface works

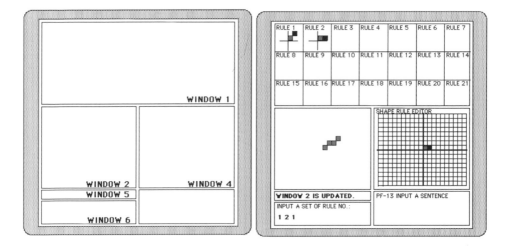

Figure 4   GRC, the graphical shape grammar rule constructor. Typical interactive screens.

exactly as in FROEBEL. At the moment, the program is restricted to two dimensions, as too many possible cases must be considered for three-dimensional input. The program is also compatible with FROEBEL and TARTAN. It is implemented, similar to the previous programs, in C and graPHIGS.

Research and Teaching
The previous sections described examples for applications of domain specific tools to routine and innovative design in theory. They are research programs with limited practical importance yet they begin to explain the notion of domain specific design tools. The following two examples are conceptually not as well defined but relate more closely to practice.

Traditional Taiwanese housing—parametric design
The example of the knowledge-based design of Taiwanese housing is based on the careful study of geometric properties of this building type. The shape-grammar paradigm is used to generate the components of traditional Taiwanese villages such as buildings, courts, rooms, walls, and components. The project is an example of routine design because the parameters of a prototype of the traditional Taiwanese house are known, formalized, and merely manipulated within well defined boundaries.

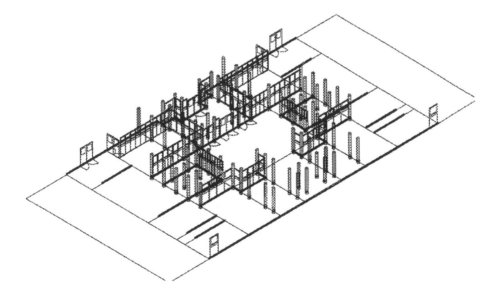

Figure 5 Axonometric of a five-bay house, showing some foundations, columns, doors, and wall panels

The prototypes consists of AutoLISP functions and association lists which together form the "design object." The program prompts the user at the beginning and during the design development for the value of important parameters which vary within certain limits for different family sizes. The *types*, however, do not change. The program performs on any IBM AT class machine but the resulting buildings and building blocks, designed and displayed three-dimensionally, are so complex that as a minimum, a SUN3 class machine is recommended. The program may be used to study the effects of parameter variation on buildings and building agglomerations, without going beyond the underlying prototype.

The significance of the program lies in the actual level of interaction between designer and computer: the dialogue takes place on a conceptual level in which family size and proportional aspects determine the shape and size of the building. Whereas the built-in knowledge may be seen as a limitation, it can be changed, and the end result of a session may be edited on the level of AutoCAD entities.

Maggi House by Mario Campi—Innovative Design

The Maggi house by the Swiss architect Mario Campi (built in 1980) is an example of the combination of prototypes and may be categorized under the heading of innovative design. The Ticino farm house prototype was combined with a rational and contemporary organizational language prototype. One could argue that either one of the prototypes was modified or adapted to the degree that innovative design resulted. However, the Maggi house is better explained by prototype combination, because the result clearly shows characteristics of both types.

The Maggi house represents a piece of architecture in spatial isolation yet set in a regional context for which the application of a knowledge-based system

Figure 6   Front and back elevation of the Maggi house by Mario Campi, with precedent prototype.

for innovative design is feasible. The accompanying program is still under development and is implemented in parallel in AutoLISP, Hypercard/Hypertalk and Smalltalk. In AutoLISP, lists of functions represent prototypes. The Hypercard implementation takes advantage of the graphical and object-oriented-like programming style of Hypertalk. The Smalltalk application makes use of the object-oriented and graphical programming environment.

Conclusions

To divide design processes into different classes is useful for understanding the complexity of design and leads to the isolation and exposure of unsolved research questions. Present commercial CAD programs and tools developed in CAD laboratories best support the routine design process. It would be wrong to assume that *any* one program could support a given design process. The different phases and types of design require a variety of conceptual and modeling aids. The second large research question, that of principled representation and reasoning techniques is not touched upon in this paper but must be solved for the communication of the individual design tools. Our experiences also show that prototype and shape grammar editors require very high computing power for visualization and execution to be perceived as the dynamic modeling methods that differentiate them from traditional methods.

The time has come to develop appropriate tools to support each type of design and to end the mismatch between application requirements and program offerings: Drafting systems are just not built for conceptual design and paint systems are unfit in the long term for detail development. As in both examples, excessive implicit knowledge is required from the viewer. All resulting interpretations are therefore ambiguous and port human problems to the machine rather than taking advantage of the computer's capabilities. Knowledge implicit in details or larger planning units should finally be made available in useful form. The definition of unified standards for product modeling may be a first step in this direction [Gielingh 89].

Acknowledgments

The author would like to thank Heng Tzu Wu, Chen-Cheng Chen, Shen-Guan Shih and Annelies Zeidler. Special thanks to Sibylla Spycher and Laura Lee. Research funding for Graphical Knowledge Acquisition, of which GPC, FROEBEL, TARTAN, and GRC are a part, is provided by IBM.

References

[Faltings 1988]   Faltings, Boi. "Qualitative Kinematics and Computer-Aided Design" In *Proceedings of the Second IFIP WG 5.2 Workshop on Intelligent CAD*, Cambridge, UK.

[Flemming 1986]   Ulrich Flemming, Robert Coyne, and Shakunthala Pithavadian. "A Pattern Book for Shadyside." Pittsburgh: Department of Architecture, Carnegie Mellon University.

[Gero 1988]   John Gero, Mary Lou Maher, and Weiguang Chunking Zhang. "Structural Design Knowledge as Prototypes." Sydney: The Architectural Computing Unit. Department of Architectural Science, University of Sydney.

[Gielingh 1989]   Ir Wim Gielingh. "Computer Integrated Construction, a Major Step Forward." In *Proceedings of the 2nd International Symposium on Computer Aided Design in Architecture and Civil Engineering.* Barcelona.

[IBM 1986]   IBM Corporation. *Understanding graPHIGS.* Kingston, NY: IBM.

[Kramer 1988]   Glenn A. Kramer and Harry G. Barrow. "An Intelligent Mixed Symbolic/Numerical System For the Design of Mechanical Linkages." In *Proceedings of the Second IFIP WG 5.2 Workshop on Intelligent CAD*, Cambridge, UK.

[Laseau 1980]   Paul Laseau. *Graphic Thinking for Architects and Designers.* New York: Van Nostrand Reinhold.

[Maher 1987]   M.L. Maher and P. Longinos. "Development of an Expert System Shell for Engineering Design." *International Journal of Applied Engineering Education.* Pergamon Press.

[Mitchell 1989]   William J.Mitchell, Robin S.Liggett, and Milton Tan. "Top-Down Knowledge-Based Design". This volume.

[Schmitt 1988]   Gerhard Schmitt. "IBDE, VIKA, ARCHPLAN: Architectures for Design Knowledge Representation, Acquisition, and Application." In *Proceedings of the Second IFIP WG 5.2 Workshop on Intelligent CAD.* Cambridge, UK.

[Stiny 1980]   George Stiny . "Introduction to Shape and Shape Grammars". pp 343-351. *Environment and Planning B .* Vol 8.

6
Tools for Exploring Associative Reasoning in Design

Richard D. Coyne

Department of Architectural and Design Science
University of Sydney

Two tools for storing and recalling information in computer systems are discussed and demonstrated in relation to design. The tools are hypermedia and neural networks. Each provides a valuable model for reasoning by the association of ideas.

Introduction

The ability to form associations between ideas appears to be an important part of design thinking. As discussed in this paper, association provides a means of navigating through information and recalling information. In this paper we will investigate two important tools for exploring associative reasoning in computer-aided design. These are (i) the use of interactive networks consisting of units of information connected by links (so called 'hypermedia') and (ii) methods of organising and storing information in computer memory as neural networks. These tools (hypermedia and neural networks) serve to highlight two widely different approaches to information processing of interest to designers. They each furnish us with useful models that may assist in the creation of computer systems for designers.

Recalling information by association can be seen as a smaller part of reasoning by analogy as a means of solving design problems and producing design decisions. Research into analogical reasoning by computer generally involves getting the computer to find solutions to problems on the basis of similarities with problems that have already been solved. Solutions and explanations of solutions are stored in a computer system, and some reasoning mechanism is used to establish associations between problems and explanations at different levels of abstraction. The theory and application of analogical reasoning is explored by Schank (1982, 1986), Mitchell at al (1986) and Dejong and Mooney (1986), and some interesting design applications are described by

Navinchandra and Sriram (1987), and Dyer et al (1986).

A full discussion of analogical reasoning and design lies beyond the scope of this paper. We will restrict ourselves to the idea of exploring associations between ideas rather than the general issue of analogical reasoning, bearing in mind that the issue fits within the broader field of study.

Association and Recall

Design relies heavily on the ability to recall ideas. Externalising design ideas as sketches can lead to further recall of useful ideas. This process can be characterised as a database problem—searching through a catalogue of graphical ideas (as pictures), and navigating through those pictures by association. It is possible to set up a computer system to demonstrate a rudimentary form of associative reasoning using the Hypercard applications program on the Apple Macintosh computer.

In essence the idea is this: information is stored as a series of 'cards' (records in a database) containing pictures. A human operator moves from picture to picture by abstracting some aspect of the current picture and asking the system to call up another picture that manifests a similar idea. In practice, the abstractions through which associations can be made are generally very simple—just some pictorial element. So if a picture shows a house with a door, it is possible to call up a picture of another artefact with a door, such as a shop or a car. The wheels on the picture of the car may prompt an association with a picture of a bicycle, and so on. In Hypercard, the linkages must be set up in advance by means of invisible buttons positioned above key pictorial elements. The user of the system operates the screen cursor to select which element is to prompt the association. Figure 1 shows the button idea. The buttons are normally invisible, but are shown here as rectangles drawn over key pictorial elements. Figure 2 shows some of the linkages between key elements and pictures within a database (a Hypercard 'stack'). The pictures were scanned from hand drawings made on site by architecture students studying the construction of a traditional Fijian *buré*.

The idea of navigating through pictures in this way has wide appeal for designers. It provides an efficient means of browsing through reference material, directories, manuals and encyclopedias. Is can also provide a structure for tutorial systems. Hypercard is able to attach text, programs, sound and animation sequences as well as static pictures to cards. Because of the interactive nature of the Hypercard environment it shows promise as a means for designers to organize and externalize their own directories of ideas and precedents.

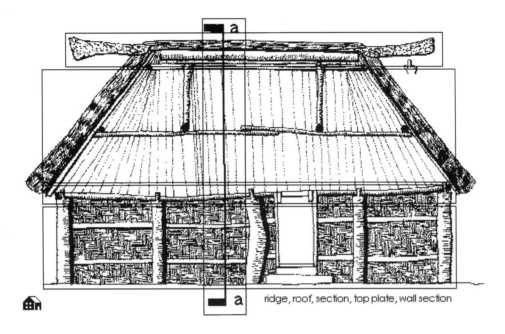

ridge, roof, section, top plate, wall section

Figure 1 A card from a Hypercard stack showing buttons for recalling other cards by association.

Hypercard is a scaled down application of hypermedia, which makes use of a range of electronic media, such as laser disk and networked communications systems. Issues in the development of hypermedia are discussed by Smith and Weiss (1988), who include a summary of its history which dates back to 1945. Of course, the full exploitation of navigating by association requires developments in the hypermedia technology beyond that currently available. In an ideal system for designers it should not be necessary for the links between pictorial ideas to be established a priori. How the system is able to form associations on the basis of arbitrary abstractions is an interesting problem in image understanding and pattern matching. Insight into this issue is provided by the second reasoning tool to be discussed here.

The Neural Network Model of Information Processing
In the hypercard approach information is stored as discrete cards (records). This approach results in useful and accessible computer systems, but it bears little relation to the way information is stored in the human brain. One of the limitations of this is that it is extremely difficult to model how associations are formed through ideas that match only approximately (a profoundly useful human capability)—for example, recalling a detailed picture of a particular house from an abstract sketch, or being prompted to recall a caravan or a dog kennel through its abstract resemblance to a house—in other words, recalling

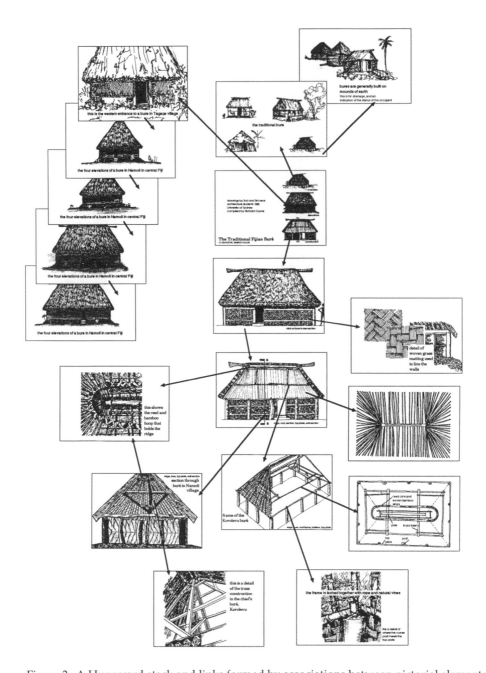

Figure 2   A Hypercard stack and links formed by associations between pictorial elements.

complete information given only approximate, abstract and incomplete information as a key.

This aspect of associative reasoning is addressed by the neural network idea. The neural network idea is powerful, but currently limited by the excessive computational cost involved in simulating parallel neural processes (as well as shortcomings in the development of the theory). In neural networks representation is at a much lower level than in a Hypercard database. Neural networks rely on simple, universal algorithms that must work very hard at a problem. Essentially these algorithms are concerned with optimizing a set of values in a network as a means of storing information (pictures). Recalling information is usually simpler and involves the simple multiplication and summation of values. McClelland et al (1986) provide a summary of techniques available for setting up neural network systems.

In essence the idea is to store patterns (pictures or records) in a data structure known as a neural network, usually as a regular matrix in a computer system. The network bears no discernable physical resemblance to the information being stored, and is intended to simulate the neural connections in the human brain. Information is stored as values of nodes and values of connections in the network. The network looks similar when there are five picture stored and when there are five hundred, though the values on the nodes and connections will be different. The number and configuration of nodes and links has considerable bearing on the types of associations that can be established between information. A large number of nodes and linkages generally means a more powerful system, but computational cost rises sharply with larger networks.

The information is stored uniformly over the entire network, in much the same way that information is thought to be stored uniformly across large parts of the brain (Rumelhart and McClelland, 1986). As a new picture is presented to the system for storage the values on most of the nodes and arcs are adjusted slightly in accordance with an algorithm. The various algorithms used generally have a stochastic component and make use of principles of thermodynamics. Storing new patterns involves many iterations of a simple algorithm and can be a slow process.

As with the Hypercard example it is currently only possible to demonstrate associative reasoning at a very rudimentary level. In the examples presented here information is simply stored as coarse bit maps, and the process of finding a match is to present the system containing the stored pictures with a partial picture. The system then recalls the closest matching picture from memory. Theoretically, it is possible to recall pictures on the basis of abstract 'features' that pictures have in common. But this requires more sophisticated algorithms and faster computers than demonstrated here.

Neural network systems are also called 'parallel distributed processing (PDP) systems'. They lend themselves to parallel computer architectures, though the whole process can be simulated with iterative computer programs using standard hardware. Parallel distributed processing machines are considered by some to closely resemble the operations of the human brain at a micro-level. As pointed out by McClelland, Rumelhart and Hinton (1986) this leads to interesting and useful analogies between cognition and computing, and interesting explanations of cognitive phenomena.

Some of these features are summarized here. Once they have learned a set of patterns PDP systems can be regarded as operating 'holistically' in producing interpretations of patterns presented to them. Input patterns are not reduced to primitives for analysis but are processed in totality. The process of discovering similarities and categorising input features is essentially automatic.

PDP models are a good way of simulating the human capacity for pattern completion. Successful recall can be accomplished with imperfect patterns. Where there is poor or ambiguous input the system will always produce some form of output from its memory. This may be an amalgamation of stored patterns or it could be the pattern corresponding most closely to the key pattern. Unlike rule-based reasoning systems, PDP systems provide at least some form of output for uncertain input. It could be said that the knowledge degrades gracefully.

PDP systems have a substantial contribution to make to machine learning. Unlike the acquisition of knowledge as rules (as exemplified by Winston [1975], Quinlan [1979] and Michalski et al [1986]), the content of the PDP network is not generally meaningful on inspection. However, the examples from which learning takes place are not lost but can be reconstructed from the network. Furthermore, the memory of past events (stored pictures) constitutes a kind of knowledge base from which the system can reason analogically. This is thought by some to present a better model of knowledge-based reasoning for expert systems than the rule-based approach (Dreyfus and Dreyfus, 1986; Stanfill and Waltz, 1986) .

An interesting parallel between the PDP method of storage and that used in the brain is that storage of information is not local. Destruction or modification to one part of the network generally results in uniform degradation of the performance of the system rather than the loss of any particular item of memory. Further parallels may be drawn with cognitive behaviour at a macro level. Rumelhart and McClelland (1986) describe an interesting experiment in which it was possible to replicate the behaviour of children learning the past tenses of verbs. The same sequence of standardizing and 'overregularizing' can apparently be observed in human behaviour and the behaviour of the PDP model.

The neural network model discussed here is much simpler than others that have been proposed (for example, the so-called 'Boltzman machine'—Hinton and Sejnowski, 1986). The network described here consists simply of a set of nodes, each connected to every other node. The nodes are arranged in an array, and the patterns to be stored and recalled constitute binary values on each of the nodes. Figure 3 shows the configuration of a network consisting of four nodes.

The parameters of the system are weights on the arcs and threshold values on the nodes. Learning, or storing, patterns of ones and zeros involves automatically adjusting the weights and threshold values. In recalling a pattern from memory given a partial pattern, the decision about whether or not a particular node should be on or off (that is, have a value of 1 or 0) is a function of the sum of the products of the weights of arcs directed towards the node and the value of the connected node. A net value greater than the threshold means that the node will 'fire' (producing a value of 1). Net values less than or equal to the threshold produce a 0. This kind of operation is propagated throughout the network to produce a configuration of values in response to a given partial pattern. The precise way in which this process occurs is described in greater detail by Coyne and Postmus (1988) based on the ideas of Rumelhart and McClelland (1986).

Spatial Applications of Neural Networks

Reducing information to binary patterns suitable for processing with a PDP system may appear somewhat limiting. However, if we configure these patterns into two-dimensional arrays the application to visual perception and design becomes apparent. Here we explore the use of two kinds of patterns: spatial patterns across a grid and patterns of relationships on a matrix.

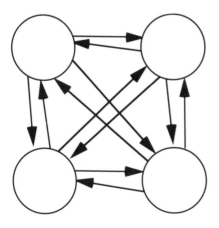

Figure 3. A neural network consisting of nodes and links.

Pattern completion in a graphical domain is demonstrated with the example in figure 4. Nine patterns are stored. Following the learning phase (that is, the stage during which patterns are stored) we present a partially complete pattern to the system (figure 5). In response the system produces the complete pattern of figure 6. The 'noise' in the image is due to the fact that parts of the partial pattern of figure 5 match more than one of the patterns of figure 4, though clearly one is more dominant than the rest. A certain amount of noise is also attributable to inaccuracies inherent in the stochastic process. The noise can be considerably reduced by feeding the noisy pattern back into the system. Half a dozen cycles of this kind generally produce a complete match.

It is interesting to observe what happens when the system is given an ambiguous pattern during the recall phase—that is, where the partial pattern contains fragments of several different stored patterns. In this case the output will be a combination of the closest matching patterns: a kind of 'fuzzy union'. This result is not always particularly informative. We can reinforce the closest match by feeding the output pattern back into the system. The result of cycling through this feedback

Figure 4. A set of patterns committed to memory by a neural network.

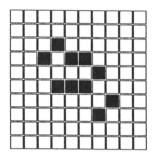

Figure 5 A partial pattern for matching against the memory of figure 4.

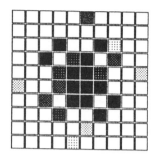

Figure 6 Completion of the pattern of figure 5.

Figure 7 The results of iterative feedback. The original pattern is at the top left corner. The system "homes in" on the closest matching pattern after successive iterations.

process for a particular input pattern six times is shown in figure 7. This operation reduces the noise due to overlapping and finds the image that matches the partial pattern most closely.

An interesting design application is where we match floor plan layouts to their performances. Because of the gross nature of pattern completion it is useful to think in terms of matching performances and types, specifically building plan forms. Figure 8 shows how the units can be configured to represent a set of plan forms and their attributes (performances). The attributes are a combination of high-level plan descriptors and the opinions of one designer as to the suitability of the various forms for certain uses and siting conditions.

Figure 8 shows nine plan types and their attributes. To be really useful we should teach the system all possible orthogonal plan forms (this is a large number but is certainly enumerable). If we then present the system with any one of the plans it will generate the attributes. It is interesting that the plan 'drawing' does not need to be perfectly accurate in order to find the right attribute match. Figure 9 shows a progression from the inaccurate, partial pattern presented to the system and the result after several feedback iterations.

Of interest to designers is the operation where we present the system with a set of attributes. The system then 'generates', or selects, a plan form. If we exploited the set theoretic properties of the system demonstrated above then we would produce loosely drawn unions of the closest matching plan types. There are three ways of treating this information. (i) It can be seen as a loose kind of synthesis for producing new types (assuming all types are not stored). Unfortunately the combination of plans rarely produces attributes that are simply derived from the union or intersection of the attributes of each of the plans. (ii) The overlapping patterns may serve to indicate the closest matching patterns from which the human operator of the system can make a choice. (iii) We can use the iterative feedback operation to produce the closest matching plan. Figure 10 demonstrates the latter approach.

In figure 10 we show the stages in the iterative feedback process by which the system 'homes in' on the closest matching plan form. Of course the iterative process need not be visible to the operator, but it is informative here in showing what the system is doing. There are three important observations we can make about this operation where we provide a partial pattern of only a small number of performances during recall. (i) We are attempting to find a matching form when there are in fact several forms. The most prominent forms appear shadowed after the first iteration in figure 10. (ii) We are attempting to complete a pattern where we supply the system with only a very small pattern

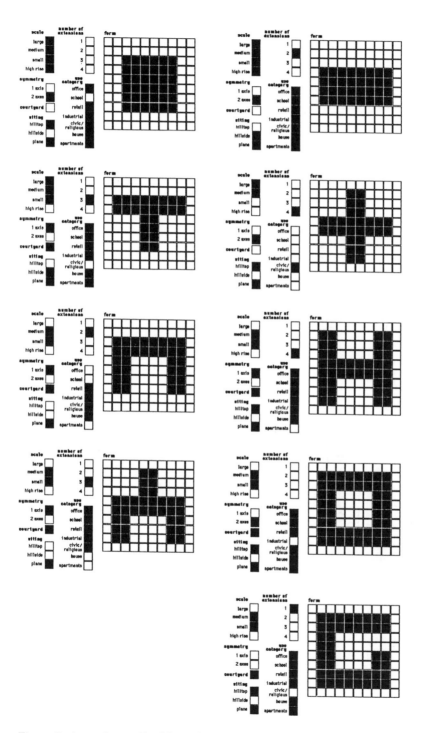

Figure 8   A typology of building plans

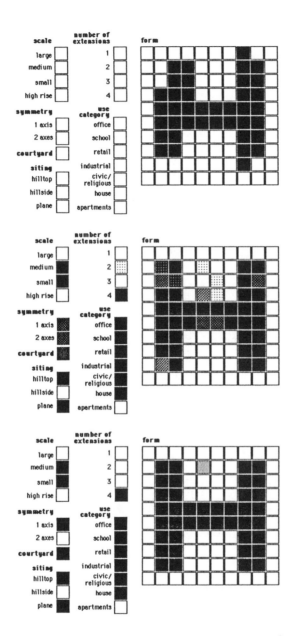

Figure 9   Matching a type from an approximate and partial image

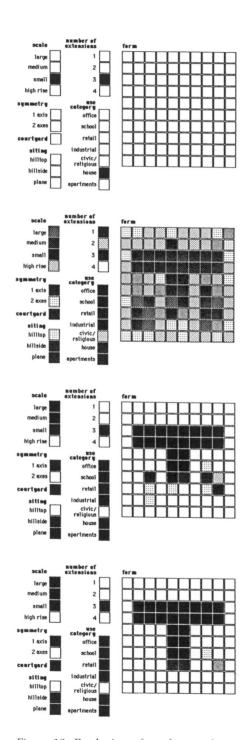

Figure 10   Producing a form from a given set of attributes

fragment. This considerably increases the noise in the result. (iii) The partial pattern may closely match with several plan forms. On successive iterations the system produces a plan shape that closely matches the combination of these plans. The resultant form may have very different performances to those specified in the original partial pattern. This can be overcome by introducing some kind of weighting factor into the representation so that one unit of performance is equal to several units on the form grid. Of course, for some applications the combination of plans may be very useful.

It is interesting to note that the neural network system described here was implemented using Hypercard and Turbo Pascal. The graphical interface to Hypercard provided a useful development environment. As well as being stored in the neural network, each of the stored pictures is retained as a record in Hypercard. Of course, it is not necessary, and indeed wasteful, to retain a database of individual pictures, as they are contained within the neural network. But the explicit storage of the individual pictures was of assistance during experimentation. It also serves to suggest that the ideas behind hypermedia and neural networks may be integrated to good purpose.

Conclusion

The idea of hypermedia provides a useful model of the storage and recall of information through associative links established a priori. It also makes use of well-established technology for storing information. However, the neural network idea accords more with the way in which information appears to be stored in the human brain. It has been demonstrated how neural networks facilitate the recall of stored patterns from partial patterns. The potential of neural networks to facilitate a crude kind of design synthesis has also been demonstrated.

In spite of its substantial history, the neural network idea is still in its infancy. Storing and recalling pictures is computationally expensive. There is considerable benefit to be gained from an integration of both approaches. Full pictorial information could be stored in hypermedia, while certain abstractions of those pictures, perhaps in the form of tables as depicted in figure 8, may be stored in a neural network representation. Navigation through the card system could be via associations established through the neural network. The integration of the two ideas poses a formidable research challenge, but may provide further insights into the design process, and assist in the production of better computer systems for designers.

Acknowledgements

This work is supported by a University of Sydney Special Project Grant. The assistance of Arthur Postmus is gratefully acknowledged.

References

Coyne, R.D. and Postmus, A.G. 1988. "Spatial Applications of Neural Networks in Computer-Aided Design". Working Paper. Sydney: Department of Architectural Science, University of Sydney.

Dejong, G. and Mooney, R. 1986. "Explanation-based learning: an alternative view". pp.145-176. *Machine Learning.* Vol.1, No.2.

Dreyfus, H. and Dreyfus, S. January 1986. "Why computers may never think like people". pp.41-46. *Technology Review.*

Dyer, M.G., Flowers, M. and Hodges, J. 1986. "EDISON: an engineering design invention system operating naively." pp.36-44. *Artificial Intelligence in Engineering.* Vol.1, No.1.

Hinton, G.E. and Sejnowski, T.J. 1986. "Learning and Relearning in Boltzmann Machines". pp 282-314. In Rumelhart, D.E. and McClelland, J.L. (eds) *Parallel Distributed Processing: Explorations in the Microstructure of Cognition. Vol. 1 .* Cambridge: MIT Press.

McClelland, J.L., Rumelhart, D.E. and Hinton, G.E. 1986. "The appeal of parallel distributed processing." pp.3-44. In Rumelhart, D.E. and McClelland, J.L. (eds) *Parallel Distributed Processing: Explorations in the Microstructure of Cognition. Vol. 1 .* Cambridge: MIT Press.

Michalski, R.S. 1983. "A theory and methodology of inductive learning." pp.111-161. *Artificial Intelligence.* Vol.20.

Mitchell, T.M., Keller, R. and Kedar-Cabelli, S. 1986. pp.47-80. "Explanation-based generalisations: a unifying view." *Machine Learning.* Vol.1, No.1.

Navinchandra, D. and Sriram, D. 1987. "Analogy-based engineering problem solving: an overview", *Artificial Intelligence in Engineering: Tools and Techniques*, D. Sriram and R.A. Adey eds, Computational Mechanics, Southampton, pp.273-285.

Quinlan, J.R. 1979. "Discovering rules by induction from large collections of examples", *Expert Systems in the Micro-Electronic Age*, D. Michie ed, Edinburgh University Press, Edinburgh, pp.168-201.

Rumelhart, D.E. and McClelland, J.L. 1986. "On learning the past tense of English verbs". In McClelland, J.L. and Rumelhart, D.E. (eds). *Parallel Distributed Processing: Explorations in the Microstructure of Cognition, Volume 2, Psychological and Biological Models*, MIT Press, Cambridge, Massachusetts, pp.216-271.

Schank, R.C. 1982. "Dynamic Memory: A Theory of Reminding and Learning." In *Computers and People.* New York: Cambridge University Press,

Schank, R.C. 1986. *Explanation Patterns: Understanding Mechanically and Creatively.*

Hillsdale, New Jersey: Lawrence Erlbaum.

Smith, J.B and Weiss, S.F.   1988. "Hypertext". pp.816-819. *Communications of the ACM*. Vol.31, No.7.

Stanfill, C. and Waltz, D. 1986. "Toward memory-based reasoning." pp.1213-1228. *Communications of the ACM*. Vol.29, No.12.

Winston, P. 1975. *The Psychology of Computer Vision*. New York: McGraw-Hill.

7
Designing with Diagrams: A Role for Computing in Design Education and Exploration

Stephen M. Ervin

Department of Architecture
School of Architecture and Urban Planning
Massachusetts Institute of Technology

Introduction

Environmental designers, design educators and design students using computers are a constituency with a set of requirements for database structure and flexibility, for knowledge representation and inference mechanisms, and for both graphical and non-graphical operations, that are now articulatable [23] and to-date largely unmet. This is especially so in the area called 'preliminary' or 'schematic' design, where our requirements are related to, but different from, those of our colleagues in mechanical and electrical engineering, whose needs have dominated the notable developments in this area. One manifestation of these needs is in the peculiar form of graphics called *diagrams* , and the ways in which environmental designers (architects, landscape architects, urban designers) use them. Our diagrams are both similar to and different from structural, circuit, or logical diagrams in important ways. These similarities and differences yield basic insights into designing and design knowledge, and provide guidance for some necessary steps in the development of the next generation of CAD systems. Diagrams as a form of knowledge representation have received little scrutiny in the literature of graphic representation and computer graphics (but see [1, 3, 5, 8, 10, 11, 13, 17, 18, 22, 25, 27, 28, 29]). In the following sections I present an overview of the theoretical basis for distinguishing and using diagrams; examine some of the computational requirements for a system of computer-aided diagramming; describe a prototype implementation called CBD (Constraint Based Diagrammer) and illustrate one example of its use; and speculate on the implications and potential applications of these ideas in computer-aided design education.

A Model of Designing with Diagrams

Real-world knowledge can be represented by many kinds of graphical constructs—photographs, sketches, maps, plans, diagrams, charts, graphs among them. The question of which kind of graphics to use in which circumstances is the usual AI question of choosing an appropriate knowledge representation formalism, guided by both the intended application and the inherent structure of the knowledge. *Pictorial graphics* (images like photographs, sketches and some maps) are powerful data that exploit our visual ability for parallel processing, but make no commitment to use or structure -- they are literal(ly) data. *Propositional graphics* (some maps, plans and diagrams, e.g.), by contrast, constitute information (or even knowledge): they embody some media-independent abstraction(s), typically are associated with some particular inference-making use(s), and require a commitment to some model(s) of the structure of the knowledge being conveyed. Categorizing graphics, however, is not a Linnaean enterprise and no hard and fast distinction can be made (see discussions in [7, 10, 17]).

Two criteria that are useful for distinguishing pictorial representations from propositional ones are their respective inferential purposes and the levels and types of abstraction they contain. I propose a simple assertion: pictorial graphics are concerned with shape, shape-like and detail attributes: color, curvature, texture, balance, proportion, e.g. ; while propositional graphics are concerned with form, and attributes that are abstract and topological (meta-shape, if you will): existence, number, magnitude, closure, connection and others. The former are appreciated visually, judged 'holistically', and generally defy symbolic translation; the latter may be represented symbolically, judged 'logically', and are designed for visual inference rather than appreciation *per se*.[1].

Definitions of design and models of designing have been many (for example, [2, 6, 20, 33]), and I'm not proposing any new one here. I take the common and uncontroversial position that designing is a process of preparing for the production of an artifact (at whatever scale, in whatever medium, at whatever level of abstraction or aggregation) subject to some set of goals and constraints. In final 'working drawings', neither goals nor constraints may be explicit—they will have been transformed into specifications on material properties. In preliminary 'design drawings', including diagrams, goals and constraints are more likely to be represented directly. In this model of designing, then, goals and constraints must be made explicit, represented graphically, and turned into specifications on material properties. The possible paths from concepts to drawings are several, and need not include diagrams, but often do.

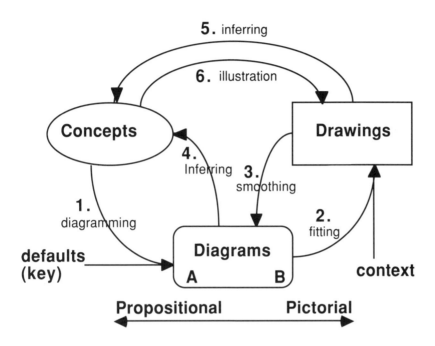

Figure 1. Concept - Diagram - Drawing Transformations.

A model of the relation between concepts and drawings—with diagrams in between—is shown in figure 1. Between the three nodes that describe forms of representation (concepts, diagrams, drawings) are six arrows, representing transformations between the representations.

This model of designing doesn't specify a starting point or any sequence of operations; nor does it require diagrams at all. There is no claim that designing always starts from concepts and proceeds to drawings, or in any other direction; the poles and the paths between them are caricatures, but they are useful. The decision about which route to take from concepts to drawings—a question about the necessity and utility of diagrams—is not resolvable by any theory. It is surely possible for designers to live without diagrams, though it might not be comfortable. This comfort derives from the place of diagrams between graphics and concepts, and their role in visual reasoning and inference.

The above assertions about graphical distinctions, design knowledge and design operations are arguable, but the question should not be "Are they right?" Rather, the question here is "Are they useful? Implementable? Testable?" I believe the answer is "Yes" to all three, which is where computing comes in.

Constraint Based Diagrammer

The diagram machine described here is the CBD (Constraint Based Diagrammer), designed to explore the ideas about designing with diagrams, and using constraints to do so. The realm I've chosen is in urban design. The foundation of this machine, though, is not urban design knowledge, but rather geometric and topological. Computing with geometry has received a lot of attention in CAD and solid modelling applications; less attention has been given to topological descriptors [15, 36]. The assumption here is that the abstraction inherent in diagrams calls for less precise descriptions than shape, size and position; that relational descriptors are the essence of the knowledge, and that particular details are generated by default only when required for display.

Propositional and Graphical Database

Clearly a diagramming machine will have a graphical component, with display and editing operations, and as such will require a commitment to a graphical database and data structures. An additional database is required that contains the propositional knowledge being conveyed by the diagram. The particular choice in the machine described below is an object-oriented approach, in which objects and the relations between them are the principal data structures.

Default Translation rules

The most distinctive component of the diagramming machine described below is a system for translating symbolic propositions into graphics. In this implementation I'm concerned with the process of going from propositions to a diagram (the arrow labelled "1—diagramming" in figure 1 above). This translation require a set of default rules for creating objects and representing class distinctions between them, a vocabulary of diagrammatic relations between objects, and a set of default rules for generating graphics from these objects and relations. A partial vocabulary is illustrated below, and defaults are expanded upon, but first I describe the mechanism for managing objects and relations between them.

Constraint Management

The constraint management paradigm [19, 21] provides a concise, flexible and expressive means for expressing relations (constraints) between objects and among classes of objects. The forms of the relations may include equations, inequalities, and one-way assignments (inferences of the 'IF-THEN' form.) These relational descriptions form the basis for the computational mechanics behind the constraint model of designing, including satisfaction, propagation, conflict resolution and block-structuring. The approach of designing with constraints has been explored in various fields, and has been applied to both preliminary and detailed design [32].

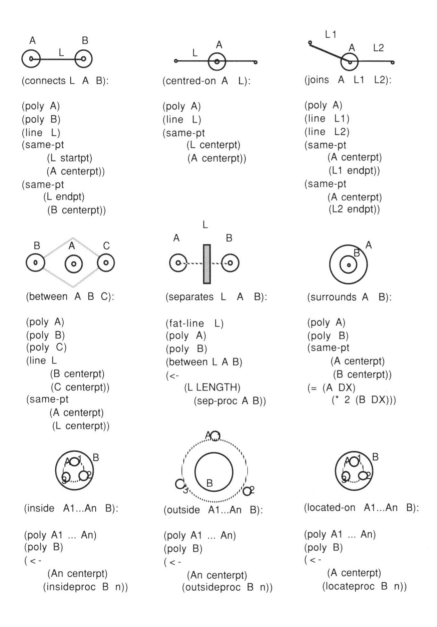

Figure 2.   Lexicon of Relations in CBD.

CM2 [14] is an implementation of a constraint manager[2], based on the principles outlined above. It has been used in the development of several design 'laboratories', micro-worlds constructed for the exploration of designing by constraints. It provides an object-oriented constraint manager with a graphic interface and basic mechanism for constraint compilation, satisfaction, propagation and conflict resolution through dependency directed backtracking. It serves as a substrate for the Constraint Based Diagrammer (CBD) described in figure 2.

Lexicon of Constraints
The vocabulary of elements and relations used by the CBD is simple. Elements are points, lines, and simple polygons (rectangles and ovals). Relations in CBD are defined as LISP procedures, in the form

(RELATION   ELEMENT1 ELEMENT2 ELEMENT3 ... ELEMENT n)

that behave as follows when entered: 1.) Check the types of ELEMENTs to make sure that they are appropriate for the relations, and signal an error if not; 2.) If the elements do not already exist, create them according to an appropriate type determined by default; 3.) Install a set of constraints between the elements, according to the rules of the constraint manager, and turn over processing to the constraint manager to check and propagate if possible. Figure 2 shows a selected set diagrammatic relationships in CBD, that have a constraint implementation.

Graphical Defaults
The CBD uses the above vocabulary of relations between elements, relying on the constraint manager (CM2) to enforce the relations numerically as required. Numerical values are required for the purposes of producing graphics, but in CBD these numeric values are secondary to the propositional relations such as those listed above. In fact, these values are instantiated as defaults—sensible values that make for a legible diagram in the chosen graphic environment, but that can be over-ridden by hand by the designer, or by calculation of the constraint manager.

CBD has both general and diagram- or context-specific defaults for graphics production. The defaults are in general values to be installed when graphics attributes with no value are specified. The choice of defaults is dependent upon a hierarchy of rules that determine the level and appropriate default decision. These defaults, and the rules that govern them, can be divided into three layers. At the top-level, are domain-specific defaults like, for example: "Where a screen is desired, use a linear element" . This is an example of domain expertise, in urban design—the choice to use a single nonlinear object, for example, might be more appropriate in a sculpture garden. The next level of defaults governs details of graphics appearance: for example, that screens are to be represented by a single wide line in a gray tone, or that the line should be vertical instead of horizontal if there is a choice. These defaults too are modifiable by the designer at will, but are decisions based more on immediate graphics feedback and fine-tuning than on domain knowledge. Finally, there are defaults that are generally stable, not usually changed by the designer, for example that a single line will be one- or two-pixels wide. This level of default is a graphic attribute that depends on the current graphics environment (size of window, extent of diagram etc.)

Defaults enable drawing of incompletely specified objects. Some example defaults in CBD are: "All objects are circles", "All dimensions are 20", "All colors are black." These defaults can be overridden at any time, by the designer or by a constraint in the system.

A library of common defaults is an important part of the domain-specific knowledge contained in environmental designers and their diagrams; although some common diagrammatic approaches exist, they are not nearly so well-defined as to be considered conventions. A computer-aided diagramming program must allow for easy user-definition of default graphical symbols and interpretations of propositions into graphics. This ability is supported by the object-oriented, interactive nature of the program, in which prototypes are easily developed, and modifications and alternatives easily explored. The following example shows some of these features at work.

Urban Design Scenario
Diagrams play an important role in all kinds of design—electrical, software, architectural, e.g.—but are especially important in urban design. Often urban designers are in the position of proposing conceptual master plans that others will fill out in more detail. The complexity of design at the urban scale particularly calls for the benefits of simplification gained through abstraction (with the proviso and warning that final decisions in the urban context must be made in cognizance of the full complexity, and not based solely on diagrammatic abstractions.)

A number of approaches have been taken to formalizing design knowledge at the site and urban scale, some proposing systems for computer aids (for example, [4, 5, 12, 16 , 24, 34, 37]). The domain of urban design provides an area in which some clear rules may be formulated for preliminary design, but the chances are very small that algorithmic or production-system solutions can be found to any but the most trivial problems. For this reason, the approach taken is an interactive one, in which computer aids are devised to support human designers at several levels: rule-based diagramming tools for conceptual design; drawing, calculating and modelling tools for design development and production. The following example illustrates the former only, and the interaction between the propositional and graphical databases in the Constraint Based Diagrammer.

New Town Example

This example describes a design process for a proposed new town, using a theory of urban design [9] based on the fundamental concepts of 'containers' and 'connectors', and including terms like 'magnet, 'axis, 'link, 'ring, etc. [3] These terms are used without formal definition, but with conventional meaning. The design anticipates districts of different uses (commercial, residential, industrial), and several types of connectors (pedestrian, automotive, transit). The sequence of propositions below describes a structure and form of the new town, without specifying a shape or details:

1. "the new town has a commercial center , located on a main axis"
2. "the main axis connects two external magnets"
3. "a main ring road surrounds the commercial center"
4. "several residential centers surround the commercial center, inside the ring road"
5. "a minor transit ring connects the residential centers"
6. "automotive links connect the residential center and the ring road"
7. "industrial centers are located outside the ring road'
8. "automotive links connect the ring road and the industrial centers"
9. "pedestrian paths connect between the residential centers"
10. "pedestrian paths connect the pedestrian path network to the industrial centers"

From these ten propositions the CBD can construct a diagram giving preliminary shape to the proposal. The diagram is a plausible, default graphical representation of the elements and their relationships.

To produce the diagram, the propositions above must be stated in the formal vocabulary and syntax of the CBD. (This 'translation' must be done by the user/designer—this implementation doesn't address questions of 'natural language' interface or automatic translation from text to propositions.) The relationships expressed in LISP syntax, follow:

```
(inbetween looprd washdc balto)
(centred_in townctr looprd)
(ringbetween transloop townctr looprd)
(located-on resarea1 transloop)
(located-on resarea3 transloop)
(located-on resarea2 transloop)
```

(located-on resarea4 transloop)
(links l1 resarea1 looprd)
(connected resarea1 resarea2)
(links l2 resarea2 looprd)
(connected resarea1 resarea3)
(links l3 resarea3 looprd)
(connected resarea1 resarea4)
(links l4 resarea4 looprd)
(connected resarea2 resarea3)
(connected resarea2 resarea4)
(connected resarea3 resarea4)
(links l5 townctr transloop)
(outside c1 looprd)
(links cl1 c1 looprd)

These propositions, in this order, result in a default diagram, which is shown in figure 3, and after some hand-manipulation to adjust shape and other graphic attributes for visual clarity in figure 4.

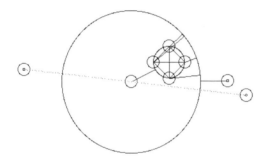

Figure 3   Default Diagram

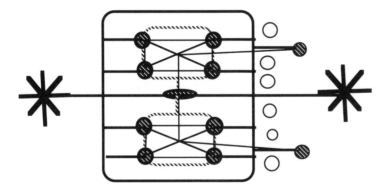

Figure 4   Hand Adjusted Graphics

The initial diagram produced by CBD, shown in figure 3, is topologically equivalent, though visually quite dissimilar to, the original source diagram. Figure 5 shows a facsimile of that diagram taken from the study mentioned above, a hand-drawn diagram illustrating the schematic organization of the new town of Columbia, Maryland. The changes required to produce figure 4 are not changes in the list of propositions themselves, but in graphic attributes of the diagrammatic elements produced by the CBD.

The reasons for these changes can be traced to two general sources. One reason is to increase the analogical and metaphorical qualities of the elements and relations in the diagram: making external magnets into asterisks, conventional symbols that contain an element of literal analogy, and making residential centers and town centers filled-in solids, for example. Another important reason for these changes is less clear, but is concerned with 'visual comfort'—making the principal axis horizontal, and the diagram generally symmetrical, and the lineweights generally heavier, for example, are all moves that result in simplicity and clarity in the diagram, thus increasing its visual appeal and inferential potential. Detailing, describing, and capturing these kinds of rules, in order to embed them into the knowledge bases and defaults procedures of the diagrammer, are all tasks for continued research, that will improve the power and utility of the CBD.

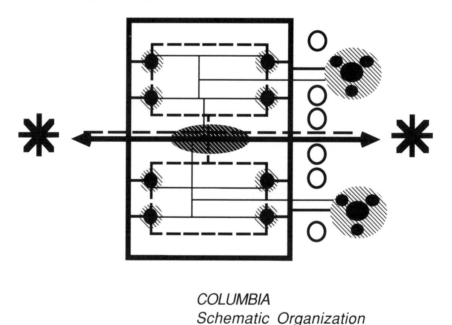

COLUMBIA
Schematic Organization

Figure 5   Original Diagram of Columbia, after Chermayeff, et al

Discussion

What are the advantages of having constructed the diagram this way? There are three principal ones. 1.) The knowledge that describes the town being designed resides in a database of propositions; from these propositions, more can be inferred, and questions can be asked. For example, without visual inspection, a geometric reasoner could determine that at some point, pedestrian paths must cross the main ring road. This in turn triggers a set of conventional responses (overpasses, underpasses, traffic lights, e.g.), and also brings the potential conflict to the attention of the designer. 2.) The graphical representation is directly manipulable, but is also tied to the database. Constraints may be observed, propagated, or modified by direct manipulation of the graphics. The conflict resolution procedures in the constraint manger make the act of graphical editing an interactive, rather than a one-way activity. 3.) The graphics can be changed without changing the propositions, just the defaults .

The sum of these advantages is that all of the usual graphical and knowledge-based examinations of the proposed design can be made, with a tight interconnection between them. Further development, into a specific design proposal, is guided by the diagram in explicit ways.

Implications for Design Exploration and Education

Claiming to aid designing is a bold claim; and even bolder in the context of design education. It may be immodest to claim that these ideas about diagramming or the program described here constitute design aids, but it is not entirely without reason. Field experience using constraint management and diagrams in design education is limited, but my expectations are not. Projecting future developments in computatational reasoning and rendering systems, we can predict the appearance of powerful and fertile systems for articulating design knowledge and manipulating that knowledge in several different representations, including diagrammatic.

Constraint Models for Design Exploration

The use of constraint models for design development and exploration puts an emphasis on conceptual understanding and reduces the impact of graphical skills on novice designers' ability to communicate. The ability to recognize and name design elements, and to articulate chains of design reasoning, is a real test of design ability. The traditional system of presentation drawings judged by jury leaves all such knowledge implicit and untested, and depends strongly on graphics to evoke discussion of design ideas. The possibility of explicitly articulating bits and pieces of design knowledge, and tying them together in defensible ways, represents a departure from traditional atelier-based design education, but one that is in tune with the opportunities presented by knowledge-based computing.

Front-End to CAD and Modelling Packages
The above is not to deny the value of "pictorial" drawings, and their role in visual inference for design development and communication. Computer graphics already offers the possibility of "levelling the playing field" between design students of varying graphical capabilities; consistent lineweights, harmonious color combinations and perspective projections are equally available to all. CAD programs are already part of the palette of modern designers and students. What corresponding advances exist in knowledge acquisition, representation and exploration? Diagrams provide an ideal front-end for developing graphical representations of formal concepts for further refinement in sophisticated 2-d and 3-d graphics modeling packages.

Knowledge Based Design Tools and Design Expertise
Diagrams may serve as a useful medium in the enterprise of knowledge engineering, extracting designers' knowledge in a form usable by rule-based and 'expert systems' of various sorts , or in new, as-yet-undeveloped systems for capturing and manipulating design knowledge [31], and so further our understanding of the forms and content of design expertise. I've indicated above that I don't hold much optimism for the enterprise traditionally described as 'expert systems' in urban design, but I do believe in the importance of knowledge-based, and to some extent rule-based, interactive design systems. Diagrams are a concise, expressive, and already-used vehicle for design knowledge and exploration. The questions that remain in this area are many and interesting. These include enumerating the principles of visual clarity and analogy that are so important to the inferential power of diagrams, as described above (and explored in some detail in [25]); methods for dealing with 'emergent form' and the related issue of 'multiple simultaneous representations' of design elements (see the discussion in [35]); as well as fundamental questions about interface and techniques of control that are essential to all designer-friendly computer systems.

Summary
I have argued that understanding diagrams and how they are used by designers is important for developers of computer-aided design tools, especially where these are to be used in design education. Diagrams are distinguished from other graphics by their essentially abstract, propositional nature, and their embodiment of graphic defaults. They are used by designers as a bridge

between concepts (propositions) and graphics, especially in preliminary design, and as a medium for visual inference and communication. A system for computer-aided diagramming must maintain both a propositional knowledge base like a traditional 'production system', a graphical data base like a traditional graphics editor, and a set of rules for default translations between the two representations; these default translations must be easily modifiable by the designer/user. A prototype implementation called CBD (Constraint Based Diagrammer) has been developed on the Macintosh computer in Allegro Object Lisp, and one example of its use was illustrated, showing how the two data bases interact in the production of a diagram of a new town.

These ideas have several implications and potential applications in design education: the use of constraint models for design development and exploration puts an emphasis on conceptual understanding and reduces the impact of graphical skills on novice designers' ability to communicate; diagrams provide an ideal front-end for rapidly developing formal concepts for further refinement in sophisticated 2D and 3D graphics modeling packages; diagrams may serve as a useful medium in the enterprise of knowledge engineering, extracting designers' knowledge in a form usable by rule-based and 'expert' systems of various sorts, and so further our understanding of the forms and content of design expertise.

The development of computational tools and techniques for the manipulation and development of diagrams, based in part on the ideas presented here, will be an important step in the pursuit of designer-friendly computer systems for design education and exploration.

Acknowledgments

The constraint manager CM2 was inspired and in large part coded by my friend and colleague Mark Gross, supported in many ways by Aaron Fleisher, and benefited from the goodwill and good work of the folks at Coral Software (makers of Allegro Common Lisp). Members of the Design Theory and Methods Group and the Design Research Seminar at MIT provided a captive audience and constructive criticism of many of the ideas presented here. The National Science Foundation and Apple Computer Co. provided partial financial support.

References

1. Albarn, K and J. Smith. 1979. *Diagram; The Instrument of Thought.* London: Thames and Hudson.

2. Alexander, C. 1966. *Notes on the Synthesis of Form.* Cambridge: Harvard University Press.

3. Alexander, C.. and M. Manheim. 1962. "The Use of Diagrams in Highway Route Location: An Experiment " Research Report R62-3. Civil Engineering Systems Laboratory. MIT.

4. Alexander, C., S. Ishakawa, and M. Silverstein. 1975. *A Pattern Language: Towns. Buildings. Construction.* New York: Oxford University Press.

5. Appleyard, D., K. Lynch., and J. Meyer. 1961. *The View from the Road.* Cambridge. Mass: MIT Press.

6. Archer, L.B. .1965. "Systematic Method for Designers". in Cross. N. (Ed.) 1984 *Developments in Design Methodology.* New York: John Wiley & Sons.

7. Arnheim, R. 1969. *Visual Thinking.* Berkeley: University of California Press.

8. Bongard, A. 1969. *Pattern Recognition.* New York: Wiley Interscience.

9. Chermayeff, S. and A. Tzonis. 1967. *Advanced Studies in Urban Environments: Toward an Urban Model.* Yale University. Institute for Applied Technology.

10. Crowe, N. and P. Laseau 1984. *Visual Notes for Architects and Designers.* New York: Van Nostrand Reinhold Co.

11. David, R.E.. 1971. "Proposal for a Diagrammatic Language for Design". in Kennedy. M. (Ed.) *Proceedings of the Kentucky Workshop in Computer Applications to Environmental Design.*

12. Dickey, J.W. and G.G.Roy "C/SI: An Idea Generating System for Urban Planning". pp 125-130. In Alexander. E. (ed.) *Proc. 1987 Conference on Planning and Design in Urban and Regional Planning*

13. Ervin, S. 1987. "Levels of Abstraction in Environmental Design: A Computational Approach". pp 91-96. *Proceedings of the 1987 Conference on Planning and Design in Urban and Regional Planning*

14. Ervin, S and M, Gross. 1989. "CM2 - A Constraint Manager for Design Exploration: User's Manual and Guide". MIT DTM Group Occasional Paper #1-89.

15. Evans, T.G. 1968. "A Program for the Solution of A Class of Geometric-Analogy Intelligence-Test Questions." pp 271-353. In Minsky. M. (ed.) Semantic Information Processing. Cambridge. Ma: MIT Press

16. Fleisher, A.. W. Porter & K. Lloyd. 1969. "DISCOURSE: Computer Assisted City Design" in Milne. M. (ed.) *Computer Graphics in Architecture and Design.* New Haven: Yale School of Art and Architecture.

17. Goodman, N. 1976. *Languages of Art.* Indianapolis: Hacket Publishing.

18. Graf, Douglas. 1985. "Diagrams". *Perspecta 22.* Yale Architectural Journal.

19. Gross, M. . 1985. "Design as the Exploration of Constraints." PhD Dissertation. MIT Department of Architecture.

20. Gross, M., S. Ervin. J. Anderson, and A. Fleisher. 1987. "Designing With Constraints". in Y. Kalay. (ed). *The Computability of Design.* New York: Wiley and Sons.

21. Gross. M., S. Ervin, J. Anderson, and A. Fleisher. July 1988. "Constraints: Knowledge Representation in Design". in *Design Studies.*

22. Herdeg, W. (ed.) 1981. *Graphis/Diagrams: The Graphic Visualization of Abstract Data.* 4th ed. Zurich: Graphis Press Corp.

23. Kalay, Y. (ed.) 1987. *Computability of Design.* New York: Wiley & Sons.

24. Kasmar, J. 1970. "The Development of a Usable Lexicon of Environmental Descriptors". *Environment and Behavior.* Vol. 2. No. 2. September.

25. Larkin, J. and H. Simon. 1987 "Why a diagram is (sometimes) worth 10.000 Words". pp. 65-69. *Cognitive Science.* Vol 11.

26. Laseau, P. 1980. *Graphic Thinking for Architects and Designers.* New York: Van Nostrand Reinhold Co.

27. M'Pherson, P.K. "Thinking with Pictures—graphics as aids to complex system design and policy analysis." pp 26-29. In Langdon. R. and G. Mallen (eds.) *Design and Information Technology: Proceedings of an international conference on design.* London: The Design Council

28. Maxwell, J.C. 1910. "Diagrams" *Encyclopedia Britannica.* Vol. 4. 11th Ed. 1910. pp. 146-149.

29. Montalvo, F. 1985. "Diagram Understanding: the Intersection of Computer Vision and Graphics". MIT AI Lab Memo No. 873.

30. Nelischer, M. and D. Hinde 1985. "A Graphic Language for Designers". pp. 60-63. *Landscape Architecture.* July/August.

31. Schön, D. July 1988. "Designing: Rules. Types and Worlds" *Design Studies.* Guildford: Butterworth & Co.

32. Serrano, D. and D. Gossard. 1987. "Constraint Management in Conceptual Design" In R.A. Adey and D. Sriram. (ed) *AI and Engineering: Planning and Design.* Computational Mechanics Press.

33. Simon, H. 1969. *The Sciences of the Artificial.* Cambridge: MIT Press.

34. Stiny, G. Fall 1985. "Computing with Form and Meaning in Architecture". *Journal of Architectural Education.*

35. Stiny, G. 1989. "What designers do that computers should.". This volume.

36. Woodbury, R. 1988. "The Knowledge Based Representation and Manipulation of Geometry". PhD Dissertation Carnegie Mellon University Department of Architecture.

37. Yessios, C. 1975. "Formal Languages for Site Planning". in Eastman. C. (ed.) *Spatial Synthesis in Computer Aided Building Design.* New York: John Wiley & Sons.

Notes

[1] I have glossed over or done damage to a number of others' thinking about these matters; the subject of graphical representations, their nature and uses, has a long history and a large literature (for example, two notable contributions in [7, 17], and an incomplete random sampling of ideas in [10, 25, 26, 29]).

[2] Running on a Macintosh computer, in Allegro Object Lisp. Development was partially funded by NSF grant #DMC86-11357. [14]

[3] These concepts (and the inspiration for this example) come from an urban design study led by Serge Chermayeff at Yale University in 1967 .[9]

8
Relational Modeling: A Basis for Computer-Assisted Design

Mark D. Gross

Design Technology Research
Cambridge Massachusetts

Today's computer assisted design (CAD) systems automate traditional ways of working with tracing paper and pencil, but they cannot represent the rules and relationships of a design. As hardware becomes faster and memory less expensive, more sophisticated fundamental software technologies will be adopted. This shift in the basis of CAD will provide powerful capabilities and offer new ways to think about designing.

Recently parametric design, a technique for describing a large class of designs with a small description in code, has become a focus of attention in architectural computing. In parametric CAD systems, design features are identified and keyed to a number of input variables. Changes in the input values result in variations of the basic design. Based on conventional software technologies, parametric design has been successfully applied in many design domains including architecture and is supported by several commercial CAD packages. A weakness of parametric techniques is the need to predetermine which properties are input parameters to be varied and which are to be derived.

Relational modeling is a simple and powerful extension of parametric design that overcomes this weakness. By viewing relations as reversible rather than one-way, any set of properties can be chosen as input parameters. For example, a relational model that calculates the shadow length of a given building can also be used to calculate the building height given a desired shadow length. In exercising a relational model the designer is not limited to a pre-selected set of input variables but can explore and experiment freely with changes in all parts of the model.

Co is a relational modeling environment under development on the Macintosh-II computer, and Co-Draw, a prototype CAD program based on Co. Co's relational engine and object-oriented database provide a powerful basis for modeling design relations. Co-Draw's interactive graphics offer a flexible medium for design exploration. Co provides tools for viewing and editing design models in various representations, including spreadsheet cards, tree and graph structures, as well as plan and elevation graphics. Co's concepts and architecture are described and the implications for design education are discussed.

Today's Computer Assisted Design

Computer tools have only begun to support architectural designing from schematic design through construction. Good at drafting and rendering tasks, they allow users to construct and edit drawings by using primitive geometric objects and parts from libraries. Current technology permits designers to work with layers, and to zoom in and out while working on a drawing. Combined with three-dimensional construction and viewing, these capabilities comprise the repertoire of most commercial packages on the architectural CAD market today.

Although today's CAD tools automate many aspects of drafting, they do not let us record the reasons for the decisions we make—the rules and relationships that govern the design. A drawing is inherently static; a design is dynamic. Drafting and rendering, while essential to architectural design, represent only the "external" aspects of designing. A complex "internal" process of reasoning and judgement lies behind every design decision. Even such a simple change as moving a window can cause far-reaching effects in a design. A drawing cannot convey these design dependencies; therefore we keep them in our head. *It would be a significant advance if computer-based design tools would enable us to record the design relationships we intend*, along with the specific decisions that accomplish these intentions.

Need For Smarter Drafting Tools

Here are three examples that illustrate the limitation of today's computer-based drafting tools: It is easy to draw two circles and make a line segment tangent to both. But once the drawing is made we cannot move or resize one of the circles and expect the line segment to adjust to maintain the tangency. Rather, we must repeat the "make tangent" operation after moving or resizing one of the circles. Likewise, in most CAD programs it is easy to select two elements and align them, for example, along their top edges. But the alignment will not be preserved if one of the elements is subsequently moved or resized. A final example is grid-gravity in which elements snap to center (or align) on grid lines. We might use this feature to locate columns at crossings in a structural grid. In today's drafting programs when we change the grid dimensions, grid lines move while elements remain as originally positioned. If elements "knew" to move with the grid then columns would remain located at grid crossings as intended.

These examples make clear the distinction between a drafting *operation* and a design *relation*. Of course, sometimes we only want to perform a one-time operation. But often we would like to declare the tangency, the alignment, or the grid-gravity as a relation, *to be remembered and maintained dynamically by the computer* as we edit the design: moving, resizing, and rotating elements.[1]

Parametric Design

Parametric design tools[2] allow the architect to describe a family of designs which vary according to certain key design variables, or parameters. A simple example is a parametric model for a stair, with height between floors and riser height as inputs. We can make a "dataflow diagram" of the model with input parameters on the left and output parameters on the right. [Figure 1].

A standard formula *(R1)* assures a comfortable stair. Dividing the height between floors by the riser-height gives the number of risers *(R2)*, from which the total stair run can be computed *(R3)*. The parametric model is really a *procedure* for designing—in this case—a stair.

A parametric model is appropriate for routine design, where we want to rapidly generate design alternatives according to a formula worked out in advance. But for conceptual design, which is characterized by interactive exploration, parametric modeling is less useful because in conceptual design *we don't want to determine in advance which properties of a design we will use as input parameters.* Suppose we need to design a stair with a given tread depth, total run, or number of steps. Our original model won't serve; its input parameters are riser-height and height between floors. We can work around this problem by building several parametric models expressing the same stair relationships, differing only in which properties are input parameters. But there are simpler and more efficient solutions.

Relational Modeling and Constraints

What we need (and what is lacking in parametric design) is a single model that can be used in several different ways, depending on which properties are to be set as inputs and which are to be calculated as outputs. This would allow us to retain desired flexibility in decision-making for conceptual design. The model would define only the relations between the stair's properties (and not which properties are to "drive" the model); at insertion time we must set a sufficient number of parameters to specify the new stair instance. (Our diagram for the relational stair would look like figure 1 without the arrows indicating the direction of data-flow.) We would use the same model to make a stair using

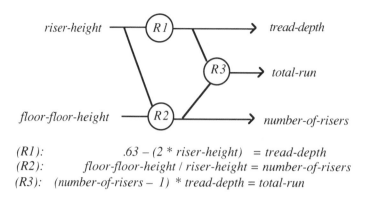

(R1):   .63 – (2 * riser-height)   = tread-depth
(R2):   floor-floor-height / riser-height = number-of-risers
(R3):   (number-of-risers – 1) * tread-depth = total-run

Figure 1   Dataflow diagram of a parametric stair model

any of the variables: floor height, riser height, tread width, number of steps, total run, or stair slope, as input parameters. This key idea, *allowing any of the variable properties of a design to become input parameters*, distinguishes relational modeling from parametric design.

Relational modeling, also called "variational" CAD, uses a software technology called "constraint-based programming"[6], first explored in Sutherland's famous Sketchpad program[14]. Research [2, 7, 8, 12, 13] has developed the concept to the point where mechanical engineering (MCAE) applications[3]software based on relational modeling has begun to appear.

In a relational model, each design object is described by *variables* and *relations*. Variables represent the object's properties, and relations, its behavior. Variables and relations are connected in a network similar to the diagram of a parametric model shown in figure 1. Unlike a parametric model, however, inputs and outputs are not determined when the model is defined, and hence the direction of data-flow through the network depends on the sequence in which variable values are supplied. The designer may freely set and change values of design variables in any order, as well as to improve or modify the model by adding and deleting relations at any time throughout the design process. Combined with object-oriented database and programming techniques, relational modeling offers a powerful and flexible medium for building computer assisted design tools.

Co-Draw

Co-Draw is a prototype for demonstrating relational modeling as a basis for computer-assisted architectural design. However relational modeling techniques are not limited to graphics—they can be employed in a wide range of domains including engineering calculations, scheduling and facilities management, and financial planning. This section describes an interactive graphics environment, Co-Draw, built using the Co relational modeling language. Figure 2 shows Co-Draw's user-interface. Drawing takes place in one or more Work Sheet windows. Command and relations menus are provided, along with a click-and-drag interface for moving and resizing elements. The part-structure, or assembly model of the design is viewed and edited in a Part Graph window.

Using the *command menu* we enter primitive graphic elements: points, lines, line-segments, rectangles, circles, arcs, and poly-lines. (Grids are defined and deployed using a separate Grid Manager module). The command menu also provides facilities for grouping, rotating, and inspecting elements. The *relations menu* offers predefined geometric relations for graphic elements including alignments and abutments, centering and edge-offsets, and dimension ratios.

Co-Draw supports relations as discussed above. If we apply "align tops" to two elements in the Work Sheet, Co-Draw maintains the relation: when we move one element, the other moves to keep the tops aligned. The relation is displayed graphically (as a red line across the element tops) but can be hidden on request. If we draw two circles and a line-segment, then apply the "tangent"

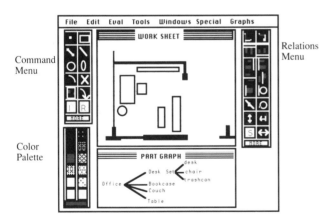

Figure 2 the Co user interface

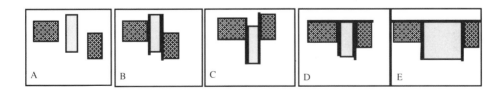

Figure 3 Co maintains alignments and abutments

relation between each circle and the segment, Co maintains the relation dynamically as we move and resize the circles. And if we fix elements to a grid, they remain in their original relationship to the grid (centered, aligned, etc.) as we change the grid-unit dimensions.

Example: abutments and alignments

A brief example shows how Co-Draw maintains geometric relations as we apply them from the menu. First we draw three rectangles (A). Next we establish relations to keep the rectangles abutting horizontally (B) but which leave them free to move vertically (C). Adding top alignment relations fixes the rectangles' relative positions (D). But if we allow the middle rectangle to vary in size then dragging the end rectangles apart will *stretch* the middle one to satisfy the abutment relations (E).

Example: a simple shed design

We might construct the simple shed design shown in figure 4, entering graphic primitives and applying relations from the menus. We draw a rectangle for the slab first and then two rectangles for walls, and enter vertical abutments (R1, R2) to fasten them to the slab. As we apply the relations, the elements move and resize themselves. We fix offset distances between the walls and the edge of the slab (R3, R4). Next, we enter a sloped line for the roof, and a "fixed slope" relation (R5). The roof and walls are not connected, so we add beams resting on top (R6) of each wall, supporting (R7) the roof and centered (R8) on the wall. Finally we add an overhang relation (R9) to keep the roof extending past the slab. Because of these relations, the shed design will "behave" in certain ways as we change dimensions and positions of its parts. If we raise the roof, the walls will become taller so as to maintain relations R6 and R7. Or, if we extend the slab towards the left, the shorter (leftmost) wall moves with it, to maintain the position relation R3. In order to maintain the roof's fixed slope

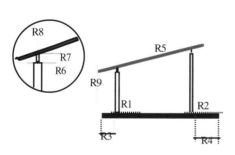

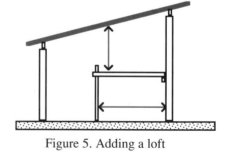

Figure 5. Adding a loft

Figure 4 A simple shed design   Figure 5   Adding a loft

R5 and support relations R6 and R7, the wall height must decrease, and the roof extends to maintain the overhang relation R9.

We can continue to add elements and relations to the design. For example, we can add minimum and maximum height constraints on the walls. We might add a loft whose interior extension is related to the height from its top to the roof (figure 5).

In this simple example we began with a simple drawing and, by applying relations between its parts, we built into it *design behavior*. Through applying the relations, lines and rectangles take on meaning; they begin to behave like the building elements that we intend them to represent. This process of assigning meaning and behavior to lines and symbols is essential to the use of drawings in design and is by no means a new concept introduced with computers. Whenever we communicate by drawing we rely on a shared understanding of the marks we make on paper, and learning to operate with this code is central to design education.

Notice that in constructing this simple model we had no need to write, compile, link, or debug any computer code; *yet we have programmed the behavior of our shed design*. We have proceeded entirely by entering graphic primitives and applying relations from the Co-Draw menus. Code describing the design behavior was generated automatically (and we can now view and edit it) but we constructed the model by adding relations interactively to the drawing.

The Co-Relational Modeling Language

Graphic elements and relations in Co-Draw are defined in the Co relational modeling language. The language integrates an object-oriented database and a "reversing" spreadsheet. The object-oriented database organizes element descriptions in a hierarchic class structure; individuals inherit default properties and behavior from class definitions. The "reversing" spreadsheet provides two-way calculation; we can work forward from design decisions to calculate performance, or backward from performance specifications to determine appropriate settings of design variables. Special "card" and "graph" windows for viewing the data-structures provide an interactive user-interface for programming. We can set and modify behavior of design elements as we explore consequences of decisions. This section introduces principal features of this language with simple examples.

Classes and Individuals

Every Co element is either a *class* or an *individual*. A class defines variables (properties) and relations (behavior) for all its members. A tree-like taxonomy organizes class definitions with specific information added in subclasses, general information stored at higher levels. For example, the class "unit-masonry" [Figure 6] describes general characteristics inherited by subclasses "brick" and "concrete-block," each of which specifies a material value inherited by its subclasses which specify dimensions, color, glazing surfaces, etc. The *Library Graph* window displays the structure of element classes, and we can make new definitions in this structure interactively. For example, we could add a new "shed" class based on the example above.

At the lowest level of this "inheritance hierarchy", every individual element is a member of one or more classes. Individuals add specific information (such as position) to the defaultvalues and relations they inherit from their classes. An individual may also *override default values* from its classes, which makes it an *exception* [1] .

Every individual is also a *part*, either of some other individual, or of a top superpart element called "World". A <u>Part Graph</u> window displays the hierarchy of part-whole relations among individuals in the design (see figure 2). The part-structure of the design is retained when we open a configuration to edit a part; when we finish editing the part we can simply close the group (unlike with MacDraw, we do not need to "group" again). The part structure can also be edited directly in the graph window by adding and deleting links.

Spreadsheet Cards
Variables and relations for each individual and class are viewed and edited using special windows called "spreadsheet cards". These cards enable us to interactively extend Co's capabilities by defining new classes of elements and relations and by modifying and adapting built-in definitions. <u>Variables Cards</u> (see figure 7) display the variables that define elements' properties: coordinates, dimensions, color, parts and superparts. We can fix and unfix

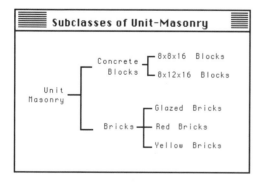

Figure 6 Library Graph

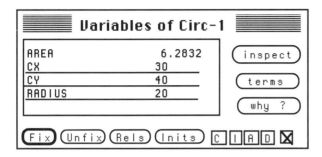

Figure 7 Variables Card for a Circle individual
showing fixed Radius and calculated Area

(retract) values, add new variables and inquire about chains of inference that
lead to derived values. The relations that define elements' behavior are
viewed and edited in *Relations Cards*. We can add and delete relations and
inquire how a relation was derived. We can control the display to show only
relations defined for a particular individual or to include all relations
inherited from superclasses.

Example: Adding Area Calculation to Circles

A Circle is defined in Co as a relational object with three variables: CX and
CY, defining its center coordinates, and RADIUS. We can extend this definition
to include an AREA calculation. In the Relations Card for the class CIRCLE, we
enter:

AREA = 3.14159 * RADIUS2

Immediately all new and existing Circle individuals will calculate their area
using this formula inherited from the CIRCLE class. Co's spreadsheet is
"reversing"; therefore the area relation can be used "backwards" to compute
RADIUS as a function of AREA. If we enter a circle into the Work Sheet and
view its Variables Card [Figure 7] we see that its RADIUS is fixed (indicated
by underlined typeface) and AREA is calculated. If we change the value of
CIRC-1's AREA, Co recomputes RADIUS, switching it from "fixed" to
"calculated" status, and updates the graphic view in the Work Sheet.

Example: Defining Element Sub-Classes

We can define new element types that inherit from the class RECTANGLE but
which have additional properties or behavior. For example, we can make
subclasses with default colors (BLUE-RECTANGLE) or dimensions (BIG-
RECTANGLE, SMALL-RECTANGLE). We can define a SQUARE subclass with
the additional relation HEIGHT = WIDTH. Or we can define a class of

elements which automatically calculate their cost based on size. We define the class MASONRY-WALL as a rectangle with the relation: COST = LINEAR-COST * LENGTH. Next we fix a default LINEAR-COST value in the MASONRY-WALL class. As we enter individual MASONRY-WALL instances (each with a different LENGTH) into a design, each individual computes its COST, multiplying the *inherited* LINEAR-COST by *its own* LENGTH. When we change the lengths of individual MASONRY-WALLS, their COST values change dynamically[4] . If we change LINEAR-COST in the MASONRY-WALL class, individual COST values also change. We can further specialize MASONRY-WALL, making subclasses BRICK-WALL and CONCRETE-WALL, and fix different default LINEAR-COST values for each.

This example suggests how we could program Co-Draw to display constantly updated totals for area, number of window, costs, etc. This ability to calculate on-the-fly and display running totals while designing offers a significant improvement over current schemes, which require the designer to leave the drawing environment and run the design through a separate costing module.

Relations, not just equations

Although many important relations can be conveyed by algebraic equations, many others cannot. Inequality relations and tolerances, for example, are needed to represent minimum and maximum dimensions, placement of elements in zones, and other concepts in architectural and engineering design. Co interprets inequality relations as interval equations, and Co's arithmetic routines support calculations with interval or range values. By introducing the symbolic value ∞ (infinity) as a special number, Co represents the inequality X $\leq$ 20 as an interval equation X = [– ∞ 20] and the relation 8 $\leq$ WIDTH $\leq$ 12 becomes the interval equation WIDTH = [8 12]. If this value is multiplied by HEIGHT = [6 10], the result is an AREA = [48 120], or 48 $\leq$ AREA $\leq$ 120.

Selecting elements from a limited set is another case where Co's support for relations goes beyond simple algebra. Building components are made certain sizes and design relations that specify dimensions must recognize this. It is easy in Co to define tables and catalogs of components and to index them relationally by size, cost, and other properties.

Finally, Co provides the ability to define new relations *that apply to objects, not only to numbers.* For example, although the internal definitions of built-in alignments and abutments relate edge coordinate values, alignments and abutments are *relations between elements*. In turn, abutments, alignments, and offsets can be combined into higher-level spatial relations. At each level the new relations hide their detailed internal definition with an *abstraction barrier*, so we can work at a level appropriate to our needs.

Applications

Laying out horizontal curves in road design is a process of placing control points connected by line segments, then inscribing curves in the angles between segments. The curves must be tangent to the line segments and road safety standards dictate additional relationships between radius of curvature, safe travel speed, and lengths of the straight segments. Once an initial road layout is made, the designer edits the layout by moving control points, changing curvatures, or by adding and deleting control points (and thus curves)[3].

In a space planning problem, a fixed program of functions is placed into a designated site, subject to certain dimensional and adjacency requirements among functions and areas of the site. For example, an entrance area has minimum and maximum dimensions and must be adjacent to the building facade. Once functions are located in the site, the designer edits the layout by adjusting room dimensions. As dimensional adjustments are made, neighboring rooms stretch and squeeze to avoid gaps or overlaps.

In structural design, a beam's cross-sectional dimensions, span, and load are related. If cross-section and span are given, the safe load can be determined; conversely, if load and span are given, the required cross-section can be derived. When the beam is placed in a building, its dimensions are related to other building components. Its span is related to column and bearing wall locations and its depth is related to storey-height. As bearing walls are moved in plan, spans may change, requiring increased beam-depths. In turn this may lower the clear-space between floor and ceiling, or raise the overall building height.

A final application is the coordination of subsystems[5]. Each system—foundation walls, structural steel, partitions, piping, electricity, HVAC—has its own selection of components and rules for assembly. Additionally, certain position relations must be maintained between elements of different systems. Subsystem placement rules can be coordinated using a grid system.

Implications for Design Education

The introduction of computers into the design curriculum offers exciting opportunities to reflect on architectural knowledge and the process of design. For many, learning to operate available software for drafting, solid-modeling, and rendering in a studio setting is a first step to understanding both the potential and limitations of today's computer tools in the profession. However if this is the full extent of engagement then we have failed to take full advantage of our opportunities.

An effective approach to employing computers in teaching mathematics asks students to write programs to carry out the algorithms they are studying. For example, in instructing the computer to test whether a given number is prime, or to find a common denominator of two fractions, the student is forced to think carefully about how to solve the problem. The computer provides a medium for expressing implicit "how to" knowledge in an explicit and testable form.

A similar approach can be applied in design education. Architects however, unlike mathematicians, are unaccustomed to expressing knowledge in concrete, algorithmic terms. Thus the student becomes a researcher engaged in an effort to capture and convey architectural knowledge to the computer, creating an *epistemology of design*. As a first step in this direction, students learn to write macros and programs to extend built-in CAD features and to automate frequently repeated actions. Constructing shape grammars and knowledge-bases for expert systems should also be classified under this rubric, as students reflect on and express architectural knowledge in a computer code where it can be examined and exercised by others.

A significant obstacle to this approach in design education is the lack of an appropriate language. Traditional computer languages such as BASIC and Pascal were developed for scientific programming and are unsuited to the expression and exploration of design knowledge. The control and data structures are restrictive and the syntax is clumsy. The programming language C and its object-oriented extensions, though popular among programmers, will not serve designers directly, nor even will symbolic languages like Lisp, Prolog, and Smalltalk.

This paper has described the Co relational modeling language and argued the benefits of the relational approach to computer assisted design in architecture. We need interactive computer languages in which we can easily express architectural design concepts. The task of inventing these languages is not easy, for it requires an explicitness that architectural design has hardly known. But if such a thing can be, then architects must participate in the inventing. That should be one goal of integrating computers in design education.

References

[1] Alves, M. and M. Ruano. 1987. "Towards Meaningful Computational Descriptions of Architectural Form." *Proc. ARECDAO International Symposium on Computer Aided Design in Architecture and Civil Engineering.*

[2] Borning, A. H. 1981. "Programming Language Aspects of ThingLab." pp 353-387. *ACM Trans. on Programming Languages and Systems* vol 3 no 4 (Oct).

[3] Ervin, S. and Gross, M. 1987. "RoadLab - A Constraint-based Laboratory for Road Design." *Artificial Intelligence and Engineering,* vol. 2 no. 4.

[4] Gross, M., S. Ervin, J. Anderson, A.Fleisher. 1988. "Constraints: Knowledge Representation in Design". *Design Studies,* vol. 9 no. 3 (July)

[5] Gross, M., Habraken, N.J., Ruano, M., Fry, C. 1988. Spatial Coordination Demonstration Program - Report to Shimizu Corporation. (unpublished).

[6] Leler, W. 1987. *Constraint Language Programming.* Reading MA: Addison Wesley.

[7] Lin, V.C., D.C. Gossard and R.A. Light 1981. "Variational Geometry in Computer Aided Design." In *Computer Graphics(15)3:171-177 SIGGRAPH Proceedings*

[8] MacCallum, K. J. and A. Duffy 1987 "An expert system for preliminary numerical design modelling." *Design Studies* Vol. 8 No 4 (October) pp 231- 237.

[9] Mitchell, W. J., R. Liggett and T. Kvan 1987. *The Art of Computer Graphics Programming .* New York: Van Nostrand Reinhold.

[10] Nelson G. 1985. "Juno—A Constraint-based Graphics System," *Computer Graphics (19)3:235-243 SIGGRAPH Proceedings*

[11] Robinson, P. April 1989. "The Design Debate." pp 101-106. *Computer Graphics World* (12) 4.

[12] Serrano, D. and Gossard, D. 1987. "Constraint Management in Conceptual Design." In R.A. Adey and D. SriramAI (eds.) . *Engineering: Planning and Design.* Southampton: Computational Mechanics Press.

[13] Steele, G. J. and Sussman, G. 1979. "CONSTRAINTS - A Language for Expressing Almost-Hierarchical Descriptions." *Artificial Intelligence* 14:1-39

[14] Sutherland, I. 1963. "Sketchpad - a Graphical Man-Machine Interface", M.I.T. Ph.D. Dissertation

[15] Weinzapfel, G. and S. Handel 1975. "IMAGE: Computer Assistant for Architectural Design." pp 61-68 . In Eastman (ed.) *Spatial Synthesis in Computer-Aided Building Design .* New York: Wiley.

Notes

This project began with my Ph.D. dissertation at M.I.T, where S. Ervin and A. Fleisher collaborated on previous related research[3,4]. The development team for this project included C. Fry, J. Habraken, and M. Ruano. I am indebted to A. Dula, J. Nilsson, M. Ruano, and H. Sayed for comments on earlier drafts of this paper. Support from Shimizu Construction Corporation, Coral Software Inc. and Apple Computer's Cambridge Advanced Technology Group is gratefully acknowledged.

[1] We sometimes annotate design drawings with instructions like "align these walls" or "keep 6' minimum clearance". These instructions are more effective at conveying design intent than measured dimensions, with which a subsequent change may inadvertently cause a desired relationship to be lost.

[2] PASCAL programs to implement parametric design techniques are discussed in Mitchell et al. [9] Parametric design templates can also be constructed using macro or programming language facilities of conventional drafting programs. Recently, commercial packages with parametric capabilities have appeared: on the high-end are ICAD's Design Language product and Wisdom Systems "Concept Modeller", which require a designer to write code to describe a family of designs. On the low end, the "Synthesis" package provides parametric design capabilities to AutoCad.

[3] Perhaps the best known is Cognition's Mechanical Advantage program. Other products that employ relational modeling techniques are described in a recent article in Computer Graphics World [11].

[4] The present implementation of the Co language is *busy*, computing all values as soon as possible. A previous implementation was *lazy*, computing values only on demand.

9
Top-Down Knowledge-Based Design

William J. Mitchell
Harvard University Graduate School of Design

Robin S. Liggett
Graduate School of Architecture and Urban Planning
University of California, Los Angeles

Milton Tan
Harvard University Graduate School of Design

Traditional computer drafting systems and three-dimensional geometric modeling systems work in bottom-up fashion. They provide a range of graphic primitives, such as vectors, arcs, and splines, together with operators for inserting, deleting, combining, and transforming instances of these. Thus they are conceptually very similar to word processors, with the difference that they operate on two-dimensional or three-dimensional patterns of graphic primitives rather than one-dimensional strings of characters.

This sort of system is effective for input and editing of drawings or models that represent existing designs, but provides little more help than a pencil when you want to construct from scratch a drawing of some complex object such as a human figure, an automobile, or a classical column: you must depend on your own knowledge of what the pieces are and how to shape them and put them together. If you already know how to draw something then a computer drafting system will help you to do so efficiently, but if you do not know how to begin, or how to develop and refine the drawing, then the efficiency that you gain is of little practical consequence. And accelerated performance, flashier color graphics, or futuristic three-dimensional modes of interaction will not help with this problem at all.

By contrast, experienced expert graphic artists and designers usually work in top-down fashion—beginning with a very schematic sketch of the whole object, then refining this, in step-by-step fashion, till the requisite level of precision and completeness is reached. For example, a figure drawing might begin as a "stick figure" schema showing lengths and angles of limbs, then be developed to show the general blocking of masses, and finally be resolved down to the finest details of contour and surface. Similarly, an architectural drawing might begin as a *parti* showing just a skeleton of construction lines, then be developed into a single-line floor plan, then a plan showing accurate wall thicknesses and openings, and finally a fully developed and detailed drawing.

"How to" drawing manuals often demonstrate this top-down stepwise refinement process in very direct and explicit fashion. For example, the famous sketchbooks of Villard de Honnecourt, Albrecht Dürer, and Leonardo da Vinci all show examples of schemata for various types of objects, together with demonstrations of how to elaborate these into fully-developed drawings (figure 1). Dürer's *Four Books of Human Proportion* (1528) sets out the method, as applied to human faces and figures, in systematic, textbook fashion. Similarly, J-N-L. Durand's architectural design method, as illustrated in the plates in his *Précis* (1802) and *Partie Graphique* (1821), proceeds from a highly schematic parti through a sequence of refinement steps (figure 2). In our own time, the books of tips for amateur artists that you can find in artists' supply stores are usually organized in much the same way.

Analogous methods are widely used in computer programming and in the development of text documents. Top-down stepwise refinement is a standard technique of structured programming, and is encouraged by the structure of languages like Pascal. The concept of a word processor has been elaborated into that of an outline processor, which supports refinement of a schematic set of headings into subheadings, and finally complete and finished text.

The idea of a computer-aided design system that supports stepwise refinement of a schematic idea into a complete and detailed design is, then, a plausible and

Figure 1   A sketch by Albrecht Dürer showing elaboration of stick-figure schemata

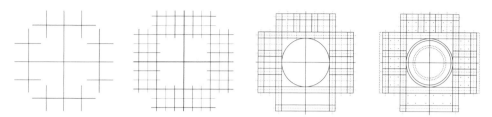

Figure 2 Durand's method for refinement of plan schemata

attractive one. Furthermore, if such a system provides a library of schemata for various types of artifacts, together with rules for refinement of schemata, it can effectively deliver knowledge of how to design these artifacts. The system becomes not merely an efficient design medium, but a design consultant that supplies at each step in the design process appropriate suggestions about what to do next. Schemata and development rules can evolve over time as they are tested in practice—much as E. H. Gombrich suggested in *Art and Illusion* (1969).

This paper describes a prototype top-down, knowledge-based design system, and illustrates its application. The system is called *Topdown*. Versions have been developed in Lightspeed Pascal for the Macintosh and in Microsoft Pascal under Microsoft Windows for the IBM PS/2, and these have been extensively used in teaching at the Harvard Graduate School of Design and the UCLA Graduate School of Architecture and Urban Planning.

Topdown can be described at three levels. From the user's viewpoint it is a highly interactive graphics system controlled by mouse operations. From the programmer's viewpoint it is an environment for encoding knowledge of how to draw or design things. At the substructure level it is a piece of software, coded in Pascal, which maintains a data structure and provides a graphics interface. We will consider these in turn.

The User Level

A designer working at the user level sees the screen shown in figure 3. There are two graphic windows—the peek window and the poke window. The peek window always shows the current state of the design, depicted as a two-dimensional composition of lines and color-filled polygons. There are the usual pan, zoom, and other basic display functions. The peek window is for viewing only: the user cannot directly select or operate upon graphic objects displayed within it.

All design interaction is accomplished via the poke window. The designer only needs to know two basic moves: substitution of a more detailed representation for a less detailed one, and parametric variation of dimensions, angles, colors, and so on. Substitution is accomplished by clicking in the poke window on the part which is to be replaced. This brings up a dialog box showing the substitution options (figure 4). When an option is selected by clicking in the dialog box it is displayed in situ in the

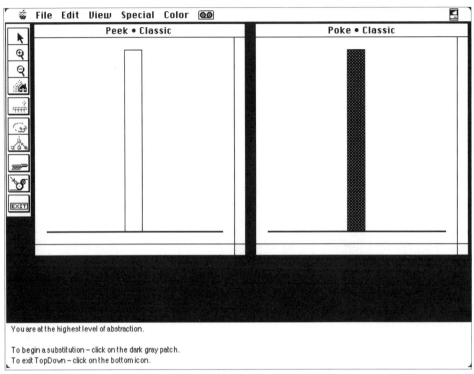

Figure 3 The *Topdown* screen with peek, poke, and message windows

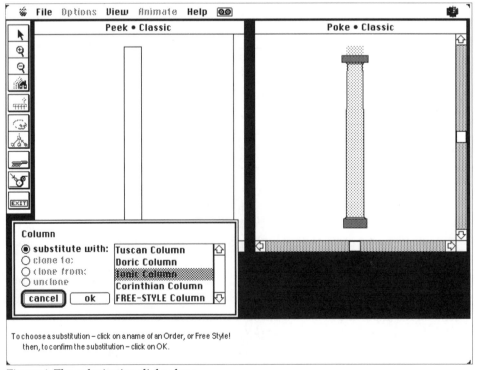

Figure 4 The substitution dialog box

poke window. Then, when ok is clicked, the selected option is substituted in the current version of the design that is displayed in the peek window, and the dialog box disappears.

Parametric variation of dimensions is accomplished by clicking on a dimension line in the poke window to bring up a control bar with a slide bar (figure 5). Dimensions are then varied, in real time, by means the slide bar. The control bar displays the name and current value of the variable that is being manipulated. When ok is clicked the current value of the variable is entered in the data structure and the control bar disappears.

The peek window always shows the design with all the detail that has so-far been established, but the user can set the poke window at any level of abstraction. Thus by setting the poke window at a high level of abstraction the user can make global decisions—to readjust overall dimensions of an object, for example—and immediately see the effects of these propagated to the details shown in the peek window. Conversely, by setting the poke window at a low level of abstraction, the user can work on details within the framework of an established design. This freedom to move freely between and work at different levels of abstraction is not provided either by physical media or by traditional CAD systems.

At all times a message window is open at the bottom of the screen. This provides

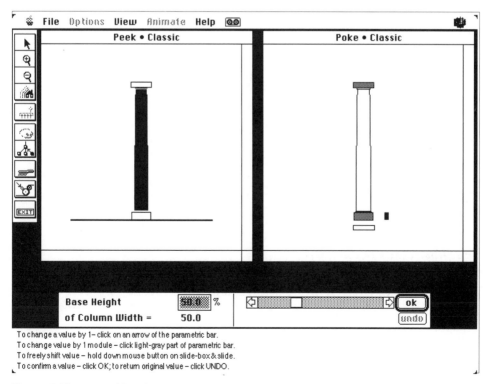

Figure 5 The control bar for parametric variation

a continuous stream of context-sensitive advice and suggestions, critical comments, and results of relevant analyses (such as area and cost calculations). It can, of course, be ignored—but some appropriate advice is always there when the user happens to give it a glance.

Essentially, then, the user sees the current state of the design in the peek window, variables and options in the poke window, and advice and criticism in the message window.

The Programmer Level

The programmer's task, in constructing a *Topdown* knowledge base, is to capture and encode knowledge of the shapes and sizes of elements and subsystems, and of how to put them together. In other words, the programmer must encode the vocabulary and syntactic rules of a parametric shape grammar (Stiny, 1980) for the type of artifact that is to be designed. The user is then able to explore designs in the language specified by that grammar.

The first step in constructing a knowledge base is to specify the vocabulary of parameterized shapes from which designs are to be assembled. Secondly, rules specifying which shapes may be substituted for a given shape must be defined. Finally, the positions and sizes of substituted shapes must be related to the positions and sizes of their predecessors by specifying how parameter values will be inherited by substituted shapes. If a detailed depiction of a window is to be substituted for a simple rectangle, for example, the window's width and height should be inherited from that rectangle.

This sort of programming might, in principle, be carried out in many different ways. In current versions of *Topdown*, which are used for teaching programming, the programmer sees an extension of Pascal. Shapes are represented by parameterized procedures (using the approach described by Mitchell, Liggett, and Kvan 1987), and there are facilities for specifying substitution possibilities and paths of inheritance of parameter values. A more sophisticated production version would take greater advantage of techniques of object-oriented programming, and would provide a point-and-click graphic method for specifying shapes and shape substitution rules.

The Substructure Level

Knowledge bases for design of different types of artifacts can be plugged into the *Topdown* shell—a piece of software that provides the interface between the user and the rules encoded by the programmer. The shell presents shape substitution rules as selectable shapes in the poke window together with substitution options in the substitution dialogue box, and it presents dimensioning variables as dimension lines in the poke window which can be selected to invoke the slide bar that is used to assign a value. It also records the user's design decisions in a data structure, and displays the current state of the design in the peek window. Finally, it provides file import, export, and print utilities.

In order to present shape substitution possibilities and perform substitution operations the shell must have some kind of structural description of a developing design as a collection of subshapes of various types in various relations to each other. Current versions of *Topdown* organize designs as strict hierarchies of subshapes within subshapes, and require the programmer to predefine this hierarchical structure. Thus they do not capture the full power and generality of the shape grammar formalism (Stiny, 1982). We expect that more sophisticated future versions will incorporate unrestricted subshape recognition capabilities, and thus allow structural descriptions to be created dynamically during a design process. Some parallel research is exploring ways to accomplish this (Nagakura 1989, Tan 1989).

The shell is designed to provide real-time performance: substitutions are performed instantly, and movement of the slide bar results in simultaneous resizing of affected elements in the peek and poke windows. This provides a qualitatively different experience from that of systems which exhibit perceptibly delayed response, and we believe that the tactile character and immediate feedback provided by a real-time system are important both to comprehension and to fluidity and spontaneity in design exploration. Designers come to think of drawings not as basically static objects that can be edited in discrete steps, but as dynamic mechanisms that can be adjusted fluently to the particular state that is desired.

In order to accomplish real-time performance on the chosen hardware platforms it was necessary to accept certain limitations. *Topdown* is two-dimensional, it can only handle designs of limited size and complexity, and at the programmer level it does not take advantage of high-level programming constructs that would impose an unacceptable computational overhead. But these are all limitations that can be eliminated as faster platforms become available at acceptable cost.

The shell software is written in Pascal, making use of the windowing and graphics functions of the various environments for which it is implemented. Thus it varies from implementation to implementation, but this variation is completely invisible both to the programmer and to the user. Knowledge bases can be transferred between implementations, and screen displays and user interaction are identical in different implementations.

An Example

A knowledge base that tells how to put together classical columns provides a particularly clear illustration of the operation of *Topdown*, since the rules for classical columns are well known, and since the traditions of classical architecture assign them a well-defined hierarchical structure (Summerson 1966, Tzonis and Lefaivre 1986, Onians 1988). Essentially, this knowledge base encodes a parallel of the orders.

At the highest level of abstraction a column is represented as a narrow vertical rectangle (figure 6). This is what the user first sees in the poke window. Clicking on it brings up a dialogue box which presents the options of developing it into a Tuscan, Doric, Ionic, Corinthian, or freestyle column. Let us assume, for the moment, that the Ionic order is selected. The poke window now shows a structure of base, shaft, and capital in correct Ionic proportions. Each of these parts can be selected for further development. When this is done, correct Ionic details are presented and can be substituted to complete the design as shown.

The part vocabulary of this knowledge base includes several types of capitals (figure 7), several types of bases (figure 8), and two types of shafts. Furthermore, some of these have alternative details (figure 9). But the substitution rules do not allow combinations that violate the integrity of a chosen order. Only if the freestyle type has been chosen will free combination of parts from different orders be allowed.

As parts are selected, dimensions and proportions are also assigned. First, overall height and diameter, and the relative sizes of base, shaft, and capital are established. Then, at the next level of detail, the internal proportions of the chosen base type, the chosen shaft type, and the chosen capital type can be adjusted. At the next level of detail the proportions of small mouldings and fillets are manipulated. Whenever the user returns to a higher level of abstraction, and alters dimensions at that level, the proportions that have been established for lower-level details are preserved as parts are resized.

The knowledge base incorporates proportioning rules. Whenever a part is first presented in the poke window its dimensions and proportions default to correct values for the particular order that has been selected to control the design. The user can specify variation from these default values (by moving the scroll bar), but only over a sanctioned range. If the freestyle type has been selected, however, proportioning rules do not apply and dimensions can be varied over wide ranges to produce bizarre results.

A comparison of figures 10 and 11 illustrates the effect of the knowledge that is provided by this knowledge base. Figure 10 shows correctly combined and proportioned classical columns that were produced in a few seconds by choosing, at a high level of abstraction, to follow the rules of a particular order. Figure 11 shows a few of the many strange mutants that can be produced by selecting the freestyle option which allows recombination of parts from different orders and unfettered variation of dimensions and proportions.

The difference in time required to design a classical column using this knowledge base rather than a traditional computer drafting system (even for an architect thoroughly familiar with the classical orders) is one of seconds compared to hours. This multiple order of magnitude speed-up results from a combination of real-time performance with use of high-level, specialized, context-specific, design operations rather than low-level, general-purpose, drawing-editing operations.

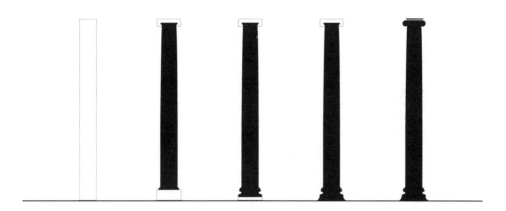

Figure 6   Steps in elaboration of an Ionic column

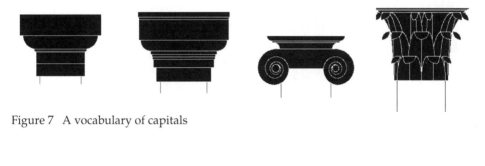

Figure 7   A vocabulary of capitals

Figure 8   A vocabulary of bases

Figure 9   Alternative ways to detail a Doric capital

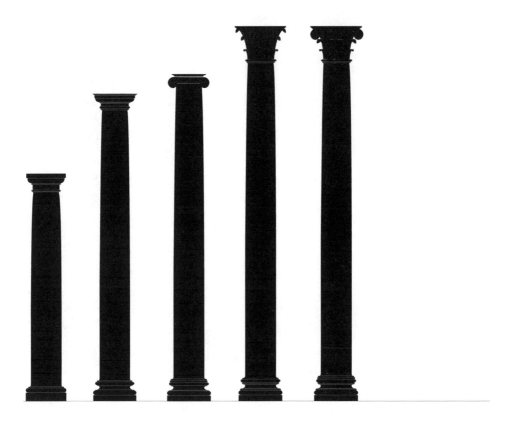

Figure 10   Correctly configured and proportioned columns:
Tuscan, Doric, Ionic, Corinthian, and Composite .

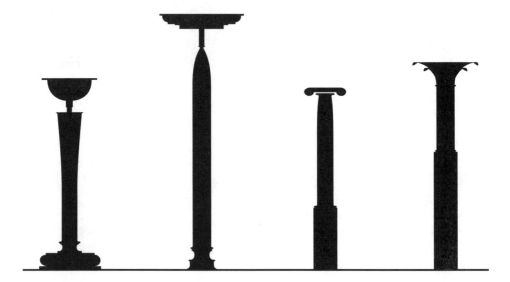

Figure 11   A variety of freestyle columns

Integration of Topdown with Traditional CAD Systems

Traditional CAD systems are content-free, general-purpose tools, whereas a particular *Topdown* knowledge base is a content-rich, special-purpose tool. Thus the two perform complementary roles, and they are best used in combination. They can be integrated effectively by treating *Topdown*, with a library of knowledge bases, as an accessory that can be invoked as needed from within a CAD system. A shape in the CAD drawing or model can then be specified as the starting shape to be developed into a detailed element or subsystem design with Topdown. When the detailed design has been developed it can be exported back to the CAD database and there substituted for the original shape. Subsequently, this detailed design can be modified as required using standard CAD system editing tools. In the current implementations this capability is approximated by providing for export of designs in standard formats such as DXF.

A library of *Topdown* knowledge bases might include tools for designing many different types of architectural subsystems, elements, and details. Our students have, for example, experimented with knowledge bases for producing schematic apartment plans, detailed layouts of kitchens and bathrooms, door and window designs, fenestration of elevations, sectional window details, trees, and human figures. When libraries of knowledge bases become large it is necessary to provide tools for finding the ones that are relevant to particular design contexts. Hypermedia techniques can be useful here. We have, for example, experimented successfully with launching *Topdown* from *Hypercard*, and organizing *Topdown* knowledge base libraries in *Hypercard* stacks.

A *Topdown* knowledge base does not have to provide flawless solutions under all conditions in order for it to be useful: it merely needs to provide a good starting point for further exploration. Nor does it need to be universal: it might provide a highly personal and idiosyncratic set of suggestions about how to develop a particular element or subsystem. The point of a *Topdown* knowledge base library is not to replace the skill and judgement of the designer, but to speed the process of design exploration by providing a wide variety of specialized tools for swift development, in alternative ways, of aspects of a design.

Conclusion

The *Topdown* prototypes have demonstrated the concept of top-down knowledge-based design, and they have shown its potential usefulness. They illustrate one way in which the knowledge captured and encoded in a shape grammar can be delivered effectively to a designer at a CAD workstation.

The prototypes have many limitations. They are restricted to two-dimensional design, they can only maintain real-time performance with designs of very limited complexity, they rely on an overly simple and rigid method of structural description, and they are relatively cumbersome to program. But none of these limitations seem fundamental: we expect them to be overcome as increasingly powerful hardware platforms become available, as more sophisticated environments for graphic, object-oriented programming emerge, and as current research on the structural description of designs comes to fruition. As the relevant technologies mature, top-down knowledge-based design systems should become important practical tools.

Traditional CAD systems are approaching a productivity plateau that is a consequence of their fundamental character: further speeding of operations and addition of features will make only a marginal difference. Use of top-down knowledge-based techniques seems one promising way to escape the limitations of traditional CAD and to carry design productivity to entirely new levels.

Notes

Durand, Jean-Nicolas-Louis. 1802. *Précis des lecons d'architecture*. Paris: Ecole Polytechnique.

Durand, Jean-Nicolas-Louis. 1821. *Partie graphique des cours d'architecture*. Paris: Ecole Polytechnique.

Dürer, Albrecht. [1528]. 1970. *Vier Bucher von menschlicher Proportion*. (Four Books of Human Proportion). London: G. M. Wagner.

Gombrich, Ernst H. 1969. *Art and Illusion: A Study in the Psychology of Pictorial Representation*. Princeton: Princeton University Press.

Mitchell, William J., Robin S. Liggett, and Thomas Kvan. 1987. *The Art of Computer Graphics Programming*. New York: Van Nostrand Reinhold.

Nagakura, Takehiko. 1989. "Shape Recognition and Transformation—A Script-Based Approach." This volume.

Onians, John. 1988. *Bearers of Meaning: The Classical Orders in Antiquity, the Middle Ages, and the Renaissance*. Princeton: Princeton University Press.

Stiny, George. 1980. "Introduction to Shape and Shape Grammars." *Environment and Planning B* 7: 343-51.

Stiny, George. 1982. "Spatial Relations and Grammars." *Environment and Planning B* 9: 113-114.

Summerson, John. 1966. *The Classical Language of Architecture*. Cambridge, Mass.: MIT Press.

Tan, Milton. 1989. "Saying What it Is by What it Is Like." This volume.

Tzonis, Alexander, and Liane Lefaivre. 1986. *Classical Architecture: The Poetics of Order*. Cambridge, Mass.: MIT Press.

10
Shape Recognition and Transformation:
A Script-Based Approach

Takehiko Nagakura

Harvard University Graduate School of Design

Design evolves. Architects deploy considerable knowledge to develop their designs from one stage to the next. Drawings play a major role in describing the "state" of design at each stage; however, they do not explicitly reveal the knowledge used to achieve the design, for the knowledge is concealed in the "process" between these stages rather than in the drawings themselves. This process involves parametric and schematic transformations as well as perception of unanticipated possibilities emerging from the drawings in progress. To make an impact on design, CAD must address these issues of design knowledge, but so far its focus has been instead on drawings as relatively static collections of graphic primitives.

This paper introduces the concepts of shapes and shape-transformation as fundamental aspects of design knowledge. It is implemented on a computer program in the form of a prototype shape-scripting language with the following features:

1. A means of describing categories of shapes: This uses a basic structure called the "object script," which identifies any category of shapes defined as a set of successive lines with interrelated parametric constraints.
2. A means of specifying transformations as intercategorical relationships: This uses a secondary structure called the "transformation script." It takes the form of an arithmetic mapping from the set of parameters of one shape category to that of another.
3. A mechanism to enable the recognition of emergent subshapes: This employs pattern-matching to find members of a specified shape category in drawings.

In summary, this language works as a shell to encode a set of shape categories and their transformations, and it enables progressive shape recognition and shape transformation in line drawings. An appropriate set of these encoded transformations may represent a body of syntactic knowledge about an architectural style. This opens up the exciting possibility of a computational implementation of a shape grammar.

Introduction to Three Problems

Drawing and Process

Drawings are the architects' preferred tool. Besides being an effective means of presentation and communication, drawings enable us to develop the first flash of an idea into the most detailed architectural form. *In other words, drawings are important to design because design develops only through the interaction between an architect and such a vehicle as drawings.* The final form of a design never springs into being *sui generis*, nor is a drawing merely its visualization. For example, figure 1 below illustrates a sequence of six drawings from left to right. If you were just copying the drawing on the far right, which you already knew from somewhere else, this sequence might simply show a way of modelling a precise copy of it without a Xerox machine. But in design you always start from scratch and you do not know what you will accomplish in the end. (You might have an image of the final form when you start the design, but our experience says it is always different from what finally comes out.) If we imagine that this sequence shows the development of an architectural design, we can see that the architect could determine the building periphery in the third drawing only on the basis of a grid layout like the one in the second drawing. The room arrangement in the fourth drawing could be accomplished only by taking into account the building periphery in the third drawing. The position of the circulations in the next drawing was designed in response to the room arrangement developed in the previous drawing. And we could never have produced the last drawing without making this series of decisions between stages.

The example shows the evolutionary nature of design occuring through the interaction of an architect with his drawing. This interaction involves at least two kinds of cognitive processes. When a drawing advances from one stage to the next, the architect first perceives and evaluates the current drawing, and then performs transformations on it. The architect is continually examining his drawing , trying to find appropriate lines to add and erase. Thus a design is an iteration of a perception-transformation cycle lodged between an architect and his drawing.

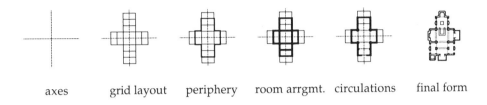

axes   grid layout   periphery   room arrgmt. circulations   final form

Figure 1 Development of a design

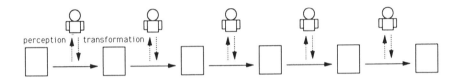

Figure 2 Diagram of a design

Such a view of design illuminates the significance of process in design as well as in drawings per se. Drawings are the major vehicle by which design happens, and design needs sophisticated processes to navigate this vehicle toward an appropriate final form. This process represents an aspect of domain-specific knowledge in architecture. In the field of design, this process of perception and transformation is usually carried out heuristically by individual architects, but until recently few attempts have been made to reveal and formalize this process in a more reusable form.

One way to formalize the knowledge used in the process of design is to apply a *production*, used in the standard problem-solving paradigm. A *production* is a set of rules in the form "If you find X, you can replace it with Y." Rules can be represented in some notation system such as language[1] or graphics. Figure 3 shows two examples of graphically represented rules of a *production*.

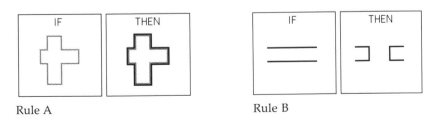

Rule A   Rule B

Figure 3 Examples of production rules

Using these rules, it is possible to describe the process that occurs between the successive drawings. In the sequence of drawings in figure 1, the movement from the second to the third drawing is accomplished by applying rule A above, and the movement from the fourth to the fifth drawing can be reduced to six elemental processes by repeatedly employing rule B.

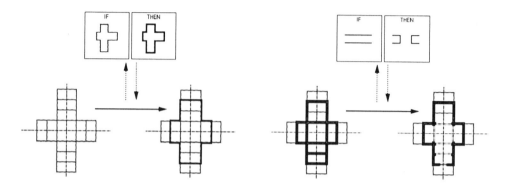

Figure 4 Development with rules

At each stage, "perception" means finding a local pattern in a drawing which matches the pattern provided in the if-clause of a rule in *production*. "Transformation" means rewriting the found pattern using the pattern provided in the then-clause of the rule; that is, erasing the left pattern and drawing the right pattern. Developments of such rule-based knowledge representation in architectural design can be found in a number of sources,[2] and generally *production* in architecture is known as a shape grammar.

Three Problems

The discussion so far applies to architectural drawings whether they happen on a sheet of yellow trace or on a computer screen. As long as these media try to serve only the drawings and not the process, and as long as this process is administered only by architects, we encounter no new difficulties. *We can draw either with a pencil on yellow trace or on a screen with a mouse.* But given the enormous potential power of the computer, it seems quite natural to think about expanding the use of the computer beyond its present role of a simple drawing medium to improve the process of design itself. One of the first steps toward this goal is to establish a way to encode these shape grammar rules into the machine so that architects can access and use various prescribed rules in their design.

An attempt to encode a shape grammar into the computer raises three major problems. Since they arise from the concept of shape grammar rules rather than from the technical implementation itself, these problems lead to a mathematical reformation of the graphic *production*. The first two problems arise from the ambiguity in the description of these rules. For instance, in figure 3, what the rules mean may seem quite obvious to architects. Rule A can be interpreted architecturally as "If you find a cross-shaped grid, you can make a cross-shaped building periphery." Rule B means "If you find a wall, you can put an opening in the middle." But here we take it for granted that the graphic patterns used in the if-clause and the then-clause in these rules do not represent only those particular graphic instances in a drawing that are exactly identical to the graphic patterns described by the rules. In fact, the cross-shaped grid in the left drawing of figure 4 is different from the if-clause of rule A in its dimensions and proportions. Thus what a shape grammar rule intends to describe is a category of shape, a set that probably includes an infinite number of instances, and yet it graphically shows only one exemplar of these instances. This may lead to a problem when a number of graphic patterns are given, as in figure 5, for there is no way to determine which of these are the cross-shapes included in the category implied by the if-clause in rule A. To encode these rules as reusable knowledge, we need a definition of shape category that is at the same time more comprehensive and more precise than a particular exemplar.

Figure 5 Cross-shapes

Ambiguity lies also in the relationships between the patterns of the if-clause and the then-clause. For example, we do not know which of the following (figure 6) might be a valid transformation resulting from the application of rule B. The shape grammar rules show only one example of correspondence between two shapes, one from the category for the if-clause and the other from the category for the then-clause, and this is not enough to specify all possible correspondences between the members of these two categories. Moreover, rules in a shape grammar often imply parametric transformations such that an instance in the category for the if-clause may be rewritten to any member of a subset of the category for the then-clause. For example, it is architecturally natural for the interpretation of rule B to allow both transformations in the left column in figure 6 as valid cases. In any case, we need a more structural way to define intercategorical mappings.

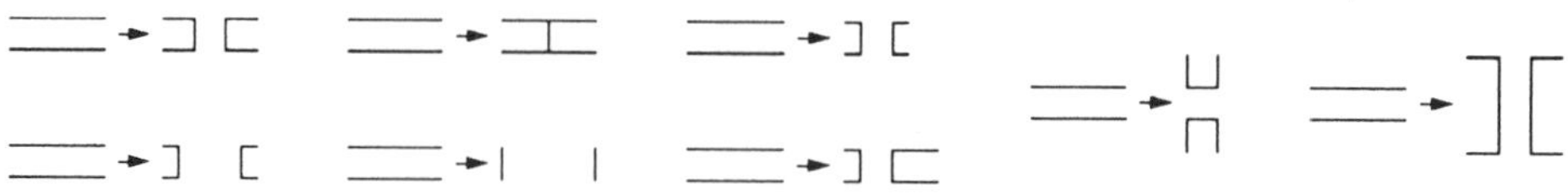

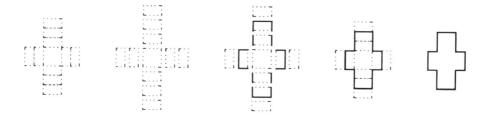

Figure 6 Transformations

The third problem lies in the perception mechanism employed in the application of these rules to drawings. In figure 4, rule A was applied to the drawing when several lines were perceived as a cross-shape, which happens to match the category for the if-clause. Although this perception is automatic to the human eye, it sometimes appears very unnatural to the computer. Suppose that originally the grid arrangement was given as eleven rectangles drawn one after another (figure 7). The original structure of this drawing is forty-four lines with four lines composing each rectangle. When the cross-shape is perceived, the human eye recognizes sixteen among these forty-four lines and recomposes them into a different structure within the same composition. Among shape grammar researchers, this phenomenon of the structural shifting of a composition is known as *emergent shape*.[3] On the other hand, this reorganization of the composition is very difficult for computer systems, for they usually do not select anything except a structural identity in the original database. More concretely, on the computer screen, any of these eleven rectangles can be selected, but most likely the fourteen lines of the cross-shape as a group would not be selected without the intentional and laborious operations of decomposing and recomposing the original structure. Finding an efficient way to automatically capture *emergent shapes* is the third problem.

Figure 7 Emergent shape

Proposal for a Shape-Scripting Language

In this section, I propose a conceptual specification of a prototype shape-scripting language in response to the three problems discussed above. This language attempts to facilitate the mathematical formalization of a shape grammar, which guides the development of drawings.

First, the language provides two unique script structures: one for describing categories of shapes and the other for defining intercategorical transformations. On top of them, the language introduces four major controls that employ these scripts to manipulate line drawings. They include finding, trasnforming, erasing, and drawing of shapes in drawings. As a whole, the language allows progressive shape-recognition and shape-transformation in architectural design.

Description of Shape Categories

Object Script and Its Hierarchy

A basic structure called the *object script* is used for representing a categorical notion of shapes. For two-dimensional line drawings, it allows any category of shapes defined as a set of successive lines with interrelating parametric constraints. There are three different states of this script structure, which establish a system with three hierarchical levels (figure 8). *Object scripts* in each level are called *generic objects*, *categorical objects*, and *instance objects*, respectively. The *generic object* is the most abstract one from which the categorical notion of shape derives, while the *instance object* is the most concrete and thus can be uniquely visualized on the world coordinate system.

An *object script* consists of four slots which store information for location, sides, parametric constraints, and bindings of the parameters. All of these slots are empty in the *generic object*. The language system treats the concept of shape as the whole set of geometry specified by the *object script* with these four slots. In the *categorical object*, the slots for location, sides, and parametric constraints are filled, with the slot for bindings left empty. An *object script* on this level represents a category of shape usually containing an infinite number of instances. Filling all four slots puts an *object script* on the instance level and makes it represent a specific instance of the category.

Sides Slot, Constraints Slot, Location Slot, and Shape Category

These three slots in the *object script* specify a *categorical object*, which represents a shape category. Each slot has its unique format and takes a set of variables and constants as its fillers. The concrete syntax for these formats are implementation specific. The following discussion is based on the prototype written in LISP notation.

First, the *location slot* establishes a local coordinate system in which all the members of the shape category are defined. The general form of the slot-filler is

(x-offset   y-offset   angle   mirror)

The values of the first two variables specify the offset of the local system's

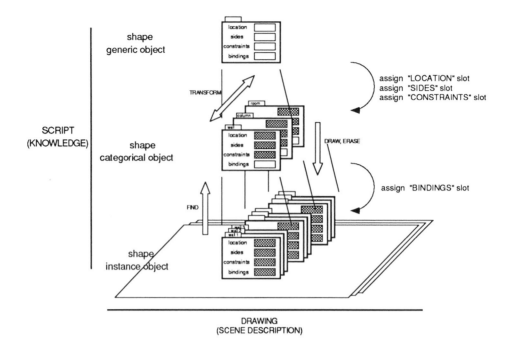

Figure 8 Object script

origin relative to the global coordinate system's origin. The values of the third variable specify the rotation of the local axes.   The last variable takes Boolean values and specifies if the relation between the ordinate and abscissa is flipped. Figure 9 illustrates some examples.

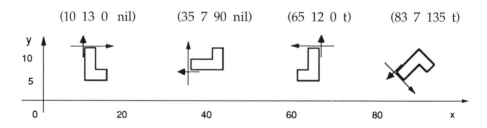

Figure 9 Location slot

The *sides slot* consists of a set of specifications for successive *sides*. A *side* is an expanded notion of a vector in the usual mathematical sense, and it represents each side of the members of the shape category. The general form of a *side* is

(primitive-type   arguments-list   label)

The primitive-type with a list of arguments represents the geometry of a side, and the *label* is reserved to attach to it any attributes other than its geometry. For now the *labels* can be thought of as line characters (see figure 10).

(line (10 0) back-side)   (line (10 0) sectional)   (line (10 0) face-side)   (line (10 0) constructional)

Figure 10 Labels

These sides in a sides slot are connected head to tail, that is, the endpoint of the previous *side* is the starting point of the next *side*. The starting point of the first *side* is placed at the origin of the local coordinate system, specified by the *location slot*.

The following example of a *sides slot* specifies the horizontal parallel lines with a length of 20 and an interval of 5.

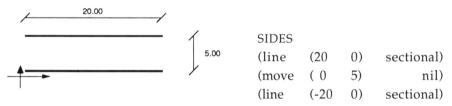

```
SIDES
(line     (20    0)    sectional)
(move     ( 0    5)    nil)
(line     (-20   0)    sectional)
```

Figure 11

Here, "line" and "move" are two predefined primitive types which take as their arguments horizontal and vertical offsets of the endpoint relative to the starting point. The primitive "move" represents an invisible line (and thus does not require any *label*).

The *constraints slot* is filled by a set of *constraints*. A *constraint* is a form of a predicate to limit the range of values of a variable called *constrained variables* by a mathematical function of other variables called *argument variables*. The general form of a *constraint* is

(predicate   *constrained-variable*   function-of-*argument-variables*)

For example,

(= wall-depth   (x 1/2 wall-bottom))

means " wall-depth = wall-bottom   x 1/2 " in ordinary mathematical notation. Also

(<   wall-depth   (x 1/2 wall-bottom))

means " wall-depth < wall-bottom x 1/2 " in the usual sense.

By allowing the use of variables in the arguments of *sides* in the *sides slot* and the *location slot*, these *constraints* specify the internal structure of the *categorical object*. In other words, bindings of variables are local within the definition of an *object script*, and when the *sides slot* and the *location slot* include variables, the *constraints slot* determines their interpretation. If a variable does not appear as a *constrained variable* in any *constraint* of an *object script*, the value of this variable takes any real number. If a variable does appear as a *constrained variable*, it should satisfy the predicate specified by the corresponding *constraint*. Thus there are two types of variables: the values of one type of variable are automatically determined by certain *constraints* when the values of other variables are assigned. The values of the other type of variable remain unassigned or ranged only when all other variables are assigned. The latter type of variable is called an *object handles*.[4]

For example, suppose that the *sides slot* and the *location slot* are filled as follows:

```
LOCATION
(  x   y   angle  nil  )
SIDES
(line   (wall-bottom     0      )  sectional)
(move  (     0     wall-depth)         nil)
(line   ( wall-top        0      )  sectional)
```

Depending on the contents of *constraints slot*, this *categorical object* may represent different shape categories as follows:

category W1 : parallel lines with fixed
dimension and fixed direction constraints
(= angle   60   )
(= wall-bottom   10   )
(= wall-depth   5   )
(= wall-top   - 10   )

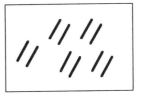

Here, the *object handles* include x and y.

category W2 : parallel lines with fixed
distance at fixed position constraints
(= x   100   )
(= y   100   )
(> wall-bottom   0   )
(= wall-depth   5   )
(= wall-top(-   wall-bottom)   )

Here, the *object handles* include angle
and wall-bottom.

category W3 : parallel lines with fixed
proportion constraints
(> wall-bottom   5   )
(= wall-depth(x 1/2 wall-bottom)   )
(= wall-top(-   wall-bottom)   )

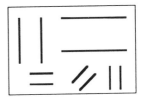

Figure 12 Shape categories

Here, the *object handles* include x, y,
angle, and wall-bottom.

Here, variables work like handles to change built-in parameters of a shape
category and like rubber bands to hold the arithmetic relations between its
sides. In this way, a *categorical object* is given a parametric generality and an
internal structure at the same time.

Bindings Slot and Instantiation
The three slots introduced above are used for the description of a shape
category that normally includes an infinite number of members. The notion of
shape in the *categorical object* is a set of line segments with some interrelating
structure on their dimensions and directions. This parametric structure is
controlled by a set of unassigned variables called *object handles*.

   At the most concrete level, the *object script* specifies each individual
member of a shape category represented by the *categorical object*. This is done
by simply assigning a real value to each *object handle* of the *categorical object*.

The *bindings slot* is used for this purpose. It is a list of pairs of a variable and a value called *binding*. The general form of a *binding* is

(variable   value)

The *bindings slot* is filled by

(variable-1   value-1)   (variable-2   value-2) . . . (variable-k   value-k)

When the *bindings slot* is filled, the values of all the variables in the *sides slot* and *location slot* are assigned, and these slots are said to be *instantiated* (with the restriction that the value of each of these variables satisfy its appropriate range, specified by the related *constraints* in the *constraints slot*). The *object script* is now an *instance object* and it can be uniquely plotted on the global coordinate system.

For example, the following illustrates instantiation of the *categorical object* W3 of figure 12.

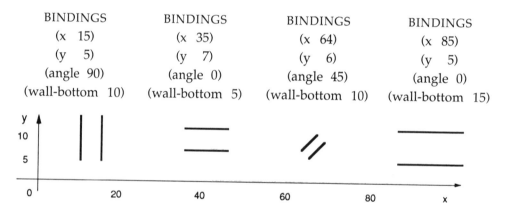

```
   BINDINGS              BINDINGS              BINDINGS              BINDINGS
     (x   15)              (x   35)              (x   64)              (x   85)
     (y    5)              (y    7)              (y    6)              (y    5)
   (angle 90)            (angle 0)            (angle 45)            (angle 0)
(wall-bottom 10)    (wall-bottom 5)    (wall-bottom 10)    (wall-bottom 15)
```

Figure 13 Shape instances

Description of Intercategorical Relationships

Transformation Script and Its Hierarchy

The *object script* makes possible a mathematical notation of a shape category. Furthermore, this notation allows us to formally specify an intercategorical relationship between any two *object scripts* which represents a transformation from one shape category to another. This simply requires us to define mappings between the *object handles* of two *object scripts*. A structure called a *transformation script* is introduced for this purpose.

Like in an *object script*, three different states of this script structure create a system with three levels of hierarchy. A *transformation script* consists of three slots that store information for two *categorical objects, mappings* between their *object handles,* and *bindings* of the parameters in transformation. These are called the *objects slot, mappings slot,* and *bindings slot,* respectively. With all these slots empty, the *transformation script* is called a *generic transformation.* Filling the *objects slot* and *mappings slot* makes a *categorical transformation,* which represents a category of transformations (usually containing a number of instances) from one *categorical object* to another. A *transformation script* with all three slots filled is called an *instance transformation,* and it specifies an instance of a transformation category that maps each member of one *categorical object* uniquely to a member of another (figure 14).

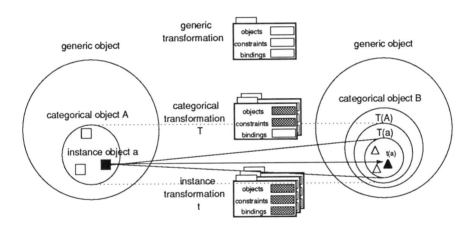

Figure 14 Transformation script

Object Slot, Mappings Slot, and Categorical Transformation
The *objects slot* specifies two *categorical objects* called a *source object* and a *destination object*. It is sufficient that the general form of this slot owns a pointer to each *object script,* as follows:

(source-object   destination-object)

The *mappings slot* specifies mathematical relationships between the *source object* and the *destination object*. Three types of variables are used here: the *object handles* of the *source object,* the *object handles* of the *destination object*, and variables unique to each *categorical transformation*. They are called *source handles*, *destination handles*, and *transformation handles* respectively.[5] The *mappings slot* consists of a set of *mappings*. A *mapping* specifies every *destination handle* as an arithmetic function of *source handles* and *transformation handles*. The general form of a *mapping* is

(destination-handle   function-of-*source-handles-and-transformation-handles*)

For example,

(handle-A   (x 2 (+ handle-B handle-C))

means " handle-A = 2 x (handle-B + handle-C) " in mathematical notation. "Handle-A" must be an *object handle* of the *destination object*, and each "handle-B" and "handle-C" must be either an *object handle* of the *source object* or a variable unique to this *categorical transformation* which is not found as an *object handle* of the *source object* or of the *destination object*.

Suppose we need to specify rule B in figure 3 when two shape categories are prepared in the form of *object scripts*, as follows:

WALL
The *object handles* include
x, y, angle, H1, and V1.

```
LOCATION
(  x      y    angle nil  )
SIDES
(line    ( H1      0   )  sectional)
(move  ( 0      V1  )           nil)
(line    ( H2      0   )  sectional)




CONSTRAINTS
(>       H1      0      )
(>       V1      0      )
(=       H2   (-  H1)  )
```

OPENING
The *object handles* include
x, y, angle, H1, H2, V1, and V1.

```
LOCATION
(  x      y    angle nil  )
SIDES
(line    ( H1      0   )  sectional)
(line    ( 0      V1 )  sectional)
(line    ( H3      0   )  sectional)
(move  ( H2      0   )           nil)
(line    ( H3      0   )  sectional)
(line    ( 0      V2 )  sectional)
(line    ( H1      0   )  sectional)
CONSTRAINTS
(>       H1      0      )
(>       V1      0      )
(=       H3   (-  H1)  )
(=       V2   (-  V1)  )
```

Figure 15 Object Scripts

The following *categorical transformation* represents a set of transformations:

RULE B

The *transformation handle* is TH.

OBJECTS	
(WALL	OPENING)
MAPPINGS	
(x	x)
(y	y)
(angle	angle)
(H1	TH)
(H2	H1)
(V1	V1)

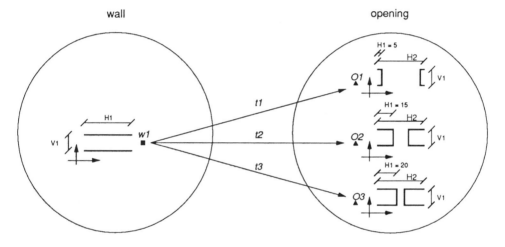

Figure 16 Categorical transformation

Note that the fourth line in the *mappings slot* means "the value of 'H1' in the OPENING object is equal to the value of 'TH'." 'TH' is a *transformation handle*, an independent variable which takes a real value. It controls the width of the opening in the wall. Furthermore, the last two lines in the *mappings slot* mean "the value of 'H2' in the OPENING object is equal to the value of 'H1' in the WALL object," and "the value of 'V1' in the OPENING object is equal to the value of 'V1' in the WALL object," according to the definition of *mapping* above. This maintains the length and thickness of the wall when an opening is perforated.

Bindings Slot and Instance Transformation

As seen above, a *categorical transformation* specifies a set of mappings between two categorical objects. That is, a member of the *source category* corresponds to a subset of the *destination category* through the set of mappings in the *categorical transformation* (figures 14, 16). Here, the *transformation handles* work as parameters to control this *categorical transformation*.

The *bindings slot* assigns values to each *transformation handle* and specifies an individual member of the *categorical transformation*. The general form of this *bindings slot* is the same as that of the *bindings slot* in the *object script*:

(variable-1 value-1) (variable-2 value-2) . . . (variable-k value-k)

Now the *mappings slot* is said to be *instantiated*, and the *transformation script* is called an *instance transformation*.

For example, filling the *bindings slot* of the *categorical transformation* of rule B as follows specifies three transformations t1, t2 and t3 of figure 15.

t1	t2	t3
BINDINGS	BINDINGS	BINDINGS
(TH 5)	(TH 15)	(TH 20)

Control Strategy and Emergent Shapes

The two script structures above, *object script* and *transformation script*, allow us to formally describe shape grammar rules. To use this rule-based knowledge, we need a way to apply these rules to drawings. For this purpose, fundamental controls to the language are provided as follows.

Minimum Scene Description

For the sake of simplicity, the discussion here assumes that the drawing used is converted to *maximum-segment notation* (although other computational notations for two-dimensional line drawings could also be used). This means that adding a new primitive which has colinear relations to existing primitives of the same *label* (line character) in the drawing concatenates the primitive with the existing colinear primitives. For example, in figure 17, adding a new primitive X to a drawing in the upper row deletes the original primitives and makes Y, as shown in the drawing in the lower row .

Thus the drawing never includes any colinear segments. The drawing in this notation is called a *minimum scene description*. The shape-scripting language has four basic control commands over this *minimum scene description* (figure 8). They include **FIND, TRANSFORM, DRAW,** and **ERASE**.

Figure 17 Minimum scene description

Controls

The control command **FIND** takes a *categorical object* and an area of the *minimum scene description* as arguments, and returns a set of its *instance objects*, which are the *subshapes* of the *minimum scene description* in the specified area. In the prototype written in LISP, the syntax is

(**FIND** categorical-object   *area*)

For this computation, a simple pattern-matching mechanism is used in conjuction with some pre-processing of the *minimum scene description*. (The details of programming technique are not presented here.)[6] The shape-scripting language provides a notion of *subshape*. Each side of a *subshape* must be defined between two points on the intersection of two primitives or at the end of a primitive. This means that the language is capable of capturing *emergent shapes* with a restriction. For example, when instances of the shape category Wall are searched in the *minimum scene description* A of figure 18, B is found as a *subshape* of the *minimum scene description*, but C is not. This restriction is assumed to match the architect's usual perception of shapes in a drawing, so that the language system does not find "too many" unnecessary *subshapes* nor "too few" feasible ones.

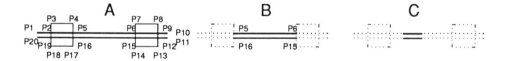

Figure 18 Subshapes

The control command TRANSFORM takes an *instance object*, a *categorical transformation*, and *bindings* for its *transformation handles* as arguments, and returns an *instance object* specified by this transformation.

(TRANSFORM *instance-object categorical-transformation   bindings*)

The control command DRAW takes an *instance object* as an argument, and adds the line segments of its sides in the *minimum scene description* while keeping the maximum-segment notation.

(DRAW   *instance-object*)

The control command ERASE takes an *instance object* as an argument, and deletes the line segments of its sides from the *minimum scene description*.

(ERASE   *instance-object*)

Again, when line segments are deleted from the *minimum scene description*, the maximum-segment notation must remain valid. This means primitives in the *minimum scene description* are trimmed or split if necessary. For example, in figure 19 the *minimum scene description* A includes ten line primitives. Erasing the *subshape* in B leaves the *minimum scene description* in the state shown in D. The primitives L1 and L2 in A are split into L1, L2, L11, and L12 in D.

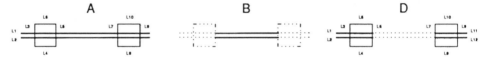

Figure 19   Rewriting process

Application

Using these four controls, we can exercise a computational shape-recognition and transformation on a drawing. At each stage of design, the system finds a shape and transforms it while it erases the found shape and draws the transformed shape in the MIMIMUM SCENE DESCRIPTION. An example of this progression appears in the appendix.

Conclusion

This language system allows development of a design based on a set of fundamental architectural design knowledge. A design is described in a series of drawings D in the form of a *minimum scene description*. Design knowledge is prepared by a set of *categorical objects* O and *categorical transformations* T, encoded in the form of scripts. A typical design development proceeds by rewriting a portion of the drawing using these scripts.

This is illustrated in figure 20 by means of a conventional state-action tree. At each stage i, the process P_i consists of three decisions. One decision is the choice of a *categorical transformation* T_i from the set T. The system then locates in the drawing D_i all the *subshapes* that match the *source object* of the selected *categorical transformation*. The control command FIND is used here.

The second decision is the selection of a *subshape* S_i among those found. The third decision is the specification of an *instance transformation* by providing a set of values for *transformation handles* in the form of *bindings* B_i. In the end, using the control command TRANSFORM, a new *subshape* is created from the selected one. To accomplish the rewriting process, the system deletes the originally selected *subshape* from the *minimum scene description* using the command ERASE and draws the new *subshape* in its place using the command DRAW. (Some architectural operations may require only the deletion of the original *subshape* or the addition of a new one.)[7]

In summary, at stage i of the design, we see

$$D_i = P_i (D_{i-1})$$

while

$$P_i = T_i + S_i + B_i.$$

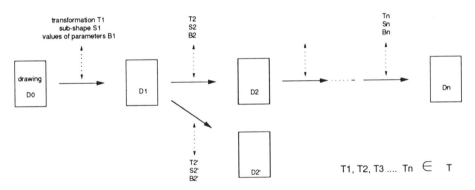

Figure 20　State-action progress and grammar

Of these three decisions, T_i is provided from the pre-encoded scripts, while S_i and B_i are parameters specified by the architect during a design. Obviously the type of knowledge these scripts can describe is very primitive. They deal only with the syntactic rewrite mechanism through pattern-matching and do not take into account any other context of the design. Yet an appropriate set of scripts is quite powerful for the generation of stylistic geometry, as implied by recent research on shape grammar,[8] and the scripts can be accumulated in digital form for information retrieval and exchange. Thus, a concept of style Style is defined by a set of *categorical transformations* T provided on top of a set of *categorical objects* O.

Style = O + T

Anyone can access this style.

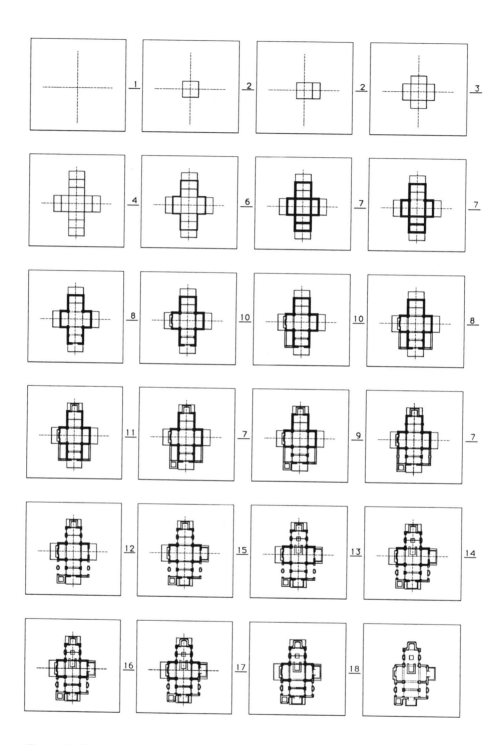

Figure 21 Transformation rules

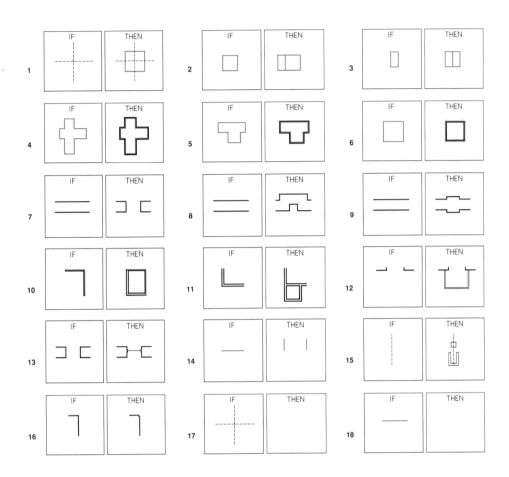

Figure 22 Derivation of a design

Background

For a discussion of the technical details of this shape-scripting language, see Nagakura, "The Shape-scripting Language" (manuscript in preparation).

Appendix : Computational Implementation

The above prototype shape-scripting language has been implemented in Common LISP on a M68020-based personal computer by Nagakura. As long as the number of primitives in the minimum scene description is relatively small (up to a few thousand), shape-recognition and transformation work interactively, just like a word-processing system with a thesaurus.

An example of the use of this language system is attached. Here, eighteen transformation scripts are prepared (figure 21), and the design proceeds by applying these rules. The illustration in figure 22 shows the derivation of a design.

Notes

Special thanks to Joy Sobeck for editorial work on this paper.

[1]   Production in linguistics was intensively studied by Noam Chomsky and others between 1950 and 1965. For example, see N. Chomsky, Syntactic Structures (The Hague: Mouton, 1951).

[2]   See, for example, G. Stiny and W. J. Mitchell, "The Palladian Grammar," *Environment and Planning B* 5:5-18.

[3]   W. J. Mitchell, "Types and Vocabularies," Chapter 6 of The Logic of Architecture (Cambridge, Mass. : MIT Press, in press).

[4]   Some restrictions are imposed on the order of reference among these variables. For details, see T. Nagakura, "The Shape-scripting Language," (Cambridge, Mass. : manuscript in preparation).

[5]   The *transformation handles* are independent variables, and a *mappings slot* can include any number of these, as long as their names do not conflict with the names of *destination handles*.

[6]   The technical details of pattern-matching in images can be found in many programing texts. For example, see P. H. Winston and B. K. P. Horn, LISP (New York: Addison-Wesley, 1988). For related theoretical foundations, see R. Krishnamurti, "The Construction of Shapes," *Environment and Planning B* 8:5-40.

[7]   See W. J. Mitchell, "Formal Representations: a Foundation for Computer-aided Design," *Environment and Planning B* 13:133-162.

[8]   Stiny and Mitchell, op. cit.

11
The Computability of Architectural Knowledge

Robert Oxman and Rivka Oxman

Faculty of Architecture and Town Planning
Technion: Israel Institute of Technology

A Theory of Design Knowledge for Design Computing

In an important contribution to the theoretical foundation of design computing, Mitchell noted "an increasingly urgent need to establish a demonstrably sound, comprehensive, rigorously formalized theoretical foundation upon which to base practical software development efforts" (Mitchell, 1986). In this paper we propose such a theoretical framework. A basic assumption of this work is that the advancement of design computing is dependent upon the emergence of a rigorous formulation of knowledge in design. We present a model of knowledge in architectural design which suggests a promising conceptual basis for dealing with knowledge in computer-aided design systems.

We require models which can represent the formal knowledge and manipulative operations of the designer in all of their complexity—that is formal models rather than just geometric models. Shape Grammars (Stiny,1980) represent an example of such models, and constitute a relatively high level of design knowledge as compared to, for example, use of symmetry operations to generate simple formal configurations. Building upon an understanding of the classes of design knowledge as the conceptual basis for formal modeling systems may contribute a new realization of the potential of the medium for design. This will require a comprehensive approach to the definition of architectural and design knowledge. We consider here the implications of a well-defined body of architectural and design knowledge for design education and the potential mutual interaction—in a knowledge-rich environment—of design learning and CAAD learning.

The computational factors connected with the representation of design knowledge and its integration in design systems are among the key problems of CAAD. Mitchell's model of knowledge in design incorporates formal knowledge in a comprehensive, multi-level, hierarchical structure in which types of knowledge are correlated with computational concepts. In the main focus of this paper we present a structured, multi-level model of design knowledge which we discuss with respect to current architectural theoretical considerations. Finally, we analyze the computational and educational relevance of such models.

Architectural Knowledge and Design Knowledge

We propose a working definition of the terms architectural knowledge and design knowledge and a discussion of these terms from an architectural theoretical point of view. Architectural knowledge may be considered a category of formal knowledge. It is the knowledge of architectural and urban form and constitutes the disciplinary core of knowledge within a larger body of professional knowledge. Architectural knowledge occupies a dominant role in design, and the acquisition of architectural knowledge may be considered one of the objectives of design education. Design knowledge manifests itself in the selection, manipulation, modification and adaptation of architectural knowledge in design. It provides the basis for integration of a disciplinary core of object descriptions with procedural, heuristic, causal and interpretive knowledge in characteristic procedures of design. The definition and formalization of both of these bodies of knowledge is a significant part of the effort to establish a theoretical foundation for CAAD.

It may well be that a limiting factor in the computation of design is not deficiency in CAD theory, but the lack of such formalized knowledge in architecture. Silvetti has described the problem of the schism caused by modernist theory's radical discontinuity and rejection of the authority of historical precedent and tradition as sources of professional knowledge (Silvetti , 1980). The current recourse to historical sources may, in a positive sense, represent a new epistemology in which an atemporal and styleless recourse to precedent becomes a means to reestablish the disciplinary basis of architectural knowledge (Hancock, 1986).

The revitalization and definition of this body of architectural knowledge has been one of the leitmotifs of European theories for the past twenty years. This effort, including the formalization of knowledge of both architectural and urban form, has been principally associated with the European Neo-Rationalists, but may now be considered a general phenomenon. Among examples of this incipient body of knowledge are typological analyses and urban form studies (Gregotti, 1985) which attempt to define the elements and fundamental processes of architectural and urban design. Of further note is the resurgence of interest in composition, a subject of methodological significance until discredited as formalist and superseded by the concept of organization . There is a strongly revived interest in theory of composition (the formal and spatial principles underlying the generation of form), and in formal analysis as a basis for identifying these principles.

Why are these developments of significance to the computation of design? In what was a relatively early theoretical statement regarding the role of a priori knowledge in design, Colquhoun suggested that the typified knowledge of prior solutions was an essential ingredient in architectural design (Colquhoun, 1969). This in contradistinction to the Functionalist emphasis upon the spatio-temporal uniqueness of each architectural problem. In the terms of our discussion, he and others since have established the integral relationship between architectural knowledge and design knowledge. It is a goal of this paper to elucidate the current rich state of architectural knowledge and its implications for design computing. As this knowledge becomes well-formulated and rigorously formalized, we can anticipate its use as a foundation for a new generation of knowledge-based CAAD systems.

A Computable Model of Design Knowledge

We describe a model of integrated architectural and design knowledge comprised of four levels. Declarative and procedural knowledge is seen as integral and linked within each level. The levels are:

Syntactic and formal elements and operations
  Elemental knowledge of architectural objects, object relationships, and
  operations on objects
Syntactic structures and compositional operations.
  Structuring of architectural elements and operations
Generic knowledge structures
  Highly structured generic knowledge organized typologically
Design paradigms and schemata
  Meta-knowledge and control knowledge for lower levels

These categories of design knowledge reflect significant subjects of current architectural thinking. As we shall see, compositional and generic knowledge forms have also begun to prove their relevance to design computing. The categories appear to be a convenient classification of knowledge with the potential for the integration of these levels in design systems. We believe that there also may be cognitive relevance to the model and that, in design, knowledge flows are reciprocally both top-down and bottom-up, within some framework such as "chunked knowledge in networks" (Newell and Simon, 1972).

How the idea of a structure of knowledge actually operates in design is a subject of some complexity. For the present argument, the implications of the concept of structured knowledge suggest certain interesting possibilities for operative characteristics in design systems. For example, should it be possible to move flexibly between levels, from a language to its modification schema, and to lower-level formal operations ?   Design may, in fact, be conceived of as a structured, and often stylized, path through knowledge structures. Design learning may be conceived as the building of such knowledge structures; and the beginning of the learning process is characterized by for the absence of such a preform of knowledge structure.

In the following section we consider successively the various levels of a structured, multi-level model of design knowledge and the computational concepts which are related to the content of each level. In the final section, we return to the question of structure in knowledge and its relationship to computation, learning and education.

A Structured Multi-level Model of Design Knowledge

Elements and Operations in Architecture

Is it possible to establish a basic level of architectural formal object descriptions which goes beyond a finite set of discrete geometric primitives— that is, an elemental and pre-compositional level of knowledge which is above the geometric and the morphological and which is uniquely architectural? We can distinguish between two classes of formal knowledge in architecture included within this level. The first of these is a general category of knowledge of object descriptions which defines architectural formal categories. This is elucidated   through formal analysis. The second is a sub-class of syntactic knowledge providing operative knowledge in design of object classes, object to object relationships, and operations on architectural objects. This is elucidated through syntactic analysis. We refer to this knowledge collectively as formal knowledge.

There is an emergent body of knowledge of categories of form. This derives from diverse sources which may be generally described as formal analyses. Such formal categories are historically unique in the sense that they are not directly derivative of the formal categories of a historical tradition, such as the formal syntax of the Classical (Tzonis and LeFaivre,1986). Design theoretical work such as that of Baker (Baker, 1984, 1987), though not rigorous in the scientific sense, begins to establish categories of architectural form relating to such characteristics as volumetric organization, circulation patterns, axes, and boundaries. A modern approach to formal analysis in architecture began to emerge in Rowe's work (Rowe,1947). This has since been developed by both researchers as well as design theoreticians such as Eisenman, whose early works emphasized the specification of categories of form and operations on form in integrated design analysis and synthesis (Eisenman, 1987). These efforts collectively begin to establish a vocabulary of form and formal relationships in architecture.

Syntax is the rigorous definition of these formal categories in an operative sense. Syntactic analysis helps us to define and classify syntactic elements and operations in architecture. Higher levels of syntactic knowledge include intermediate abstractions as media for structuring relationships in architecture, and transformational processes as operations on sets of objects. Shape Grammars provide a method for syntactic analysis as well as a formalism for representing the knowledge. The elements of syntax function both in the analysis and synthesis of designs, and in the work of Stiny as in that of Eisenman and others there is no abrupt transition between analysis and synthesis. Contemporary formal analysis may be seen to be contributing to a new architectural epistemology, a reformalization of architectural knowledge beyond tradition. However, we still lack a general, comprehensive theory of formal objects and operations in architecture. Once such theory becomes a rigorous body of knowledge, it may provide a foundation level in CAAD systems for formal processing. Like contemporary computer drafting systems, such systems would provide a predetermined range of object categories and relationships as the basis for construction of architectural objects.

With respect to a basic level of syntactic operations in design, existing CAAD systems are already very sophisticated in the provision of formal operations. Various kinds of symmetry operations, figure-ground, and layering are common features, and parametric transformations of elements can be developed (Mitchell, Liggett, Kvan, 1987). The questions related to the operational capacity of formal manipulative systems again seems not so much a CAAD problem as one of the formalization of architectural knowledge. What operations do architects require in their processing of architectural form ? We may develop a classification of procedures of architectural syntactic operations in various ways. Configurative operations are additive operations, including Boolean operations, which construct form from geometric elements. Stiny's analysis of the Froebel gifts is a good example of an approach to classifying configurative procedures (Stiny, 1980). Another type of classification system might derive from the analysis of operations undertaken by professionals in the construction of traditional complex architectural representations, such as the elevation. Habraken has such an approach in Form Writing (Habraken,1983). He attempts to define the basic operations for combining, substituting, modifying and transforming object to object relationships at a pre-compositional level. Current architectural interest in shearing, partial forms, strip relationships, scaling, layering, superpositions and other transformations suggest the potential richness of an architectural, as compared to computational, establishment of categories of operations.

An additional problem exists—that of the computational representation of forms. New operations demand new internal representations. Syntactic operations should be represented in an architectural computing system as forms of architectural knowledge. At this level, emergent forms, created by such operations as overlapping (Stiny, 1982) should be capable of flexible detachment through editing mechanisms not a minor computational problem. But the goal of providing such flexible editing tools is inherent in the idea of formal processing and we must be able to solve the computational problems involved. This necessitates specifying the repertoire of form processing procedures in architecture as both the conceptual basis and content of formal modeling systems. It is necessary to transcend the purely configurative operations of CAD systems in order to achieve true formal processing. To figure may be as significant in architectural design as to configure.

Syntactic Structures and Compositional Operations

This level of knowledge includes the properties of structure of sets of objects and the operative knowledge of nested operations. These structures and the ordering of operations into nested procedures may be represented in the computer as complex sequences of architectural syntactic operations. This is traditionally referred to as knowledge of composition. Composition is the establishment of formal relationships between the elements of architecture. Organization, a complementary concept, is the formation of relationships between the functional, circulatory and spatial elements of architecture. Composition is generally the formal disposition of elements relative to a referential system. Therefore, composition is traditionally, as well as computationally, the result of higher level entities employed in defining relationships between formal vocabulary elements. We can describe the elements, the processes for establishing the relationships relative to an underlying structure, and kinds of variations and transformations possible. Composition is also seen as possessing a unifying coherence derived from the superposition of a unitary ordering structure such as a grid, axial system, or modular system. Design may also be seen as a rule-based inflection of the ordering system. The ordering system may be an internal, underlying abstraction as in Classical building, or it may be realized and observable in the physical fabric of the building. These concepts underlie important descriptive work, such as the description of bodies of architectural work by menas of shape grammars, in which configurative relationships, or instances of differentiation and refinement within unitary structures, are described procedurally.

Now let us consider some contemporary work in which the aggregative and differentiative logic of an underlying unitary structure may be inadequate for description and representation. Libeskind has described "a changed consciousness about the making of architecture" (Libeskind, 1984). In place of the classical concepts of order and coherence, we find a new sense of ordering which denies pre-established coherence. Eisenman, Tschumi and others have emphasized that the analysis of complex formal operations in composition is integrally related to design generation (Eisenman, 1984; Tschumi,1988). Transformational orders of design are established mainly through analytical procedures which become formalized as compositional strategies.

What is significant is that these theoretical developments pose a challenge to the unitary logic underlying both our ideas of composition and, by implication, to the associated conceptual basis of computer-aided design. This defines a shift, characteristic of an important body of design thinking, away from the idea of a unitary order underlying composition. A new compositional paradigm is emerging which is syntactic, transformational, and non-unitary (Whiteman, 1986). In this new compositional logic, there are multiple orders or no apparent order. Composition strategies include complex sequences of transformations such as shifting, shearing and cropping. There is a new composition which is, in spirit, related to the Modernist techniques of montage and collage. In place of the classical grid, contemporary orders are compound, twisted, sheared, shifted, fragmented and superimposed. An example is Meier's Crafts Museum in Frankfurt in which, within an underlying syntactic order of great complexity, both figurative and configurative strategies are employed in the generation of the composition. We are beginning to see attempts to classify the strategies of this new mode of composition. Architecturally, this may also involve a new representational paradigm (Whiteman,1987). The objects of design representations are frequently the series of successive states of a compositional transformation. The intermediate states of transformational procedures, are represented, and also, materialized in the design.

What is relevant in the context of our analysis is that it seems to contradict some of the current theory and practice of CAAD. The representation of architectural and urban form by geometric primitives and regular ordering systems, by parametric variations and geometric transformations is challenged by the richness of contemporary composition. Much work is required in order to define, formalize, and represent this vocabulary of structures and compositional strategies. We require other means of representation and a new computational

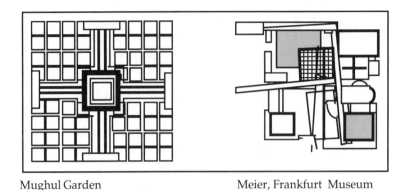

Mughul Garden   Meier, Frankfurt Museum

Figure 1   Unitary structure and complex compositional structure

approach for dealing with the classes of formal manipulations that are involved. There is beginning to be a recognition of the computational significance of these design-theoretical developments, and of the computational problems such as the need for "dynamic editing" (McCullough, 1988) in order to loosen the graphic gestalt in situations of emerging form. Obviously the idea of a new liberty in the computational capability of computer graphics systems is one of the challenging goals of software development.

Archetype, Type, Prototype
The generalization of typological knowledge from experience is one of the characteristic processes of design (Rowe, 1987). Architectural traditions may define relevant knowledge in the form of relevant types of problems and solutions, for example in the case of the Ecole des Beaux Arts. We will employ the term precedent, to describe such forms of higher-level generic knowledge. One of the major efforts of the current generation of architectural theoreticians has been to re-validate the precedent as a fundamental source of architectural knowledge without recourse to historic stylistic justification.   Precedent becomes a form of atemporal generic architectural knowledge.   This interpretation of precedent differs from the idea of canonic exemplars. The precedent is a generalized   encoding of characteristic solution modes emphasizing the salient morphological characteristics.   Here we encounter an extremely rich body of architectural knowledge in an incipient state of formalization.   Within the scope of this paper, we can only suggest the theoretical and computational significance of these concepts.

The focal concept is that of the type and of knowledge generated through typological analysis. There exists a large body of literature on typological

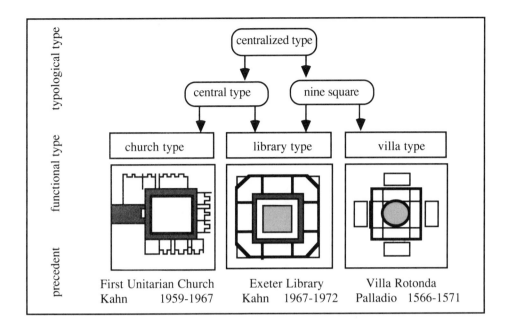

Figure 2   Precedents, functional types, high level typological concepts

analysis of both urban and architectural form. For Hancock, the type derives from "culturally rooted form-function analogies" (Hancock, 1986). The typological distillation of essences from building morphology through synchronic historical analysis has established a rich body of architectural knowledge. Archetypes are the expression of such essences with the connotation of basic, recurrent type-forms and underlying morphological diagrams, such as the nine-square plan type. Generalization and typification process may typify the function or the context (situation) as well as the objects of design. All of this is encapsulated in the term type—the encoding of the salient features of a design object in a form which permits its application in current designs with modifications and variations. A good introduction to the term and its history can be found in Moneo (1978).

In types, we have a complex body of knowledge which includes the characteristics of the type, associated knowledge of procedures for the modification and refinement of the type, as well as semantic control of these procedures. This grammar of the type includes such knowledge as design heuristics, procedures for variations, and knowledge of the key design variables and their main states. As in formal languages, configurative steps for describing and modifying a type can be described as a rule system. Formal generation may be related to instances of a type as particular sets of syntactic

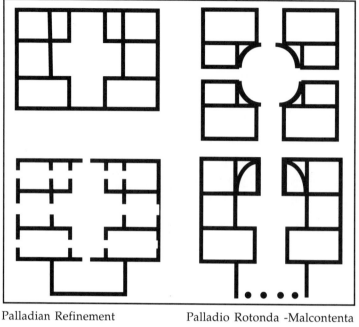

Palladian Refinement   Palladio Rotonda -Malcontenta
(Stiny and Mitchell)   Adaptation (Lerup)

Figure 3   Refinement and adaptation of the prototype

rule chains. From a computational point of view, the major achievements in the representation of this level and its implementation in design systems has been in the area of formal languages and knowledge-based systems.

The prototype is a relatively recent computer concept for encoding the salient characteristics of the type, its refinement schema and some semantic basis for control of the refinement, modification and adaptation of the prototype (Gero, 1987; Oxman and Gero, 1988). In knowledge-based systems prototype schemata can be represented by such structures as frames. Such prototype schemata can then be incorporated in design systems (Oxman and Gero, 1987). These concepts provide a way to encode architectural and design knowledge in CAD systems. The prototype is a concept rich in potential for supporting top-down recursive refinement. Particularly promising is the ability to represent nested concepts in typological structures of knowledge. Given the generative capability of grammars, and the reasoning capabilities of knowledge based systems, their integration in future prototype based design systems is most promising (Oxman, 1989).

Paradigms and Schemata

Paradigms and schemata are highly structured networks of knowledge. Design knowledge becomes paradigmatic when the types are general types or general problem classes rather than specific building types. Paradigmatic knowledge is a form of higher-level knowledge which derives from a class of architectural problems and is relevant to all members of the class regardless of the particular building type. Knowledge of the heuristics of all problem types in which the basic generative functional elements are repetitive, such as the dwelling and the dormitory, is such a paradigmatic class.

Paradigmatic knowledge is holistic, high level knowledge of problem classes. This is meta-knowledge in which the concept of class may contain a common philosophy which identifies relevant problems of the class, their characteristics, appropriate methods, definition of goals,etc. Functionalism might be considered such a design paradigm carrying associated value systems as part of the knowledge of the paradigm. Little work has been done on the formalization of paradigmatic knowledge. The incorporation of meta-knowledge in design systems has been experimented with in knowledge-based systems. This level of knowledge provides the linkage back in the chain of paradigms, precedents, compositional strategies, and formal elements and operations.

The Design and Computational Significance of the Multi-Level Model

It is our assumption that knowledge in design is structured and that there is a meaningful relationship between levels, or types of knowledge. There appears to be a significant cognitive role of generic structures of knowledge in controlling syntactic operations at lower levels in design. That is, typological knowledge provides not only a classification system, but the generic classes of usage of complex syntactical operations. It is a generic source of syntactical operations, that is, the experienced designer knows how to operate differently on different classes of plans. We should be able to represent and encode such multi-level knowledge in a computer system (Oxman, 1989).

A multi-level model of design knowledge has significant potential implications for the operating characteristics of design systems. Future design systems may integrate these levels and permit both top-down and bottom-up operation. Ultimately such systems, must go beyond the simple provision of an enhanced capacity for formal manipulation. They must also integrate both interpretive knowledge as well as causal knowledge in the form of algorithms.

We can identify three important classes of research which are necessary for the realization of integrated design systems with enhanced formal processing capacity. The first is the formalization, representation and encoding of architectural and design knowledge for both two-dimensional and three-dimensional modeling in a manner which solves the computer graphics problems, such as those of emergent form. We require further experimentation and development of multi-level systems (Mitchell, Liggett, Tan, 1989) of multi-mode operation in design systems (Oxman and Gero, 1987), and with integrating algorithmic computation with knowledge-based reasoning. Knowledge-based systems appear to provide important potential as knowledge-integrators in design systems.

Conclusions

Design Knowledge: the Educational Implications
Such a structured model of design knowledge would appear to have an important relationship to a theory of design learning. We have already mentioned our supposition that knowledge acquisition and design memory are probably related to the the concept of structured knowledge. This is generally supported by current research in AI and cognition (Galambos, Abelson, 1988). Design learning involves the generalization and classification of the salient aspects of design experience (or design teaching) according to some existing schemata of knowledge. The acquisition and modification of design experience is dependent upon the schema. Knowledge of the solution space enables the experienced designer to efficiently define current problems. In young students, lacking such pre-structures of knowledge, it is increasingly important to convey well-formalized design knowledge. We might postulate that for early design education it would be preferable to inculcate the structure of knowledge, the principles, rather than the detailed content of specific chunks. The model of design knowledge which we have suggested, with its emphasis on formal and procedural knowledge, might become the explicit content of design education.

The Relevance of CAAD Education for Design Education
This paper has attempted to demonstrate the important linkage between architectural theories and the computerization of design. We would now like to argue that CAAD education has relevance as a medium of design education. This has been demonstrated by a generation of educational experience in CAAD. Design learning requires the abilities to formalize and to generalize design experience. Dealing explicitly with the formalization of design knowledge is one way of improving design teaching. Encoding architectural knowledge for CAAD and programming can help the designer-user understand

and use this knowledge more effectively in design. Mitchell has spoken of the "computer-trained imagination" (Mitchell,1984). Teaching architectural knowledge as computational principles and encountering design knowledge through the electronic processing of architectural formal content is an important medium for teaching design principles (Oxman,Radford, Oxman,1987). There appears to be rich potential for the integration of modalities between design teaching and design computation.

The Medium and the Designed Artifact

The computation of designs is dependent upon the underlying systems of conception, representation and notation of architectural form which are implicitly reflected in the conceptual schemata of CAAD systems. Perhaps the converse may also be true, and the medium may demonstrate its potential as a creative way of designing. Here a theory of design for computers begins to emerge as a computational theory of design. We have briefly reviewed the changes in the conception and vocabulary of architectural and design knowledge. Much work on the formalization of this knowledge is necessary, as is research into the internal representations which are required to represent compositional structure in design systems. As there is creative potential for these new representational systems in design, so there is in design computing. If design computing should become responsive to the importance of the concept of formal modeling, then computers as interactive knowledge processors may be capable of becoming truly capable partners in design.

Acknowledgement

This research was supported be a grant from the VPR Fund, Technion

References

Baker, G. H. 1984. *Le Corbusier—An Analysis of Form*. New York: Van Nostrand Reinhold.

Baker, G. H. 1987. "A Formal Analysis". pp.68-79. *AD Profile #65*. London: Academy Editions.

Clark, R.H. and Pause.M. 1985. *Precedents in Architecture*. New York: Van Nostrand Reinhold.

Colquhoun, A. 1985. "Typology and Design Method". *In Essays in Architectural Criticism*   Cambridge: M.I.T. Press.

Eisenman, P. 1984. "The Futility of Objects:Decomposition and the Process of Difference". pp. 65-82. *Harvard Architectural Review 3*. Cambridge: M.I.T. Press.

Eisenman, P. 1987. *Houses of Cards*. New York: Oxford University Press.

Galambos, J.A., Abelson R.P., Black, J.B. 1986. *Knowledge Structures*. Lawrence Erlbaum.Hillsdale.N.J.

Gero, J.S. 1987. "Prototypes: A New Schema for Knowledge Based Design". Working Paper. Architectural Computing Unit. Dept. of Architectural Science. University of Sydney.

Gregotti, V., (ed). 1985. "The Grounds of Typology". pp.1-111. Casabella 509-510.

Habraken, N.J. 1983. *Writing Form*. Draft Manuscript. MIT.

Hancock, J.E. 1986. "Between History and Tradition". *Harvard Architectural Review 5*. New York: Rizzoli.

Lerup, L. 1989. "On Eden.the Geography of Villas and Dolf Schnebli's Villa Meyer". pp. 62-71. A+U. 2.

Libeskind, D. 1984. "Peter Eisenman and the Myth of Futility ". pp. 61-64. *Harvard Architectural Review 3*. Cambridge: M.I.T. Press.

McCullough, M. 1988. "Representation in the Computer Aided Design Studio" pp. 163-174. In Bancroft,P.J.ed. *ACADIA 88 Proceedings* . Ann Arbor.

Mitchell, W.J. 1986. "Formal Representations: A Foundation for Computer Aided Architectural Design". pp. 133-162. *Environment and Planning B.*vol. 13.

Mitchell, W.J.. 1984. "Computing the Form of Things Unknown". pp. 48-51. *Arts and Architecture*. 3 1.

Mitchell,W.J., Liggett,R.S., Kvan,T. 1987. *The Art of Computer Graphics Programming*. New York: Van Nostrand Reinhold.

Mitchell, W.J., Liggett, R.S., Tan,M. 1989. ""Top-Down Knowledge-Based Design". This volume.

Moneo, R. 1978. " On Typology". *Oppositions 13* . Cambridge: M.I.T. Press.

Newell, A. and Simon, H. 1972. *Human Problem Solving*. New Jersey: Prentice Hall.

Oxman, R. M. Radford,A, , Oxman, R.E.. 1987. *The Language of Architectural Plans*. Red Hill: Royal Australian Institute of Architects.

Oxman, R.E. 1989. "Architectural Knowledge Structures as Design Shells". This volume.

Oxman, R.E. and Gero,J.S. 1987. "Using an Expert System for Design Diagnosis and Design Synthesis". pp.4-5. Expert Systems. 4 1.

Oxman, R.E. and Gero,J.S. 1988. "Designing by Prototype Refinement in Architecture". in Gero.J.S. ed.. Artificial Intelligence in Engineering Design. Amsterdam: Elsevier.

Rowe, C. 1976. "The Mathematics of the Ideal Villa". In *The Mathematics of the Ideal Villa*. Cambridge: M.I.T. Press.

Rowe, P.G. 1987. *Design Thinking*. Cambridge: M.I.T. Press.

Silvetti, J. 1980. "On Realism in Architecture". pp. 11-32. *Harvard Architectural Review 1*. Cambridge: M.I.T. Press..

Stiny, G.. 1980. "Kindergarten Grammars: Designing with Froebel's Building Gifts". pp. 409-462. *Environment and Planning B*. vol. 7.

Stiny, G.. 1982. "Shapes Are Individuals". pp.359-367. *Environment and Planning B*. vol.9.

Tschumi, B. 1988. Notes Towards a Theory of Architectural Disjunction". pp. 13-57. *A+U*. 9.

Tzonis, A. and Lefaivre, L. 1986. *Classical Architecture: The Poetics of Order*. Cambridge: M.I.T. Press.

Whiteman, J. 1986. "Site Unscene—Notes on Architecture and the Concept of Fiction". pp. 76-84. *AA Files 12*.

Whiteman, J. 1987. "Criticism. Representation and Experience in Contemporary Architecture: Architecture and Drawing in an Age of Criticism". pp.137-147. *Harvard Architectural Review 6*. New York: Rizzoli.

12
Architectural Knowledge Structures as "Design Shells": A Knowledge-Based View of Design and CAAD Education

Rivka Oxman

Faculty of Architecture and Town Planning
Technion: Israel Institute of Technology

The concept of a knowledge based design shell *is proposed as a basis for teaching design. The significance of the concept of design shell is discussed with respect to formalization, implementation, application and operation. GPRS—a generative prototype refinement design shell—is proposed, defined and elaborated. A plan type is introduced as one significant kind of structure of knowledge in architectural design is introduced. A method for representing syntactic and the semantic content to be used in design refinement is proposed. The method exploits the characteristics of both rules and frames, and integrates them in a prototype-based design system. This is demonstrated in a system called PRODS. Finally, the significance of such an approach in teaching is discussed.*

Knowledge-Based Design Shells as a Vehicle in Design and CAAD Teaching

Teaching computer-aided design should be coupled with teaching design. It has been shown that teaching programming can be mapped directly into certain types of architectural knowledge (Mitchell, Liggett and Kvan, 1987). The *Topdown* system has demonstrated its use in design teaching (Mitchell, Liggett and Tan, 1989) by providing programming tools to encode the rules of a kind of parametric shape grammar. Emerging tools from the field of artificial intelligence, such as expert system shells, may serve as a step forward in the adaptation of this approach to CAAD and design education. The promising idea of a shell can be further developed in order to accommodate the characteristics of knowledge in design. A design shell would be an extension of the traditional concept of a shell which could be adapted to the structure of a particular body of design knowledge. Knowledge-based design should provide means for encoding architectural knowledge as pre-defined structures which are delivered to the CAAD user by means of design shells.

The purpose of this paper is to develop the concept of empty design shells, to present a generative shell for prototype refinement in design, and to describe its potential in teaching and research on the following four levels:

—Teaching about structures of design knowledge
—Teaching about implementing these structures as empty design shells
—Developing specific domain applications for these structures
—exploring different designs with these applications.

GPRS : A Generative Prototype Refinement Shell

Design knowledge should be available in a form which utilizes its generic characteristics. The use of terms, such as schema, and type in the design professions suggests the cognitive value of such generic forms of knowledge. One such form of generic structures is the design prototype. Such prototypes encode knowledge of the salient features of a generic solution type. With respect to knowledge-based design systems, the use of the prototype as a knowledge structure, provides a basis for the organization of design knowledge. A prototype may be defined (Gero, 1987) as parametrized design description generator, a set of interpretations, a set of design elements which are the basis for design description and knowledge relating design description and its interpretations. A prototype is selected and specialized to the task at hand by providing values to parameters. The significance of such generic knowledge structures in design can be seen in the possibility of multiple derivations from high-level abstractions of the prototype.

GPRS—A generative prototype refinement shell proposed by the author, provides a structure for refinement processes by representing formal knowledge of a generative structure, its generic vocabulary, and syntactic operations, as well as their meanings, and a design description generator, all within a single schema. It is based on the idea that the shape grammar formalism (Stiny, 1980) can form the basis for a design description generator within a prototype. It contains knowledge of pre-defined rules which can be applied for refinement of designs in a top-down fashion. There are various examples (Stiny and Mitchell, 1978), (Flemming,1981) which treat specific designs, or a style, as a knowledge structure with generative capabilities. The distinction between GPRS representation and shape grammar representation is that the latter supports formal refinements in which goals and constraints are embedded implicitly within the syntactical rules while the generative prototype provides ways to represent and use explicit constraints and goals in a reasoning process for guiding the refinement. It deals with formal knowledge in which the design generator is controlled by the interpretations of its refinement steps.

In the following section the structure of the generative prototype refinement shell will be described in relation to the following four issues:

—The formalization of design structure
—Implementation of the design shell
—Development of applications for the shells
—Providing interfaces for the applications.

Knowledge Formalization for GPRS

An assumption of this work is that designers have the ability to typify both situation and solution types. Typification is the recognition of characteristic and recurrent types of constraints in a design domain. Design can be seen as a matching process relating typified design situations and design solutions. A design situation is given by a set of conditions and requirements which are then typified as overriding goals and constraints. olution refinement can be seen as a process of matching typified design conditions to design steps of formal generation and refinement. The formalization of knowledge in GPRS, which is described below, reflects these assumptions.

Figure 1 indicates the successive stages of a refinement process. At each refinement stage conditions are typified and provide knowledge for instantiations of attributes of a subtype at a particular level of refinement. Various types of knowledge are employed in a generative prototype refinement process. GPRS represents a way of structuring all these types of knowledge in a single schema. These may be defined as follows:

a. *Typological knowledge of the prototype, subtype and their properties*: typological knowledge is the knowledge of the hierarchical relationship between the prototype and its subtype.

b. *Topological knowledge of the type:* topological relations between components of the type. Each component can have its own typological hierarchy.

c. *Interpretive knowledge of design constraints*: knowledge of constraints that effect decisions about refinement steps. These are typified constraints that capture experiential knowledge related to meanings in certain situations.

d. *Generative knowledge of the type:* knowledge about successive steps in a refinement process. Each stage of refinement causes instantiation of a subtype in the typological hierarchy. The refinement process is executed by operations which produce parametrized design descriptions in the subtype.

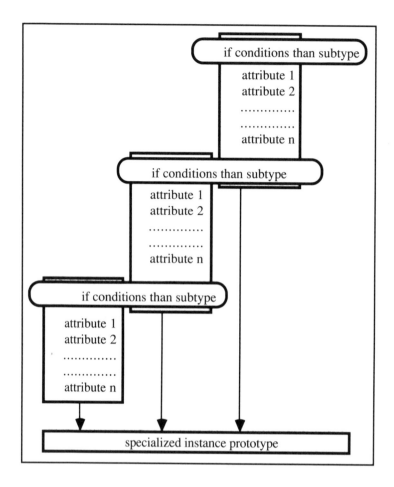

Figure 1   Description of refinement and instantiation process of instance-type

Implementation Level of GPRS

Various approaches to encoding knowledge have been proposed by artificial intelligence researchers (Minsky,1975; Schank and Abelson,1977). They have developed structures such as frames and scripts. GPRS is a holistic structure capable of containing various types of knowledge. It provide means to generate solutions by reasoning from relevant knowledge bases in order to activate design operators for producing design descriptions. Representational methods were chosen according to the following criteria:

—Suitability for rendering the knowledge explicit
—Ease of encoding
—Ease of maintenance

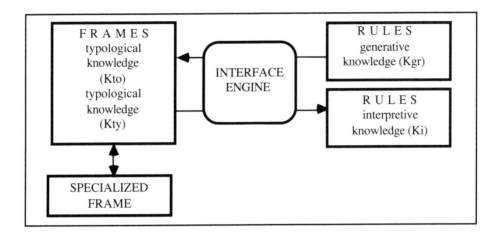

Figure 2   Refinement and instantiation process of instance-type using rules and frames in GPRS.

A hybrid representation which combined different methods according to their suitability to specific types of knowledge was selected. A special hybrid representation was developed which combined the advantages of frames as structured representations for objects or classes of objects production rules as a formalism for describing generative patterns (Gips and Stiny, 1980) and a rule-based formalism for describing causal heuristic knowledge. Figure 2 demonstrates a diagram of the different kinds of knowledge represented as rules and frames in the proposed schema. An interface module supports the flow of knowledge between rules and frames. The following section elaborates the representational method which was selected for each of the types of knowledge and the manner in which it operates as a design shell.

Rules Represent Generative Knowledge
Generative knowledge of a prototype =can be represented by production rules. A rule-chaining mechanism such as a shape grammar can provide a medium for successive refinement. This process can be guided and controlled by interpretive knowledge of the refinement stages.

Frames Represent Typological and Topological Knowledge
Typological knowledge and topological knowledge of a prototype are handled by the frame in its traditional use. The frame provides a scheme which enables a generic description to support hierarchical inheritance of attributes in the process of typological refinement. It describes its attributes and passes them, through the inheritance mechanism, to its subtypes. It also supports the notion of specifying default values in the frame. Thus, it is unnecessary to

specify all the information at each level. We assume that an instance inherits the properties of its superclass unless specified otherwise. Frames enables us to use *abstraction levels* in representation of attributes.

Rules Embedded in Frames Represent Interpretive Knowledge
Most systems dealing with objects obtain their values by means of procedures which specify the attributes. Usually a system must perform some diagnostic tasks in order to accomplish this. In a prototypical design situation, certain heuristic knowledge is associated with the situation. The system described here may consult relevant experiential knowledge in the form of situation-conclusion pairs in order to establish the instance attributes. The basic advantage of combining rules and frames in this case is that the frame structure provides explicit representation of the context in which production rules can be used for reasoning. In this way, each prototype represented in the frame formalism can direct the use of a set of rules to a specialized sub-class.

Frames Supply Generative and Interpretive Knowledge
Frames are used in a way that provides descriptions of the objects being reasoned about by the rules (Rosenman, Manago and Gero, 1986), in the context of a generative refinement process. They are used to encode a model of the prototype described by the generative rules. They provide a structure storing and supplying information associated with the abstract concepts reasoned about the rules. Interpretive knowledge is associated with the frame slots in a way that enables the frame to link relevant supplementary knowledge bases to its attributes. These knowledge bases, which are invoked by the frame, employ a rule mechanism and provide information back to the frame structure. This mechaninism operates with the generative model which specifies stages of refinement at different levels of abstraction in a top-down fashion. Each hierarchical level is then described by a sub-type frame. Each sub-type frame contains and invokes a specific knowledge base which is relevant to that particular refinement stage. At any step, the instance type contains the specific values of its attributes which are added at each stage.

System Operation of GPRS
GPRS uses a system controller in the form of an expert system rather than an object-oriented programming environment. BUILD—an existing rule-based expert system (Rosenman, 1986)—was used. It includes a frame system for representing the prototypes, and an interface engine which controls all system interactions. It passes control between the rule-based and the frame-based inference engines and provides communication between rule and frame representations.

Application Level of GPRS: A Row House Plan Type
A design prototype, such as an architectural plan type, can be formulated by establishing stages of refinement. These start with high level concepts, each of which provides associated refinement decisions which lead to formal operations.

Generative Knowledge of a Row-House
The generative knowledge of a row-house plan type is represented by rules that indicate the order in which decisions are taken in a typical design refinement process. This application is based on an existing typology (Sherwood, 1978). The first classification level of a row-house type is based on decisions about its number of floors. This results in a formal decision about the row house section. The next level deals with the zoning of the plan. There are two options for making a decision about zoning. These are defined as: exterior-interior-exterior zoning, and exterior-exterior zoning. The first type of zoning, does not provide an outside orientation for the interior zone. The functional implication of such a zoning diagram is that the wet functions, such as toilets, are usually located in that zone. In the second type of zoning, the exterior-exterior type, the two zones each have an outside access. The next decision level is built about vertical and horizontal circulation, followed by kitchen core location, etc. Figure 3 demonstrates a generative representation of a row-house plan type in GPRS.

Typological and Topological Knowledge of a Row-House
Typological knowledge (knowledge of the salient characteristics of the type organized hierarchically into types and sub-types) and topological knowledge (knowledge of the relationships between the components of the type) of the row-house are described by the frame. For example, the class Row_House is a superclass of Double_Storey_Row_House and Double_Storey_Row_House_1 is an instance within the class. The attributes such as number of floors or the basic orientation of the walls etc., have been specified for the class, while no information about the instance has been specified directly. In this way, each level contains only the relevant attributes of that level.

Interpretive Knowledge of Row Houses
The basic advantage of combining rules and frames in this case is that the frames provide a generic model of the row-house as well as the knowledge by which interpretations for formal decisions are made. For example, A row house prototype, contains relevant rules for decisions about number of floors, zoning

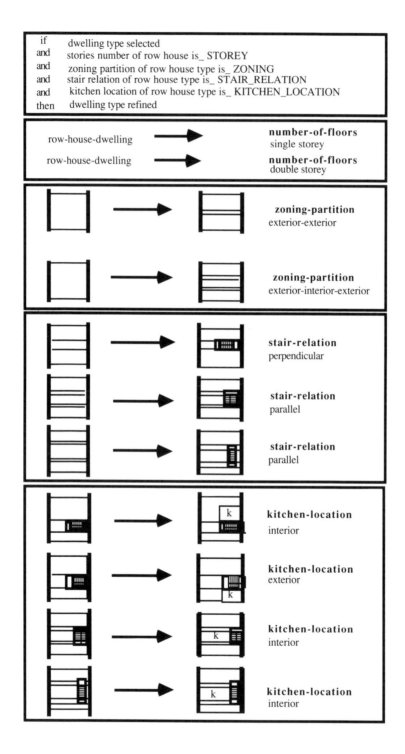

Figure 3   A generative representation of a row house plan type in GPRS

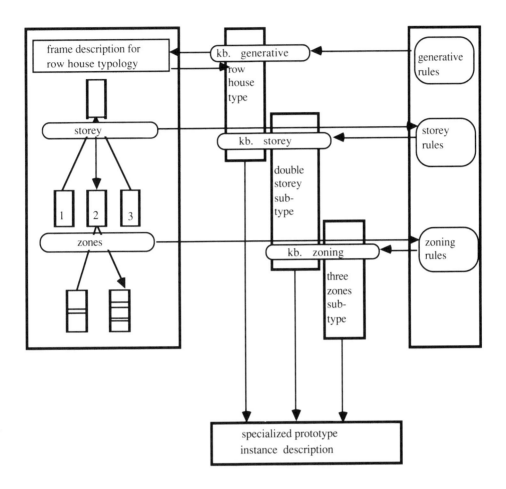

Figure 4   Knowledge flow between rule bases and frame bases in GPRS

partitioning, stair location, kitchen location, etc. These knowledge bases are activated by the 'if_needed' mechanism which is provided by the frame inference engine.

The knowledge bases which are embedded in the frames are rules about meanings of formal decisions in the refinement process of a sub-type. For example, in order to decide about attributes such as number of floors, a special reasoning process about the available width condition takes place by consulting a specific rule base called 'knowledge_base_storey'.

Flow of Knowledge Between Rules and Frames
The row house frame is used to describe a model of the plan type to which the generative rules refer. For example a double storey row-house, a three-zone row-house type, etc., eachhave their own plan characteristics. Each of them is described by a sub-type-frame. At any step, the instance type contains

attributes which are added at each stage of the refinement process. Figure 4 demonstrates the flow of knowledge between the rules and frames of a row-house prototype. The rules are activated according to the frame-model.

Using the Application Level: Demonstration of the 'GPRS' in a Design Context
PRODS (Prototype-Based Design System) is an application system which demonstrates design by prototype refinement in architecture (Oxman and Gero, 1988). PRODS utilizes GPRS in a design context. A design situation defined by conditions specifications and requirements can provide a contextual environment for specific instantiations of a design solution type. The design process consists of the following stages:

—Context definition by input of data through which site specifications and design requirements can be specified
—Typification of design situation as intrinsic constraints
—Typifications of design solution types as extrinsic constraints or design goals
—Prototype selection by matching between constraints types
—Refinement process as successive steps of generation of the solution type.

Figure 5 shows a screen display of a design session carried out with the system in which instantiations of the prototype instances are made by consulting 'kb. zoning'—rule based-knowledge which supports decisions about zoning.

```
The dwelling organization typification is_ ? - enter value
(how/why/explain)
the options for dwelling organization typification are:
1. compact organization, wetcore  is not provided by outside
orientation
2. loose organization, wetcore  is provided by outside orientation
? 1.
-------------------------------------------------------------------------------------
dwelling organization typification is_  compact
-------------------------------------------------------------------------------------
*************************************************************
dwelling zoning typification is_ exterior-interior-exterior
*************************************************************
zoning refinement is_true
*************************************************************
kb.zoning returned
```

Figure 5   Design session :   refinement stage reasoning with a zoning knowledge base

Modes of Interaction with a Design Shell

Once a knowledge structure is defined another practical question is raised: how does the designer interact with a design shell in a design process? Three modes of interaction have been suggested (Oxman, 1988). The first one, termed a design critic, allows the user to interact with the structure, explore formal variations, and derive a semantic description from the system. The second is termed the design generator mode. This mode allows the user to interact with the system, give a semantic description of a design, and have the system operate as a design generator. The system then produces a formal result. There is a combined mode of interaction with a system, which was termed, critic-generator. This mode allows the user to suggest a schematic formal design as a partial design, and lets the system, at any stage, check it and accomplish the detailed design automatically. This approach was demonstrated by the PREDIKT system (Oxman and Gero, 1987).

Conclusions: Some Educational Implications of the Design Shells Approach

A major research effort is required to connect the field of architectural theory and the field of CAAD theory.

The four levels of developing and interacting with design shells as described previously are: knowledge formulation, implementation, generic application, and design usage. These represent four levels and types of knowledge which are of interest in CAAD education. At the lowest level, that of usage, we learn through employing the system without modifications. The capacity to convey principles of design or computation derives from the way in which the system interacts with the user. With a tutorial kind of user interface the design decision making process, effect of design variables upon design, etc. become transparent to the user. Thus, even at this lowest level, there is considerable potential educational value.

The next level is that of *applications*. In a shell system, this implies the personalization of the shell through the 'filling in' of specific design content. This requires the ability to understand the concept of a structure of levels of knowledge. The user formalizes a specific level of knowledge within the higher level of knowledge of the shell. From a conceptual point of view, the personalization of shells provides exposure to generic knowledge, its role in design, and dealing with it computationally.

Implementations require a high level of knowledge of computer programming and knowledge-based systems technology. Knowledge formalization requires a high level of knowledge of design theory. Systems are time-consuming to design and develop.

The knowledge provided in low-level drawing systems is basically knowledge of pre-defined primitives and operations. The degree of freedom left to the user is very high, but, the user is not supported with knowledge by the system. It is, however, in the usage of a knowledge based view of design in which the major educational advantages of the design shell exist. To interact with stylistic or typological knowledge bases is to interact with an expert teacher in a specific design realm. The computer acts as design tutor and design critic, with the advantage of being transparent in exposing the design reasoning processes. Thus we might consider the shell as providing knowledge-based design tutorials as a fringe benefit to using them in design applications. In a knowledge-based approach to design education, the shell concept offers a new environment for CAAD education.

Acknowledgments

This work was undertaken in the Design Computing Unit, Department of Architectural Sciences,University of Sydney and at the Faculty of Architecture and Town Planning, Technion. It was supported by a continuing grant from the Australian Research Grants Scheme, and by the VPR Fund, Technion.

References

Flemming, U. 1981. "The secret of the Casa Guiliani Frigerio". *Environment and Planning B*. Vol.8. pp.97-114.

Gips. J., and Stiny. G. 1980. "Production systems and grammars: a uniform characterization". pp.399-408. *Environment and Planning B*. Vol.7.

Gero, J.S. 1987. "Prototypes: a new schema for knowledge-based design". Working Paper. Architectural Computing Unit. Department of Architectural Science. University of Sydney.

Minsky, M. 1975. "A framework for representing knowledge". pp.211-277. in P.H. Winston (ed.). *The Psychology of Computer Vision*. McGraw-Hill. New York.

Mitchell,W.J., Liggett,R.S., Kvan,T. 1987. *The Art of Computer Graphics Programming*. New York: Van Nostrand Reinhold.

Mitchell, W.J., Liggett, R.S., Tan,M. 1989. ""Top-Down Knowledge-Based Design". This volume.

Oxman, R.E. and Gero, J.S. 1987. "Using an expert system for design diagnosis and design synthesis". *Expert Systems* 4 1: 4-5

Oxman, R.E. and Gero,J.S. 1988. "Designing by Prototype Refinement in Architecture". In Gero.J.S. ed.. *Artificial Intelligence in Engineering Design*. Amsterdam: Elsevier.

Oxman, R.E. 1988. "Expert System for Generation and Evaluation in Architectural Design. D.Sc". Thesis. Faculty of Architecture and Town Planing. Technion. Israel.

Rosenman, M.A. 1986. *The BUILD Manual*. Sydney: Architectural Computing Unit. Department of Architectural Science. University of Sydney.

Rosenman, M.A.. Manago. C. and Gero. J.S. 1986. "A model-based expert system shell". IAAI'86. pp.c:1:1-15.

Schank, R.C.. and Abelson, R.P. 1977. *Scripts. Plans. Goals and Understanding*. New York: Lawrence Erlbaum Associates.

Sherwood, R. 1978. *Modern Housing Prototypes*. Cambridge: Harvard University Press.

Stiny, G., and Mitchell, W.J. 1978. "The Palladian Grammar". pp.5-18. *Environment and Planning B*. Vol.5.

Stiny, G. 1980. "Introduction to shape and shape grammar". pp.343-351. *Environment and planning B*. Vol.7.

13
Saying What It *Is* by What It Is *Like*
—Describing Shapes Using Line Relationships

Milton Tan

Harvard University
Graduate School of Arts & Sciences / Graduate School of Design

Shapes – taken as well-defined collections of lines – are fundamental building blocks in architectural drawings. From doodles to shop drawings, shapes are used to denote ideas and represent elements of design, many of which ultimately translate into actual objects. But because designs evolve, the shapes representing a design are seldom static – instead, they are perpetually open to transformations. And since transformations involve relationships, conventional methods of describing shapes as sets of discrete endpoints may not provide anappropriate foundation for schematic design.

This paper begins with a review of the perception of shapes and its significance in design. In particular, it argues that juxtapositions and inter-relationships of shapes are important seedbeds for creative development of designs. It is clear that conventional representation of shapes as sets of discrete lines does not cope with these 'emergent' subshapes; the most basic of which arise out of intersecting and colinear lines. Attempts to redress this by using 'reduction rules' based on traditional point-and-line data structures are encumbered by computational problems of precision and shape specification. Basically, this means that some 'close' cases of sub-shapes may escape detection and their specifications are difficult to use in substitution operations.

The paper presents the findings of a computer project – Emergence II – which explored a 'relational' description of shapes based on the concept of construction lines. It builds on the notion that architectural shapes are constructed in a graphic contextand that, at a basic compositional level, the context can be set by construction lines. Accordingly, the interface enables the delineation of line segments with reference to pre-established construction lines. This results in a simple data structure where the knowledge of shapes is centralized in a look-up table of all its construction lines rather than dispersed in the specifications of line segments. Taking this approach, the prototype software shows the ease and efficiency of applying 'reduction rules' for intersection and colinear conditions, and for finding emergent sub-shapes by simply tracking the construction lines delimiting the ends of line segments.

Introduction

There are 'external facts', and we can say what they are. What we cannot say – because it makes no sense – is what the facts are independent of all conceptual choices.[1]

It goes almost without saying that the representation of architectural ideas on drawing – all the way from tentative doodles to precise 'working' drawings – depends considerably on the use of shapes. Ordinarily, shapes define edges or boundaries by using an integrated collection of lines and curves. They can be used to denote space – such as a room – or building elements – such as columns and beams – or, indeed, more abstract concepts like criculation patterns or spatial relationships.

If a designer produces shapes in a process analogous to a musician playing a musical composition, then shapes are little more than passive end-products. But shapes have a far more significant role in the design process than simply being 'static' building blocks for drawings; they are active ingredients in design transformation.

The basic idea behind design transformation is a simple one – designs evolve. Although the concept is simple, its implications are profound. The most significant, though subtle, is that design evolution requires not only that shapes be definable but that they be retrievable (in whole or part) for subsequent transformations.

This paper begins with an investigation into the demands of shape definition and recognition. It then deals with shape transformation, specifically in terms of parametric variation and shape substitution; leading to the problem – or opportunity – of emergent subshapes. Taking a relational approach, it presents a project to manage shape definition and recognition based on line relationships rather than the conventional end-point specifications of discrete lines. In this sense it attempts to describe shapes by what they are like, by-passing the encumbrance of specifying what they are.

Shapes – why we need to be able to define them

Shapes can be constructed using a variety of instruments and on different media; this does not exclude freehand, of course. But, unless there is access to their defining parameters, they will, in effect, remain fixed templates – actual or imaginary – and their reusability for shape transformation limited. The seriousness of this limitation is probably best contrasted by the richness of 'parametric variation'.

An example of parametric variation is the computer program *Miesing About*[2]. It encodes the parameters of the wall alignments of Mies's Brick Country House as variable line segments along the common edges of the 'spiraling' rectangles that characterize many Cubist work[3]. Figure 1 shows the wall configuration of the original house plan whilst Figures 2a shows a variation using the program.

Parametric variation is only a small aspect of shape transformation. As demonstrated in the program *TopDown*,[4] it also includes standard Euclidean operations –

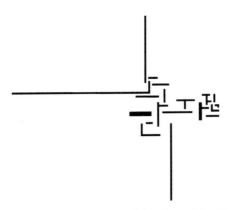

Figure 1 Reconstruction of the plan of the "Project for a Brick Country House (1923)" by Mies van der Rohe.

Figure 2a: Variation on Mies's Brick Country House produced using *Miesing About*.

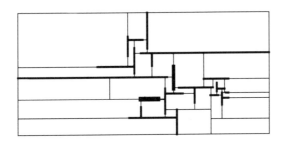

Figure 2b: The underlying rectangle 'alignments' for fig. 2a in *Miesing About*.

translation (moving of the whole shape), reflection, rotation and scaling – resulting in a wide repertoire of transformation methods to create instances of types.

But, parametric variation, particularly when localized to a part of a shape, can change its character considerably. Although this is precisely what one often desires, it can reach a point where, at best, the shape is better defined in some other terms or, worse, the shape looses its principal characteristic altogether. The first is illustrated by a triangle with a 'sliding' vertex[5]:

Although figures 3a and 3e are 'right-angled triangles', 3b and 3d are better classified as 'isosceles triangles' and 3c as another 'isosceles triangle' (or an 'equilat-

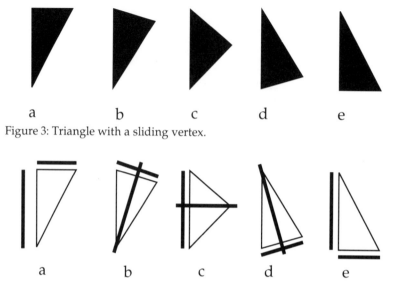

Figure 3: Triangle with a sliding vertex.

Figure 4: Dominant axes of the five triangles from figure 3.

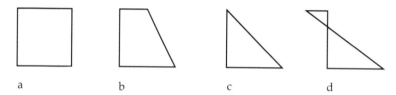

Figure 5: Parametric variation on a length of a side of a square.

eral triangle' if its three angles or sides are equal) as indicated in figure 4.

Taken further, parametric variation can be even more destructive. For example, figure 5 shows the effect of progressively reducing the length of a side of a square.

Initial reduction of the side transforms the original square into a trapezium but reduces to a triangle when the length reaches zero; the shape becoming two similar triangles when the side takes on a negative value.

So, what started out as an innocent move to create variations of a shape can end up in 'total' transformation from a shape to another. But, from a creative design point of view, this is by no means an undesirable thing! The practical implications of taking this seriously is, however, more sobering. Before going on to examine them, the complementary aspect of shape recognition needs to be addressed.

Shapes – why we need to be able to recognize them

Parametric variation is generally confined within a scheme – defined here as a collection of shapes. Although a shape's characteristics can drastically change, as noted above, the overall 'density' of the scheme remains largely the same, ie parametric variation does not normally change the number of constituents in a shape or scheme. So, although parametric variation affords degrees of freedom for shapes to flex their profiles, it does not handle the more drastic transformations needed to bring schemes to different levels of resolution. These require shape substitutions.

Shape substitution is the mechanism to raise (or lower, as the case may be) the level of detail or elaboration of a design. It basically takes the context of a shape and introduces a new shape with or without the removal of the original. For a design to remain coherent, the substitute shape should, of course, enhance its new context. Figure 6 shows the substitution of the abstract capital of a classical column by a Tuscan capital using the program *Topdown*.

Shape substitution presupposes that the shapes to be substituted can be explicitly located in the first place. For a system which maintains a list of all the discrete shapes that make up the scheme, this is a simple task of searching the list for the required shape; that is, if all that you ever need to look for are shapes which have been explicitly defined previously. Unfortunately, that is not all the shapes that there are, and definitely not all the interesting ones!

Emergent Shapes

The human imagination is capable of finding recondite or unlikely relationships between seemingly disconnected things, then rallying support within itself to stabilize and defend them, often against all odds. There is a curious satisfaction in being able to seek out novel shapes from a familiar scene; indeed, if shapes are synonymous with problems, what characterize creativity more is not 'shape-solving' but shape-finding[6]. In the simple case of two overlapping triangles – figure 7 – the initial set of 'emergent shapes' are the contiguous closed sub-shapes of the scheme (figures 8a - 8e); these can be combined in groups of 2 to 5 of the contiguous closed sub-shapes as shown in figures 8f - 8p.[7] (There are, of course, another range of sub-shapes comprising 'open' figures with varying number of line segments; and yet another with disconnected juxtapositions of varying numbers of lines or closed shapes.)

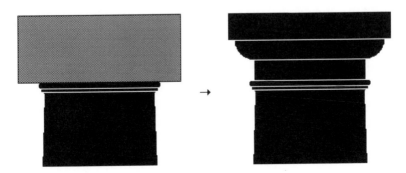

Figure 6: Substituting a Tuscan capital using *Topdown*.

Figure 7 Overlying two equilateral triangles

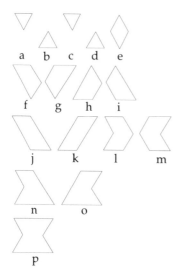

Figure 8 Closed sub-shapes from figure 7

Figure 8b: 'Phantom Figure' by Bradley & Petry.

Gestalt psychologists have long maintained that there are 'natural' and more immediate recognition of certain types of shapes over others. But there is no compelling reason why they should be preferred by designers other than perhaps their simplicity; in fact, a creative tendency would be to seek 'non-gestalt' emergent shapes! In any case, emergent subshapes can be important to design and, specifically, to shape transformation and therefore cannot be ruled out of the repertoire of the shape-using designer.

There are many ways in which emergent sub-shapes are formed. In one extreme they may only be implied by some aspects of the geometry of other shapes as in figure 8b.

In another extreme, an emergent shape may be suppressed or enhanced through the use of labels – applied distinctions to categorize them differently from otherwise similar shapes. These labels can take different forms, eg the use of graphic styles to denote material represented, or the attachment of symbols. In this paper, however, the concern is for a more basic but nevertheless important representation of shapes: contiguous line segments connected at end-points or intersections as in a chain. At the heart of this are two fundamental line-relationship conditions:

1   Intersection
2   Colinearity

Emergent Shapes by Intersection

When two lines cross each other – an X-intersection – four emergent line segments are formed with the point of intersection and the end-points of the contributing lines (figure 9), resulting in a total of six lines.

In a T-intersection (a special case of an X-intersection), if an end-point of line B lies on line A, two emergent line segments are formed with the point of intersection and the end-points of A (figure 10), giving a total of four lines.

Emergent Shapes by Colinearity

There are four general conditions of colinearity which produces contiguous line segments (figure 11):

The 'reduction rules' for the intersection conditions produce emergent shapes by division whereas for the colinear conditions they are both by division and addition (or union). Either condition can easily be created by piecemeal construction of shapes or the manipulation of existing ones – eg by parametric variation and shape substitution.

In practice, the detection of the two conditions are not without problems; particularly in going beyond gross simplifications such as a confinement to orthogonal lines. One of the most serious of these is the precision needed to establish cases of line intersection and colinerity.

Figure 9: The X-intersection of two lines.

Figure 10: The T-intersection of two lines.

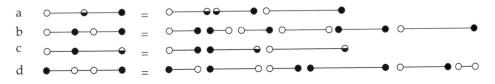

● = coincident point

Figure 11: The four colinear conditions producing contiguous line segments.

Describing shapes

The popular approach in describing shapes[7] depends on the definition of a line segment, l, in terms of a pair of end-points, pa and pb:

l = (pa, pb), where

pa = (xa,ya), and

pb = (xb,yb), and where

xa = x-coordinate of point a,

ya = y-coordinate of point a,

xb = x-coordinate of point b, and

yb = y-coordinate of point b.

Since there is a heavy reliance on the coordinates, the accuracy of determining whether an intersection or colinear condition exists in the first place, depends on how tolerances are compounded at the coordinate level – the bane of all who work with serious computer graphics! Often, an intersection should be recognized when it is, informally speaking, "close enough". The problem is illustrated in figures 12 and 13.

The problem diminishes, or even disappears, if manual intervention is permitted – typically by tracing all or part of a shape in question – as in the implementation by Chase (1989) where three points have to be selected on a shape so that a transformation can be mapped onto it. But the challenge, rather, is for a system to find the required shape automatically to satisfy the condition of the transformation rule.

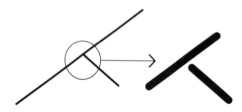

Figure 12: Is this an intersection?

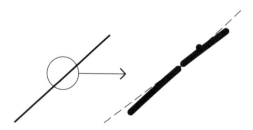

Figure 13: Is this a pair of coincident and colinear lines?

Emergence II

Emergence II was a project set up specifically to circumvent the tolerance issue in automatic shape recognition. Its point of departure from the current trend is to formulate a higher-level descriptor to define line segments (instead of resorting to a lower-level point-coordinate specification). The impetus for this comes from the hypothesis that relationships between lines, not its limits of specification, is the key to handling shape transformation.

The basic concept in Emergence II is that underlying every line segment is a construction line, as in traditional drafting. Moreover, each end of a line segment is marked by an intersection with another construction line. Therefore, a line segment – SLine – is simply defined in terms of three construction lines – CLines:

A line segment, Sa = (C1, C2, C3), where

C1 is the the 'host' construction line and

C2 and C3 are the delimiting construction lines.

The interface enables the creation of 'maximal' construction lines by clicking the 'mouse' at two points in the screen. Line segments are created by using the mouse to pick a 'host' construction line followed by two delimiting construction lines.

Then, a construction line is defined conventionally using a codescriptor, cd, in turn defined as the description of the equation of the CLine:

cd(C1) = (x), if the line Cl is vertical; otherwise

cd(C1)= (s, i), where s and i are the slope and y-intercept, respectively, of the CLine Cl according to the line equation $y = sx + i$.

To reduce rounding errors, the slope, s, is maintained as a pair of integers, rn and rd – its numerator and denominator (reduced to its primitive form using Euclid's algorithm for the greatest common denominator):

s = (rn, rd)

The comparison of slopes, s(l1) and s(l2), for equality is simply a direct test of equality of the corresponding two integer values, ie (s(l1).rn = s(l2).rn) and (s(l1).rd = s(l2).rd).

Only four basic functions are needed to handle emergent shapes

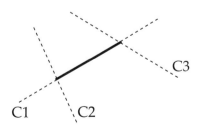

Figure 14: Definition of a line segment in terms of a reference line (C1) and two delimiting lines (C2 & C3).

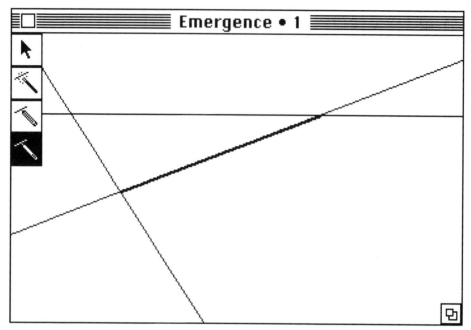

Figure 15: A 'window' in Emergence II, showing the construction of a line segment (thick line) with reference to three construction lines.

Function 1: Point (l1, l2)
If the coordinates of a point of intersection is needed, it can be determined by solving the equations of the two contributing lines, l1 and l2.

Function 2: Coincident (p, l)
The test for a point, p, lying on a line segment, l, returns true if the coordinates of p satisfies the line equation of l and that its x-coordinate lies between the x-coordinates of the intersections between the construction line of l and its delimiting construction lines.

Function 3: Intersection (l1, l2)
The test for an Intersection (both X and T) between SLines l1 and l2 returns true if the following are true:
a   The host CLines are not the same:
      CLine (l1, 1) ≠ Cline (l2, 1)
b   The point of intersection between l1 and l2 are coincident with l1 and l2:
      (Coincident (Point (l1, l2), l1)) and (Coincident (Point (l1, l2), l2)).

If an Intersection exists, a total of 4 possible emergent Slines are produced:

(CLine (l1, 1), CLine (l2, 1), CLine (l1, 2))

(CLine (l1, 1), CLine (l2, 1), CLine (l1, 3))

(CLine (l2, 1), CLine (l1, 1), CLine (l2, 2))

(CLine (l2, 1), CLine (l1, 1), CLine (l2, 3))

For a T-intersection (ie when a delimiting CLine = a host CLine) two of these are eliminated.

Function 4: Colinear (l1, l2)

The Colinear function returns true if the following are true:

a   l1 and l2 share the same host CLine:

CLine(l1, 1) = CLine(l2, 1)

b   One of the CLines of l1 is the same as one of the CLines of L2:

CLine(l1, 2) = CLine(l2, 2) or

CLine(l1, 2) = CLine(l2, 3) or

CLine(l1, 3) = CLine(l2, 2) or

CLine(l1, 3) = CLine(l2, 3)

This produces the emergent line segment:

(CLine (l1, 1), CLine(l1, 3), CLine (l2, 3)) or

(CLine (l1, 1), CLine(l1, 3), CLine (l2, 2)) or

(CLine (l1, 1), CLine(l1, 2), CLine (l2, 3)) or

(CLine (l1, 1), CLine(l1, 2), CLine (l2, 2)), respectively

Functions 3 and 4 show how emergent line segments are specified entirely with reference to the construction lines which define the 'parent' lines. In cases involving more than two lines, recursive applications of the process checks for all combinations of emergent line segments to be enumerated.

So far, only the reduction process is complete. The next phase involves a search for the required shape. The interface enables the shape to be defined as a list of contiguous line segments in the following form (for an x-sided shape)[9]:

(L1.length, L1.angle L2.length, L2.angle L3.length, L3.angle

... Lx.length, Lx.angle)

The search procedure then merely attempts to match the definition by testing each item on the list against contiguous line segments in the scheme. Since the definition of every line segment has references to the delimiting lines the next potential line segment will have a host construction line similar to one of them. Because the reduction process has taken into account the intersection and colinear cases, the search includes emergent shapes.

The 'parser' developed to handle this shape definition can accept either an absolute or relative value for either the length or angle entries, as well as arithmetic expressions[10], eg

'128,45' specifies a line segment 128 units long and at 45 degrees (clockwise from vertical).

'a,30' specifies a line of any length, a, at 30 degrees, if 'a' is encountered for the first time in the list, otherwise 'a' takes on a value assigned to it when it was matched to the length of a test line for the first time.

'b*2,x+180' specifies a line of length 2 x b and at the direction x+180 degrees (ie opposite to direction x degrees).

Future plans to develop the search-shape specification will most likely move away from this rather rigid sequential declaration towards a more hierarchical system capable of responding to priorities. Among other things, it would be better suited to handle disjoint and 'network' shapes. Also, it has been anticipated that the interface should enable a graphic method of specifying a search shape, at least at the outset; the lowest response of which is the 'reverse' of the present drawing and search process.

Conclusion

Describing shapes in terms of how their component lines relate to each other has the advantage that 'lo-level' calculations involving coordinates of points can be effectively postponed until they absolutely matter. It also enables a significant amount of searches and tests necessary for shape recognition – particularly for emergent shapes – to be pre-processed. This approach suggests that intermediate representation and formal structures of shape description can be usefully exploited to make the computation of shape transformation and combination more tractable.

Acknowledgements
My thanks to Professor Bill Mitchell (Harvard Graduate School of Design) for his encouragement and constant source of good ideas; also to A/Professor Mark Friedell (Harvard Graduate School of Arts and Sciences – Computer Science) for putting up with this project!

Notes

1   Putnam 1987.

2   Tan 1987.

3   Compare the parametized cruciform method for the same project in Mitchell, Liggett & Kvan (1987); p198.

4   Ref. Mitchell, Liggett & Tan 1988, 1989.

5   After Arnheim (1974); pp93 & 94.

6   Csikszentmihalyi (1987) concluded from studies on creativity that "problem-finding" rather than problem-solving is more characteristic of creative lives.

7   For a formal treatment of 'ambiguous forms' ref. Stiny 1989.

8   In the context of shape grammar, see Krishnamurti 1980 and 1981; for a computer implementation see Chase 1989.

9   cf shape 'script' in Nagakura 1989.

10   For an example of this technique, refer to Winston & Horn (1989); pp 353-356, 455-470.

References

Arnheim R, 1974, Art and Visual Perception. University of California Press, Berkeley & Los Angeles. (Originally published 1954.)

Chase S, 1989, "Shapes and Shape Grammars: from mathematical model to computer implementation." Environment and Planning B: Planning and Design, v16, pp 216-242.

Krishnamurti R, 1980, "The arithmetic of shapes." Environment and Planning B: Planning and Design, v7, pp463-484.

Krishnamurti R, 1981, "The construction of shapes." Environment and Planning B: Planning and Design, v8, pp5-40.

Krishnamurti R, Giraud C, 1986, "Towards a shape editor: the implementation of a shape generation system." Environment and Planning B: Planning and Design, v13, pp391-404.

Mitchell W, Liggett R & Kvan T, 1987, The Art of Computer Graphics Programming. Van Nostrand Reinhold, NY.

Mitchell W, Liggett R & Tan M, 1988, "The Topdown System and its Use in Teaching – an exploration of structured, knowledge-based design." Proceedings of the Association of Computer-aided Design in Architecture Workshop '88.

Mitchell W, Liggett R & Tan M, 1989, "On Teaching Designers to Program and Programmers to Design." Proceedings of the 1989 CAAD Futures Conference. MIT Press, Cambridge, MA.

Nagakura T, 1989, "Shape Recognition & Transformation – a Script-based Approach". Proceedings of the 1989 CAAD Futures Conference. MIT Press, Cambridge.

Putnam H, 1987, Many Faces of Realism. Open Court, LaSalle, Il.

Stiny G, 1989, "What Designers Do that Computers Should". Proceedings of the 1989 CAAD Futures Conference. MIT Press, Cambridge, MA.

Tan M, 1987, "Miesing About – a computer program to investigate parametric variation of the 'Project for a Brick Country House', 1923, by Mies van der Rohe." Unpublished project.

Winston P & Horn, 1989, LISP (3rd. edition). Addison-Wesley, Reading, MA.

14
A CAAD Model for Use in Early Design Phases

Mark de Vries
Harry Wagter

Department of Architecture and Building Science
Eindhoven University of Technology
The Netherlands

In this paper we present a model for handling design information in the early design phases. This model can be used for representing both vague and exact defined information. The first part describes the difficulties involved in using CAD in the architectural design process and the characteristics of that process. Then we give a description of the design information and its representation during the design process. Next an overview of the architectural design process describes how design information is added and manipulated during the design process in order to achieve an effective result. Finally, we include a brief description of a simple prototype program to illustrate how this theory acts in practice.

Introduction
Computer-aided design technology has been adopted widely as a useful tool for speeding up and improving the design process. It is already normal practice for parts of machines or complete chemical plants to be designed mainly on a CAD system. A notable exception is the field of architectural design. Today CAD systems are being used more often as a drafting package, but most attempts to use this technology to improve architectural design have failed. There are two major reasons for this failure.

In the first place a designer uses vague concepts, especially in the early phase of the design process. Computer programs are not yet capable of handling this kind of data and require that theinformation be exact. Unfortunately this kind of precise information is not available until relatively late in the design process. At that point the information that can be generated by using CAAD tools can no longer be used effectively to improve the design, as it is already almost completed. Major modifications at this stage will lead to unacceptable financial, technical,or aesthetical costs.

We find that most CAAD tools currently available concentrate on the late design phases. The designer can provide the necessary information for calculation of cost, strength, heat balance, and so on. For the early phase of the design process no such programs are available, although here they can be used more effectively to improve the design.

The second problem with using CAAD is its constant interruption of the design process. To use a CAAD tool the user must normally supply a geometric description of the design and a list of characteristics (material) for each part of the design. This means that the designer must temporarily stop the design process to translate his mental representation of the design into a form more suitable for the tool he is intending to use. This new representation must then be entered into the computer. After the program finishes, the designer must try to link the results to his own mental representation of the design in order to decide how the design must be improved. This process has a number of drawbacks. First, it takes much too long. In early design stages new alternative solutions can be generated within a few seconds. Application of a CAAD tool may interrupt this for ten minutes or more, which is not acceptable.

The designer must also concentrate on a different representation of the design. This makes it very difficult to relate the result of the tool to the design. Therefore the CAAD tool is not very useful, as the designer has great difficulties in using the information it generates.

Finally, the CAAD tool interrupts the "association link." During the design process every step is evaluated and may lead to new steps and new alternatives. Every attempt brings up ideas for improvements. Interruption of these steps for a long period makes it very difficult for the designer to find creative solutions to the problems he/she encounters. It is difficult to regain a line of thought and concentrating on one solution tends to block creative search for alternative solutions.

Using available CAAD tools in the early design phase thus raises severe difficulties for a designer. Basically these difficulties are caused by the specific nature of the architectural design process. A brief summary of these characteristics may help to explain the model of architectural design and design process presented in this paper.

The Architectural Design Process
There are three characteristics of the architectural design process which together make it different from all other kinds of design processes.

First, the architectural design process is ill structured. It is not possible to describe a series of steps that will finally lead to a successful solution for a design problem. The best that a designer can do in such a process is to create a solution and verify that it satisfies the constraints.

It is also very difficult to predict which modification will lead to an improvement of the design and which modification will not. This is possible for only a very small part of the design at a time. Such part must have a limited number of constraints.

Experienced designers know about a large number of solutions and their weak and strong points. They can use this knowledge to choose a primary solution that best suits the problem.

Second, the architectural design process is open-ended. A design is never completed and can always be further improved. During the design process the designer continues to work on the design until a deadline or budget limit is reached. It is very rare for a designer to stop the design process because he feels he cannot further improve the design. This is because each design is an optimization of a large number of partially conflicting constraints and requirements. Each improvement of one of these will also affect most of the others, either positively or negatively.

The designer decides which constraints he/she considers most important and optimizes the design accordingly. More important constraints are improved, even if this means that other less important requirements are not met. Choosing which constraints will be considered depends not only on the design problem, but also on the preferences of the designer and the principal.

There is a second form in which the design process is open-ended. Especially in the early design phase, there is no real goal the designer can work toward. As a starting point there is only a common idea about the building that is going to be designed (its "type"). This common idea must be extended by the designer to satisfy the particular needs of the principal. This occurs during the design process, so in the early phase the designer has to make a design without knowing exactly what he/she is supposed to design.

Third, the designer has no fixed starting point. This characteristic relates to the preceding one. Usually the designer must start with a design brief and a given site. These two are not fixed. The design brief is usually global and incomplete, and the site can be adjusted if needed. Before the design process starts, the designer must make a number of assumptions about the design objectives. These assumptions include the shape and appearance of the design and how it is going to be used. When the design is completed to such a level that it can be appraised by the principal, these assumptions can be evaluated properly.

Most theories of the design process concentrate on the design process for mechanical engineering. This differs in two ways from the architectural design process. It is less open-ended and it is better structured.

Criteria used with design for mechanical engineering can commonly be quantified. It is therefore possible to a large extent to describe the design goal early during the design process. This also simplifies the design process, since it is easier to check if a design is satisfactory and to know which modifications will improve it. In the architectural design process, the later phases are similar to the stages of the design process in mechanical engineering. CAAD tools developed for that kind of design process can be used very well in the later phases of the architectural design process.

Architectural designers use some special techniques to overcome the problems of vagueness and complexity that inhere in the architectural design process. Two techniques most frequently used to control the design process are decreasing the number of requirements to an acceptable level and superimposing some ordering principle on the design.

The number of requirements cannot really be decreased, but, conveniently, most requirements influence only a part of the entire design. In the early phase of the design process only those requirements that influence major parts of the design need to be considered. They can be combined into groups of requirements that have essentially the same effect on the design. In effect this means that in the early design stages the designer does not need to consider all requirements in depth but can look at a very small subset. Later in the design process the designer can and must consider more requirements in more detail. When he/she does so, those requirements will not affect the entire design.

The following schematic example may clarify this concept. When deciding the building shape, the designer may follow one of two tendencies: to minimize the building envelope or to maximize it. Both tendencies stem from a number of requirements. External walls are relatively expensive and cause heat loss; therefor, the smaller the elevation the better. On the other hand, it is better to have as many rooms as possible situated on the exterior wall because such rooms require less artificial lighting and air conditioning and are more pleasant places.

In the early design phase it is sufficient to choose a shape that allows enough rooms to be situated near the external wall of the building without creating an envelope that is too large. The designer does not need to consider all the individual requirements for these two tendencies. Later in the design process the designer will optimize cost for the exterior walls and the internal climate but does not reconsider the building shape.

The second technique, superimposing an ordering principle, is used to provide a starting point for the design process. Furthermore, it gives a set of criteria that can be used to evaluate the earliest designs. This aspect is especially important because in the early phases there is no information that can be used for a more conventional numerical evaluation of the design.

The ordering principle is in a sense a minimal design. It consists of an abstraction of the essential parts of a design, considering only one or two requirements. Because it is so limited it can be designed fairly easily. The only important rule is that it is both simple and consistent with a basic idea for the building. The structure can be used to generate design alternatives and variations and extensions of the structure. It can also be used to evaluate the design alternatives. Each alternative must obey the rules that are laid out in the principle, otherwise a design derived from that alternative will not be acceptable because it will be inconsistent.

An ordering principle can take many different forms; for instance, a routing scheme, a construction in which the building must be fitted, a cell of which the building will be composed, or a geometric form.

Each CAAD tool intended for use in the early design phase must allow the user to apply these techniques. Otherwise the use of these tools will obstruct the design process. These tools must also allow the use of vague information to avoid requiring specificity too early in the design process.

Design Information
During the design process the designer builds a mental model of the design. Simultaneaously, he/she makes sketches of the design. Observations of designers lead to the following conclusions:

1. The sketches act as memory aids and contain only the most important parts of the mental model.
2. The mental model is based on decisions about units of the design and not on objects. This is true particularly in the early stages of the architectural design process. Later the difference between decision and object is not as clear.

Basing the model on decisions instead of objects allows a much more flexible approach to the design process. Intentions and relations, for instance, can be expressed only in this form since there is no physical translation for them that can be used in an object-based model. Decisions are also a better basis for roughly describing a design. Later in the design process the design can be made more specific by adding more accurate decisions about the same units or their composite parts. This is possible for the entire design as well as for a part of it.

The units about which the decisions are made are not simply the objects of which a building is composed. In the early design phase a more global unit is used. Decisions are made about compositions of properties and requirements

Figure 1 Form follows structure as an ordering principle: Church, Barcelona, by A. Gaudi

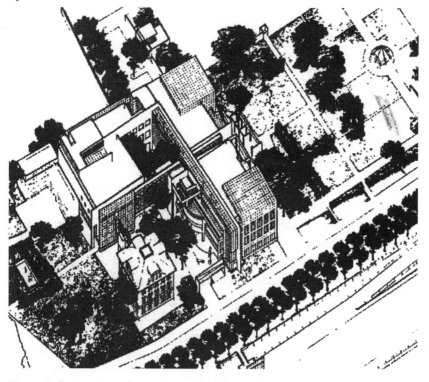

Figure 2 Geometric ordering principles: Museum, Frankfurt am Main, by R, Meier

that have specific architectural meaning. This can either be a "function" or a "building property." Both lead eventually in the final design to an arrangement of spaces and materials that suits the specific requirements of the unit. A "living room" and a "stair" are typical examples of functional units, whereas an "axis of symmetry" and a "vista" are common units about properties.

A building houses several kinds of activity specific to the building type, such as "sleeping" and "going upstairs' in a house. These kinds of activity need special provisions, such as a separate space of certain size with regulated internal climate and connections to external spaces via doors, windows, telephone, or television. All these requirements for functions and many more are combined in a single architectural unit.

A different kind of unit is used for decisions about the entire building—the way it is shaped, how its should look, and so on. These decisions are usually made early in the design process because they affect all other requirements and properties in the design.

Levels of Accuracy

The decisions that are made by the designer during the design process vary greatly in accuracy. In the early design phase they are very rough and concern large parts of the design at a global scale without any detail. The decisions in the latest phase of the design process are very precise, at a scale of millimeters, and concern very detailed parts of the design.

In the earliest stages decisions are often made about units without the designer knowing exactly how these units are composed. Decisions in this stage are normally expressed in terms of earlier decisions. For instance, a decision about size could be that a certain division occupies about "half the building." After having made the major decisions, the designer can make new decisions about smaller parts of the building. These decisions can be more accurate, which indirectly makes the major decisions more accurate. Use of a design grid is typical for this stage. The grid size can range from very small (30 centimeters) to over 10 meters for very big buildings. The size of a step (about 1 meter) is most commonly used. In this stage a size will already be expressed in measurable quantities like "6 meters," although this still is not very accurate.

Final decisions are made at the same level of accuracy as the building materials, normally in multiples of 10 millimeters.

Symbols

The design sketches are not the main representation of the design. Still they play an essential role in the design process. Observations showed that a designer sketches a symbol for each decision he/she makes. This symbol contains a graphical description of the essential parts of the decision. Figure 3a shows a typical symbol for a functional unit sketched very early in the design process. Figure 3b shows the parts of the decision and the way they are represented in the symbol.

If the designer reviews this symbol later in the design process, he/she remembers the decision it represents and, more importantly, the reason for that decision. Different symbols represent different kinds of decisions, each dependent on the properties of the architectural units.

For most decisions more than one type of symbol can be drawn. The different symbols for the same decisions are necessary to represent the accuracy of the decision. A more precise decision is represented using a more detailed symbol. Figure 4 shows a more accurate symbol of the same architectural unit as in figure 3. The main difference between the symbols is that in the accurate decision the composite parts are also considered and therefore can be found in the symbol.

Context

This way of using symbols representing decisions raises one problem. There are far more possible decisions than there are different symbols to represent them. Designers seem to use the following way around this problem. Associated with each decision is a set of other decisions that must be present before the decision can be made. We have called this the "context" of a decision. No two decisions represented with the same symbol can have the same context. Within a certain context all symbols therefore must unambiguously represent a decision. Consider the following example. Figure 5a shows a very simple design consisting of one rectangular and three round shapes. Now assume that the rectangular shape represents a decision about the building shape and that a round shape can represent a decision about either a room or a tree. The sketch can have only one meaning because a room can never occur outside the building and a tree can never occur inside it. This mechanism removes most ambiguities from the design sketches.

The Architectural Design Process

Most theories of the design process are based on a variation of the Analysis-Synthesis-Evaluation cycle. The theories differ in the number of steps used in each cycle and in the number of phases in the process. The basic idea is that the cycle is repeated until the design is completed. These theories cannot adequately describe the early phase of the architectural design process. They describe design processess with objective and fixed requirements that are fairly well structured. None of this applies to the architectural design process.

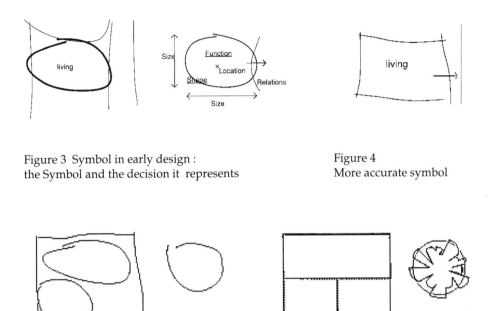

Figure 3 Symbol in early design :   Figure 4
the Symbol and the decision it represents   More accurate symbol

Figure 5   Context sketch: Interpretation

A theory to describe the architectural design process in the early stages must be less rigid and include mechanisms to state goals and criteria during the design process.

Observations of design processess reveals that the architectural designer uses synthesis-evaluation cycles in a rather unstructured way. At first sight there appears to be no relationship between the successive steps in the process. Each step stands on its own, and correction of unsatisfactory designs does not seem to occur very often. The design process takes place very rapidly but at irregular intervals and may be interrupted for a longer period of time. Furthermore, it appears that the designer is working on several parts of the design simultaneously, thereby constantly moving between the different drawings.

Underlying this seemingly chaotic process is a complicated though logical structure. The design process cannot be thought of as a single cycle that is repeated. Instead, it must be considered as three nested synthesis-evaluation cycles.

The fastest and innermost cycle is the "decision" cycle. Most design decisions are made in this cycle. The outermost cycle is the "development" cycle, in which the development of the design is controlled. Between those two is the "structuring" cycle.

The Decision Cycle
This is a simple synthesis-evaluation cycle. It can normally be completed within a few seconds. The cycle consists of only two steps. No analysis step is included

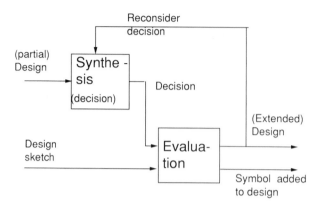

Figure 6 The decision cycle

because the vague and unstructured nature of the process at this stage makes analysis of a problem difficult.

In the synthesis step the designer makes a decision about an architectural unit. He/she then immediately enters the evaluation step to check if his decision meets the requirements. During this evaluation the designer sketches the symbol for the decision. The evaluation focuses on the properties of the decision itself and less on the relationship to other decisions. If a decision is not satisfactory, the designer will reconsider it.

The Structuring Cycle

This cycle is slightly more complicated than the previous one. In the synthesis step of this cycle the designer performs a number of decision cycles for different architectural units. This creates an appearance of chaos. Another side effect is that the complexity of each decision grows rapidly because each decision is influenced by most earlier decisions. At a certain point the complexity becomes too great for the designer to continue. When this point is reached depends on the complexity of the relations between the various decisions, but it is normally reached after four to eight decisions. The designer then enters the evaluation step of the development cycle. The first thing he/she will do is evaluate all decisions again, this time focusing on their relations. This process is more complicated than evaluation of a simple decision and may take some time.

When the decisions are all correct, the designer finally groups all newly added decisions together into one new decision. This allows for new decisions to be made because the designer has to consider only the relation to the group decision.

This process can be repeated only a limited number of times because these grouped decisions have very complex relationships. A typical design can contain about thirty decisions and four groups.

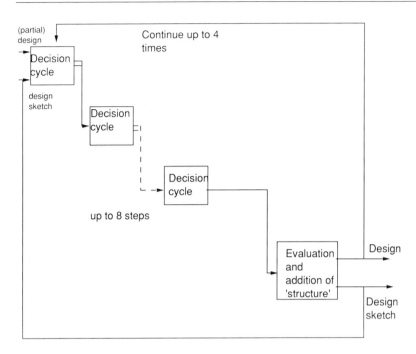

Figure 7 The structuring cycle

The Development Cycle

This is not a real synthesis-evaluation cycle since it contains no separate evaluation step. Each step in this cycle is in fact a completed "structuring" cycle. The first step is an analysis of the design brief and site. The analysis of the brief will define which functional units are needed in the design, and the analysis of the site will lead to a number of units about properties. In the next step the designer makes a conceptual design based on the units that were defined in the first step. The third step is the most important partial design: the main floor plan. In the beginning this plan is a translation of the conceptual design in architectural units. Later in the design process this will gradually be improved. All other partial designs will be derived directly from this plan, and all major modifications will be made only in this plan. The fourth step is for the plans of other floors. Though presented here as a single step, there can in fact be any number of plans in this step. The final step is for partial designs fulfilling other requirements. In the early design there are usually two partial designs: a section for height and construction and an elevation for appearance and volumes. Later in the design process more requirements are considered and so there are more partial designs in this step. When all steps are successfully completed, the designer returns to the main floor plan. He/she will redesign it, this time considering more

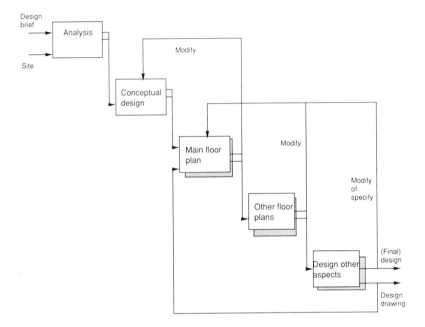

Figure 8 The development cycle

requirements and making decisions with a higher level of accuracy. This
process can continue until some external force like a time limit forces the
designer to stop. If, on the other hand, during one of the evaluations a problem
occurs that cannot be solved by reconsidering the last decisions, the designer
must stop. He/she will return to the main floor plan and make a modification
that will prevent the problem. After this the designer must check all decisions
to see if they are still correct. Sometimes it is not possible to make a
modification to the main floor plan that will prevent a problem. In that case
the designer must return to the conceptual design and alter it. This brings the
design process back to the start. The accumulated knowledge from the aborted
design process may help the designer move more quickly through the first steps
of the new attempt.

Prototype

We wrote a prototype program to demonstrate the use of this theory for
architectural design. Our main objective prototype was to make a computer
program capable of handling vague design information. A secondary goal was
to create a user interface that could interpret sketched information and would
not need commands or dialogue to guide the process.

Figure 9   Sequence of automated sketch design interpretation

The prototype is written in a dialect of the Lisp language. It uses keyword association lists to store the design information. This also means that a number of data formats are acceptable for most entries in the lists. The program is limited to the first three steps of the development cycle and can therefore not interpret different levels of accuracy. Furthermore, it can recognize only three different shapes: rectangular, round, and linear. In different contexts these shapes can represent decisions about the following architectural units: lot, alignment, tree, building, corridor, elevators, and rooms for four different functions. Additionally, the program can recognize and maintain the following relation: coincidence, partial overlap of two symbols, and complete overlap, which is interpreted as replacement of the older decision. Two properties, "size" and "function" are used by the program to check some simple design rules. For instance, rooms should not be too small, and a washroom should not normally be placed in a corridor. The program warns if a decision fails on these rules but does not attempt to correct them.

If the designer sketches a symbol that violates the context rules, the program will warn the designer. He/she must state which symbol was intended. The program will modify the sketch so that it is located entirely in the correct context.

Future Plans

We are preparing a new study to investigate three subjects closely related to this study.

First is a more extensive study of the architectural units. Knowledge about these units is essential for understanding what decisions a designer makes during the design process. This study must also reveal more details about the properties of the different decisions and about the context in which they are made.

Second, the model has to be enhanced. It is not now capable of explaining the hierarchical structure of the design decisions. During the design process each decision is gradually replaced by a number of more detailed decisions. The new decisions are more detailed not only because they are more accurate, but also because they cover a wider range of properties and requirements. This process of specification and the relations between the decisions involved must be explained by the theory.

Third is a new study of the best way to represent in a computer database the vague and nonprecise information that is created by the designer. This requires among other things a study of the levels of accuracy and of ostensible default values for unspecified values. The same problem occurs when generating output. This must refer to architectural units and their properties and may not be too specific in the early stages of the design process.

The objective of the new study is to improve the theory of the architectural design process and to create an new prototype program for a CAAD user interface. This must support the entire design process and should not require any input other than the design sketches. During the design process a data base must be filled that at any moment can be used as input for CAAD tools for appraisal of a design.

Information Delivery Systems for Design

15
Light Table: An Interface To Visual Information Systems

Patrick Purcell
Dan Applebaum

The Media Laboratory
Massachusetts Institute of Technology

Introduction

A primary aim of the Light Table project was to see if a combination of the optical laser disc, local area networks, and interactive videographic work-station technology could bring a major visual collection, (such as the Rotch Visual Collections of the Massachusetts Institute of Technology), to a campus-wide population of undergraduate users.

VIS (Visual Information System) is the name being given to the new genre of information technology. Much research and development effort is currently being applied to areas where the image has a special significance, for example in architecture and planning, in graphic and fine arts, in biology, in medicine, and in photography.

One particular advance in the technology of VIS has been the facility to access visual information across a distributed computer system via LAN (Local Area Networks) and video delivery systems, (such as campus TV cable). This advance allows users to retrieve images from both local and remote sources, dispatching the image search through the LAN, and receiving the images back at their workstation via dedicated channels on the campus TV cable.

Light Table is the title of a system that acts as a computer-based interactive videographic interface to a variety of visual information systems described in the body of this paper. It takes its name from the traditional, back-lit, translucent light table that lecturers use to assemble and view collections of slides for talks and seminars. The component of Light Table which is being reported in greatest detail here, a software outcome called Galatea, is a versatile and robust system capable of controlling video devices in a networked environment.

Context for Light Table: MIT Project Athena

The context for these developments has been Project Athena, a comprehensive educational program, launched at MIT in 1983, with the collaboration and support of DEC (Digital Equipment Corp) and IBM (International Business Machines), to develop a new technical infrastructure for under-graduate use (recently extended to graduates) across campus in the coming decade (Murman 1989).

While Athena's primary mission is educational enhancement, its technical goals have been several. One goal is coherence, namely to achieve a uniform operating system at the Athena user interface. Unix (AT&T) was the choice as the operating environment (Leffler et.al. 1989). Another goal has been to develop a digital network which would accommodate the campus-wide computing activities of hundreds of workstations, together with file servers, mail servers and printers. Athena has also sponsored new courseware and teaching strategies to take advantage of this computing context of unprecedented scale and complexity. The standard Athena Workstation is a 32 bit, 1-3 MIPS CPU with 4-8 MB of RAM, a hard disc, a monochrome megapixel display, a mouse and an Ethernet interface. The present deployment of approximately 800 machines, is a mix of DEC VAXstations and IBM PC/RTs. Selected workstations are configured with color displays and have multimedia capability.

In the technical area, there have been many interesting spin-offs, with potential well beyond the original Athena agenda. Among the most prominent has been a window system called "X" (Scheifler and Gettys 1987), a powerful network-transparent windowing program and the environment for Light Table.

Athena's educational mission has yielded a number of distinctive and interesting results, including computer-aided design tools, and interfaces to laboratory experiments. Multimedia applications having agendas in education, entertainment and communications, promise to be among the most significant Athena outcomes (Mackay and Davenport 1989).

The Visual Information System

The focus of this paper is the electronic Light Table as a highly interactive videographic interface connected to different visual information systems. So far, the VIS source images have almost entirely come from the MIT Rotch Visual Collections.

Rotch Visual Collection

The Rotch Visual Collection is a library of approximately 300,000 images in the form of slides, photographs, drawings, and microfiche. Covering the areas of architecture, urbanism, art and photography, it serves as a research and educational resource to faculty and graduate students. The progressive transfer of visual images from this important source to electronic media will make a radical change in the role of the Collection at MIT by making it accessible to undergraduates using Athena workstations across the campus.

The image banks accessed by Light Table include Archfile, Picassofile and the Boston Project. Archfile is an architectural image library that is comprised of approximately 5,500 records of architectural design. Each record in Archfile is divided into nine fields in the following manner. Fields 1 and 2 define the location of the building or project. Field 3 assigns the building as one of eight architectural types, (including religious, residential, medical, public, educational and commercial). Picassofile (Purcell and Okun 1983) is the name given to a small, but detailed image bank and data base built around the works of Pablo Picasso. The Boston collection (Smith 1987) is the most recent of the databased image collections to have been compiled. It consists of approximately 7,000 examples of significant architectural design or planning projects in the metropolitan Boston area. Its parameters of search and the organization include fields such as architect, location, frame number, year of construction etc. For example, a search to show the work of architect I.M. Pei in Boston generates 32 references and associated images. To constrain the search further the user may wish to specify a year of construction, or specify a building type (for example "residential"), or specify a particular precinct in metropolitan Boston, or combine all of the above.

Light Table

Light Table, begun in 1978, presents multiple images on the screen, as independent entities, each with its own border. Goals of the project have included portability, distributed use, and efficient use of resources.

To enhance portability for Light Table, (especially for different resolutions and for both DEC and IBM platforms), the X Window System was chosen to control the graphics output. Since X-Windows was designed to provide a machine- and device-independent method of creating interactive graphics, it was on its way to being adopted as an industry standard. Its use made it possible to develop a single program that would run both on the variety of hardware utilized by Project Athena and later in outside environments as well. The first version of Light Table was created using the X Window System, version 10. This first version only used digital representation of stored images. These images could be stored in a one bit, eight bit, or twenty four bit format. Images from any of the three storage formats were converted for display on either one bit or eight bit display depths.

Figure 1 General view of Athena video workstation showing the electronic "light table".

Figure 2 MIT Rotch Visual Collection, with conventional light table.

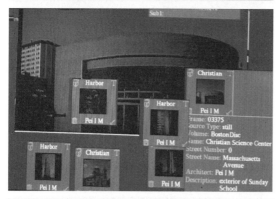

Figure 3 Images being retrieved on light table interface. Collages of images at various scales are shown.

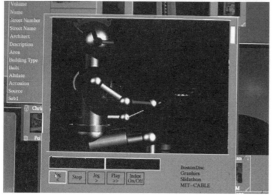

Figure 4 Light Table window running a digital videographic animation "beat dedication" (Sabiston—Visible Language Workshop)

The user interface for this system contained individual slides for each image plus a database control window. Each slide was comprised of several components. The primary component was a miniature version of the image. Around this was a wide border with several icons, a title, and the artist's name. The icons, located in the corners, could display the slide's image at full size, delete the slide, or protect the slide against accidental deletion. The database search window, (outside of the slides), controlled which images would be loaded into slides.

Although providing a good user interface for a slide library, the prohibitive cost of digital image storage required that an alternate storage method be found. The early version of Light Table was modified to take advantage of videodisc storage technology. In addition to using images stored on the file system, the program could search to a single image frame on a videodisc stored in a videodisc player connected to the computer with an RS232 serial line. Displaying an image found in this manner on a video monitor next to the main graphics display was not a very good substitute for the slide metaphor used earlier. A method of digitizing the analog videodisc images was required. The solution entailed using the Parallax Graphics model 1280 videographic subsystem to digitize the analog video directly into the frame buffer, so that the images were displayed at the same location and size as the digitally stored images.

To provide a distributed operating environment, the videodisc control method had to change from a local control system to a network-based control system. An experimental program was designed to listen to access requests from other programs and to control the videodisc players accordingly. Since this program program served the needs of other programs, it was called a "server." This program remained running at all times, making it a "daemon" process. Light Table was redesigned so that it sent commands to this videodisc server, instead of sending commands directly to the videodisc players, hence, making it a "client" for the videodisc "server." The commands issued to the videodisc server were independent of the brand of videodisc player being used; the server was responsible for adapting to the particular player being used. As new players were added, only the server required modification.

As the server could respond to requests from multiple clients, and manage switching between clients, users could share the videodisc players. Since the video digitizing process takes only about one thirtieth of a second, a client only needed a frame kept on the player for a short time. By allowing users to share the videodiscs and players, a more efficient use of relatively scarce resources was accomplished. Two videodisc players, controlled by a workstation and feeding an audio/video switch, were installed in the Rotch Visual Collection. The output of the switch was modulated to be sent out over the MIT campus cable television system. Users taking advantage of Light Table could access 108,000 frames of visual information from many locations on the campus. Once the experimental server was completed, work began on a more powerful and more flexible videodisc control system which would be available for other projects around the campus. This system would later be called Galatea.

The other piece to be changed from local access to network access was the database retrieval system. In the original system, the program simply read the information about the available images out of a file in the computer's file system. To provide remote access to this database and to prevent duplicate copies of what could now be a very large file, a database search server was created. This server responded to requests over the network for information about the images that were available in databases pertaining to architecture, art and documentary video.

At the same time as the database server and Galatea were developed, the decision was reached to rewrite Light Table from scratch to utilize the new version of the X Window System, version 11, which was established as an industry standard, and which would permit work with the latest equipment from many vendors. This new Light Table required virtually no local resource, but used network servers almost exclusively. The graphics output was through the X Window System, using network capability to retrieve information from the custom database server. The videodiscs were controlled through the "Galatea Network Video Device Control System."

Galatea

Galatea (Applebaum 1989) was designed not only to provide remote access to centralized video devices, but also to handle a distributed arrangement of video resources. Shared devices did not all need to be located on a "master" server, but could be located at several sites. This distributed flexibility was essential in the Project Athena environment, since each videographic workstation usually had its own local video resources, in addition to its access to the remote central server. In order to control the local resources, usually a videodisc player and an audio/video switch, a Galatea server was run on the videographic workstation. This server was also capable of forwarding requests for video resources to other Galatea servers on the network, the most common of which was the primary campus video server, located centrally, in the Rotch Visual Collection.

Naturally, keeping track of how all of the video devices were wired together was one of the main tasks of a Galatea server. Each server managed a collection of videodisc players and audio/video switchers. A Galatea server was capable of providing several outputs. If the audio/video switch in a system could handle such routing, a single videodisc server could be configured

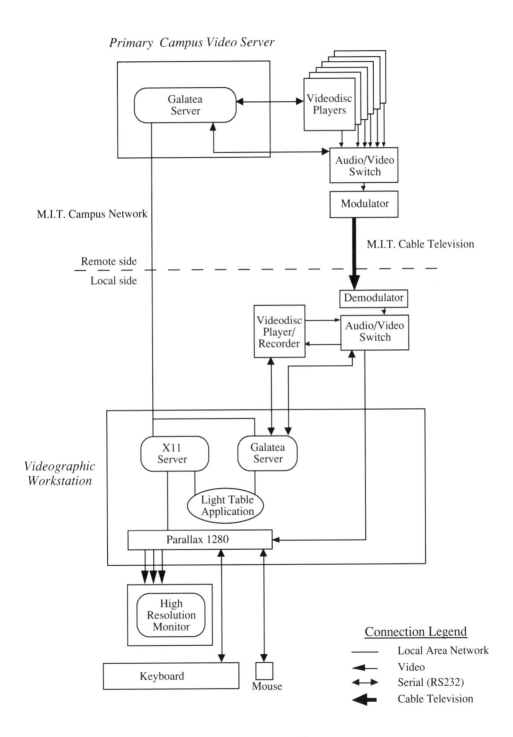

Figure 5 Diagram of Light Table system including Galatea

to send the output of any of several videodisc players to any of several different destinations. By supporting multiple "virtual" server outputs, a single server could support several channels on a cable television system, or several displays on a single videographic workstation. In order to make the configuration even more flexible, switchers could be chained. An output of one switcher could feed an input to another switcher. For example, two "four input, one output" switchers could be combined into one "seven input, one output" switcher by passing the output of one of the switchers into an input on the second switcher.

All of the details of the routing system were hidden from client programs, such as Light Table. When a client first connected to a Galatea server, it established which of the server's "virtual" outputs it wished to use. The server then passed the client a list of disc volumes that could be routed to the specified output. Once the client had this information, it needed only to indicate to the server which volume was desired, and the server would handle all of the specific audio and video routing.

The client's task was also simplified because a Galatea server could actually combine several copies of a single disc into one volume. If two copies of the Archfile disc were present, the server would provide the clients with the information that the Archfile volume was available. Normally, the server would guarantee that the multiple copies of the disc would appear to all the clients as just one. For a frame search, however, the Galatea server would first query all of the copies of a volume as to which player containing a copy of the disc was closest to the requested frame. To reduce the time needed to perform a search, the server would then use the closest player.

A major effort has been made to enable the Galatea servers to compensate for device failures. Network crashes, workstation crashes, failure of videodisc player and failure of audio/video switch were all handled automatically, with no intervention necessary from an operator. The usual method of dealing with the indication of a video device failure was for a server to clear all its internal device tables and rebuild its device information from scratch. It then proceeded to notify any other servers and clients that relied on its volume information that a volume table rebuild took place. Failures of networks and workstations required much more complicated compensating techniques. When a server served other Galatea servers, it maintained a file containing the network addresses of those other servers. If its workstation crashed and was rebooted, the Galatea server would notify each of the servers listed in that file that it was back on line. This technique could compensate for workstation crashes. Network crashes were slightly more complex. When a local server detected that a remote server became unavailable, it would undertake a volume table rebuild. If the remote server did not respond during the rebuild, it would not be recorded in the volume table. However, the local server would periodically check to see if the remote server was available by sending out small network packets requesting a response. If a response was received, another volume table rebuild would be performed so that the remote server, with its associated video devices, could be used again.

Although originally designed for the Light Table project, Galatea has been extended to perform well in many other contexts. Galatea can handle live video control requests, seamless splicing, and recording onto write-once video media. The live video requests can be used to view discs which contain motion video segments. The seamless splicing code can sequence several segments and, through a series of pre-rolls and video switches, can provide the seamless playback of the segments. The recording functions can be used to do frame by frame recording of computer generated animations. Alternately, the record functions can be used to take snapshots of the workstation user to send to other persons, or to copy a personal video tape into the main storage for use by others.

Galatea is an attempt to standardize access to video resources, so that various video client programs can work together on a single workstation, and so client programs are portable from site to site. Currently there are about one dozen universities and corporations using Galatea as the video device control system for their research. Galatea's built-in management of the various types of failures is a significant improvement over previous server designs. In summary then, it can be said that the Light Table interface, combined with Galatea and the database server provide reliable image delivery and effective portability. Galatea, which has grown to become an entire project, was the key to creating a system with these characteristics. The power of Galatea to provide disparate forms of video access was also essential in its deployment, so that many projects can share video resources for long periods without human intervention.

Acknowledgements
The concepts of the visual information system and the development of a versatile user interface to such systems owe much to our colleagues at MIT and elsewhere. Osnat Ron was the developer of the prototype Archfile system. Morissa Miller, Carter Pfaelzer and Paul Paternoster developed the second generation of Archfile. Thanks to Henry Okun, author of Picassofile, whose art historical erudition was the basis of the Picassofile data base. A special mention for Merrill Smith, originator of the Boston Project, and erstwhile Head of the MIT Rotch Visual Collections. Thanks to Fang Pin Lee for sustained contribution to the Boston Project. Christopher Thorman made many contributions including the "Image Delivery System". Several persons have helped in

the development of Galatea. Hal Birkeland has made considerable improvements and corrections to the server implementation. With Ben Rubin, he wrote the code for seamless splicing in the system. The input of Ben Rubin and Paul Boutin has led to the implementation of many features in the current version. Russ Sassnett provided the model and most of the underlying device control system. The special database server for networked environments was a creation of Jenifer Tidwell. Overall, Glorianna Davenport's constant encouragement, ideas and suggestions were essential to the proper development of the system. Light Table and its server Galatea have been sponsored by MIT Project Athena. The facilities provided to Light Table project by Muriel Cooper and colleagues in the Visible Language Workshop and by other colleagues in the MIT Media Laboratory were greatly appreciated.

References

Applebaum, DI. 1989. "The Galatea Network Video Device Control System". Cambridge: MIT Media Laboratory.

Leffler, SH, MK McKusick, MJ Karels, and JS Quarterman. 1989. *The Design and Implementation of the 4.3BSD UNIX Operating System.* Reading MA: Addison-Wesley.

Lippman, A. 1980. "Movie Maps: An Application of the Optical Video Disc to Computer Graphics". In *SIGGRAPH '80 Proceedings*. New York: ACM.

Mackay, WE, and G Davenport. 1989. "Virtual Video Editing in Interactive Multimedia Applications". *Comm. ACM* Vol 32/7. New York: ACM.

Murman, EM. 1989. "The Athena Project: Goals. Philosophy Status and Experiences". *MIT Athena Report.* Cambridge.

Purcell, PA, MW Smith, and CP Thorman. Sept. 1986. "The Image Delivery System". *Report to the Council for Library Resources.* Washington.

Purcell, PA, and H. Okun. 1983. "Information Technology and Visual Images: Some Trends and Developments". In proc conf *International Federation of Arts Libraries.* Munich.

Scheifler, RW, and J Gettys. April 1987. "The X Window System". *ACM Transactions on Graphics* 5(2) pp 79-109. New York: ACM .

Smith, MW. 1987. "The Boston Project". Internal Paper. Cambridge: MIT Dept of Architecture.

16
Messina 1908: The Invisible City

Sergio De Cola

De Cola Associates, Messina

Bruno De Cola
Francesco Pentasuglia

Faculty of Architecture
University of Reggio Calabria

Introduction

The initial purposes of this work were to build a 3D model of the old city of Messina and to reconstruct a walk through it; to understand the "Ghost city," the parts that form it, and the rules of its plan, which are explicit in some cases but hidden most of the time; to measure its space, appreciate the similarities to and differences from modern city plans, and use the information to improve the plans of tomorrow.

It might seem a useless study of a nonexistent city, and yet during the months of detailed work, of patient reconstruction from the surveys and photographs of the city destroyed in 1908, we began to consider how it was still possible to obtain spatial values of and to project behaviors in the lost city, in other words, to practice tests on memory that are very interesting for people working in a context in which memory no longer exists.

The work presented here is the first stage of a more complex research project still to be carried out on Messina as it was at the end of the nineteenth century. Here we constructed a 3D model of some parts of the city prior to the earthquake of 1908 and made a five-minute video, using cartoon techniques, of an "impossible" walk through the city. The fragments of the city were reconstructed from available documentary sources, primarily photographic images, which tended to be of the most important places in the city.

Methodology and Work Steps

The construction of the model required distinct work phases, which resulted in a correspondent series of products that can be considered autonomously.

First, we began with the digitization of the cadastral pre-earthquake cartography (on the scale of 1 to 1.000), distinguishing, on different layers, the contours of the buildings, the internal cadastral partitions, and, even if not finalized in the construction of the model, the lines of the plan for the reconstruction of the destroyed city. We obtained the city plan by assembling the individual small maps; this was the first step in reconstruction of the volumetry and thus of facades which determine the rebuilt urban scenes. The procedure employed for the acquisition of the cartography, permitted us to give, distinct or superimposed, the cadastral planimetry of the city and/or the planimetry of the reconstruction plan.

The second step was to research sources for the reconstruction of the sizes and layout of the buildings. As the original plots of the projects were missing, we fell back on photographs and illustrated postcards of the era. Those were, of course, devoted primarily to the important places of the city at that time. Most of the images came from the the Regional Library of Messina, and others came from the historical archives of the Commune of Messina and from private collections.

Unfortunately, though, there were few buildings (and above all urban contexts) that we could redesign accurately and rich in detail. Furthermore, along the most important road networks, the images show the buildings greatly foreshortened and often permit only an approximate reconstruction of the volumes.

The third step was the reconstruction from the photographic images of layouts and volumes. The facade tracings were reconstructed at a scale of 1 to 50. To reconstruct the 3D facades on the computer, we needed some graphic libraries. This led to an analysis of the architectonic elements, through a study of the recurrent elements. We thus arrived at a sort of collection of the typologies of the elements making up the facades; this collection can be considered an essential "dictionary" of the elementary forms of the architecture in eighteenth-century Messina.

It is important to point out that it there was a problem of simplification in the building of the 3D models. This resulted as much from technical constraints and from the limits of available means as from the aims for which the complete model was constructed. The simplification and schematizations we built into the design of the elements of the graphic libraries allowed and guaranteed a uniform approximation of each facade and of the rebuilt urban areas.

The next step of the task was the construction of the building facades using, and adapting when necessary, the various elements of the dictionary. All the work relating to every building whose facade was redesigned was set out on index cards; each one giving the elements of the cadastral identification, a synthetic description taken from texts of the time, the relevant bibliographic indications, two reproductions of some documentary photos, the a view at the scale 1:200, and the images of the model in 3D of the facade. At the same time, we designed the volumes of the model. Finally, all the facades that it was possible to redesign were inserted into the wire frame model.

At this time part of the "invisible city" was rebuilt, and we began to choose the routes, to illuminate several of the scenes, and to assign colors to the individual buildings. This set the stage for the animated walk through the city. The completed video shows a walk through the model on a route that starts at the railway station and crosses the most important squares of the time, which were completely different from those of today. We produced about 1400 images in succession for the walk. The individual views were processed with a 35 mm single-shot movie camera and then transferred to videotape.

Conclusion

We consider this a work in progress, and at this stage it is incomplete in both appearance and in structural and technical characteristics. The finished model is susceptible to further definition and development, in addition to improvements in its formal qualities, utilizing instruments more sophisticated than those we have used so far.

But above all we want to consider this an open work because of the several conjectures that it suggests to us, even if sometimes in a problematic way. For instance, a further elaboration could be the building of a database for the separate cadastral units, so that we could have an interactive system with numerous reports of increasing complexity: from the elaboration of a thematic map, up to graphic and alpha-numeric index cards for separate buildings and groups of monuments, to the cataloging and documentation of the artistic objects contained in the better ones, to the bibliographic connections and documentary sources.

Upon reflection, we also had the idea of setting up and creating a "laboratory museum" of urban history. It would be an institutional structure that could produce material simulating the set up condition, the place, and the monuments of the city at different times. It is an idea we think particularly efficacious above all in a situation like that of Messina, which today has virtually no tangible signs of its history.

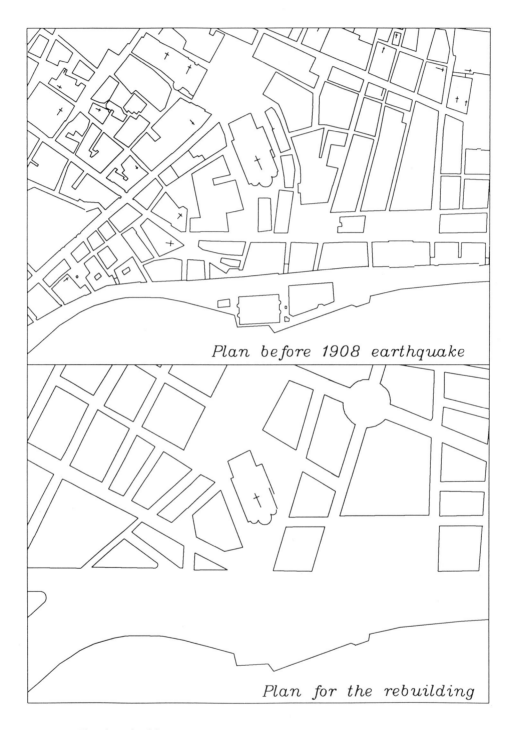

Figure 1 Plan for rebuilding

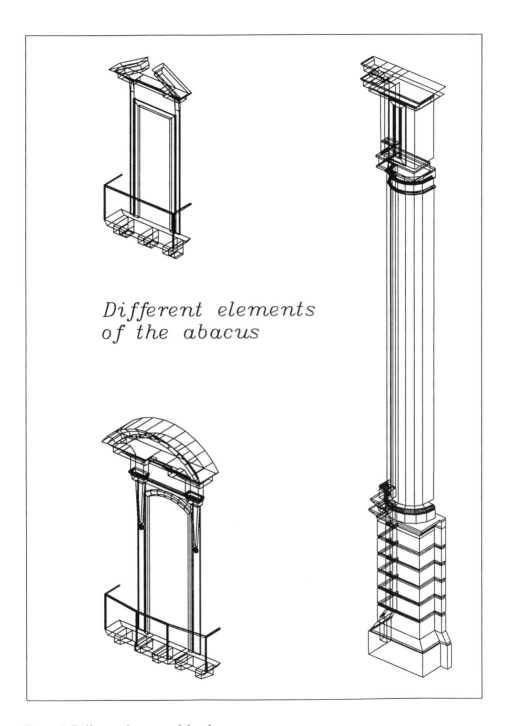

Figure 2 Different elements of the abacus

Figure 3 Perspective

Figure 4 Perspective

Figure 5 Perspective

Figure 6   Perspective

Technical Notes:

Photos and images of the archives utilized: 106.
Redesigned facades :10
Amount of data: 3D model:45 Mb; animation:350 Mb.
Computation time (on Compaq 386/25): 200 hours
Hardware: Compaq 386/25, (80387, 4Mb RAM); IBM AT, (Intel Inboard386/16, 80387,
   1.6 Mb RAM) ; Graphics boards: IBM PGA, Artist 12 GT, EGA, VGA
Software: Autocad (release 9.0), Autoshade (release 1.0), and Autoflix (release 1.0),
   from Autodesk Inc.

17
Supporting Reflection-in-Action
in the Janus Design Environment

Raymond McCall

College of Environmental Design
University of Colorado, Boulder

Gerhard Fischer & Anders Morch

Department of Computer Science
University of Colorado, Boulder

Introduction

We have developed a computer-based design aid called Janus, which is based on a model of computer-supported design that we think has significance for the future of architectural education. Janus utilizes a knowledge-based approach to link a graphic construction system to hypertext. This allows the computer to make useful comments on the solutions that students construct in a CAD-like environment. These comments contain information intended to make students think more carefully about what they are doing while they are doing it. In other words, Janus promotes what Donald Schon has called "reflection-in-action" (Schon, 1983).

The Janus design environment is named for the Roman god with a pair of faces looking in opposite directions. In our case the faces correspond to complementary design activities we call construction and argumentation. Construction is the activity of graphically creating the form of the solution—e.g., a building. Traditionally this has been done with tracing paper, pencils, and pens. Argumentation is the activity of reasoning about the problem and its solution. This includes such things as considering what to do next, what alternative courses of action are available, and which course of action to choose. Argumentation is mostly verbal but partly graphical.

As an initial approximation, we can say that construction corresponds to what Schon calls action, while argumentation corresponds to what he calls reflection. Janus promotes reflection-in-action by providing computer support for argumentation about construction during construction. Janus integrates computer-support for both construction and argumentation, the former in the form of a graphic construction kit, the latter in the form of IBIS hypertext. It accomplishes this integration using a knowledge-based approach.

In this article we first describe precursors of Janus and then Janus itself. Finally, we explain the relevance of Janus to Schon's theory of architectural education.

The efforts to develop computer support for construction and for argumentation have proceeded in parallel with little or no interaction between them. The former is associated with CAD (computer-aided design), the latter with hypertext—in particular what is known as IBIS hypertext.

Work in CAD dates back more than twenty-five years and is well-known in architectural circles. Almost invariably, the term CAD is construed to mean computer graphics, though not all graphics systems support the design activity we are calling construction. Many graphics systems support only drafting or rendering of already designed—i.e., constructed—forms. Nevertheless, there are systems, such as solids modeling systems, whose central purpose is to aid construction of complex objects, such as buildings.

Work in hypertext is nearly as old as that in CAD but until a few years ago was considered exotic and was pursued by only a small number of researchers (Conklin, 1987). Within the last year there has been an explosion of interest in hypertext. This is largely due to Apple's HyperCard and to periodicals, such as *Byte* (October 1988) and *Communications of the ACM* (July 1988), which have devoted issues to hypertext. Even so, its past and potential impacts on computing are still not widely understood. Thus, for example, it seems that relatively few people realize that both the word processor and the mouse are spinoffs of hypertext research.

Work on software that developed into IBIS hypertext began about 1976 and until 1984 was pursued mostly in Europe. In this article we assume that the reader is familiar with CAD but not with the concepts of IBIS hypertext. We therefore start by explaining the IBIS approach underlying Janus and the hyperext technology which implements it.

Ibis Hypertext

In the mid-1970s advocates of the so-called argumentative approach to design methodology began development of computer support for design argumentation. By the early 1980s this resulted in hypertext based on the IBIS method.

The IBIS Design Method

In the late 1960s Rittel developed the notion that design problems were wicked problems (Rittel, 1972). This meant they were intrinsically open-ended, situation specific, and controversial in ways that defeated attempts to treat them like problems of science or mathematics. To deal with this wickedness Rittel called for an argumentative approach to design, an approach that acknowledged and promoted the judgmental, political, and creative nature of design. The aim of the argumentative approach was to support the designer's reasoning without trying to automate it. To implement this approach Rittel developed the IBIS (Issue-Based Information Systems) method (Kunz and Rittel, 1970).

IBIS centers on the deliberation of issues arising in design; these issues are framed as questions. By deliberation we mean

1. identifying alternative answers to issues
2. stating arguments for and/or against the proposed answers
3. resolving the issues by selecting answers on the basis of the arguments.

In Rittel's IBIS issues are linked together by various relationships. These include an issue's being similar to, more general than, temporal successor to, and logical successor to (giving rise to) other issues.

PHI (Procedural Hierarchy of Issues) (McCall, 1979, 1987) extends IBIS by broadening the scope of the concept issue and by altering the structure relating issues, answers, and arguments. In Rittel's IBIS an issue is a question which is deliberated. In PHI every design question is counted as an issue, regardless of whether or not it is deliberated. PHI dispenses with the various inter-issue relationships of the original IBIS and uses instead only so-called serve relationships. These indicate that the resolution of one issue influences the resolution of another issue. "Subissue of" is the main serve relationship.

The overall structure of a PHI issue base, i.e., hypertext databases of issue discussion, is a quasi-hierarchy of issues with subissues, i.e., a tree-like structure such as that shown in figure 1. PHI also allows and encourages the development of quasi-hierarchies of answers with subanswers and of arguments with subarguments.

The changes in scope and structure which PHI introduces to IBIS allow creation and effective use of far larger issue bases. They also increase the range of situations to which IBIS is applicable. In fact, there is a descriptive theory of design, called Issue-serve Systems (McCall, 1986), which predicts that PHI can model all the describable processes and information of design.

Hypertext

Hypertext is software for managing nonlinear structures of information (Conklin, 1987). A linear structure is purely sequential, such as in a novel. A nonlinear structure is a graph with labelled links. In this graph the nodes contain information—e.g., text—and the links correspond to relationships between the nodes. A common example of a nonlinear structure of information would be a reference manual with many cross references—e.g., "see also."

In many hypertext systems the nodes can also contain nontextual information, including graphics, animation, video, sounds, and even executable code. Sometimes the term hypermedia is used to designate such systems; but the term hypertext is usually taken to include these as well.

Besides nonlinear structure, the other defining characteristic of hypertext is navigation. Navigation means moving around in the hypertext graph by traversing its links. Usually this works as follows. The contents of a node—e.g., text—are displayed on the computer screen along with labels denoting its links to other nodes. Clicking on a link label with the mouse causes display of the contents of the node that the link points to. Repeated application of this link traveral allows the user to travel around in the information "hyperspace."

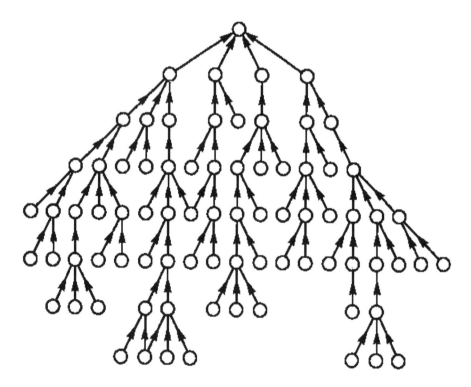

Figure 1   A quasi-hierarchy of issues with subissues

Previous Implementations of IBIS Hypertext

The MIKROPLIS hypertext project began in 1980 as a means for implementing the PHI approach to IBIS. A prototype was finished in 1985 and has since been in testing at the University of Colorado, Boulder. MIKROPLIS (McCall, 1987) is a text-only system that superficially resembles an outline processor. Actually, it has full-blown database management capabilities and can handle graphs with labelled links and tens of thousands of nodes. At the nodes are texts of essentially arbitrary length. Clusters of nodes are displayed in outline format. Retrieval is by navigation and/or by use of an English-like applicative—i.e., functional—query language. This allows the retrieval of complex substructures of the hypertext issue graph using key terms that are numbers, indexed terms, or substrings.

MIKROPLIS supports both exploration and creation of large and complex PHI issue bases. To date it has been used to construct issue bases on a range of subjects, including the design of housing projects, individual houses, neighborhood shopping areas, kitchens, and even health care policy. The largest of these is the equivalent of about 500 single-spaced pages in length but uses only a small fraction of the capacity of the MIKROPLIS system.

Rittel himself developed an IBIS hypertext system on his Apple II in the early 1980s (Conklin, 1987). This was a small-scale system that displayed only one text—e.g., one issue—at a time and had limited retrieval capabilities. It was nevertheless of great significance as the inspiration for the gIBIS system developed at MCC.

GIBIS, recently featured in an article in *Byte* magazine (Begeman and Conklin, 1988), was developed by Jeff Conklin and Michael Begeman of the Software Technology Program at MCC (Microelectronic and Computer Technology Corporation). Based on Rittel's original IBIS, gIBIS has a sophisticated graphics interface and allows concurrent use of a single issue base through a local area network.

ViewPoints is a hypertext application based on PHI and implemented in HyperCard on the MacIntosh computer. It was developed as part of the initial exploration of principles for Janus. It has fewer retrieval capabilities than MIKROPLIS but has graphic capabilities not available in MIKROPLIS. ViewPoints can be regarded as the direct conceptual precursor of the hypertext component of Janus. In particular, ViewPoints uses an issue base for kitchen design that is essentially the same as the one used for Janus.

Evolution of the Janus Design Environment

Deficiencies of Separate Computer Support for Construction and Argumentation
Computer-supported construction facilitates design. The problem is that it
facilitates both good and bad design. To create good design designers need
knowledge about how to evaluate what is constructed, i.e., knowledge about
criteria such as utility, safety, aesthetics, social value, and cost. To increase
the likelihood of good design a computer-aided design system should therefore
supplement support for construction with a store of evaluative knowledge. But
adding such knowledge to a construction support system would not in itself be
enough. For, as Schon has argued, good design requires that designers have
more than knowledge. It also requires that they reflect-in-action, i.e., think
about what they are doing while this thinking can still make a difference to
what they do. Ideally, a computer-aided design system should promote and
support such reflection-in-action.

Computer-supported argumentation, in the form of PHI hypertext, is a
natural complement to a construction system. An issue base for the problem
domain can contain much of the knowledge students need. The PHI-IBIS
method also provides a natural stimulus to and vehicle for reflection. It might
therefore seem sufficient to provide the student with a stand-alone PHI system,
such as MIKROPLIS or ViewPoints, to use during construction. Our experience,
however, suggests that this strategy is ineffective.

With a stand-alone PHI system one has to interrupt construction and search
for relevant argumentation in the issue base, just as one would if using a book.
Our experiences suggest that, for a number of reasons, students will tend not to do
this. One reason is that the interruptions are disruptive. A second is that
searching for useful argumentation will not always pay off and students have
no way of knowing when it will. A third is that students are often unaware
that they need information and thus do not search for it.

Stand-alone construction and PHI hypertext systems leave a gap between
action and reflection. Bridging this gap requires an integration of computer
support for construction and argumentation. But how is this integration to be
accomplished? An answer to this question was derived from the CRACK
project.

CRACK: From Construction System to Design Environment
Student designers need systems that both support construction and contain
knowledge for distinguishing good from bad in construction. We call such
systems design environments (Fischer, Lemke 1987–88). CRACK (CRitiquing
Approach to Cooperative Kitchen design) (Fischer and Morch, 1988) is a design

environment that is a direct precursor of Janus. It consists of two components: a construction kit for kitchen floor plan layout, and a knowledge-based critic for evaluating these layouts.

A construction kit has a palette of parts and a work area for assembling these parts into complex designs. The parts are appropriate to a particular problem domain. In CRACK the domain is kitchen design and the palette contains kitchen equipment—such as sinks and stoves—and architectural fixtures—such as walls and windows. A set of operations on these parts are defined, such as move, rotate, and scale. Users design by using the mouse to select parts from the palette and arranging them in the work area. This allows them to work directly in the problem domain, without having to type or to build objects from lines and simple shapes.

The knowledge-based critics in a design environment detect and criticize partially constructed solutions on the basis of knowledge of design principles. The critics in CRACK are state-driven condition-action rules which take action when nonsatisfying partial designs are detected. The action they take is to display criticism based on principles of kitchen design derived from reference books and protocols of professional designers.

CRACK is knowledge-based but not an expert system. It aims to inform and support the judgment of designers, not to "de-skill" them by judging or designing for them. Thus the CRACK user is free to ignore, turn off, or even, within limits, to alter the criticism displayed.

From CRACK to JANUS

CRACK's criticism is really what we have been calling argumentation. In CRACK, however, this is not in PHI form nor is there any hypertext component. CRACK's argumentation also has a superficial "cookbook" character and does not show the complex argumentative background that an issue base can show. Nevertheless, CRACK demonstrates how to connect construction and argumentation using a knowledge-based approach.

The Janus design project began with the observation that the "critiquing approach" of CRACK could be used to connect a construction kit to a full-blown PHI hypertext system. In particular, CRACK's context-sensitive mechanism for triggering criticism could provide entry into precisely that point in the hypertext issue base where the relevant argumentation lies. The system could then display the argumentation relevant to the current construction situation without the user's having to search or even ask for it. This solves two problems: how to improve the argumentation capabilities of CRACK, and how to make PHI inform construction.

Basically, Janus works as follows. The user constructs a kitchen layout with the construction kit. After each part from the palette is placed in the work area, the system analyzes that placement. Brief criticism is displayed by the system if a design principle has been violated. Should the user want to see the argumentation underlying this criticism—e.g., to understand or challenge it— he or she can activate the hypertext system. Janus will then display the relevant section of the issue base. This display can be used as the starting point for further exploration of the issue base by navigation. When finished exploring, the user can return and complete the construction task.

Conceptually, Janus is an integration of two separate software systems: CRACK and ViewPoints. There are, however, differences in implementation details. In particular, the "ViewPoints" part is implemented in Concordia/Document Examiner, rather than HyperCard. The Document Examiner is a hypertext system developed by Symbolics Corporation for users to browse through its system documentation on line. Concordia is the authoring system that allows the user to create documents that can be browsed using the Document Examiner.

The screen layout for CRACK, the construction face of Janus, is shown in figure 2. Th\e "Palette" in the upper left window contains the parts of the kitchen, called design units (DUs). These include both kitchen equipment— sinks, stoves, refrigerators, etc.—and architectural features—walls, windows, and doors. The upper right window shows the "Work Area," where the actual construction takes place. A partially constructed kitchen is shown in this area. Construction is accomplished in the same manner as in CRACK: by using the mouse to select DUs from the "Palette" and position them in the "Work Area." Students can also reuse and redesign complete floor plans by selecting one of several examples from the "Catalog," which contains a varied collection of finished floor plans. After each placement—or repositioning—of a DU, critics analyze the layout and display any relevant criticism in the "Messages" window.

So far Janus functions like the original CRACK system. But the transition to the full-blown hypertext argumentation is made merely by clicking on one of the texts (criticisms) displayed in the "Messages" window. This provides entry into the hypertext at the relevant portion of the issue base.

The screen layout for ViewPoints, the argumentation face of Janus, is shown in figure 3. Different types of views of the PHI argumentation are shown in three windows. The "Viewer" window shows the actual argumentation in the relevant section of the issue base, including both text and graphics. Text is displayed in outline format and can include issues, answers and arguments. The "Outline" pane shows the identity of the issue being dealt with and the structure of its deliberation. "Visited Nodes" shows names of the sections of the issue base that have already been retrieved by the user. Each type of view provides areas which when "clicked on" will cause the display of some other section of the argumentation, which in turn contains mouse-sensitive areas. This is "navigation," the hallmark of hypertext.

Computer Supported Reflection-in-Action

Schon defines reflection-in-action as thinking about how to act in a situation while the situation is at hand and action can still make a difference to it. We interpret each situation at hand as being associated with an issue that the designer is trying to resolve—for example, the issue "Where should the sink be located in the kitchen?" Janus "knows," or rather assumes, that this issue is being addressed when the user selects a sink from the "Palette" and places it in the "Work Area." It presents relevant argumentation while this can still make a difference to the decision taken on the issue.

Janus promotes two kinds of learning by doing: learning design principles and learning to reflect-in-action. It also promotes two kinds of reflection-in-action: reflection triggered by violation of principles of design and reflection on the principles of design themselves.

Reflection Triggered by Violations of Principles of Design

Schon sees good design as "a reflective conversation with the situation," in which the designer acts and the situation "talks back." A goal of studio education is to get students to engage in such reflective conversations. Students have difficulty doing so because they cannot "hear" what the situation is "saying." In other words, they do not see the unintended consequences of their construction actions. Schon points out that such unintended consequences— pleasant or unpleasant—are the crucial stimulus to reflection. Unfortunately, for neophyte designers the problem situation does not speak for itself: it needs a spokesman, i.e., a critic. When available, studio teachers play that role and thus lead students to reflect. Janus supplements the work of these teachers with knowledge-based critics and does so while decisions about construction are actually being made—something that teachers often cannot do. By informing students when principles of kitchen design have been violated, it prompts them to rethink their designs.

Reflection on Principles of Design

Schon stresses that design is far more than the application of standard "principles." It is also professional artistry: the ability to reflect on situations that are conflictual, uncertain, and/or unique. In these "intermediate zones" principles do not suffice. The assumptions underlying them may be violated,

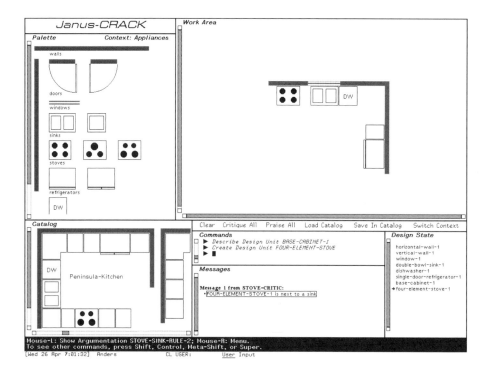

Figure 2

CRACK: Janus's Construction Face Construction in Janus-CRACK is based on a direct manipulation interaction style, i.e., using the mouse, although commands can also be entered by keyboard in the "Commands" pane. Building blocks (Design Units) are selected from the "Palette" and can be moved around with the mouse to desired locations inside the "Work Area." Students can also reuse and redesign complete floorplans by selecting one of several examples from the "Catalog." The "Messages" pane displays criticism by the knowledge-based system. Clicking on a criticism with the mouse will bring the student into the ViewPoints hypertext (see figure 3).

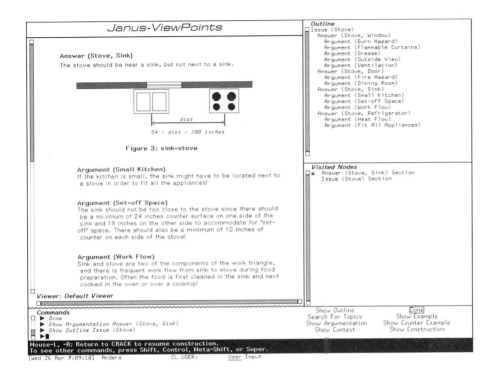

Figure 3

ViewPoints: Janus's Argumentation Face Janus's argumentation component is a PHI-IBIS hypertext system implemented using the Symbolics Document Examiner. When students click with the mouse on criticism in the "Messages" pane in CRACK, the construction face of Janus (see figure 2), they are brought into ViewPoints at the point where the relevant argumentation is to be found. The "Viewer" pane shows argumentation on an answer suggested by the criticism. (Note that this pane can be scrolled.) The "Outline" pane shows the identity of the issue being dealt with and the structure of its deliberation. "Visited Nodes" shows names of the sections of the issue base that have already been retrieved by the user. In this example, the issue is "Where should the stove be located?" The student has evoked criticism from the knowledge-based system by placing the stove near the sink. The ViewPoints system shows the user various pros and cons of placing the stove near the sink.

the "experts" may disagree, or there may be no principles at all. In such cases, which are not "in the book" or for which there is no consensus, the designer must reflect carefully on how to act.

Few of the standard "principles of design" are inviolable. They are merely rules of thumb whose appropriateness must be judged by the designer in each new situation. In other words, the designer must not reflect merely on how to apply principles, but also on whether the principles should be applied as is, modified for the particular situation, or simply abandoned.

IBIS is a natural stimulus to and vehicle for such reflection. It was designed to deal with the controversiality, open-endedness, and essential uniqueness of Wicked Problems. This fits well with Schon's characterization of the "intermediate zones" of design as "conflictual, uncertain and unique."

An issue base can supply a variety of information to stimulate and improve reflection. This includes not only design principles, but also issues, alternative answers, and arguments that help the student to decide whether standard principles are applicable to a situation at hand. Where exceptions must be made to such principles, the argumentation underlying them can provide a basis for reasoning about how to deviate from them.

Janus can also display useful information for situations where no principles exist. This information includes issues to consider and possible answers as well as relevant criteria and other arguments. All of these require students to judge for themselves. They inform student judgment but do not judge for the students.

Conclusion

There is much that can and should be done to extend the work described above. We need to expand the current issue base on kitchen design to include more social, psychological, aesthetic, and monetary criteria. We need to develop issue bases in other problem domains so that Janus can be applied to these domains. While kitchen design has been a useful starting point, the significance of the Janus approach will lie in its applicability to a wide range of problems.

In working with Janus we have discovered several additional ways of connecting the construction and argumentation. Implementing these will further promote reflection-in-action and extend the range of problem domains to which Janus is applicable.

Much can be done to make Janus a better aid to the designer's ability to understand the consequences of construction decisions. Inclusion of color, 3D graphics, and multiple views are perhaps the most important. Computer-based analysis—e.g., of lighting—as well as simulation and gaming of use situations would also be useful.

These and other considerations indicate to us that exploration of the Janus approach has only begun. The Roman deity, Janus, was the god of gateways. It is our hope that the Janus design environment is a gateway into a new area of research on computer-aided reflection-in-action.

References

Begeman, M., and J. Conklin. "The Right Tool for the Job." *Byte* (September 1988).

Conklin, J. "Hypertext: An Introduction and Survey." *IEEE Computer* 20:9 (September 1987).

Fischer, G., and A. Lemke. "Construction Kits and Design Environments: Steps toward Human Problem Domain Communication." *Human-Computer Interaction Journal* 3:3 (1987–88), pp. 179–222.

Fischer, G., and A. Morch. "CRACK: A Critiquing Approach to Cooperative Kitchen Design." *Proceedings of the International Conference on Intelligent Tutoring Systems* (June 1988).

Kunz, W., and H. Rittel. "Issues as Elements of Information Systems." Working Paper 131. Stuttgart: Institut fuer Grundlagen der Plannung, 1970.

McCall, R. "On the Structure and Use of Issue Systems in Design." Dissertation, University of California, Berkeley, 1979.

McCall, R. "Issue-Serve Systems: A Descriptive Theory of Design." *Design Methods and Theories* 20:3 (1986).

McCall, R. "PHIBIS: Procedurally Hierarchical Issue-Based Information Systems." *Proceedings of the Conference on Architecture at the International Congress on Planning and Design Theory.* New York: American Sociey of Mechanical Engineers, 1987.

Rittel, H. "On the Planning Crisis: Systems Approaches of the First and Second Generation." *Bedriftokonomen* 8:390 (1972).

Schon, D. *The Reflective Practitioner.* New York: Basic Books, 1983.

18
Image Collections in the Design Studio

Dave van Bakergem

Urban Research and Design Center
School of Architecture, Washington University

No matter what the medium, architects are constantly using images in all aspects of design thinking. Whether it is the perception of the environment, an image in the mind's eye, an abstract drawing or a photographic record, designers use images to conceive of, and manipulate their design ideas. Managing these image collections occurs at a variety of levels in the creative process and is dependent on the type of image that is called upon for reference. The most basic example would be the image collection residing in the mind's memory which is a result of the designer's world experiences and the relative impressiveness of each experience. Clearly, personal memory plays a significant role in the use of imagery in design, but it is unreliable and can be abstracted in uncontrollable ways. The sketchbook and later photographic collections of the grand tour were the beginnings of efforts to manage and utilize image collections as an aid to drawing and thinking about design. Now the capacity to use electronic means of creating, altering, storing, and retrieving images will enable designers to effectively use large image collections in ways that have not been possible before.

This paper describes current work at the School of Architecture at Washington University in a graduate design studio. The students use a powerful 3D modeling CAD system (HOKDraw) to design and present their studio projects. In addition, we are experimenting with an image storage and retrieval system which is directly linked to the CAD model through a relational database (INGRES). Access to the database and images is instantly available through the command language and graphic display. The CAD model in effect becomes a 3D menu to an extensive image database stored on an optical memory disc recorder.

Several collections are available to the studio members: the library's slide collection which relates to the studio project, specific photographs and drawings of the project site, and personal image collections stored by individuals for their own reference. The commonly accessible images are basically background material and images collected by the students to document the site, urban context and building typology. The personal images collections are any images (drawings, photographs, published images, CAD images) created or collected by the students for purposes of informing their design thinking.

This work relates to the use of precedents and typology in architecture as a point of departure as well as in development of design ideas.

Introduction

What is the source of design ideas? Clearly this question is not easy to answer but it is safe to assume that designers bring to each project a set of enabling prejudices and corresponding enabling images. These prejudices and images are derived from world experiences and are stored in memory to be called on in the mind's eye. A mature, experienced designer may have a vast and extensive collection of images which provide a source of knowledge about a place, about architecture, about formal concepts, etc. An architectural student may have a comparatively tiny collection to call upon as a source of ideas from outside the problem context—a handicap in part overcome by the usual rush to the library at the start of a studio. These trips to the library are documented by copies of relevant images which form the beginning of an image collection for a design project. Tack boards fill up, work areas become scattered with photos, drawings and other images. The use of images can be compared to the use of study drawings which play an essential role in thinking about design but are mostly used by habit and circumstance rather than organized and managed in any coherent way. Once completed, study drawings join the collection which provides a short-term pool of images to back up design activities. The process is informal but it is a critical part of building the knowledge which a designer brings to a project.

An attempt to manage this process of building an image collection for a design project was recently pursued in a graduate design studio. The project was the recent ACSA student design competition "London: Designing in the Historical Context". Five students participated in the studio for which the program was a large mixed use commercial development on the Thames River just west of the Tower of London. Part of the studio's tasks was to create an image collection which would be shared over a computer network and would be project specific. The objective of the experiment was to explore the role that images play in design when a small group focuses on the same problem and develops both a communal and personal image collection.

The process of formalizing and managing the collections raised issues of terminology and typology. Labels, notes and terms were required for both communal and personal collections. The act of naming an architectural object is a process that typifies through language. Through the process of assigning names and labels the images were grouped by certain inherent similarities and the students faced some fundamental issues of typology. The use of images as a vehicle to explore types was not meant to encourage a literal copy-and-paste approach to models but to encourage an interpretive approach—to seek the essential elements that provide an idea for change or transformation. In " On Typology" Professor Rafael Moneo wrote "Architecture. . . is not only described by types, it is also produced through them. If this notion can be accepted, it can be understood why and how an architect identifies his work with a precise type. He is initially trapped by the type because it is the way he knows. Later he can act on it; he can destroy it, transform it, respect it. But he starts from the type. The design process is a way of bringing elements of a typology—the ideas of a formal structure—into the precise state that characterizes the singular work." Typology as a point of departure is a powerful teaching tool which can be effectively enhanced by the use of image collections.

Types of Collections

Three types of collections can be identified: general, communal, personal. These types can be distinguished by the sorts of images included in the collection and the purposes for which they were collected.

General collection

This type is a collection which attempts to be comprehensive for a specific discipline. Typically, a library's slide collection is a general architectural collection which provides basic reference images for a wide range of subject matter and is organized by building type, architect and/or location. The architectural periodicals in the library could also be thought of as a general collection.

Communal collection

This collection is the central project-specific image collection to which all members of the studio make contributions. It grows as more information is gathered and includes site documentation, local and regional history, building types and other images and is meant to be a shared resource for all users. It is located on the disc in a designated location with expansion room.

Studio tack board

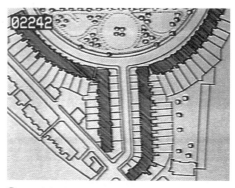

Cresent type

Studio tack board

Image from library collection

Site documentation

Tower Bridge

London Custom House

Geo-referenced image—All Hallows Church

Personal collection
The personal collection is a group of images which may only have meaning to the designer

Functional types
Images of buildings or special rooms which the user might wish to record as an example of a functional type constitute this category. For example, in the studio the program called for hotel, office commercial and retail commercial space. Students collected images of these building types in an effort to understand the range of typical forms that these building types might take.

Well-known places
These images might be part of the designer's personal collection of places that are used for references of scale and sense of place. Places that are known from personal experience might be local places which have been recently visited or which are frequently encountered, such as a local urban plaza or university quadrangle.

Impressionistic images
These images are the most open-ended and free of any literal interpretation. Images which provide any reference for the designer in the most personal manner might be included in the collection. For example, a late nineteenth century painting of boats in the river might provide a point of departure for architectural form.

Designers' sketches
Designers produce images in the from of sketches, drawings, collages and models. Schematic sketches and other study drawings can be made part of the on-going collection process in which progress toward the final design becomes part of the collection. Looking back at early sketches is a common technique for designers when faced with an impasse.

Image Collection System
The image collection system is essentially a hypermedia environment in which the CAD window is the primary access to graphics and text. It is a working environment which provides links between images, text and three dimensional CAD models. The most significant aspect of this system is the connection between graphic objects in the CAD model and photographic images stored on an optical disc. The CAD system used for this project is HOKDraw and it has

Reference project from personal collection

19th century painting / river edge

Trafalgar Square

Tower of London

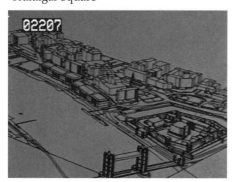

Student sketch of project site

Image in personal collection

Figure ground project site

St. Paul's Cathedral

access through its command language to Ingres, a relational database. Lines polygons and symbols in libraries can be linked by unique identification numbers to entities in the graphic database. This functionality is common in many CAD systems and seems to be most frequently used in facilities management applications and other applications in which attributes are assigned to polygons and other graphic entities. In the image collection system those attributes include a videodisc frame number which links the entity to an image as well as text files, labels, keywords and notes. With this connectivity, any symbol or part of a CAD model can be linked to anything that can be photographed including motion video with stereo sound.

The image storage device used was a Panasonic Optical Memory Disc Recorder which is a direct read-after-write NTSC video medium. The capability of recording single still frames from any NTSC video source made it a convenient and easy-to-use device. The disc capacity is 24,000 frames of high resolution, full color video. Search time for any frame is less than two seconds and it can play image sequences at any speed up to 30 frames per second. The analog videodisc medium was chosen because of the large capacity and its capability of rapidly displaying sequences of images which permits the important function of browsing the disc. Image input was accomplished by a high resolution video camera on a copy stand and a video slide processor. This set up permits flat artwork, photos, images from books and periodicals, drawings and color slides to be quickly transferred to the video disc.

The CAD program runs on a local area VAX cluster (Vaxstation 2000's). All functions of the CAD program, the relational database and the videodisc player/recorder are controlled through the command language or pop-up menus in the CAD program. CAD images are displayed on the workstation monitor and images from the videodisc are displayed on the NTSC video monitor.

Using the Collection System
There are two basic modes in using the system: building the collection and searching/personalizing the collection.

Building the collection
Recording images, inputting symbols and creating links are functions with which the users establish their studio collection. In order to encourage extensive use and to discourage early elimination of images in the preselection process the system was set up to be as convenient as possible with the copy stand and slide processor constantly available in the studio. Any image created in the studio, found in a publication or recorded on the site could easily be included in the collection. The links to the graphic database were accomplished by inputting a graphic symbol with a name related to the class or subclass of

Garden gate

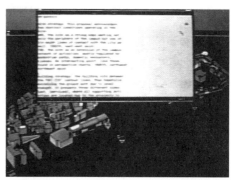

Text file window associated with image

Symbols for geo-referenced image

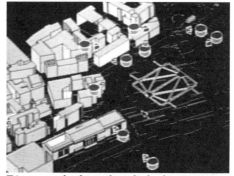

Diagram of urban plaza linked to image

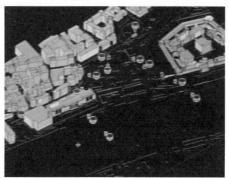

Pop-up menu for image selection

Piazza San Marco / well known place

Image from personal collection

Early London map showing site

images, for example, arcades, entries, St. Paul's. The shape, size and color of the symbol provide visual cues as to the type of image to which it is linked. For example, photos of the site which are geo-referenced images were linked with an arrow indicating the location of the photographer and the direction of the photograph. Links to the relational database were accomplished by Ingres's query-by-forms function which allows the user to make notes and labels associated with each image or group of images. These notes and labels would become one of several means of selecting the images by keyword searches. The label field was established as an objective description of the image, such as "Kew Gardens;gate" while the note field was left open for subjective, personalized adjectives and nouns which the user might find useful in returning to that type of image, such as, "grand entry; best example".

Searching/Personalizing the Collection
There are several types of actions which a user might take in searching the collection: selecting symbols in the graphic database, performing a keyword search of the tables in the relational database and browsing the image collection on the videodisc.

Selecting symbols provides a direct link to a single image or group of images. The user graphically picks a symbol or polygon, a pop-up menu displays the images' labels associated with that symbol, the user selects a label, and the video monitor displays the image while a workstation window displays the text file associated with that image. Other display options include a sequence such as surrogate travel through the site. Photographs of the site, historic drawings and maps, plans of an existing church, and other miscellaneous photos were available to the students in the studio through the graphic selection mode. Other applications might include the creation of an abstract memory place that may or may not be associated with the specific place in which the project is located. Personal drawings and images could be linked to objects in three dimensional space in a "memory annex" to the project's physical description and the designer's own mental memory.

Keyword searches of the tables offer another means of selecting images from the collection. Because of the small, specialized nature of this collection, the terminology conventions for labels were kept very simple by identifying the images according to functional types, place names and, possibly, location; these labels were typically assigned to the images by someone other than the users (labels on slide mounts, captions from publications, an editor's judgement). On the other other hand, the notes field was allowed to consist of highly personalized descriptions—based solely on the user's terminology, as though no one else would ever use the collection. Note fields can be edited and amended as the user's understanding of the collection matures.

The browsing function permits the users to rapidly display the images in the sequence in which they were recorded on the disc—visually scanning the collection at speeds up to ten frames per second. Within the browsing mode the user can select an image and view the associated database (labels, notes, text files).

Personalizing the collection is accomplished through a process of progressive elimination and the creation of tables of images created for a specific purpose. By means of a "like/don't like" choice the user can create a temporary subgroup of images under a new name. For example a small subgroup might be started under the name "my plaza" and images selected through a keyword search or browsing the disc might be included. The collection could be added to over time and reviewed at any time by requesting the display of all images in "my plaza". These small sub-collections were meant to be specific and personal and not necessarily shared over the network.

One powerful selection mechanism was the connection of an image to a symbol in the CAD library, which can then be placed in the graphic model. This capability was used as a means to compare the scale and size of well known places to the project site. For example, a user might search the collection with the keywords "urban plaza" and find an image of the Piazza San Marco; selecting the image the CAD system calls up an abstract diagram of the Piazza which the user places in the location for the desired comparison. Both the diagram and the photograph can be viewed at the same time. A future development might include an image collection associated with an extensive knowledge base of architectural and urban elements that could be selected by searching an image database of the objects' form at default parameters.

Summary
As the concept of hypermedia working environments expands to include the discipline of architecture and urban design, quick and easy access to large image collections will become an integral function of the designer's workstation. Linking images to the graphic data permits the working model to become a dynamic 3d menu for organizing information about a project and providing students with a powerful tool for developing their personal image collection—both on the workstation and in their minds.

References

Herbert, Daniel. 1988. "Study Drawings in Architectural Design: Their Properties as a Graphic Medium". *Journal of Architectural Education*. Vol. 41.Number 2. Winter

Moneo, Rafael. 1978. "On Typology." pp. 22-45. *Oppositions 13.*. Published for the Institute for Architectural and Urban Studies. Cambridge: MIT Press.

Rowe, Peter. 1987. *Design Thinking*. Cambridge: MIT Press.

Soergel, Sagobert. 1985. *Organizing Information: Principles of Database and Retrieval Systems*. New York: Academic Press.

19
CALinCAD: Computer-Aided Learning in CAAD

Rob van Zutphen

Department of Architecture and Building Science
Eindhoven University of Technology

Calibre, Eindhoven University of Technology, ABACUS, University of Strathclyde, and LEMA, University of Liege, investigate whether it is possible to teach the architectural design process, using different CAAD techniques in a more integrated way. The research is funded by the EC in the European Comettproject.

The architectural design process is a complex, multidisciplinary process in which we have to deal with the many regulations, standards, and procedures of different participants and companies. There are also constraints in time and costs. This complexity makes teaching CAAD difficult. The design process itself is still not completely understood. Several models of the design process have been developed; most of them, including the "Analysis-Synthesis-Evaluation" model by Maver that we used in our work, are based on or influenced by the model developed by Asimov in his "Introduction to Design."

Partitioning is often used to cope with problems of such large scale. But when we focus the attention of students on one aspect of the design problem at a time, as is done in many schools of architecture and universities, the highly complex, holistic nature of the design seems to get scant attention.

Our aim is to bring the different disciplines together into a workable whole, using the powerful and flexible possibilities of modern computer aids. The first goal will be to develop an open framework with only a few design constraints. Then new parts will be attached, making the model ever more mature and realistic. The openness of the model allows this attachment to be made by people from other departments or other universities and schools of architecture.

CALinCAD Project

CALinCAD stands for Computer-Aided Learning in Computer-Aided Design. It is a computer-aided learning system intended to inform and excite students in schools of architecture and those in architectural practice about computer-aided architectural design. Our philosophy is that the urgent need for education and training in CAAD is best met by deploying it. Our goal is not to write a commercial program but to develop courseware for education and training.

CALinCAD involves integrating CAAD, CAL, and system design and development into one system (figure 1). This demands knowledge not only about CAAD, but also about teaching methods and software engineering. All three universities working on this project have a broad range of experience in using computer technology in the building environment and in architectural design. Contacts with educationalists within Eindhoven University provide the working group with the necessary information in the area of education.

Computer-Aided Learning

Computer systems can serve not only as sophisticated tools in architectural design, but also as powerful learning aids. Some important advantages to using computer systems in education are:

— Students can work at their own pace, selecting their own learning path through the program.
— Computers are good for students' confidence (computers don't laugh when errors are made).
— Computers are time efficient for teachers.
— In general computers offer all the advantages of the individual teaching style.

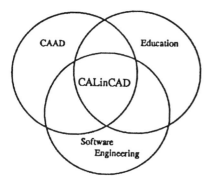

Figure 1 CALinCAD

It is possible in CALinCAD to record the student's actions, resulting in a history of the learning process. This can be used to improve the courseware, to assess the student, or just as a demonstration (playback).

There are five major types of computer-based instruction programs. They are: Tutorials, Drills, Simulations, Games, and Tests

Simulation of the design suited our needs best (figure 2). Simulations typically have three major advantages over the other instruction types: they enhance motivation, have better transfer of learning, and are more efficient.

In general a simulation is a simplified imitation of the real world, in our case the complex design. On a highly interactive base students learn to solve design problems in a integrative way, to make evaluations, and to make appropriate decisions. They learn about architectural procedures, come to understand and to use the characteristic computer aids like drawing, calculating, data-management. The idea is that students are not only highly motivated by simulations, but also learn by interacting with them in a manner similar to the way they would react in real situations.

User Interface

Whether the computer is used as a tool in architectural design or as a tool in teaching, the success or failure of the program depends to a great extent on the design and implementation of the user interface. If, for example, you don't get the attention of the student, he/she will not be motivated, resulting in anineffective education.

Figure 2 Cyclic sequences in simulation

Well- designed screen layouts, fast responses, graphics, and a wide range of help functions are all involved in designing a good user interface. In general there are four major components: the human factor, the task to be performed, the environment, and the machine. Much research is still needed in this area.

Software Engineering

The program CALinCAD as included in this paper is a prototype used to gather information about how students and teachers respond to this way of teaching design. We are using SDM, System Development Method, which has been developed by some large companies and software houses in the Netherlands. SDM describes the process of software development from the first idea through maintenance, dividing it into six phases. They are:

Definition study (GOAL)
Functional specifications (WHAT)
Technical specifications (HOW/WITH)
Implemention
Testing
Distribution and maintenance

At present, the project is at the end of the second phase. We developed a prototype version of the computer program and used it in our curriculum to define the different functional specifications.

SDM has in fact some similarities to the architectural design process, which is not surprising if you look at both processes as being a production line with a final product, e.g. a building or a computer program. Both processes are partitioned to make them controllable and workable. The main difference is the higher level of uncertainty in architectural design.

CAAD

As mentioned above, we used the "Analysis-Synthesis-Evaluation" model as a suitable theoretical base for CAAD. First, a search for information relevant to solve the design problem takes place. Using this information, a design is created. During the evaluation phase the design is tested against the design parameters.

If the design does not fulfill these parameters, the designer must decide whether to accept it or to adjust the parameters.

Each time we go through the phases of analysis, synthesis, and evaluation, the design gets more detailed. The process goes from draft design to preliminary design to final design. As a tool for the designer, CAD techniques can be used in a responsible way only after the design process is very well described in a more formal matter. The decomposition of design can lead to several distinct, defined processes in which the mutual relations and information flows are set. The descriptions of the subprocesses, their relations, and information together comprise a so-called information system.

The Computer Program

To get a clear understanding of the way computer systems can be used to support decision-making in design, we first developed a prototype of the computer program CALinCAD (figure 3). We used this prototype to define the functional specifications of computer- aided learning in CAAD. The prototype has a small database and limited constraints.

The program consists of three modules (figure 4). The most important one is the Design module. In this module the student has to design a single-room school building. There are some design objectives, such as the required floor area, the type of wall elements to use, the building and running costs, the annual energy consumption, and the daylight factor.

The second part is the Application module, which is divided into several submodules that each focus on a particular design objective. Implemented on the PC are the submodules "heat transfer" and "thermal comfort." Other submodules, "layout" and "structure," run on other computer systems.

The third module of the prototype, the Protocol module, ought to give a first introduction to several parts of computer systems and CAD techniques (D for drawing). Lack of time made it necessary to skip most of the planned submodules. Only a small paint package and a part of the visualisation methods have been implemented. We did, however, get the required feedback through the use of other existing software.

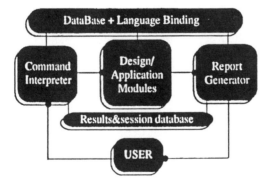

Figure 3 Concept of CALinCAD

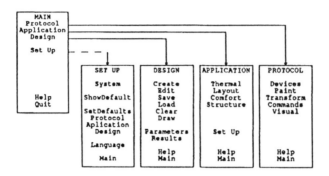

Figure 4 The menu structure

The Design Module

The student first sizes the room and then specifies the four walls (figure 5). He/she can choose from a limited number of prefab elements of different size and type. These are solid elements, window elements, and door elements, each with their specific features such as cost and U-value. There are also a number of general features—such as energy cost per kWh, the interest, and the inside and outside temperatures—stored in the database.

As the design is finished, the computer calculates all the required results for the different targets which are then available for evaluation by the designer (figures 6, 7). Each design target is characterized by its required input data, a calculation method, and the output data. The output data from one process can be the input for one or more other processes. For instance, the area of glass is an input parameter necessary not only for calculation of the daylight factor but also of the cost and the energy needs. Globally this means that when a certain parameter such as the area of glass is changed (figure 8), other results will also change because of the relationship between the different parameters. The CALinCAD program offers the student the possibility of exploring quickly and simply the consequences of the action he or she takes by changing the different parameters. In this way he/she can concentrate on the design while the computer takes care of the calculations. The design process can be seen as a decision- making process in which modern computer techniques can be of great help and support, though the final decision will always be made by the designer.

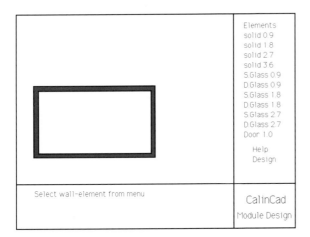

Figure 5 Design of walls, using prefab elements

Energy Consumption	RESULTS
# Transmission	
Northside [KWH]: 2340	Daylight
Eastside [KWH]: 2305	* Energy Cons
Southside [KWH]: 10202	Costs
Westside [KWH]: 3808	Geometry
Floor [KWH]: 2713	
Roof [KWH]: 4521	Resume
# Sunlight	Saveresults
# Annual Heating Energy : 28540	Help
	Design
Select option from menu	CalinCad
	Module Design

Figure 6 Example of calculation results—Energy

*** Costs ***	RESULTS
	Daylight
Foundation [ECU]: 2677	Energy Cons
Floor [ECU]: 5594	# Costs
Wall Elements [ECU]: 10202	Geometry
Roof [ECU]: 7408	
Sunlight [ECU]: 6271	Resume
Finishing [ECU]: 1588	
# Sub Capital Costs	Saveresults
# Other Costs	
# Capital Costs	Help
	Design
Rent & Depreciation	
Select option from menu	CalinCad
	Module Design

Figure 7 Example of calculation results—Costs

The Application Module

The Application module is divided into submodules that give the designer a closer view of the different aspects of building design. Each module deals with a single aspect, giving the student an opportunity to learn interactively the sensitivity for the different parameters involved. For instance, he/she can learn about the heat transmission through a wall element whose construction he/she designed by first defining the number of layers and then selecting from different basic materials such as concrete, bricks, or wood (figure 9).

The computer calculates the amount of energy transmitted through the wall. By changing the thickness of, for instance, the insulation material, the user gets a good feeling for the relations between the energy transmission and the type of material. Other factors that influence the calculation of the heat transfer, such as inside and outside temperature, have a default value that can always be changed. The advantage of using default values is the ability to keep the necessary input for the calculation to a minimum. In this way results for evaluation are quick at hand. The use of default values is used not only in the application modules but throughout the whole program.

Other examples of submodules are: a module for a beam built from different materials, which is tested on its stiffness and strength with different forces, and a module in which we calculate the degree of use of space in, for instance, a bathroom with different sanitary appliances. The placement, size, and number of appliances are chosen by the user. In another submodule students explore the thermal comfort (PMV-Predicted Mean Vote) within a room (Figure 10). The degree of thermal comfort depends on six parameters: the room temperature, the mean radiant temperature, the air velocity, the humidity, the human activity (sitting, walking, learning, etc.), and the clothes the occupants wear. Every parameter can be changed. The mean radiant temperature depends on the construction of the walls. It is important to realize that first- and second-year students do not know each value for the different parameters. As much as possible, we let students enter parameters by name and not by value. For example, the thermal comfort calculation requires the thermal clothing resistance. It must be given in CLO units. The student does not need to know about CLO values, but can just select the menu "clothing" and make a choice from options like "Summer," "Winter," and "Business clothes."

In the Design module we have used the computer system mainly for decision-supported designing, but in the application module the computer gives the students information about the design aspects. The aim is that each design parameter in the Design module can be explained or explored in the Application module.

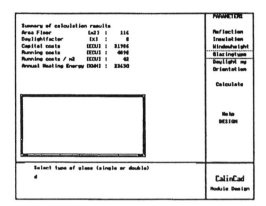

Figure 8   After user changes design parameters, the calculation results are immediately available for evaluation.

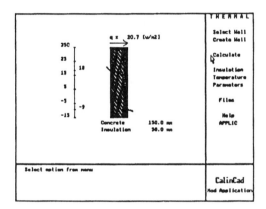

Figure 9   An example of an Application submodule. Here students explore the thermal transmission through a multilayer wall.

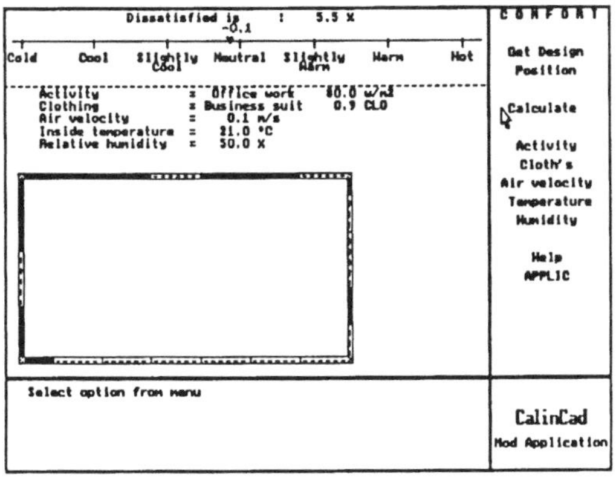

Figure 10 Another example of an Application submodule. Here the calculation of the thermal comfort.

Figure 11   The intelligent teacher?

Future Developments

Students experienced the single-room building in this prototype as one of the greatest limitations of the program. The project team will use a multiroom, single-story building model in the new program. Another limitation was the constrained set of wall elements. In the future there will be not only prefab construction elements but also other common construction methods for walls as well as for the roof and foundation. There will also be more design targets and parameters, but the team has not yet decided what these will be.

These changes are intended to make the model of the building more realistic. Our aim is to use the computer more and more as an intelligent design assistant and perhaps in the (far?) future as a more intelligent teacher (figure 11).

All the design objectives in the present prototype were of a quantitative nature, which is why the implementation has been done with a third-generation computer language (Pascal) using an algorithmic approach. In reality, however, architectural design involves many qualitative aspects which need a more heuristic approach. Decisions will then be based not only on numbers but also on rules.

The heuristic techniques can also be used for computerized evaluation methods, making it possible, for example, to compare an old design with a new one. The first step toward an intelligant assistant would be to leave the computer to do a first evaluation and let it make a suggestion for improving the design. Thinking of today's chess computers will give you an idea of what we have in mind.

Although the project team is still in the second phase (SDM), research has already been done about how to program the new functional specifications. Object-oriented programming seems to be very promising (SmallTalk or C++). We are also looking at the possibility of using existing software like Autocad in a multitasking environment (SUN 386i).

20
Hypertext: A Computer Tool to Assist Building Design

Dana J. Vanier

Institute for Research in Construction
National Research Council of Canada

This paper shows how hypertext, an electronic information transfer medium, can assist accessing the large volumes of architectural and engineering technical information needed in decision-making phase of building design. A technical paper on architectural details serves as a model for demonstrating the capabilities of hypertext. This example consists mostly of graphics and illustrates how the hypertext medium could act as an information source for designers in the construction industry. The objectives of the paper are to illustrate the potential of hypertext to create, disseminate, and access technical information, and to identify an electronic format for construction industry technical publications. The paper identifies the capabilities of the medium, some advantages and disadvantages of hypertext, and the potential of the medium for construction information transfer. The author suggests that hypertext systems can assist technical information transfer in the construction industry.

Introduction

The quality of decision-making in architectural and engineering design has a major effect on the performance and cost of buildings [MacKinder]. Generally, early design-decisions have the greatest effect on the direction of the design and the cost of construction and are often made with the least amount of supporting technical information [Brewer]. Despite the fact there is more than adequate information available to make sound decisions [MacKinder], that information is under-utilized. This may be due to the time constraints in the design phase, to an intuitive rather than a scientific approach to problem-solving, or to the lack of access to a proper technical library. Elaborate construction information archival and retrieval systems [Giertz 81] [Giertz 82] [Ray-Jones] and computer systems [Holmes] [ITEC] have been developed to assist designers, but still the first, and sometimes only, readily-available sources for technical information are professional colleagues and manufacturers' literature [MacKinder] [Brewer].

Computer tools are currently available to assist the dissemination of technical information to designers. Computer-aided design drafting (CADD) systems, spreadsheets, word processors, and databases, have all altered the way the construction industry uses technical data. As computer technologies mature other tools are becoming readily available. Hypertext[1] is a provocative electronic tool for developing information bases[2] and for quickly searching and retrieving data. It employs micro-computers, high resolution graphics, database technology, and fast-access text searches. It is a medium that can be summarized as a non-sequential retrieval system that permits rapid access to large amounts of textual and complex graphical information.

This paper shows how hypertext can be used to gain access to architectural and engineering technical information in the decision-making phases of building design. It describes using hypertext as a medium to assist in the design of external walls, windows and roofs. The information base was developed from an illustrated, technical text on *Architectural Details for a Cold Climate* [Brand]. With this tool there is also the possibility of integrating any number of associated texts, such as *Canadian Building Digests*, *National Building Code*, and *Canadian Building Abstracts*, into a cohesive construction information source. The use of the proposed integrated information is not restricted to building designers, but would be invaluable in the educational sector and to building occupants.

There are over 100 cards in the existing information base. The ADCC HyperCard stack is available from the author[3].

Objective

The objective of this paper is to illustrate the potential of hypertext to create, store, and retrieve technical information for the construction industry. I will attempt to outline a tool for technical information transfer for the construction industry. I will also suggest formats for technical information transfer, illustrate capabilities of the hypertext medium, and discuss interesting and helpful user interface designs, and identify the advantages and disadvantages of hypertext. The paper will also illustrate the advantages of this tool for the teaching sector.

Architectural Details for a Cold Climate (ADCC), will be used to demonstrate hypertext. This text was selected because it epitomizes technical information needs of the construction industry. These are 'high resolution' graphics, strong relationships between graphics and text, a comprehensive database structure, references to associated technical information, and modification or expansion on a continuing basis.

Brand provides architectural detailing for building enclosure design and construction. In the present form the publication consists of more than 200 drawings, heavily cross-referred by Brand to other chapters, sections, and other publications. Brand believes that if designers are provided with technically correct details and they modify these to specific location requirements, they will not need to develop these from first principles for every task. The goal of the project was to automate the existing traditional publication maintaining all of the manual features and augmenting these with the capabilities of hypertext.

Hypertext Background

Before describing the application, it is necessary to summarize the evolution of hypertext. It evolved from work initiated by Doug Englebart [Englebart] and Ted Nelson [Nelson] in the 1960's to address the needs for rapid text searching[4]. Hypertext systems were available as early as the late 1960's [Conklin] and these have evolved into today's commercial systems. Dr Peter J. Brown's [Brown] work at the University of Kent led to the development of Owl Guide [Owl] on the IBM PC and Apple Macintosh, Bill Atkinson's work led to HyperCard on the Apple Macintosh, and research and development of ZOG led to the marketing of KMS [Akscyn] on a wide variety of machines. There are similar products on other computer systems, such as Business FileVision on the Macintosh, Document Examiner on the Symbolics Lisp machine, and KnowledgePro on the IBM PC [Byte]. This is not an exhaustive list but it does indicate that the technology is available for a variety of machines. Numerous demonstration prototypes are in existence, including Notecards from Xerox PARC [Halasz], Hyperties from University of Maryland [Marchionini], Intermedia from Brown University [Yankelovich], and ZOG from Carnegie-Mellon University [Akscyn].

Hypertext has become a 'hot' topic in the last year due primarily to Apple's release of HyperCard [Smith] [Goodman], to the proliferation of powerful micro-computers, to the user-friendliness of the interface [Marchionini] and to the availability of large, fast storage devices. The main targets of the developers of hypertext systems are producers and distributors of large volumes of information. Their product target is oriented towards the $5 \, 1/4$" CD ROM (Compact Disk—Read Only Memory) holding over 500 megabytes of read-only data. This is equivalent to approximately 250,000 pages of encoded text, 5,000 pages of facsimile information, or 2,000 video images[5].

Although commercial hypertext products are relatively new, the technology could revolutionize the way we handle textual and graphical information. This revolution could be similar to the way spreadsheets altered numerical calculation: Large, complex and unmanageable batch programs running on mainframes were replaced with personalized software available on inexpensive desktop machines. "Hypertext systems will change the way people read and write" [Marchionini].

Hypertext Description

Hypertext can be many things to information suppliers and users. For the hypertext user (normally an information seeker) it can offer rapid access, user-friendly information retrieval. For the hypertext author (in this case the technology expert developing an information base) it is a complete environment for creating, linking, storing, and retrieving information. The major feature of the medium is that information access is not sequential: the possible information routes are pre-determined by the hypertext author, and the hypertext user does not have to follow a specific routing to search information. Not unlike the print medium, the user can peruse the information in any way desired—following the text sequentially to maintain continuity or searching randomly[6] to pick up key words, phrases, or graphics.

The visual presentation of hypertext systems and applications is a straightforward point-and-click interface. Hypertext applications depend heavily on both the implementation of the technology by the hypertext systems designers and the application design by the hypertext author. As an example, HyperCard is heavily graphical, user-friendly, and card-based, but other hypertext systems may possess these and other features. Some applications may resemble word processors, others may mimic databases, and some will imitate flash cards, but generally all hypertext systems contain the following characteristics [Akscyn] [Conklin] [Marchionini]:

- Small chunks of self-sufficient information (nodes)
- Relationships between associated nodes (links)
- Quick traversing of networks of nodes (hyper)
- Direct manipulation interface (buttons)
- Conceptual data model representing user's mental model of information

In summary, hypertext should augment rather than replace traditional retrieval systems, and should be viewed as an electronic source for the same printed word. The application for ADCC was implemented on an Apple Macintosh, but could have been developed on a number of other machines or software. In describing this application, I will remain generic in the description of the capabilities of hypertext.

The basic information packet in hypertext (see figure 1) is a 'node'. It may be called a card, frame, or record in other systems. 'Contexts' are analogous to files or 'stacks' of related cards or records. Access to additional or related

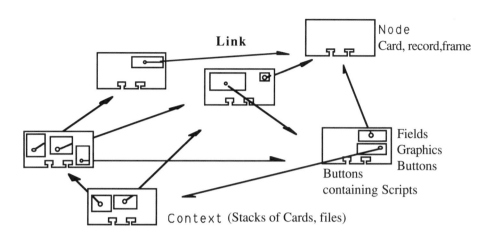

Figure 1   Hypertext concept

information is made by 'Links' to other nodes. The basic components of a node are fields, graphics, and buttons. The fields are conventional data fields that are created and normally filled by the author. The data can be augmented by the user or can be browsed by the user by searching key words in all or specific fields on a card. The graphics are bitmap[7] or object[8] drawings done in the hypertext application or imported from other packages. Once the graphics are imported into HyperCard they remain in bitmap format; however, other hypertext systems permit importing both paint and object drawings (Eg. Owl Guide). A button is designed to look like a push button or can be a designated transparent area, depicted as dashed boxes in figure 2. Buttons are graphical areas on a node that initiate actions such as pointing to another file or location; popping up an interactive message on the computer screen; opening another file; or returning the user to a specific location. Most of the features mentioned above are available on all hypertext systems.

HyperCard Authoring
The hypertext author does not need to be a computer programmer as most hypertext software tools can easily be learned in a few hours and mastered in days. The software tools available for hypertext application design consist of fields, graphics[9], and buttons mentioned above (see figure 2), as well as a scripting language. In HyperCard each field, card, stack, or button can contain a unique 'script' which will initiate an action; this is analogous to the action or method[10] of an object in object-oriented programming [Goodman]. These scripts utilize a full computer programming language that permits both the hypertext author and user to customize the application to meet their specific needs. The object-oriented language in HyperCard is an English-like programming

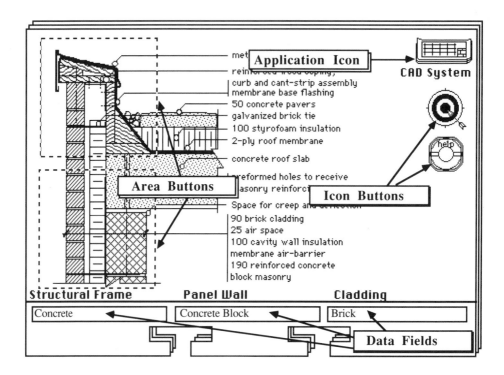

Figure 2 Detail card

environment of over 200 functions, commands, control structures, properties, constants, operators, and control structures [Gewirtz] such as: *if...then...else*, *deleteCard*, *mouseDown*, *messageBox*, *dial*[modem], *find*, *play*[notes], and *write*. Most hypertext systems also have this type of high level programming language that is accessible to hypertext authors and users.

The node presented to the user consists of layered graphics and data. The author can create a background and foreground overlay for the cards, and can overlay the fields, graphics, or buttons in any order. The hypertext author can reduce the data entry time and create a standard user interface by creating standard backgrounds. In figure 2 the entire image, with the exception of the construction detail, is a background template. Most hypertext systems have an equivalent feature for designing standard templates.

Cards in the HyperCard system are designed and entered by the hypertext author in any order and the relationships of cards and buttons can be established at any time. Cards that are closely related can be placed in the same stack by the author to consolidate and simplify access to that information. It must be stressed, however that an overall system design is necessary before any hypertext application is started [Marchionini] [Yankelovich].

Data Modeling - Architectural Details for a Cold Climate

The text and graphics of ADCC is a compendium of building science knowledge for architects, design technologists, technicians, and drafters. It is not the intention of this paper to present a comprehensive view of detailing and enclosure design; but rather to demonstrate the possibilities of the hypertext medium using a well-defined information source and its inter-connection to other technical documents. The information presented in this paper will be a representative sample of this work and will address the full depth of the information base for a limited number of details.

The final data concept is illustrated in figure 3. It was modelled in consultation with Brand, to satisfy the following requirements:

- The computer graphics must be an accurate representation of the details
- Access to CADD drawings must be possible to permit user modification
- References to other sections must be inherent in the system
- References to other publications must be possible
- Key word index and lexicon of technical terms must be available
- The information base must permit modification and addition by the user
- The completed package must run on an inexpensive computer

The ADCC information base is divided into three major components (Detail Cards, Graphics Cards, and Building Science Cards) and three related information stacks (CADD Drawings, Lexicon, and Technical Papers).

Detail Cards

The Detail Card shown earlier in figure 2 presents an overall view of the architectural detail and shows the juxtaposition and dimensions of the assembly components. However, the graphical resolution of the overall Detail

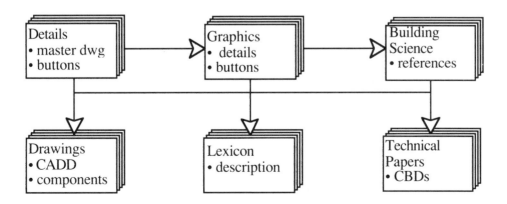

Figure 3   System model

Card is insufficient to view the finer construction detail. As in to most CADD systems, a zoom or 'blow-up' function is available via transparent buttons on the card. This zoom points to a Graphics Card containing a more detailed view of the drawing. The user can quickly move between these different scale drawings to view either the overall context or the detail.

The original CADD detail can also be accessed via a button in the top right corner of the Detail Card. The drawings for the computerized *Architectural Details for a Cold Climate* were first drawn using a CADD package and were then moved to the hypertext system. The patterns and hatching were entered in HyperCard, but could have been entered in any paint application. Other hypertext systems can display both bitmap and object drawings but may not support the editing of these images within the hypertext system.

Graphics Cards
The Graphics Card in figure 4 is an accurate architectural representation of the detail. The importance of the drawing resolution cannot be over-emphasized as design decisions have to be made based on the accuracy and the resolution of the drawing at hand. This means that the designer must be able to discern the extent of building components, follow them continuously on the drawing, and detect the topology of the components. Transparent buttons (depicted as dashed lines in figure 4) superimposed on building components and the corresponding component names are linked to Building Science Cards.

Building Science Cards
The Building Science Cards are an electronic version of the Brand layout where a text description refers to a specific area or component, identifies potential construction problems, provides building science knowledge, or suggests additional sources of information. In the HyperCard version, the Building Science Card displays an isolated view of the component(s) and has scrolling text to provide the additional information (See figure 5).

CADD Drawings
A mandatory requirement of the hypertext ADCC is to provide access to drawings that can be edited by the user. This is accomplished in HyperCard by launching a CADD application containing a pointer to the appropriate detail. The CADD representations of details are stored as PICT format files on the Macintosh, or an IBM hypertext implementation the drawings could store the detail in AUTOCAD. These are all well-known *de facto* drawing standards for microcomputers. The CADD drawings for a specific detail are accessed by clicking the CADD button in the upper right corner of the Detail Card shown in figure 2. This will immediately launch a CADD application package with

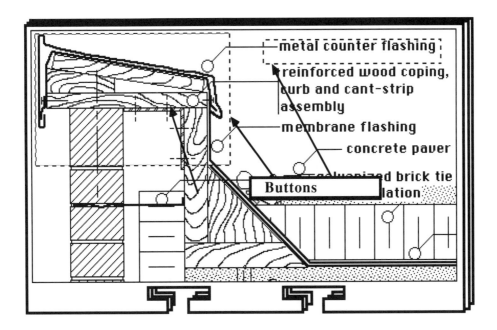

Figure 4   Graphics card

that architectural detail and permit the user to view, modify, and save the detail to meet specific requirements. The user will be returned immediately to the same Detail Card on quitting the application.

Related Technical Information
Graphics and text from any number of publications can be accessed to provide backup information to the user. This can be available in other sections or cards of the existing stack or in related stacks such as the *National Building Code*, *Canadian Building Digests*, and *Canadian Building Abstracts*. The purpose of this feature is to provide a wide and deep information base ranging from *National Building Code* articles to source documents from building science research. A feature of the design is that the user is automatically returned to the exact location of departure from the original stack.

Lexicon Stack
The Lexicon cards permit the user to seek information on terminology without leaving hypertext. This can be viewed as comprehensive HELP function for construction terms. This is also an auto-returning stack.

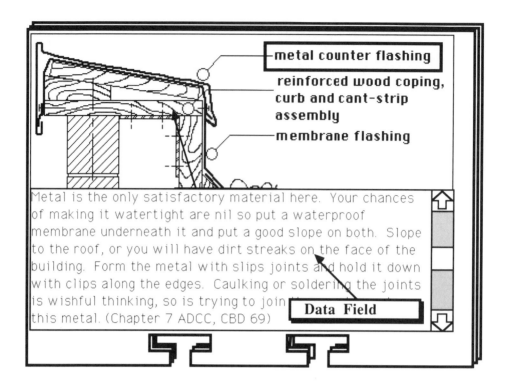

Figure 5 - Building science card

Additional Features:

A 'saver' stack is incorporated to save selected cards for later referral. This eliminates the need to search for a specific detail viewed earlier and allows the user to print the entire 'saver' stack when desired.

Pros and Cons of Hypertext for Information Transfer

The pros and cons of hypertext for specific applications [Akscyn] or for generic application [Halasz] are given in related papers on the topic. The list below is directly related to the requirements for technical information transfer for the construction industry.

Fast Access

Hypertext provides fast access, search and retrieval capabilities for a wide variety of textual and graphical information sources. Rough benchmarks in HyperCard for specific key word searches indicate the possibility of finding a single word among 20 000 words (20 K document) in 2 seconds[11]. Hypertext systems designers strive to reduce the time to find and display random frames to below 0.5 seconds and some systems are able to access frames in 0.25 seconds [Akscyn]. Because the key word search time for hypertext systems is dependent on the implementation of the search algorithm and the variety of words, hypertext systems cannot be directly compared to conventional word processing text searches. Every word in a hypertext application is indexed, thereby providing near-instantaneous search and find. Because they are indexed, if specific words do not exist in the text the user is immediately notified and a 'search and find' is averted.

User Interface Design
As mentioned earlier, principal components of the hypertext system are the direct manipulation interface and the conceptual data model representing the user's mental model of information. Studies have shown that point-and-click operations (i.e. direct manipulation) speed up user interaction by 50 % over typical pull-down menus [Akscyn]. These types of interface provide a fast access, user-friendly environment that enhances information browsing for both the occasional and the 'heavy' user.

Quick Prototypes
The inherent flexibility of most hypertext systems permits quick alteration of the data structure and the user interface. This provides an excellent tool for prototyping data models and a quick, easy-to-learn database for developer/users of small personalized systems.

Popular Technology
Interest in most hypertext systems has increased drastically over the past years. The number of technical papers on hypertext systems has increased substantially and most computer magazines have published special issues devoted to hypertext. All major Macintosh journals now feature sections on HyperCard; stacks are exchanged in clubs, universities, and companies; and numerous companies are selling HyperCard development expertise. This all indicates that software systems will continue to improve and costs for software and related hardware will decrease.

Graphic and text data
The construction industry relies on graphical information to explain which components are to be used and how construction components are assembled. Hypertext answers these needs for graphical representation, as well as the need for showing the graphics in conjunction with text. Methods should be developed to provide designers with the ability to search occurrences of words or components (i.e. find insulation) in text on drawings. Object drawings in place of bitmap pictures in the hypertext system would make this possible, as the text on the graphic would be identified as such and the location could easily be found.

Graphical Context
Current high resolution screens provide acceptable resolution for displaying conventional graphics but are restricted because of the finite number of addressable pixels, normally around 512 by 512. In ADCC the restricting resolution was circumvented by providing similar views of the details at differing scales and permitting the user to move back and forth between the desired views. This is a deficiency of the medium, viewing tools are needed to enable users to infinitely zoom and pan around a drawing. The use of object drawings in the hypertext systems would make this readily available.

HyperCAD
The concept of hypertext combined with computer-aided design was hinted in a paper entitled "Neptune: a Hypertext System for CAD Applications" [Delisle], but unfortunately the paper did not delve into the possibility of hypertext addressing the needs of integrated computer-aided design [Vanier]. Hypertext's frame-based data structure, user-friendly access, robust user interface, and rapid network traversing could prove to be a radical, useful tool addressing many integrated computer-aided design requirements.

Controlled Vocabulary
Full text searches provide an easy-to-implement data structure [Halasz]; however, the need for key words and indices still exists. Without a controlled vocabulary for information search, the users are randomly trying for 'word hits' based on their knowledge of the field and of the information base [Marchionini]. This works well for small information bases, stacks with non-similar terms, or for technologies with well-defined vocabulary; however this is not the case in construction. To illustrate the complexity of the construction vocabulary, one only has to look at the extent and depth of the *Canadian Thesaurus of Construction Science and Technology* [Thesaurus] and imagine a user looking for general information on paints in gigabytes of construction data. The implementation of a vocabulary or thesaurus in conjunction with large information bases is therefore mandatory for construction hypertext systems. This would focus word searches, decrease search time, reduce successive 'hits' of similar, but unrelated, terms, and reduce user frustration.

Easy Implementation
Existing manuals can be documented on hypertext systems with relative ease as most books already contain the structure and layout required for proper hypertext implementation. The sections, paragraphs, and chapters provide the fundamental layout; graphics and photos are related to specific locations in

the text, and references and footnotes are already established. Already many of these publications are in electronic form.

Integrated Construction Information
The construction industry has primary information sources: design handbooks, master specifications, national standards, and other technical publications and guidelines from government offices. Secondary sources include engineering and architectural graphs and tables, manufacturers' technical information (i.e. windows, doors), and trade journals. These could all form part of an overall construction information source. Project information (i.e. contract documents, maintenance records, and even contract drawings) could be included in the hypertext system and would be useful to designers. Access to the information base could be guided by thesauri or controlled vocabularies. These could all be separate stacks in an integrated construction information base. A suggested layout for a large construction information base is shown as figure 6. Multimedia information is now a technical possibility—with computer graphics, video, and text all forming part of the entire information base. Because of the storage capacities of CD ROMs, this information is readily accessible by the user.

Multi-Media Information
A multi-media information base could include all forms of data, including text, graphics, facsimile data, animation, and voice. The development of large integrated information sources will necessitate standards for the presentation and dissemination of data. Although researchers have identified the need for standards [van Dam] [Halasz], the only standard is that there is no standard.

Hypertext as a Teaching Aid
Research [Marchionini] has indicated that the users of hypertext information bases are more likely to browse wider selections of information than users of conventional paper documents. It also indicated that in some cases that information was better understood and better retained by the users. In addition, hypertext systems would be a boon to the educational sector because the information could be more current, would be properly cross-referred, and is less susceptible to theft than paper documents.

Lost in Hyperspace
A problem identified by many [Akscyn] [Smith] [van Dam] is getting lost in a large information base. Lost in hyperspace involves not knowing where one is, not knowing how much information is available, not knowing when to stop

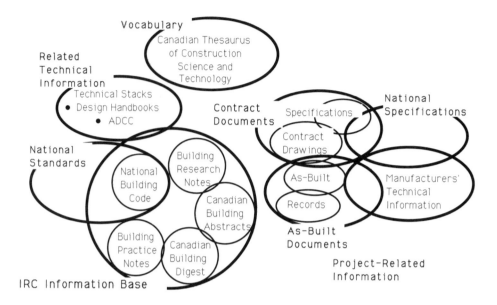

Figure 6   Integrated construction information source

looking for new leads, and not knowing when all possible leads are exhausted.
This problem can be reduced in scope with the use of a strong data structure for
the information and the use of global maps [Conklin].

CD ROM Technology
As CD ROM readers become more popular (prices are below $ 1000 CDN at this
time), users will standardize on this technology for information storage and
retrieval. Read/Write disks are rumoured to be only two years away from
commercialization. The CD ROM technology has numerous advantages over
both traditional publication methods [Hartley] and other computer
technologies (remote data services, magnetic media, etc.) including:
* Low mastering and copying costs as compared to traditional publications
* Information is protected and access can be controlled by distributor
* Compact disks are robust and can withstand physical abuse (Eg mailing)
* Standard interfaces for data retrieval can be provided to users
* User has control over all parts of the workstation and information base
* Multiple CD ROM disks can be stacked for gigabytes of on-line storage
* Stacks can be updated regularly on CD and addenda updated on magnetic
  media when required

Maintaining Information
The introduction of new technologies, such as hypertext, requires a re-thinking
of how information flows, to whom, and when. Updates by the supplier and
modification by the user are areas that need to be investigated. Supplier

updates could be issued as new stacks (on compact disks preferably) and supplemental information on magnetic medium could automatically augment or supersede the original data. However, if the original information base has been updated by the users to reflect their specific requirements, then that additional information would have to be transferred to the new supplier edition. This may prove to be a large task for the information supplier and user. It could also be accomplished in an automated fashion similar to the existing manual method: check your old *National Building Code* and transcribe your handwritten notes to the newest edition.

Many of the problems listed have been identified by hypertext researchers [Halasz] [Akscyn] [Marchionini] [van Dam] [Delisle]. They feel that advances in the technology and a clearer understanding of the user needs will eliminate a large portion of the current hypertext limitations [Smith]. Problems identified in these and related texts, including problems of concurrent access of frames by multiple users [Halasz], static links in a dynamic environment [Halasz], identification of the proper node size for specific application [Marchionini], and intuitive versus cognitive-intensive systems [Conklin], are exciting research questions, but unfortunately are all still unresolved.

Conclusions

The prototype for *Architectural Details for a Cold Climate* demonstrates that the medium addresses a large portion of the needs of the construction industry for electronic technical information transfer. Hypertext technology can help building designers access the large volumes of architectural and engineering technical information needed in decision-making phases of building design. An integrated construction information source could provide a solid knowledge base for educators, students and design professionals that could be easily updated and quickly browsed. The robustness of the hypertext medium permits even novice computer users to add to existing information bases and to create and prototype applications quickly and efficiently. There are still numerous disadvantages of the hypertext technology, but many of these will be corrected as hypertext developers become more familiar with user needs, as user interfaces become more refined, and as the cost to store large information bases is reduced.

Hypertext technology is a new tool for developers and users of information in the construction industry. It can be the medium for an integrated information source by providing a robust, powerful user environment on a micro-computer workstation.

References

[Akscyn]   Robert M. Akscyn, Donald L. McCracken and Elise A. Yoder. "KMS: a Distributed Hypermedia System for Managing Knowledge in Organizations". *Communications of the ACM*. Vol 31. No. 7.

[Brand]   RG. Brand. 1987. Architectural Details for a Cold Climate. Doctoral Thesis. Université de Montréal. to be published by Van Nostrand Reinhold.

[Brewer]   Ron Brewer and Chris Snow. 1988."Technical Publications: The Design Professionals' Response". *Building Research and Practice*. Vol. 21 No. 1.

[Brown]   P.J. Brown. 1986. "Interactive Documentation ". *Software - Practice and Experience*. Vol. 16(3) March.

[Byte]   October 1988. "Hyper Activity ". *Byte Magazine*.

[Conklin]   E. Jeffrey Conklin. 1987. "Hypertext: An Introduction and Survey ". *IEEE Journal Computer*. September.

[Englebart]   Doug Englebart. 1963. "A Conceptual Framework for Augmentation of Man's Intellect". *Vistas in Information Handling* Vol I. Sparta Books. Washington. D.C.

[Delisle]   Norman Delisle and Mayer Swartz. 1986. "Neptune: a Hypertext System for CAD Applications". *Proceedings of the ACM SIGMOD '86*. Washington D.C.

[Gewirtz]   Davis Allen Gewirtz. 1988. *Hypertalk and the External Commands*. Foster City. CA: Hyperpress Publishing.

[Giertz 81]   Lassé M. Giertz and Nöel J. Hughes. 1981. *Abridged Building Classification (ABC)*. Dublin: An Foras Forbartha. St. Martin's House.

[Giertz 82]   Lassé M. Giertz. 1982. *SfB and its Development*. Dublin: An Foras Forbartha. St. Martin's House.

[Goodman]   Danny Goodman. 1987. *The Complete HyperCard Handbook*. New York: Bantam Books.

[Halasz]   Frank G. Halasz. "Reflections on Notecards: Seven Issues for the Next Generation of Hypermedia Systems". *Communications of the ACM*. Vol. 31. No. 7

[Hartley]   Jill Hartley, Amanda Noonan and Stan Metcalfe. 1987. *New Electronic Information Services*. Aldershot. U.K. : Gower Publishing Company Ltd..

[Holmes 70]   B.W. Holmes. 1970. *BEAM Program - Construction Information System*. Department of Industry. Trade and Commerce Canada. Ottawa. Internal Report

[ITEC]   1987. Intitut de Technologia de la Construccio de Catalunya. "Structured Data–bank of Constructive Elements". *Proceedings of ARECDAO'87*. Barcelona.

[MacKinder]   Margaret MacKinder and Heather Marvin. 1982. *Decision making in Architectural Practice*. Institute of Advanced Architectural Studies. York University (UK).

[Marchionini]   Gary Marchionini and Ben Shneiderman. 1988. "Finding Facts vs. Browsing Knowledge in Hypertext Systems". *IEE Journal Computer*.

[Nelson]   Theodor H Nelson. *Literary Machines*. 5th ed. Swarthmore. Pa.

[Owl]   *Owl Guide User's Manual.* Owl International. Seattle. WA

[Ray-Jones]   Alan Ray-Jones. 1976. *Construction Indexing Manual.* London: RIBA Publications Ltd.

[Schmucker]   Kurt A. Schmucker. 1986. *Object-Oriented Programming for the Macintosh.* New Jersey: Hayden Book Company.

[Smith]   . John B. Smith. Weiss. Stephen F. "Hypertext". *Communications of the ACM.* Vol.31 No. 7.

[Thesaurus]   *Canadian Thesaurus of Construction Science and Technology.* Ottawa: Industry Trade and Commerce Canada.

[van Dam]   Andries van Dam. "Hypertext '87 Keynote Address". *Communications of the ACM.* Vol. 31(7)

[Vanier]   Dana J. Vanier and Murray W. Grabinsky. 1987. "Integrated Computer-Aided Building Design Systemss". *Proceedings of ARECDAO'87.* Barcelona.

[Yankelovich]   Nicole Yankelovich and Norman Meyrowitz and Andries van Dam. 1985. "Reading and Writing the Electronic Books". *IEEE Journal Computer.* October.

Notes

1   The term 'hypertext' will be used to denote the generic technology, 'hypertext application' to mean a specific application, 'hypertext author' to mean the designer of the hypertext application, and 'hypertext user' to mean the application end-user.

2' Database' will be used throughout the text to mean a database shell or a container for data.   The term 'information base' is used to denote a database containing information and the required links between information packets.

3   A sample stack is available for development review. Please provide an initialized 800k Macintosh diskette.

4   An excellent introduction and survey of hypertext systems is included in [Conklin].

5   These figures are based on 2000 characters or bytes per page of text, 300 dots per inch for a facsimile document, and 8-bits of colour on a 500 vertical by 460 horizontal video image.

6   'Browsing' in hypertext jargon

7   Bitmap or paint drawings are a representation of graphical data using computer screen picture elements (pixels), normally monochromatic, to designate shape and shading. For Hypercard on the Macintosh the resolution is 72 pixels per inch and it does not currently support colour or shades of gray.

8   Object drawing implies "object-oriented graphics" meaning the representation of information as the combination of both data and procedure. Objects not only know what they are but also how they should act under certain conditions. Examples of objects include: polygon, circle, rectangle, and text and examples of procedures are stretch object, move vertex, and centre text.

9   Figures 2, 4, and 5 are printed output from HyperCard and all these figures appear on the screen in the same scale and at the same resolution as shown.

10   Message passing is a feature of object-orient programming that initiates a method (a specific sequence of actions) for a class of objects. The object then produces the desired results.

11   This varies for different text files (even in one hypertext system) depending on the similarity of words in the text index.

Case Studies:
Electronic Media in the Design Studio

21
Computational Design Instruction: Toward a Pedagogy

Ömer Akin

Department of Architecture
Carnegie-Mellon University

The computer offers enormous potential both in and out of the classroom that is realized only in limited ways through the applications available to us today. In the early days of the computer it was generally argued that it would replace the architect. When this idea became obsolete, the prevailing opinion of proponents and opponents alike shifted to the notion of the computer as merely adding to present design capabilities. This idea is so ingrained in our thinking that we still speak of "aiding" design with computers. It is clear to those who grasp the real potential of this still new technology—as in the case of many other major technological innovations—that it continues to change the way we design, rather than to merely augment or replace human designers.

In the classroom the computer has the potential to radically change three fundamental ingredients: student, instruction, and instructor. It is obvious that changes of this kind spell out a commensurate change in design pedagogy. If the computer is going to be more than a passive instrument in the design studio, then design pedagogy will have to be changed, fundamentally. While the practice of computing in the studio continues to be a significant [1] aspect of architectural education, articulation of viable pedagogy for use in the design studio is truly rare.

In this paper the question of pedagogy in the CAD studio will be considered first. Then one particular design studio taught during Fall 1988 at Carnegie-Mellon University will be presented. Finally, we shall return to issues of change in the student, instruction, and instructor, as highlighted by this particular experience.

Paradigms for Computational Design Pedagogy

Representation-based Paradigms

Perhaps the clearest and earliest statement of pedagogic intent in this area can be found in William Mitchell's write-up in *Pioneers of CAD* (Mitchell, 1985). He advocates "awakening students to the insights that they can get by formulating design issues in computational terms" in lieu of learning the "details of associated computer technologies." His pedagogy goes beyond the generality of this statement and argues for a specific approach to computational design. In this approach, students start by understanding the basic notions of computing, algorithms, and data structures. Then they learn, through the use of these, to generate the "primitives" of a language of graphics—points, lines, two-dimensional compositions—which correspond in some form to architectonic elements we use as designers. Next, students are introduced to elements of composition, proportion, repetition, rhythm, and geometric transformations. Each of these concepts of design correspond to equally basic functionalities in computation, such as mathematical expressions, loops, conditionals, and recursion. Mitchell goes on to show how other more complex issues—three-dimensional design, colors, textures—can be introduced using the same principle.

The basis of this pedagogy is the existing isomorphisms between representations we use in architecture and constructs used in computing. Mitchell's pedagogy capitalizes on this isomorphism, reinforcing, even justifying, the legitimacy of these constructs and representations by showing their mutual agreement.

Design Product-based Paradigms

Another category of approaches to pedagogy in the CAD studio is offered by Flemming and Schmitt (1986). Schmitt bases his pedagogy on the principle of complementing students' evaluative abilities by providing a "work bench" of analysis tools, such as cost, heating load, cooling load, electrical load, structural feasibility, circulation efficiency, visual comfort, and contextual responsiveness. This allows students to objectively evaluate their designs once they are generated, by necessity on the computer, so that these tools can be applied to them. It is the computational power of the medium in analyzing properties of the designed object that gives rise to the pedagogic content of the studio.

Flemming's approach to CAD is generative rather than evaluative. He uses the parametric manipulation of basic architectonic elements—walls, openings, etc.—to mimic different architectural "languages"—elementary wall architecture, mass architecture, layered transparent architecture, and structure/infill architecture (Flemming, 1989). Starting from a theoretical understanding of the syntax of these languages, Flemming builds a link to computational capabilities in the computer, which in turn enables the student to explore systematically, and with relative ease and precision, the design instances in a given language category. Here, as in Schmitt's approach, the computational advantages of the medium are used to understand design in terms of the designed object.

Design Process-based Paradigms

The studio that I offer presents yet another paradigm for computational design instruction. Mitchell's approach outlines the way in which instruction stems from basic compositions or designs that in their making correspond to computational functions. Flemming's and Schmitt's approaches show how qualities of the object being produced form the basis of computational strategies. Here the aim is to consider the qualities of the design process and how the computer can be used to improve it.

An important premise of this approach is that several attributes of the traditional design studio which arise from manual forms of representation cannot be supported by the computer. More specifically, the computational medium, unlike its manual counterpart, imposes no hierarchy of representations based on scale; is not bounded by representational conventions to any particular hierarchy of issues; requires considerable front-end input time before a critical mass of information, sufficient for design, is accumulated; and does not particularly support, in the levels of precision in representing objects, a top-down, hierarchical design strategy. (But see Mitchell, Liggett, and Tan 1989).

In the traditional design studio the process adopted is a top-down hierarchical one, defined by conventions of practice and by drawing (Ledewitz, 1985). The design development process and most design pedagogies advocate that design start with a concept of the whole and then progress toward greater detail through the formalized steps of preliminary design, design development, and working drawings. The central difficulty with this approach as a pedagogic tool is that while experienced designers are cognizant of the requirements of each phase of the design delivery process and thus can anticipate the "precautions" that need to be taken during early phases on behalf of issues that will come up during later phases (proactive design), students are usually unaware of such dependencies between design and do not know how to anticipate them (reactive design) (Akin, 1986). Consequently, students are given unnecessary opportunity to fail and to use time ineffectively.

A related but different difficulty arises from the continuity in the sizes of objects and scales of representations in the computer as opposed to those of manual drawings. Most design delivery practices are codified in the conventions of particular drawing scales: engineering scales for the site, 32nd or 16th scale for preliminary design, 8th scale for design development, 8th scale and up for working drawings, and so on [2]. Furthermore, specific decisions are considered only in certain drawings—exterior appearance in elevations, riser tread relations in sections, and so on—and there are generally understood dependencies between decisions taken while considering different drawings— proportions of volumes relating sections and plan, and so on. On the other hand, sizes and scales of objects in the computer are continuous. While this permits the mimicking of the manual mode—i.e., fixing the scales in a computer application to correspond to those of the manual domain—it also permits the consideration of scaleless, or at best ambiguously scaled, objects. The distinctions established through the conventions of different manual representations get blurred in the computer. All decisions without any obvious hierarchic order can be considered on the nondiscriminating medium of the computer screen.

In approaching this studio, I considered the discrepencies between the manual and computational design modes a central pedagogic issue. The studio was structured through a series of sketch problems explicitly specifying the order and content of partial solutions to be generated. Students were allowed to use solutions generated for earlier sketch problems, but were restricted each time to certain patches of site—specified by a given, actual size—and a fixed set of design issues. During the second half of the studio the students were asked to return to a top-down design process. The results of this approach were:

1. Design commenced with a manageably small part of the site. This eliminated the consideration of the entire universe of design scales all at once and imposed a certain hierarchy of representations based on scale.

2. Each sketch problem introduced new issues along with scales in increments. This imposed a specific agenda of design issues and maintained the entire design problem at a manageable level.

3. The sequence of sketch problems allowed the incremental building of designs from scratch. This allowed the students to rely less on manual sketching and more on computer-generated designs.

4. Sketch problems constituted a bottom-up strategy, which is so often missing from the student's experience and which provides a counterpoint to the traditional top-down design strategy. This aided students in anticipating low-level concerns once they started their top-down design process.

Conduct of the Studio at CMU

Before we return to questions about the nature of computational futures for design, let me describe briefly the parameters of the design studio offered during Fall 1989 at Carnegie-Mellon University.

Objectives

The major factor determining the conduct of this studio was that it was in the mainstream of the "design sequence" of the department of architecture. That is, it was not differentiated in terms of its educational objectives from any of the other studios at the same level. It was placed in the fourth year of a five-year bachelor of architecture program.

The studio was designed to teach generation of alternative design solutions on the basis of geometric principles and programmatic requirements; use of basic structural and energy analysis packages to help evaluate and select solutions from alternatives;[3] presentation of work through electronically produced objects and the electronic media; and use of computers, in general, in the process of design and production of analytical and presentation documents.

Facilities

Seven Sun/60s were dedicated to the studio. Five of them were driven by independent disk drives. The remaining two were hosted by one of the five disk drives, the one dedicated to the instructor of the course. To facilitate file transfer and flexibility in saving large drawing files, all Suns were networked through the CMU campus network system.

An HP-plotter was dedicated to the studio. In addition a "jetstream" color printer was made available to the students to ease plot queues during submission times. Digitizer tablets and mouse input were not available. Site data was entered at the department's research lab and copied into the studio's file area over the campus-net. While being able to transfer files through the network was a great advantage, being on campus-net also made the studio's operating system overly complicated. We began to expect regular breakdowns of the network, and they became permanent toward the end.

Software

The software used was Autocad , version-9. Although there were plans to obtain additional software, particularly Autocad version-10, Autoshade , and HVAC and structural-analysis packages compatible with Autocad , a last-minute cut in the studio's budget prevented their purchase.

Setup

It was intended that software and hardware acquisition and installation be complete by June 1988, in preparation for the Fall 1988 semester. Due to ubiquitous delays in delivery and setup, these installations were not in place until the third week of the Fall semester. This made preparation of special software, algorithms for generation of standard shapes, analysis packages, and general-skill development exercises impossible. In addition, much of the system unreliability resulted from late and hasty setup procedures.

Staffing

The studio was taught by a full-time faculty member experienced in both CAD and design instruction. Two part-time teaching assistants, one a senior in the Bachelor of Architecture program who had taken a similar studio in the past and the other a graduate student with considerable Autocad experience, were assigned to help the studio with Autocad instruction.

Departmental priority was established to make sure that the facility was kept in working order twenty-four hours a day. Nevertheless, hardware problems caused considerable disruption of work. At the end of the studio,when the final presentation work was being done, the manager of the departmental lab left his position. This was a considerable hardship for the studio and negatively influenced the final documentation of work.

Design Problem

The studio was structured around a primary design problem selected to emphasize two key issues: geometry and designing with programmatic requirements that are both repetitive and diverse. The program used was a regional Islamic Center complex. The Islamic tradition of using geometry both as applied pattern and as generator of form in most public buildings was intended to set up the former objective. The selection of the functions of the Islamic complex to include a variety of room sizes and span conditions with many repeated functions—i.e., mosque, school, library, performance center, exhibition hall, administration—was intended to set up the latter objective.

The studio was structured in two parts. In the first part, which lasted seven weeks, students were given short sketch problems. Each one focused on an aspect of the problem in a bottom-up order. The first sketch problem required students to design an Islamic niche at 1/2" = 1' - 0" scale. The second covered a larger area of the site at 1/4" = 1' - 0" scale and focused on a garden or building containing the niche. The third through sixth sketch problems focused on increasingly larger parts of the site and dealt with solar, structural, circulation, and site organization issues, respectively.

In the second part of the studio, which was eight weeks long, a top-down approach was taken, starting with site plan and working down to building and interior design, as in the traditional manner. At this stage the students were expected to achieve better integration between the issues germane to different scales and the top-down versus bottom-up approaches to design.

Students

Students[4] were introduced to computing through two previous courses: an introductory modeling course and a Pascal programming course. This provided some degree of familiarity with the computer systems on campus and basic programming skills. However, as both courses are required in the first years of the undergraduate program, most students did not show a great deal of retention of the material at the time they entered the studio.

By and large, the students who were enrolled in this course elected to be in it. This meant that many of them were motivated to learn to use the computer, and the others were already knowledgeable about computers. This in many respects made up for the operational difficulties cited earlier.

No more than ten students were allowed to enroll in this studio because of the additional instruction time needed to cover technical aspects of using the computer and of the limited number of workstations that could be dedicated to the students.

Projects

Eight of the ten students enrolled in the course completed their projects on the computer. (The remaining two decided to drop the studio from their course load). Figures 1-7 show a selection of student drawings [5]. Below is a synopsis of each student's performance.

S1. A strong design student, who accepted parameters of the studio readily and grasped computer's capabilities and limitations. Used both traditional and computer media simultaneously, keeping a top-down as well as a bottom-up strategy alive throughout. Adopted a strict convention of scales and design issues. Final design shows the cumulative effect of incremental design decisions. Produced a strong design.

S2. A strong design student, enthusiastic about CAD. Used the computer exclusively to design. Became the studio's in-house technical expert, which was a burden on him. Worked well with each problem but was unable to integrate the top-down and bottom-up strategies. Could not manage to keep the different scales of design separate. Was unable to develop a solution in the site scale. Produced a weak design.

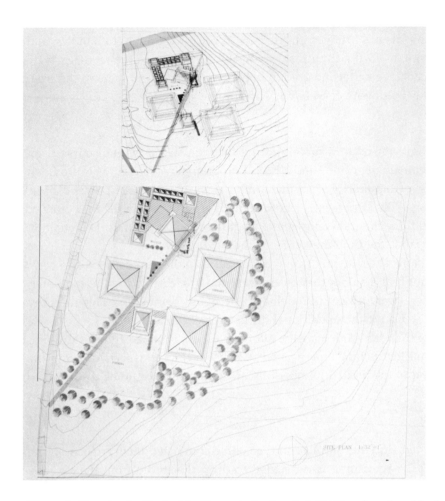

Figure 1   Drawing by Student-1. Generated using AutoCAD and rendered by hand. Plan view and axonometric of 2 1/2 D model of site plan.

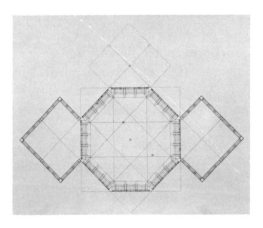

Figure 2   Drawing by Student-3. Generated using AutoCAD . Plan view of partial 2 1/2 D model of mosque.

S3. A competent design student, enthusiastic about CAD. Did not work very hard and did not gain enough momentum with the new medium. Could not bridge the bottom-up and top-down approaches. Did not succeed in integrating partial solutions into the final design. His files were lost during a system crash just before final submission deadline. Submitted an incomplete and late project.

S4. A competent design student, who kept a manual process going in parallel with the computer. Did most design manually. Was unable to bridge the top-down and bottom-up processes. Developed some parts of the project with great skill. Kept a clear decomposition of the problem by scale. Produced an inconsistent design.

S5. A competent design student, who developed a redundant process duplicating manual and computer output. Was unable to bridge the top-down and bottom-up processes. Developed some parts of the project with great skill. Kept a clear decomposition of the problem by scale. Produced an inconsistent design.

S6. A weak design student, unable to control scale of the design both on and off the computer. The geometric and repetitive capabilities of the computer proved to be overwhelming. Produced a poor design.

S7. A weak design student, who gained computer skills quickly and utilized its geometric and repetitive capabilities well. Kept a strict scalar decomposition and integrated top-down and bottom-up strategies. Was able to integrate partial solutions cumulatively in the final design. Produced a strong design.

S8. A competent design student, who adapted to the medium perfectly. Maintained a clear scalar decomposition. Built design incrementally by integrating new partial solutions into the overall design. Was able to benefit from the top-down/bottom-up strategies. Produced a strong design.

S9. A competent design student (worked with S10). Was unable to adapt to the studio and dropped it.

S10. A strong design student (worked with S9). Was unable to adapt to the studio and dropped it.

Many, if not all, of the students were disappointed by the constant inconvenience caused by hardware and software problems in the studio. This in general contributed a great deal to the performance slump in the studio, particularly toward the end of the semester.

Conclusions: Expectations for Computational Design

Let us now return to some of the issues outlined in the introduction and examine those characteristics of the student, the instruction, and the instructor which are expected to change through the use of the computer in the design studio.

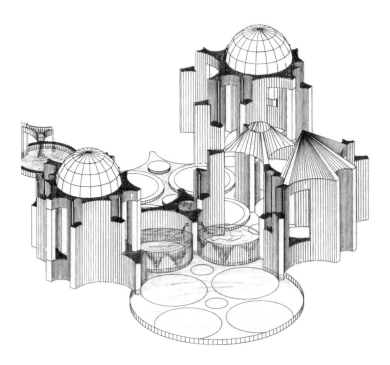

Figure 3   Drawing by Student-4.   Generated using AutoCAD and rendered by hand. Axonometric view of 2 1/2 D model of graveyard and mausolea.   Hidden lines removed.

Figure 4   Drawing by Student-5.   Generated using AutoCAD and rendered by hand. Axonometric view of partial 2 1/2 D model of mosque and entry court.   Hidden lines removed.

Student in the Computational Design Mode

Several changes for the student in the design mode can be predicted: *self-reliance, process consciousness,* and *technological sophistication.*

The student is likely to become more *self-reliant*, able to explore and verify ideas independently, within the new medium, which is technically more robust and consistent than any other medium he/she knows, particularly in terms of geometric manipulations and permutations of form. In these areas the computer automatically extends the skills and knowledge of the designer.

In the CMU studio this manifested itself primarily in the form of an overriding presence of geometric manipulation of forms. This, however, should not be construed as across-the-board sophistication with geometry. In some cases, such as S7, it indeed meant that the entire design became a geometric idea. A sense of Islamic design was achieved through the use of geometry. In another instance (S6), geometry was a thin veil behind which chaos reigned. A false sense of credibility was induced by the computer, particularly in this case, lulling the student to inaction. Ultimately, geometry became a crutch for a weak design.

As discussed earlier, there are fundamental differences between the design processes normally used in the studio and those compatible with a computing environment. If they are to benefit from this medium, students are expected to become more self-conscious about their *process* and to adapt it to the offerings of the computer. The results in the studio were mixed in this respect as well. S8 made the best adjustment to the medium and used the computer to generate formal ideas, as well as to examine and manipulate them in the computer. S1, also in control of his process, did not modify it, however, other than to multiply his effort and use the computer only as a representational and evaluative medium. S9 and S10, on the other hand, tried desperately, and without success, to integrate the computer into their process. This caused them to drop the studio.

The computer, regardless of the friendliness of the software and the abundance of user consultants and maintenance crews—which was not the case in this studio—requires some *technological sophistication* from the user, particularly in the case of nontrivial networking setups and computation environments. Often the student is required to troubleshoot and perform basic maintenance tasks. In fact this sort of relationship with the medium is desirable, particularly in "creative" fields such as design. No one can predict the day when "craft" will leave the practice of architecture [6]. As any craftsman, the designer using the computer should have the ability to manipulate with skill his/her tools as well as his/her products.

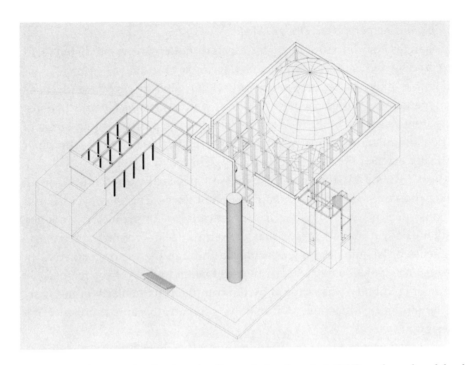

Figure 5   Drawing by Student-6. Generated using AutoCAD and rendered by hand. Axonometric of 2 1/2 D model of mosque. Hidden lines removed.

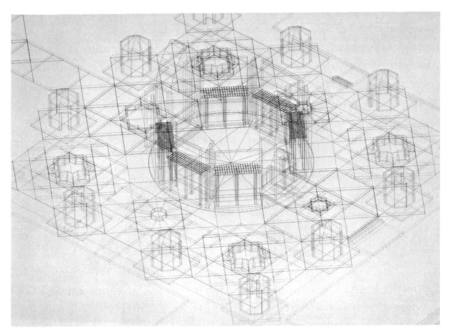

Figure 6   Drawing by Student-7. Generated using AutoCAD and rendered by hand. Axonometric view of partial 2 1/2 D model of outdoor mosque, graveyard and mausolea.

One student in the studio ventured in this direction (S2). He was a talented designer, and his instincts compelled him to try to master the medium. However, a lack of technical support in the studio and demands for technical help from his peers created problems. This student eventually became the in-house expert and spent most of his time helping his peers by searching for files, transferring files, setting up peripheral devices, and discovering new ways of modeling form in the limited 2-1/2-d world of Autocad. As a result his design suffered.

Instruction in the Computational Design Mode
Instruction is also bound to undergo fundamental changes in the computer environment. Primarily, issues of *design process* will become more explicit. *Design problems* that capitalize on the advantages of computing will be preferred over others. *Standard information* about codes, details, and quantifiable computations will readily be assumed to exist as part of the designers' capabilities. Time will have to be allocated to the instruction of operations specific to the *medium* [7].

The contention here is that by virtue of the new medium the *design process* will become radically different for the designer who strives to employ the full potential of the computer. Earlier I outlined the difference the computer makes in the design process. I argued that in the computational design studio, unlike its manual counterpart, design should commence with a manageably small part of the site; each subsequent step should introduce a new issue commensurate with the scale used; the sequence of design steps should help the accumulation of sufficient information to make designing on the computer as palatable and as quick as possible; and a bottom-up strategy should be induced to provide a counterpoint to the traditional top-down design strategy.

The studio showed that the first three recommendations work reasonably well. Working with the computer, students can gain sufficient momentum through a sequence of carefully selected subproblems and gain both confidence and insight. The primary difficulty was the bottom-up approach, which most of the students had never used before and had a hard time accepting.

The type of *design problem* suitable for the computational studio context is also an important issue. It is essential that the problem type offers the computer medium some advantage. In this studio, geometry and geometric manipulation were the principal criteria, which led to the decision to use a program, an Islamic Center complex, which traditionally is derived from geometric concepts. Other options include complex institutional buildings for the building performance analysis approach used by Schmitt, the syntactic analysis of landmark buildings by famous architects used by Flemming, and basic design exercises used by Mitchell.

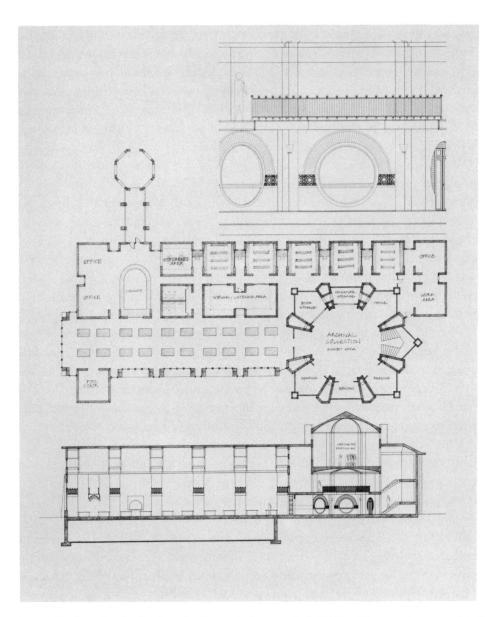

Figure 7 Drawing by Student-8. Generated using AutoCAD . Plan, section, and detail elevation of library.

There are other important design criteria for the computational design studio, which, for circumstantial reasons, we were not able to use to full advantage. One of these is the incorporation of standard information—codes, details, and other analysis algorithms—in a central database for all students to share. In our case there was not enough time to set up such an environment. Some of this spontaneously developed in the studio through shared, standard shapes, including both structural and cosmetic elements—such as domes, arches, vaults, human figures, trees figures, and so on. Inclusion of standard analysis packages in a central database can improve the students' ability to conduct fast, accurate analysis of structures, HVAC, and the like. This would have necessarily modified the expectations from students and increased the number of design criteria to be satisfied by a design.

Finally, an important factor in any computational design instruction context is the time invested in learning about the *medium*. In our case one week was allocated to refreshing students' memory of Autocad commands and introducing them to version-9. This was adequate but would not have been so had we been also tackled issues of solids modeling and building performance analysis in this studio.

Instructor in the Computational Design Mode

Perhaps the most critical change in the educational context is needed in this category. Yet there is very little to say about it, specifically. The instructor by default has to deal with all of the above issues: he/she needs to design the course, establish its pedagogic objectives, configure its computational milieu, monitor the students' progress through the course, and be the judge of how well he/she is doing as an instructor.

More pointedly, the instructor is expected to learn about the functionalities of the computer and design operations compatible with computation. He/she must be able to define processes of design that encourage productive use of the computer during both design and presentation. Also, the instructor will have to acquire new skills or aids to supplement his/her knowledge about technical functionalities of the computer—such as, geometric manipulations of form, technical analysis of buildings, and general competence with the use of the medium of representation. This is a nontrivial body of knowledge.

References

Akin, Ömer. 1986. *Psychology of Architectural Design*. London: Pion Ltd.,

Flemming, Ulrich. 1989. "Syntactic Structures in Architecture". This volume.

Flemming, Ulrich, and Gerhard Schmitt. 1986. "The Computer in the Design Studio. Ideas and Exercises that Go Beyond Automated Drafting." *ACADIA Proceedings*. '86.

Ledewitz, Stefani. 1985. "Models of Design in Studio Teaching." *Journal of Architectural Education* 38, pp. 2–7.

Mitchell, William J. 1985. "A Computational Approach to Basic Design." In *Pioneers of CAD in Architecture*. A. Kemper (ed.), Pacifica, CA: Hurland/Swenson Publishers.

Mitchell, William, Robin S Liggett ,and Milton Tan. 1989. "Top-Down Knowledge-Based Design". This volume.

Notes

1. At the time *Pioneers of CAD in Architecture* was published in 1985, ten schools reported their pedagogic activities: UCLA, Carnegie-Mellon University, Harvard University, University of Houston, Iowa State University, University of Michigan, SUNY Buffalo, North Carolina State University, Ohio State University, Rensselaer Polytechnic Institute, and Virginia Polytechnic Institute. It is safe to assume that this is at best a conservative estimate of the total number of schools teaching CAD. It does not include the token CAD instruction that extraneous demands sometimes elicit, such as NAAB requirements, public relations, and so on. Even so, and not taking into account the growth since 1985, which could double or quadruple the earlier number, it is fair to say that a significant number of accredited schools of architecture in the nation have a serious commitment to CAD.

2. The specific scales may differ from project to project; however, their relative values remain fairly constant.

3. This was de-emphasized later because of the unavailability of funds to obtain needed software.

4. In this study students will be treated as subjects taking part in surveys and empirical experiments. Their identity is suppressed to protect them from possible unwarranted or undesirable exposure. Thus, from here on they are referred to as S1 (Student-1), S2, S3, S4, S5, S6, S7, S8, S9, and S10. To acknowledge their work, however, I wish to credit them by name: Azizan Abdul Aziz, Dan Cohen, Mathew Carter, Catherine McCall, Steven Park, Glynnis Patterson, Steven Shanley, Andrew Grossi, Henry Altman, and Al DeSantis.

5. All of these figures are replicated from hard-line drawings produced on the HP plotter; some are augmented by renderings by hand.

6. Even in the case of computer applications, we see the effect of manual dexterity, particularly in presentation drawings.

7. These include the basic command structure of a given software to create operations that correspond to manual design acts, such as drafting, symbolic manipulation, simulating, manipulating, evaluating, selecting, etc.

22
The Computerized Design Firm

Fernando Catalano

Harvard University Graduate School of Design

This paper is not just about the future of computerized design practice. It is about what to do today in contemplation of tomorrow—the issues of computer-centered practice and the courses of action open to us can be discerned by the careful observer.

The realities of computerized design practice are different from the issues on which design education still fixes its attention. To educators, the present paper recommends further clinical research on computerized design firms and suggests that case studies on the matter be developed and utilized as teaching material.

Research conducted by the author of this paper indicates that a new form of design firm is emerging—the computerized design firm—totally supported and augmented by the new information technology.

The present paper proceeds by introducing an abridged case study of an actual totally electronic, computerized design practice.

Then, the paper concentrates on modelling the computerized design firm as an intelligent system, indicating non-trivial changes in its structure and strategy brought about by the introduction of the new information technology into its operations—among other considerations, different strategies and diverse conceptions of management and workgroup roles are highlighted.

In particular, this paper points out that these structural and strategic changes reflect back on the technology of information with pressures to redirect present emphasis on the individual designer, working alone in an isolated workstation, to a more realistic conception of the designer as a member of an electronic workgroup.

Finally, the paper underlines that this non-trivial conception demands that new hardware and software be developed to meet the needs of the electronic workgroup—which raises issues of human-machine interface.

Further, it raises the key issues of how to represent and expose knowledge to users in intelligent information-sharing systems, designed to include not only good user interfaces for supporting problem-solving activities of individuals, but also good organizational interfaces for supporting the problem-solving activities of groups.

The paper closes by charting promising directions for further research and with a few remarks about the computerized design firm's (near) future.

Introduction

The new information technology is shaping the structure and strategy of design firms, and not only their products. Further, the new information technology— computers and communications—is affecting competition within crucial industries, among them the metal-working and the building industries, and within the professional services. Thus, it is affecting the essence of strategy formulation for design firms. Concomitantly, it is changing the entire process by which these firms create their products and services, while reshaping the product itself—the entire package of goods, services, and information which they provide to create value for their clients. A new form of design firm is emerging—the computerized design firm—totally supported and augmented by the new information technology.

To set a background to the discussion of these key issues, the introductory section of this paper summarizes non-trivial changes in the structure and strategy of design firms brought about by the incorporation of the new information technology into their operations. In particular, this section delineates diverse conceptions of management and workgroups roles, and different strategies open to a computerized design practice.

The computerized design firm is a structurally flexible, knowledge-based organization where the emphasis is placed on information creation, and work is performed by computerized experts brought together electronically in spontaneous workgroups. These workgroups' assignments, composition, and leadership are decided on a case-by-case, project-by-project basis.

In today's demanding business environment the new information technology gives design firms a competitive advantage. This is done by increasing productivity, thereby facilitating cost reduction strategies. Further, it is done by increasing the breadth of their value-creating activities, enabling diversification strategies to take place, and by otherwise supporting differentiation strategies leading to a premium price.

Certainly, and most importantly, the computerized design firm poses its own special management problems and opportunities. It presents problems and opportunities such as creating a vision that can unify an organization of highly trained computerized experts, willing to discipline themselves while enjoying a considerable degree of interpretative freedom; motivating and rewarding them; devising a management structure that works well with task forces; and ensuring the supply, preparation, and testing of management well acquainted with the process of technological development—to name just a few.

Solving these kinds of structural problems, along with those pertaining to strategy formulation under the impact of the new information technology, seems to be the management challenge for the rest of the century. Blaming the technology is of no use; it is management that makes the difference —and what is to be managed are intellectual assets, not just equipment.

In this context, success comes to those firms and those managers able to incorporate strategically the power of the new information technology:

1. To augment the capacity of the human mind to deal with demanding knowledge work.

2. To create information, and to process effectively large volumes of information.

3. To achieve continuous improvements through organizational learning and experimentation.

In managing the computerized design firm we cannot ignore the social implications of our technical progress. The optimum design for either a tool system or a human system is dependent on the match it must make with the other. The high degree of mutual dependence implies that a balanced evolution of both is necessary.

We are compelled to learn new roles, change attitudes, and adopt different methods because of the technological development we, ourselves, introduced. Organizational structures need to evolve concomitant with the new information technology to achieve mutual impact. Over the last forty years, the computer industry changed us; of late, we are changing it.

The work of implementing the new information technology is uncovering a distinctive set of opportunities, problems, dilemmas, and challenges—not the least, the task of creating intelligent organizations, flexible enough to adjust, adapt, and learn continuously.

To this end, those managers who introduce innovations of this technological kind into design firms should engage knowledgeably in a process of technological development, and be able to function as intelligent change agents in the concomitant organizational self-renewal process.

The Computerized Design Firm Examined: A Case Study

Current computer-aided design education is largely lacking in the study of these key issues. Again, these are not trivial changes, and we ignore them at our peril.

To further research in this context, this paper concentrates now on the computerized design firm as the natural place to bring together the task, the mind, and the machine, to analyze their synergy and to examine how this kind of technological development may be understood, enhanced and managed. Special attention is being given to:

1.   The inherent synergies between people and computers—between the human system and the tool system—and how these synergies have been exploited in relation to the value activities.
2.   The kind of learning that took place, and how the firm evolved as a total intelligent system with capacity for learning and for displaying other forms of adaptive behavior.

Unlike cognitive experiments in the controlled environment of a laboratory, this paper advocates that the research methods utilized to examine computerized professional design practice be of a clinical nature, given the important aspects of complexity, contingencies, and the fundamental organizational learning involved.

Needless to say, more clinical studies of this kind are needed to help to address the fundamental question of how the new information technology can best be made useful in the development and application of technological know-how.

These concepts are of particular importance. Moreover, this paper proposes to model the computerized design firm as an intelligent system, broadly defined as a dynamic organization with capacity for learning and for exploiting the synergy between three sets of elements—formal (hardware and software), human (mind, workgroups), and activities (value operations, tasks, sub-tasks). It also suggests recognition of this system as a distinct class for purposes of management.

Along these lines and under a grant from Harvard University, the author of this paper has conducted research on professional design practice and, largely as a by-product, has developed case studies of computerized design firms to support the much needed class discussion of these issues. Consequently, these case studies were utilized as teaching material in both graduate and professional development courses of instruction at Harvard.

These case studies combine systems, behavioral and decision-making approaches to the study of computerized design firms, and they are categorized as either "Problem/Opportunity-Identifying Cases" or, more frequently, "Ground-Breaking Cases." The later category engages everyone involved in its analysis as an exploratory mission, covering new ground.

The terrain to be covered is certainly new, because the business situations the computerized design firms face are largely new, and the underlying opportunities and problems are frequently unclear.

Relevant concepts, teaching objectives, and approaches to the design and business problems or opportunities posed by the new situation, have not yet been clearly identified. Consequently, everyone involved in the analysis of these case studies must be capable of extending—not just applying—existing, tangentially-related theory and practices in order to build upon existing knowledge. Simultaneously, they must be ready to structure and organize the cases' data in new ways bearing little resemblance to existing concepts.

In order to highlight some of these issues, an abridged case study of an actual small computerized design firm follows. Shaped as an interview with the firm's founder and principal, this case study touches on issues of a technological, structural, and strategic nature. It reflects the point-of-view of the manager in charge of introducing new information technology and engaging the firm in a process of technological development.

This case is intended to convey opportunities, problems, and managerial dilemmas as perceived by the firm's management rather than to illustrate either effective or ineffective handling of an administrative situation.

Case Study: The Computerized Design Firm in Action

The computerized design firm operates quietly through the snowy winter morning.   Its mezzanine, perceived as a glass cube gliding over the calm glow of the workstation's monitors below, is occupied by the electronic conference room—networked megascreen and video projector, computers and communications equipment, infra-red lighting controls and electronic remote-control shutters. . .

There, the interviewer, sitting comfortably in a black leather reclining armchair, is located in the intended vantage point that allows one to observe the firm in action and to be observed—at once he realizes this firm is conceived as a single workspace composed of computers and communications equipment, people, and activities relating mind, space and time. A single, well- proportioned workspace; a node in a wide electronic network.

A place in which all the familiar sights of the professional practice of design are conspicuously absent. No drafting tables, no triangles, no pencils, no cardboard models, no desk lamps. . . all the workspace has ambient and task lighting with electronic preset dimming plus infra-red controls tuned to provide at all times the right kind of background to the monitors in the spine of workstations. In the center of the workspace and in full view from the conference room above, this spine of networked workstations truly performs as an electronic round table—no partitions separate the designers from one another. . . or from the world.

The feeling of the place is that of a well-run operation—serene, smooth, crisp, precise, efficient and yet relaxed and informally youthful. The interviewer smiles and turns on his tape recorder knowing that the firm's founder has strong convictions with clear-cut opinions, and is about to share them.

"Our 12-person workgroup represents an example of a totally electronic, computerized design practice increasing its value as a small business through commitment to state-of-the-art information technology—from network computing linking us with clients, consultants and manufacturers, to in-house developed software for solid modelling and animation, to expert and decision support systems, to multimedia. . . "

"We started thinking about computerization about 1980 while doing several projects for manufacturers of computer equipment. This work gave us the opportunity to see up close the advantages and limitations of the technology. It also took us over the threshold by contractual obligation, requiring of us to go ahead and begin computerizing our operations. So, we purchased the first drafting software to run on two personal computers—fit to a very small firm, like ours was at the time."

"Gradually we upgraded the hardware and acquired more applications programs. By 1984, workstation prices had dropped some tenfold, enough to arouse my interest in network configuration rather than stand-alone operations. But there is more to it than hardware and hardware cost. Early on I realized that we should be going into the computerization effort full force if we were to make it work for us properly."

"So, first, we acquired two mid-range workstations at a cost of approximately $18,000, which gave us not only networking capabilities but also multi-tasking plus a powerful operating system that communicates with the personal computers' operating system as well; the new equipment allowed us to port drawings between old and new equipment in order to preserve the investment in earlier hardware and software packages."

"And, second, as soon as we had a bunch of information technology equipment in here, I realized that we had to have a way to keep this equipment alive at all times. So I hired our first computer engineer; our firm was about seven people at the time, and for a firm that size to add a computer engineer was unheard of. But we realized very early on that we were going to have staff that was really outside the traditional roles for a design firm; so, we added first a computer engineer and, later on, an electrical engineer and computer programmer to our full time staff—that insures that the system is up and running all the time. Because we are a truly electronic firm. You pull the plug on us and that is it—we are dead."

"But, equally important, I also realized that there were certain necessary adjustments to be made to my traditional image of a design firm and how it is supposed to operate. And this behavioral change becomes very significant over the course of time. Now, I did not have this grand vision that I embarked on; I got burned and adjusted the course accordingly, but I was not afraid to stray off the old path."

"So, as we grew successfully with our design practice, I understood that rather than go and rent more workspace and hire more designers, computers would allow me to keep the talented people of the firm augmented by a powerful set of tools—we would not expand or contract the staff, just augment our existing knowledge workers. So, we gave computers to all our designers, and still call them what they are—design professionals with powerful tools."

"We always thought of our firm as being horizontally integrated; now, with computers it is absolutely horizontal—there is no need for most of the levels of the hierarchy—the designers are actually in control of all the information. Everyone has access to the databases; they are not only responsible for them but, for example, they are capable of conceptualizing the design and then of executing it in 3-D, animation, etc., and still then of conducting a very articulate networked discussion with the client, consultants or manufacturers."

"In fact, in our firm, work is being performed by computerized experts with a generalist outlook, brought together electronically in spontaneous workgroups—it really depends on how the project or problem gets defined to decide who is going to be the leader, who is going to be in charge of what value activity, and the like. And it changes not only from one project to the next but sometimes within the same project. . . It depends."

"Our firm is not a traditional, command-and-control organization mostly because of the way we are organized around the information technology. We are a series of task forces. . . workgroups in which the person who talks to the client is the same "project manager" that later talks to the foreman or to the consultants. As a result, we are more like the organization of a law firm—people manage their own projects; you have your own cases, you have co-workers, and you have para-legals who are almost your equals. And you have secretaries and other support staff. All muscle and no fat. . . A lean, adaptable workgroup."

"And the interesting thing is that we actually have the capability to produce the work of fifty people using manual techniques—among other things this means that when we get very busy we do not have to hire help, and when the business is slow we are still only twelve people."

"Yet, a problem in our firm is inter-personal communication, people talking to other people—informal contact and the like does not come easy. Our people are the firm's true assets. . . and they get to be so good in computer-aided design that eventually we lose some of them to larger firms with better money. In fact, my lawyers are exploring right now ways to retain them—"golden handcuffs" they are called. But their leaving does not have anything to do with fear of computers, quite the contrary. Although we have had cases like that 24-year-old guy who graduated with honors from a prestigious design school and who, when shown a computer, froze. I find that shocking, and this person realized that he had just spent a fortune for an education that was, in many respects, irrelevant."

"In our firm we mean to have a progressive attitude about our business, our professional practice. Let me give you a couple of examples. We just have held conversations with a very large investment bank. In fact, we are interesting them in the notion of strategic control of their real estate division by consolidating in one system all the financial information, the design information, the facilities management information, and so on. We see our professional service to them as suppliers of information-integration technology—which is beyond what people think of traditional design firms' doing. Another example: Once I realized we had considerable in-house expertise on information technology and that this technology is very expensive, it became clear to me that the best way to finance our own technological development was to turn around and sell it."

"Since I was afraid neither of computers nor to stray off the traditional path, I became a hardware and software dealer. For us, this occupation has the added advantage of remaining on-line with the manufacturers for first-hand information about new equipment and software.. So, in 1988, our firm elicited considerable response by offering turnkey CAD solutions to other design firms. I even have engaged in completely non-traditional professional behavior by taking a booth on the floor of a designers' convention, along with all the other vendors that sell equipment to designers.

"And, yes, I smiled and shook hands as any good old used-car salesman would do. Well, I also quickly found out that most designers are very confused about information technology, how to get it, how to use it, etc. . . and I soon realized that if we were going to sell this technology to designers we would have to run some kind of education program—an expensive proposition. Nowadays, we are doing more business in this area with large corporations; they tend to have engineers on their staff—and the engineers understand what we are talking about."

"Incidentally, in addition to developing our own CAD sales division and expanding into facilities management services and the like, the firm has also successfully integrated multimedia techniques into its design and presentation strategies—as you can see there are no drafting tables or cardboard models in our office. With our video equipment, 2-D and 3-D and walk-through elements can be developed into real-time, unedited computer presentations for projection via video projector here, in the conference room. For speedy presentations we prepare computer runs. Our firm uses video for recording site details. Loaded into the computer, individual frames may be worked on and used for meetings with clients and so on."

"Finally, I must say that we have become a curious commodity. We have such a spare capacity. I have created a monster for myself—this hungry machine. Now, being a group of twelve persons that produces like a firm fifty strong, we are too big to be small and too small to be big. The perception of us, as a design firm, is becoming a problem because we do not fit into any sort of traditional category. In fact, we are a new category—the totally computerized design firm. Clients that are out there shopping for big firms with, let's say, fifty people and ten offices around the country, do not look at us because they think we cannot compete—but we can, to a point, and do compete well."

"So, I have been advised by my lawyers to seek a merger, which will further capitalize on the firm's resources. But there is a price to be paid by following that path, too—loss of our identity as independent designers."

In departing, the interviewer finds himself taking mental notes of a set of questions raised by his visit to this computerized design firm, some of which will be now posed to the readers of this case. What kind of firm is this today? What set of decisions made it this way? What is your reaction to the approach and ideas of the firm's founder and principal on the matter? What do you think about the way the new information technology was decided upon, selected, introduced and implemented in this firm? How would you say this firm is to develop in terms of its organizational structure? If you were a member in a lean, adaptable workgroup at this firm, what would you think the next strategic move should be in order to preserve and augment the firm's competitive edge?

The Computerized Design Firm as an Intelligent System

This case study, representing a fairly typical computerized design firm, touches upon several important issues of technology, structure, and strategy. What follows is an attempt to highlight some of those issues, based on modelling the design firm as an intelligent system.

Modelled as an intelligent system, it can and does simultaneously hold both the conception of technology as science—as a formal system based on procedures, logic and reasoning—and that of technology as expertise—as an informal or human system based on experience, judgement, intuition and skill. Thus, the computerized design firm is functional in exploiting the synergy of science and expertise, in ways that allow for a sequential move to a higher stage of knowledge, which is at the essence of an intelligent system.

This leads us to focus on two contrasting philosophies of system development. So far, the developers of computer systems for design firms have been drawn heavily from the ranks of computer science rather than from the design domain, and they naturally feel that if the narrowly defined computer science issues have been dealt with, the system as a whole is essentially done. At this stage, the initial developers typically withdraw from the system and move on to something else, dismissing lack of practical application due to failure of the end user.

The cognitive and domain-specific issues that concern these end users, however, are of legitimate and integral concern for the design firm system as a whole—the formal elements may or may not be adequate in terms of true complements to the other elements, that is people and value activities. For example, the design and development of procedures, and of training programs for people, are almost always ignored until the formal element is finished and transferred.

This is very different from the philosophy of system development suggested in this paper—developing a computerized design firm from its conception as a total intelligent system, broadly defined. Such a philosophy advocates that all elements, from the formal, to the human, to the value activities, should be set up in parallel to fit together, reinforce each other's strength and complement each other's weaknesses. As in the case studied, development of such a system should be directed by experts in the design domain acquainted with the formal system—and enough of the original development team should remain with the system to enable it to evolve as the design domain, itself, evolves.

The case study further indicates that a computerized design firm conceived and developed as a total intelligent system also exploits effectively the synergy between human cognitive operations, formal signal processing and value activities, by emphasizing and relating both the spatial and electronic architecture of the workspace.

As reflected in the case study, the computerized design firms that have mastered the new information technology struggle to recombine effort and intelligence internally—even to the point to dislike dependence on outside vendors or organizations for expertise. While respecting and utilizing the capabilities of others, they want to develop their own formal elements, value activities and people. Great effort goes into recruiting, training, and retaining highly skilled computerized experts.

Most important is the fact that computerized design firms must be managed differently; their novelty and complexity coupled with the very dynamic situations for which they must be designed, do make managing them more difficult. However, a considerable amount can be learned from the management of earlier systems, such as the one represented in this case.

Radical changes in technology come along only once every generation or so; when one appears there is little expertise that managers can draw on. So, the most common mistake that design firms make is to treat their newly introduced information technology simply as physical assets. Yes, they are buying the hardware of programmable automatization—but are using it very poorly. In many cases the firm ends up performing worse than with the conventional technology.

Again, the technology itself is not to blame; it is management with its conception of the technology that makes the difference. Very soon, management discovers that programmable automatization demands a more interactive decision-making process and a tight integration among the firm's functions. It also discovers that the new information technology demands attention to non-financial long-term considerations and, in particular, to its impact on the firm's intellectual assets.

The new information technology not only creates the conditions for programmable automatization of conventional manual operations to take place. More important, it also creates information—and if this information is made available to each workstation, and if knowledge workers are trained and encouraged to use it, then the new hardware and software becomes a powerful mean for augmenting and enhancing knowledge.

This bears a direct connection to our observation that the computerized design firm is made up of multidisciplinary workgroups with powerful computation and communications tools. Such workgroups—intelligent organizations in themselves—are spontaneous and ephemeral structures, formed when projects surface and disbanded when they are concluded; in their network computing they include clients, consultants, manufacturers and other elements from outside the firm. Exploiting the information potential of these dynamic coalitions becomes a new managerial challenge—the managers should push at the margins of their expertise striving to shape dynamic learning coalitions.

In fact, as seen in the case study, most principals and managers are having difficulty reaping the advantages of the new information technology and continue behaving "as before" its introduction and deployment. With this new technology, though, "as before" can mean disaster. If principals and managers fail to understand and prepare for the revolutionary capabilities of the technology, it will become as much a liability as an asset—and considerably more expensive.

This new technology provides added freedom, but it also makes possible more ways to succeed or to fail. Therefore, it requires new skills on the part of managers—an integrative imagination, a passion for detail—and a quantum jump in a design organization's precision and integration.

To maximize the capabilities of the firm, managers must learn to think more as computer programmers—people who break down production into a sequence of microsteps—and at the same time to perform as cross-disciplinary generalists, with a true designer's skill for creation and integration.

They must also learn to direct highly educated knowledge workers performing in a small, tightly-knit workgroup; and they must facilitate organizational learning, harmonizing the effort of computerized experts willing to discipline themselves.

Traditional managerial attitudes, manifested in hierarchical decision-making, piecemeal changes, and a "bottom-line" mentality are incompatible with the requirements and unique capabilities of the new technology. Until these attitudes change, design firms will be slow to adopt and change the new technology.

For both small start-ups and well established design firms, such attitudes cannot change at a basic level without meaning changes in capital budgeting, performance measurement procedures, and human resource management. At the next level, change means new organizational structures that can accommodate more interactive and cooperative working relationships.

At a next level still, it means that externally the firm relates to a constellation of other computerized organizations, tending to constitute a tightly integrated network, structurally flat, self-managing, and highly responsive to evolving market needs. Services or products can be elaborated efficiently, in relative small quantities, and to order.

Some principals and managers of design firms have argued that because the new information technologies are evolving so rapidly, they should hold off investing in them until the rate of technological progress slows down. Perhaps what is behind this kind of rationalization is not the fear of technological instability as much as the fear of these technologies' tendencies to destabilize the chain of command. The inter-functionality engendered by the new technology does mean more informal cooperation at the operating levels of the organization.

This kind of spontaneous team work is unnatural behavior for design firms whose structures, staffing policies, and performance measures operate according to the traditional command-and-control mentality, where relations among people are only conceived as vertical in nature, and information technology tends to be perceived as physical assets.

Moreover, to reduce the risks that come with change, design firms often seek piecemeal improvements of their operations via "islands of automatization"—informatization is not considered. Consequently, these firms are often upgraded technologically through a series of independent projects, each justifiable in its own dollar terms until, eventually, a way is found to link those individual islands into a profitable whole—the desired returns are expected to materialize only when all these technological advances are in place. But, in fact, a design firm does not learn to exploit the full potential of advanced hardware and software unless and until it is organized to do so—unless and until changes in its structure and strategy occur.

Unfortunately, most design firms regard their choice of information technology hardware and software as non-strategic investments, even though it will change the company's cost structure, improve its ability to introduce new products, and affect the way it interacts with its clients, consultants, and manufacturers, as has been exemplified in the case study.

Understanding these basic strategy issues is paramount to understanding the computerized design firm's actions. Consequently, the rest of this section will focus on issues of strategy for computerized design practice.

For industry, design is a strategic activity—it influences everything from the efficiency of manufacturing to the flexibility of sales strategies. And it is hard to underestimate the significance of the new information technology for strategic product design.

Now this technology is transforming not only the nature of design products—and the design process itself—but more fundamentally, it is transforming the nature of competition within industries crucial to national economic performance, such as the metal-working industry which produces from coffee grinders to jet-fighter engines; the building industry; and the professional services.

The new information technology is thus affecting the essence of strategy formulation for design firms in three vital ways:

1. It changes industry structure and, in so doing, alters the rules of competition.
2. It creates competitive advantage by giving firms new ways to out-perform their rivals.
3. It spawns entirely new business, often from within a firm's existing operations.

So, every design firm has no choice but to understand the structural effects and strategic implications of the new information technology, and how it can create substantial and sustainable competitive advantage for even the smallest of firms.

In fact, a design firm is profitable if the value it creates exceeds the cost of performing the value-creating activities. Therefore, to gain competitive advantage over its rivals, a firm must either perform these value-creating activities at a lower cost or perform them in a way that leads to differentiation and to a premium price for more value added.

A design firm's ability to differentiate itself reflects, in essence, the contribution of each value activity toward client satisfaction, in the particular markets in which the firm is operating. By employing a broad vertical scope, a design firm can exploit the potential benefits of performing more value activities internally, rather than using outside suppliers—as reflected in the case study. Alternatively, by selecting a narrow scope of value activities, a firm may be able to tailor its chain of value activities to a particular target segment of the market.

Therefore, the new information technology—computers and communications, from inexpensive but powerful microprocessors and integrated software, to expert and decision support systems, to networks, groupware and multimedia—gives design firms competitive advantage not only in terms of cost reduction by increasing productivity, but also in terms of allowing them to diversify the breadth of their value activities by facilitating vertical or horizontal integration.

And, equally important in terms of supporting differentiation strategies, it gives competitive advantage by allowing an ever-increasing bundling of quality information in the package delivered to the client.

There is an unmistakable trend towards expanding the information content of the design firm's products and services, as seen in the case study. This trend combines with changes in the firm's chain of value activities to underline the increasingly strategic role of the new information technology.

This technology not only affects how individual value activities are performed but, through new information flows, it greatly enhances the firm's ability to exploit linkages among activities both within and outside the firm. Now the computerized design firm can and does coordinate its actions more closely with those of its clients, consultants, and manufacturers, conforming true electronic workgroups across the firm's boundaries.

Also, the new information technology does alter the relationship between competitive scope and competitive advantage—the technology increases the design firm's ability to coordinate its value activities regionally, nationally, and globally, unlocking the power of a broad geographical scope to create competitive advantage.

Finally, the managerial choice of emphasis on either of the technology's two capabilities—supporting automatization or informatization—leading to cost reduction, diversification or other differentiation formulations, is above all a basic question of strategy for design firms. Clearly, it derives from management's conception of the contribution of the new technology to the business.

The Computerized Design Firm's (Near) Future

As the new information technology is unfreezing the structure and the strategy of crucial industries, creating the need and the opportunity for change, design firms that anticipate, incorporate, and change this technology—becoming total intelligent systems—will have a better chance of being in control. Those that do not, will be forced to accept changes that others initiate and will find themselves at a competitive disadvantage.

But, again, this paper is not just about the future of computerized design practice. It is about what to do today in contemplation of tomorrow—the issues and the courses of action open to us can be discerned by the careful observer.

Modelling the computerized design firm as an intelligent system, this paper's focus has been upon the changes in the structure and strategy of design firms brought about by the introduction of the new information technology into their operations. The paper closes now by indicating some ways in which these structural and strategic changes reflect back on the technology of information.

The present paper has described how design firms become computerized following discernible patterns in the process of introducing the new information technology into their operations, and how this technology is shaping the structure and strategy of design firms, and not only their products.

Long in the making, the same developments that are reshaping the powerful computer industry, itself, are setting the patterns of design firm's technological innovation:

1. Microcomputers have become so powerful and affordable that they can perform many of the functions once reserved for minicomputers and even mainframes. This convergence leads firms to focus on special-purpose chips (graphics, voice), and on efficiency issues.
2. Firms have become adamant that computers and communications equipment manufacturers make their systems work together—the focus is shifting to network computing and related coordination and control issues.
3. Once companies have sophisticated computer networks in place they move beyond the automatization of operations like drafting or accounting to connect

people to information, to informatize designers. Automation yields to informatization and the firm's technology, structure, and strategy are transformed radically.

The informatization of designers implies shifting the conception of the computer as machine-tool to that of a knowledge-based system that augments the capacity of the mind to deal with complex issues. Truly smart machines meet smart people in the accomplishment of smarter value activities, and the firm starts realizing the importance of the new information technologies, not primarily to compute things, but primarily to coordinate value activities. Among other considerations, this leads the firm to a different conception of management roles.

Introducing technological innovation of this nature into a design firm presents a different set of challenges to management than does the work of competent traditional project administration. Those who manage this kind of technological change in design firms often serve as technical developers and implementers. But, as the competitive environment of the firm changes rapidly and the strategic effect of the new information technologies becomes more pronounced, the work of implementing those technologies is imposing a distinctive set of organizational challenges, not the least of which is the task of creating organizations flexible enough to adjust, adapt and learn continuously—the design firm, itself, is conceived as an intelligent system.

Success comes to those firms and those managers able to incorporate strategically the information creation potential of the new information technologies, and able to achieve continuous process improvements through organizational learning and experimentation. To this end, those who manage this kind of technological innovation in design firms should be able to serve as change agents in the organization's self-renewal process—as seen in this paper.

Interestingly enough, these structural and strategic changes reflect back on the technology of information with pressures to redirect present emphasis on the individual designer working alone in an isolated workstation, to a more realistic conception of the designer as a member of an electronic workgroup.

This non-trivial conception demands that new hardware and software be developed to meet the needs of the electronic workgroup—which raises issues of human-machine interface. Further, it raises the key issues of how to represent and expose knowledge to users in intelligent information-sharing systems, designed to include not only good user interfaces for supporting problem-solving activities of individuals, but also good organizational interfaces for supporting the problem-solving activities of groups.

The call is out in academic and professional circles for an emphasis on semiformal systems, which can be defined as computer systems that have the following properties:

1.   They represent and automatically process certain information in formally specified ways.
2.   They represent and make it easy for humans to process the same or other information in ways that are not formally specified.
3.   They allow the boundary between formal processing by computers and informal processing by people to be easily changed.

Semiformal systems are most useful when enough is understood to formalize in a computer system some, but not all, of the knowledge relevant to acting in a given situation. Such systems are useful in supporting individual work. They are especially important, however, in supporting cooperative work, where there are usually some well-understood patterns in people's behavior, but where there is usually also a very large amount of other knowledge that is potentially relevant and difficult to specify.

In order to create such a flexible semiformal system, the knowledge embodied in the system must be exposed to users in a way that is both visible and changeable—users must be able to easily see and change the information and the processing rules included in the system.

For example, passive information can be represented in semistructured objects with template-based interfaces, while active rules for processing information could be represented in semiautonomous agents.

Semiautonomous agents provide a natural way of partitioning the tasks to be performed automatically by the system; when a semiautonomous agent is triggered, it applies a set of rules to a specified collection of objects, while remaining always under the control of the user.

In combination with electronic networking and workgroup computing, these and other recent developments in interface technologies, such as the notable advance in voice recognition, will have a broad impact on the operations, structure and strategy of the computerized design firm over the next few years.

23
Computer Integrated Design:
Transformation as Process

Mark Cigolle
Kim Coleman

School of Architecture
University of Southern California

Introduction

"The search is what everyone would undertake if he were not stuck in the everydayness of his own life. To be aware of the possibility of the search is to be onto something. Not to be onto something is to be in despair." [1]

To bring together poetry, magic and science, to explore beyond preconceptions, to invent spaces and forms which re-form and inform man's experience, these are the possibilities of architecture. Computer integrated design offers a means for extending the search, one which integrates both conceptual and perceptual issues in the making of architecture. The computer may assist in generating constructs which would not have been created by conventional methods.

The application of computer techniques to design has to date been focused primarily on production aspects, an area which is already highly organizable and communicable. In conceptual and perceptual aspects of design, computer techniques remain underdeveloped. Since the impetus for the development of computer applications has come from the immediate economics of practice rather than a theoretically based strategy, computer-aided design is currently biased toward the replication of conventional techniques rather than the exploration of new potentials.

Over the last two years we have been involved in experimentation with methodologies which engage the computer in formative explorations of the design idea. Work produced from investigations by 4th and 5th year undergraduate students in computer integrated design studios that we have been teaching at the University of Southern California demonstrates the potential for the use of the computer as a principal tool in the exploration of syntax and perception, space and program. The challenge is to approach the making of architecture as an innovative act, one which does not rely on preconceived notions of design.

Design Methodology

Transformation
In the frontispiece of the story "The Library of Babel", Jorge Luis Borges wrote, "By this art you may contemplate the variation of the 23 letters. . . " [2] In the library of Borges, the alphabet provides language with a set of characters from which an unlimited number of texts may be randomly generated. For the designer, the number of available elements or geometries are infinite; as well, there is no lexicon of prescribed forms. The analogy of architecture to language, while perhaps powerful as metaphor, creates difficulty as the problem of meaning is confronted. The designer is faced, at each step in the process, with a number of options which may be selected or directions which may be chosen. Transformation as process, applied to any given form or formal structure, generates open-ended variations. The integration of the computer into the design process expands the opportunity to explore options, but, as well, helps to identify and categorize them, enabling the formation of constructs that would have remained unseen without it.   Figure 1 illustrates a series of transformations which have as their origin Philip Johnson's Glass House, developed by a student who had documented and analyzed the work. In this exploration, architectural elements are loosened from their Platonic confinement and unpinned from the modernist grid. As in the labyrinthine library of Borges, the computer poses a framework which may be engaged to assist in the generation through combination and transformation of an unlimited set of possible project structures. These structures are made as syntactic patterns or diagrams, empty of architectonic content.

Order
Juxtaposed to this infinitely extended process of design through transformation is the notion of inherent order. Michel Foucault described order as that which

"*at one and the same time. . . is given in things as their inner law, the hidden network that determines the way they confront one another, and that which has no existence except in the grid created by a glance, an examination, a language; and it is only in the blank spaces of this grid that order manifests itself in depth as though already there, waiting in silence for the moment of its expression.*" [3]

It is the search for order that brings purpose to the formation of a design. In architecture, the process of design generation is overlaid with a matrix of intentions or rules, formed by the designer in response to project requirements or hypotheses, which enable the designer to make decisions while allowing experimentation with a range of alternatives. The formulation and testing of a hypothesis and the imposition of architectonic intention differentiates the design process from formal pattern making. The hidden order in the world referred to by Foucault is not singular or simply definable, not static or representable as a whole. In architecture, ordering systems may exist simultaneously, each overlaid to establish its domain, in combinations which are simple or complex, complete or unfinished, aligned or chaotic.

Code

As the seasons passed and his missions continued, Marco mastered the Tartar language and the national idioms and tribal dialects. Now his accounts were the most precise and detailed that the Great Kahn could wish and there was no question or curiosity which they did not satisfy. And yet each piece of information about a place recalled to the emperor's mind that first gesture or object with which Marco had designated the place. The new fact received a meaning from that emblem and also added to the emblem a new meaning. Perhaps, Kublai thought, the empire is nothing but a zodiac of the mind's phantasms.

"On the day when I know all the emblems," he asked Marco, "shall I be able to possess my empire, at last?"

"And the Venetian answered: "Sire, do not believe it. On that day you will be an emblem among emblems." [4]

As Marco Polo designates a gesture as an emblem to denote a generative idea, the coding of essence or underlying order opens it to the receipt of other information. Design intention is encrypted into emblematic diagrams, the form and structure of which implies the formation of a particular project program. The forms which encode the project become the repository of meaning which goes beyond functional requirements. The designer seeks an essence, an underlying order, and, giving it specificity, brings the project to the surface. The emblem implies function and directs development in the work. In this elusive realm lies a domain for experimentation.

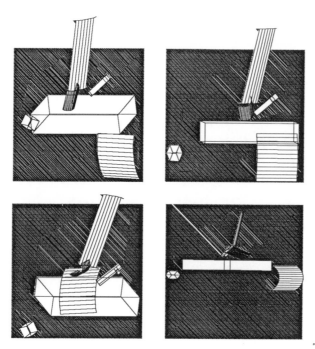

Figure 1   YMCA transformation (Nazneen Cooper)

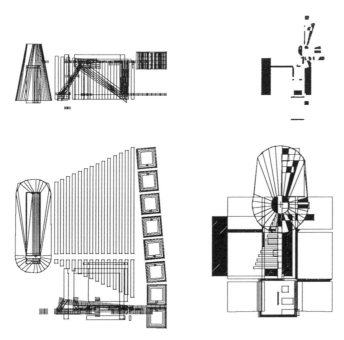

Figure 2   Single parent housing model   (Andrew Wong)

Abstraction

The quantity of things that could be read in a little piece of smooth and empty wood overwhelmed Kublai; Polo was already talking about ebony forests, about rafts laden with logs that come down the rivers, of docks, of women at the windows. . . [5]

The information that Marco Polo can interpret from looking at a chessboard of inlaid wood parallels the information potentially derived from a designer's reading of a diagrammatic image. The reading of syntax embedded in drawings of an architectural project may be seen as precedent, not in a literal sense of an immediately accessible representation, but as a response to a set of abstract relationships or traces which embody the path of culture and experience and, by extension, the history of architecture. In figure 2, a series of analytical transformations, which began with the documentation and analysis of Aldo Rossi's Cemetery at Modena and Andrea Palladio's Invention LIII from the Second Book of Architecture, generates a self referential construct which was later interpreted as an emblem for single-parent housing, day care and workshops.

Abstraction is applied not only to formal syntax but also to the essential architectural issues of program, site, and tectonics. Design is an interactive process which moves between conceptual and perceptual issues. A conceptual idea is tested and explored through a series of perceptual transformations; conceptual issues are then reformulated and new perceptions of those ideas are explored. Possibilities, variations and aspects emerge, and new perceptions evolve the concepts. Figure 3 illustrates a sequence whereby a section, derived from a sequence transforming the form of John Hejduk's Bye House to that of Le Corbusier's Salvation Army Hostel, was reconceived as a plan diagram for an urban nunnery. Interpretation of program, of the nun's dual need for extension into the community and contraction into a private world of faith, guided the transformation of the initial construct into a plan diagram of program organization. The reading of intention or function from abstract forms gives form life, creating a dialogue between the intentions of its maker and the implications for a solution.

Computer Integrated Design

Abstraction and the Computer

The more a design problem may be stated in abstract and conceptual terms, the more readily it may be manipulated within the medium of the computer. To integrate the computer into design in a substantial way, it is essential to use it at the earliest stages of design conception. Understood as a tool for design

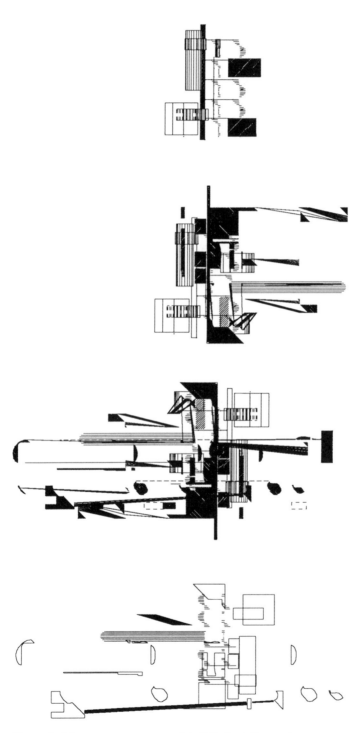

Figure 3   Nunnery program model (Elisabeth Leung)

experimentation, the computer facilitates the manipulation of formal syntax or spatial systems to generate a series of alternatives through a process of critical intention, evaluation, and transformation. The integration of the computer into the design process places the syntactic structure of its program next to that of the architectural project; the parallel conceptual structure of the computer program will impact the conceptual structure of the design project.

Computer Syntax
Each aspect of an architectural project, such as program, site, or load bearing structure, has an underlying syntax. Similarly, computers and computer programs are ordered according to a logic and set of rules which establish a syntax for the type, structure and sequence of operations that may be performed. The syntactic structure of the computer poses a framework for design which may be manipulated to generate an almost limitless set of possible project structures within a given domain. These structures are seen as syntactic patterns or diagrams, empty of architectonic content. A matrix of rules, structured by project intentions or hypotheses, overlays the process of transformational generation; the designer makes decisions while experimenting with alternatives within a critical framework. The formulation and testing of hypotheses or the imposition of architectonic intention differentiates the design process from pattern making. The reading of formal intention from figural or emblematic diagrams establishes the threshold for design process.

The imposed order of the computer environment necessitates critical thinking in the development of both project intentions and architectural systems. A tendency to consider only a few design options is displaced by an ability to readily explore a wide range of potential options through a process of transformation. In Figure 4 a series of alternatives was generated; the student used, as precedent, documentation drawings of Palladio's Villa Pisani and Villa Thiene. Computer supported design enables the designer to rapidly generate a serial progression of two- and three-dimensional studies as solid or planar models, wire frame or line drawings, orthographic or projected views, which explore the potential of the design. The computer medium itself acts to change perception, enabling experimentation with formal and spatial alternatives that would be too difficult or time consuming to represent through conventional techniques. The ability to design in perspective and to design simultaneously in two and three dimensions in a continuous process, transforms the process itself.

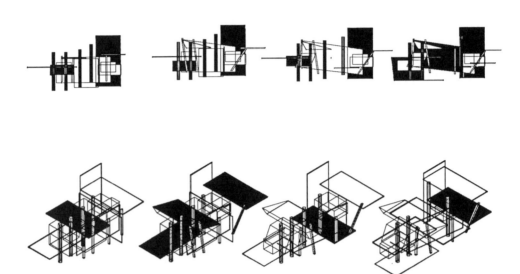

Figure 4 Urban oasis housing model (Anita To)

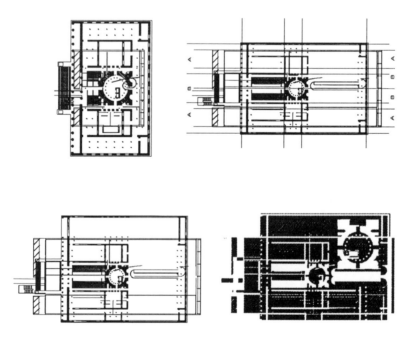

Figure 5 Urban design transformation (Maria Baldenegro)

Conventions and Representation

The particular form or spatial configuration that an architectural proposal may take is directly connected to the conventions by which it is represented. Architectural conventions, such as the plan, section, axonometric or perspective drawing, have specific implications for the design product. The means and techniques utilized to represent architectural work, whether ink line drawings, watercolor washes, or white cardboard or unpainted wood models, also critically effect the message and the perception of the work. Similarly, the computer is not a neutral medium. It can be used to develop techniques for analysis and design, establishing new conventions for representation and expanding the bounds of perception of space, form and design process.

The stereotypical expectation of the computer-generated image carries implied or anticipated precision. From the first image produced, an autonomous and absolute reading is conveyed. This precision can inhibit exploration with "sketch" studies, through which fundamental ideas evolve before details are resolved. As computer techniques are applied to design, awareness and control of the drawing intent is critical. One way that the computer medium imposes itself on the process is in the designer's tendency to organize elements as autonomous objects within the file structure of the computer environment. Reforming project files or superimposing new spatial readings may break organizational boundaries imposed by the information structure developed in the initial stages of design.

Computer drawing should not necessarily be directed to the replication of conventional techniques. Computer techniques include solid models, three dimensional x-ray drawing, animation, video overlay, and simultaneous orthographic and perspective projections. These techniques expand the designer's ability to visualize the design and extend perception, investigate the implications of decisions, and allow a more fluid process of project development as design information is manipulated.

The Design Studio

Curriculum

The intent of the studio curriculum is to describe a method for animating the design process, to reveal ordering principles embedded in the work, and to support and direct the making of architectural form. The aim of this methodology is to explore, invent, simulate a process of making architecture according to the rules of its own discourse. The design curriculum is structured according to a sequence which begins with abstract studies and proceeds to more concrete considerations.

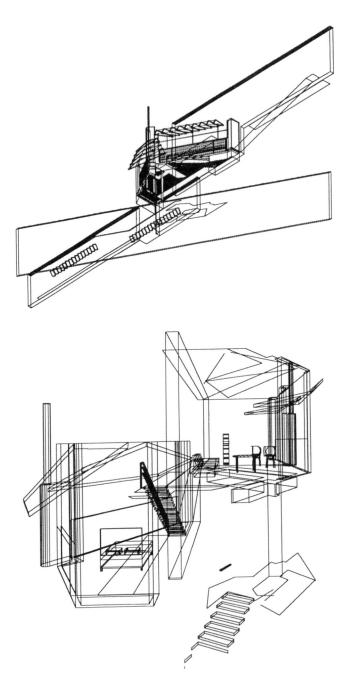

Figure 6   Los Angeles house (Sammy Wong)

Documentation & Analysis

The fundamentals of computer integrated design are taught through a series of exercises in which each student documents an assigned existing work of architecture entirely with the computer using Point Line software. In the exercise students are expected to go beyond merely replicating existing documentation to explore the work analytically. Critical analysis is therefore understood as an essential component of the design process from the outset. Computer techniques are explored as they support ideas discovered in the work. A wide variety of representational formats are explored.

Syntactic Transformation

Existing architectural works studied in the documentation phase are decomposed and transformed according to rules inherent in their order to explore alternative configurations. Alternative ordering systems may be superimposed. These exercises illustrate the power of the transformational process and develop notational conventions for representing perceived ordering structures and architectonic configurations. In Figure 5 a series of analytical transformations pairs diagrams of Schinkel's Altes Museum and Le Corbusier's Millowners Association and performs operations to overlay, stretch, expand, and invert them, in response to a desired set of syntactic relationships.

The first exercises are open-ended; a series of suggested operations as defined by the computer program are explored. In subsequent exercises each student develops a series of transformations directed by a set of project rules or intentions which they have established. The framework of the assigned building may form the syntactic structure of the work, or the introduction of a second building or second syntactic structure may overlay, combine or transform the initial project.

Context Formation

The formation of a design solution must confront the definition of the problem to be solved, the domain to be engaged, and the actions to be taken. The formation of the problem context is a direct statement of the cultural, ecological and technological context in which the specific program and site are situated.

The Chinese philosopher, Laotse, is credited with saying: "Doors and windows are cut out of the walls of a house, but the ultimate use of a house depends on the parts where nothing exists." A design solution is formed from within, considering variables of project scenario and program definition; the range of human actions which the designer considers is established. Relationships established between parts of the program form a model of program syntax, which represents ideas about hierarchy and function, human needs and aspirations, the transmission of ideas and ways of living, and considerations of the culture of the place and the culture of architecture.

A site is understood to have a context in both the physical realm of place and the conceptual one of culture. The rhythms of time and history are evaluated. An analysis of existing, pre-existing, and projected site conditions leads to development of a model of site syntax, establishing relationships intrinsic to place.

Project Synthesis

Models of program and site syntax are overlaid to create a new order, a composite context model, while maintaining fundamental relationships to the syntactic structures developed in the previous steps. The process is synthesized, and the design is made specific; the project is placed within its site. Technological considerations, physical dimensions as a result of functional requirements, spatial objectives, and the tectonics of building systems (building materials, construction techniques, structural systems) are overlaid and developed as an integral part of the architectural idea. Figure 6 shows a projection and an interior x-ray projection of a Los Angeles House. At this point in a project's development, the initial architectural precedents are not apparent at the surface, but traces derived from transformation of those precedents are embedded in the new project. Spatial studies designed with three dimensional computer models depict relationships at an experiential scale.

Conclusion

The medium of the computer enables a change in process and perception which has the potential to alter spatial or formal understanding of the making of architecture as powerfully as did the idea of perspective in the Renaissance. As the Renaissance concept of perspective construction, understood as technique, altered the relationship between the conventions for representation of buildings and their physical manifestation, techniques inherent in computer integrated design establish new dimensions in design exploration, which may be grafted onto conventional understanding.

The abstract yet complete nature of a computer sketch enables it to exist both as the representation of an idea and as an artifact, existing apart from the set of intentions which caused it to be made. It is able to be retrieved, reproduced or transformed as information in a data base. The computer medium expands both the domain of experimentation and the potential for generating design alternatives. In seeking a model for computer-integrated design, we speculate on a process which extends the dialogue between form, program, and culture towards the making of a new architecture.

The catalogue of forms is endless: until every shape has found its city, new cities will continue to be born. When the forms exhaust their variety and come apart, the end of cities begins. In the last pages of the atlas there is an outpouring of networks without beginning or end, cities in the shape of Los Angeles, in the shape of Kyoto-Osaka, without shape. [6]

Notes

1   Percy, Walker. <u>The Moviegoer</u>.

2   Borges, Jorge Luis. The Anatomy of Melancholy, "The Library of Babel", <u>Labyrinths</u>.

3   Foucault, Michel, <u>The Order of Things.</u>

4   Calvino, Italo. <u>Invisible Cities</u>.

5   Calvino, Italo. <u>Invisible Cities</u>.

6   Calvino, Italo. <u>Invisible Cities</u>.

24
Some Years' Experience Teaching CAAD

Roberto Cipriani, Anna Decri Lagomarsino, Anna Stagnaro, Elisabetta Valenti, and Tiziana Sambolino

Facoltà di Architettura, Istituto di Progettazione
Università degli Studi di Genova
Italy

Introduction

In the conventional way of teaching architecture, it is common to think of design as the final synthesis of an intellectual process (*composizione* in Italian) integrating different elements from different curriculum subjects: history, structural analysis, technology, regional and urban planning, and so on. These elements, being comprehensive of their specific domains, together build *the project*.

This process is supported by a long tradition[1] that cannot easily be modified; however, we must not consider it to be the only one. Architectural practice should be much more. The *Scuole di Architettura* has walked a long and difficult road in the last thirty years, with a significant widening of interest in social, political, and economic issues. There have been recurring attempts at epistemological reformulation in some areas. There has been an acknowledgment of a crisis in contemporary town planning and a dimming of several certitudes that had developed with the birth and growth of the modernist school. And there has been a weakening of the promises that had given life to the vigorous discussion about town and regional planning. All of this leads to a reconsideration of the meaning and the deeper assumptions that *the project* implies, a question mark at the center of the human sciences that architectural practice involves.

The old tradition, which assigned composition a central role in the project, is no longer sufficient because it is related to a reductive reading of epistemology that views human sciences as defining segments of *physical* knowledge of the actual world. Contemporary reflection on the difference between *understanding* and *unfolding*, together with the attention given to

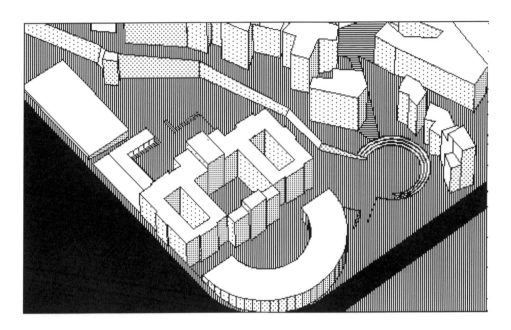

Figure 1   New use of a public building—Heliodonic perspective [perspective from the point of view of the sun], drawn by means of Space Edit and Full Paint. Example of verification of the disposition of masses to the scale of a neighbourhood.

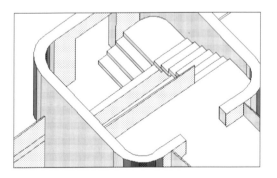

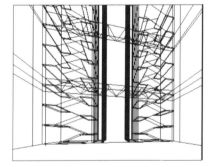

Figure 2   Design of a railway station, Genoa-Nervi. Axonometric of the internal part of a communication tower, drawn by means of Space Edit and Full Paint.

Figure 3   Study of the vertical circulation paths for a students' residence.

interpreting a moment as compared to purely *describing* one, gives to the project the task of inquiry instead of solution.

Choice of CAAD

This idea of architecture requires particular attention in teaching. Our didactic objective is to teach an organizational method addressed to the problems of evaluation, identification, definition, and control of the spatial qualities of a design, as well as to provide the instruments required to carry out the verifications of the design. It is within this context that we felt the necessity to include the organized teaching of CAAD techniques.[2]

From Research to Didactics

This research originated in our interest in using a digital computer in architecture merely as a technical tool, as happened more-or-less in the whole architectural world. These first experiences and interests go back to the early 1970s, when one of the authors, Roberto Cipriani, was working on his graduate thesis. For several years, work on the computer was confined to a very few theses, which, as a result of the availability of ever more advanced and suitable machines and programs, were able to focus on specifically design-related interests in meaning, communication, and language that today find clearer expression in our didactics.

The first thesis carried out with the aid of the computer as a drawing machine was completed by G. Rossi, under the guidance of R. Cipriani, in 1979. The study looked at the graphic possibilities offered by the state-of-the-art equipment at that time. Rossi drew the hull of a sailboat by, for the first time in Italy, developing algorithms[3] and writing the necessary software in FORTRAN for the PDP 11/45 with a Tektronics storage-tube graphic terminal and a plotter. This thesis demonstrated that it was possible to process complex objects from a formal point of view; the work was published in the Italian magazine *Domus* in 1980.

Later theses studied the organization of databases necessary to describe buildings, in particular to produce the drawings of spatial structures. The most interesting result, obtained from consideration of all this work, was to convince us that an architecture department is not the right place to write software; rather, it is the right place to write the performance specifications to be met by the programs that software specialists create. This realization has been confirmed by the fact that an increasing number of programs suitable for design are becoming available (even though many were not conceived for architectural design). Therefore, our focus has shifted to analyzing and evaluating available software, especially the software available on small machines—the ever-improving personal micro-computers.

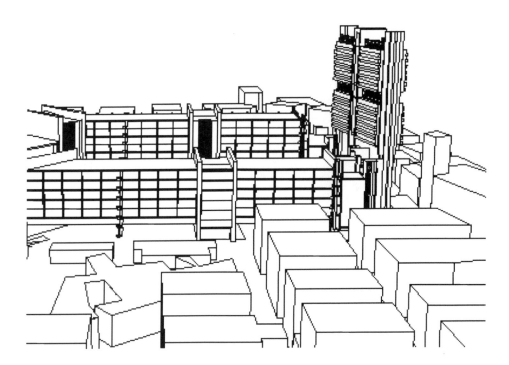

Figure 4   Design of a university campus in Genoa. Perspective showing relationship to context. Unlike the previous images, this drawing was been obtained from amathematical model, which contained all information relevant to the design.

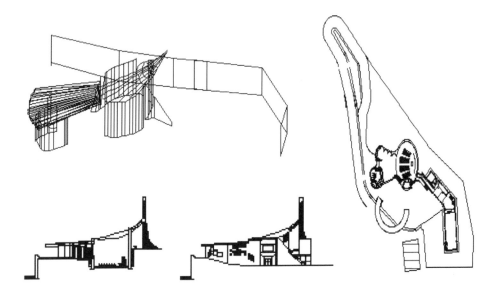

Figure 5   Representation of a Church by means of Space Edit

One of the authors, Anna Decri, completed a thesis in 1986 that offered our department the opportunity to obtain its first Macintosh. The thesis analyzed the software available at that time, and so guided the subsequent choices. Moreover, it clarified and defined precisely the meaning and the implications of CAAD through a comprehensive bibliographic search of the most important international texts and the leading work being done in Italy, using as a basis W. J. Mitchell's work. Documenting this experience at the Fourth European Conference on Teaching and Research Experience with CAAD, held in Rome in 1986, we presented a paper entitled "Approaching CAAD at Facoltà di Architettura, Genova."

Subsequent work, particularly the theses of Alfio di Bella and Paola Gualeni in 1989, explored in depth the possibility of using for architectural design the several programs available for the various models of the Macintosh. They sought to evaluate the limits of this software. At the same time, and recognizing the maturity of these systems, we tackled mass teaching with an institutional course on architectural computer-aided design.

Programs and Themes

In our department there are five design courses, one for each year. Every teacher takes a turn at being in charge of each of the courses, in the following order: second, third, first, fourth, fifth. The sequence keeps a student from having the same teacher for more than two consecutive years. The syllabi of the architectural design courses include design theory and practice; however, given the nature of these subjects,[4] what is taught, and how it is taught, varies according to the cultural position, within the current architectural debate, of the individual teachers. Our approach focuses on the language of architecture and the meaning of the project. To achieve our objectives and to meet a high standard of quality, we use the CAAD techniques that we teach in our other technical courses.

Organization of Our Teaching

During the last academic year, our course was offered to fifth-year students. We taught at the same time architectural design and the use of CAAD programs. As far as we know, this was the first time that such an experiment had been tried in any Italian department of architecture; in fact, the teaching of CAAD has always been separate from the teaching of design.

Taking for granted that the fifth-year students had already reached a certain specialization of interests, we allowed them to choose freely their design theme, though we encouraged them to concentrate on meaningful three-dimensional space. Besides critiques of their work, we also gave a series of theoretical lessons on the language of modern and contemporary architecture.

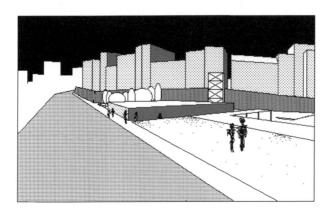

Figure 6.   Perspective drawn by means of Space Edit and Full Paint

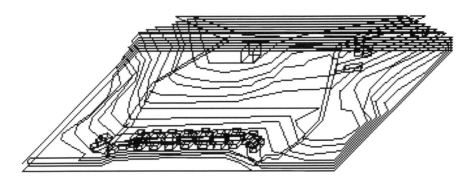

Figure 7   Axonometric of a sloping site drawn by means of Space Edit in order to study the siting of the project

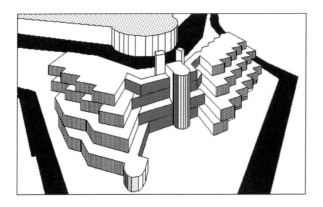

Figure 8   Old people's home in Genoa. Perspective, drawn with Space Edit and edited with Full Paint in order to correct the hidden-line removal errors

This year we are in charge of a second-year design course, which we will continue through the end of the students' third year. In the part of the course that strictly concerns design, we give a basic training in design, identifying certain fundamental elements[5] and developing a more in-depth approach from the theoretical point of view. In the part of the course concerned with computers, we proceed in parallel, teaching a course suitable for the hardware and software we have chosen, with the objective of having the students acquire familiarity with the system and independence in handling it. Next year we shall try to integrate the two aspects of our teaching, with a more in-depth approach to theoretical aspects of the design methodology. We will attempt a design that is drafted entirely by means of CAAD.

Choice of Hardware

We selected Macintosh personal computers four years ago, at the same time as programs of architectural interest began to be available. We are interested in personal computers because they may be accessible to an average Italian architectural office, both with respect to the scale and the quantity of work.

We also chose the Macintosh because the man/machine relationship is more attuned to the architect's way of working, particularly since it communicates through graphic images. Moreover, the CAD programs for MS-DOS, at least the programs such as AutoCAD that are normally used and tested by other groups in our department, are more suitable for mechanical drawing, which of course is very different from architectural drawing: it is in fact the drawing of symbols. We are not interested in the mechanical accuracy of the description of the object, but rather in the expressiveness of the detailing, in its capacity to make the whole architectural design into an organism that speaks.

At present, we use five Apple Macintosh personal computers for these exercises: three Pluses and two SEs, all with 1 Mb RAM. This quantity of memory is sufficient only for carrying out simple exercises: we envison upgrading to 2.5 Mb for each computer. The two SEs are each fitted with a 60 Mb Rodime hard disk, while two of the Pluses are fitted with an external floppy disk drive, and one with an internal floppy disk drive alone. These five computers are linked by an AppleTalk network, using Tops 2.1 software and using the operating system of 6.0.2. level.

Special configurations of the system allow us to have enough free storage space on the disk so as not to hinder the normal printing operations, especially for the Mac Plus computers that are not fitted with hard disks. Printing is carried out by means of an Apple ImageWriter LQ printer, which is also linked

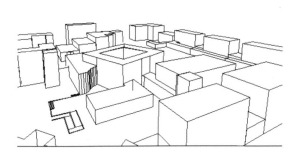

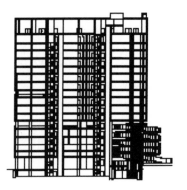

Figure 9 Perspective made in order to study the relationship with the surroundings of the designed mass (at the centre of the image). The impossibility of highlighting the mass, together with the lack of precision of the algorithm for the removal of the hidden lines, make this image of little use.

Figure 10 Cross section of a building, drawn by means of RadarCh. Since this program is a true 3D solid modeller, it is possible to obtain cross sections drawn cut at any plane.

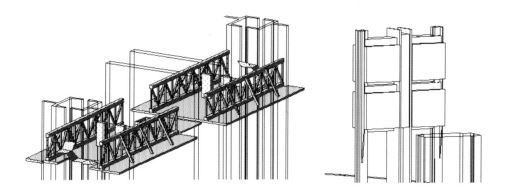

Figure 11   Axonometric of a detail of the building shown in figure 4. These are different views of the same mathematical model.

with LocalTalk. It is supplied with a large quantity of fonts in many sizes. We also have a Kodak DataShow liquid crystal screen that may be used for overhead projections. On these computers, we use Diehl Graphsoft's Minicad+ 1.0 as graphic software and MacWrite 5.1 for wordprocessing.

For research, which takes places mainly through the writing of graduation theses, we use a Macintosh II with 2 Mb RAM, a 40 Mb hard disk, and a monochrome monitor and a Macintosh IIcx with 5 Mb RAM and a 40+60 MB hard disk and an 8-bit color monitor, also linked to an Apple scanner. The whole system is linked over a LocalTalk network and uses as printers an Apple Imagewriter LQ and a Laserwriter II. [6]

Choice of Software

Since we mean to teach that architecture is essentially a creation and a use of spaces, we chose to use only three-dimensional software. We prefer, in this category, the less specific and more general programs, so that it is possible to carry out effective exercises without having to bring definition of the object to a final stage; that is, the situation in which the designer, and even more so the student, finds him or her self during the conception stage. Since if it is true, as we believe, that the architect must think in terms of assemblies of actual objects, it appears to us that it is limiting to decide beforehand the characteristics of these objects while the spaces are being conceived: one is still in the first stages of the design.

Several very specialized packages, each for a particular market, have appeared since the old days of MacDraw. For instance, RadarCh (also known as ArchiCad outside Italy) was devised exclusively for the design of buildings, MGM Station for industrial design, and MacCad for the design of printed circuits. We have been able to test in depth SpaceEdit, RadarCh, and MiniCad, and we have seen the operation of such programs as Swivel 3D, PowerDraw, and Mac3D.

SpaceEdit is a professional drafting package that permits drawing and representations in both 2D and 3D. Objects may be viewed from any vantage point. It can show the three Monge projections (plan and elevations) together with an axonometric view, all at the same time on the same screen. It provides powerful zooming features, exploded views, and walkthroughs.

RadarCh is a powerful program for the design of building objects. Actually, although RadarCh is a superb program for final presentations, it is necessary to begin and prepare the design using traditional pencil and paper methods, since it is not possible to leave details incomplete. This program is the one preferred by professional offices for producing final drawings, but it is not very useful for the beginning stages.

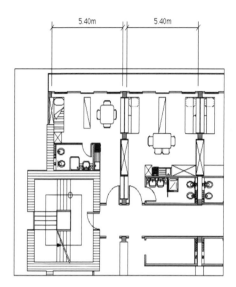

Figure 12   Another image obtained from the same database from which figures 4 and 11 were obtained. Drawn by means of Minicad+ 1.0.

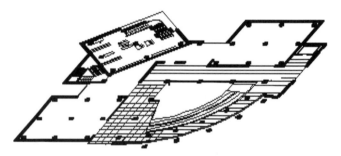

Figure 13   Example of unsuitable use of a 3D program: plan of a project for a museum. It would have been better to create a three-dimensional object.

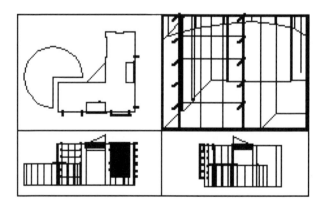

Figure 14   Example of suitable use of a 3D program: unlike the previous image the object is here described in three dimensions, even though without full details

Minicad+ is a complete program for generic drawing, although only partially oriented to architectural drawing. It is three-dimensional, it employs color, it is object oriented and it supports calculations through a built-in spreadsheet. Moreover, the ability to program it in Pascal and to export the data in various formats makes it a flexible and powerful tool.

The students learned SpaceEdit first but then moved on to Minicad+, because SpaceEdit permitted no more than the definition of masses and the embellishing of the drawing with FullPaint, a paint system. Only a very few students, with very considerable effort, managed to describe their building objects in much detail.

CAAD Teaching Methods

In the two courses that we have taught so far, we have dealt with two different types of student. The first course was for students in their last year before the graduation thesis; they were at the end of their course of studies and had four years of study in the traditional methodologies of design and drawing. Students of this type are convinced that they have their own method and language; they are attached to traditional forms of drawing and verification of the ideas they are developing, such as the freehand sketch and the scale model. With the second course, the situation was different. This was a two-year course, which allowed us to plan a much more gradual learning of the new techniques, and had students with only one experience of design according to traditional techniques.

None of our students had any specific training in nor any previous experience with the use of computers. They had these different attitudes because of their past experiences; therefore, we attempted two different teaching strategies, both affected by the characteristics of the Macintosh world, which above all requires personal experience.

In our first experiment, we gave three lessons to each of 46 working groups, into which the 146 students of the course were divided. The idea was to give students a hands-on experience. This approach seemed to be effective; however, problems developed as soon as the students were left alone to work with the machines.

In our second experiment, we gave theoretical lectures followed by direct, hands-on experience for the students, which was reinforced during the following lesson by feedback questions and further explanation of the software. This was much more useful for students who had already tried to use the software. This global question-and-answer type of teaching, according to the first results, appears to be much more effective, because the Macintosh is best learned by experience rather than through theoretical explanations.

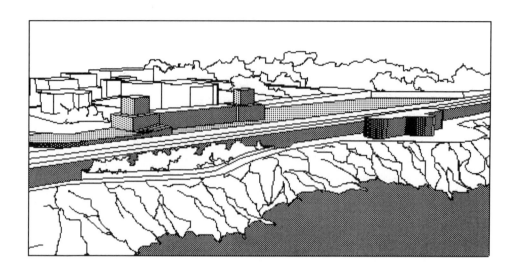

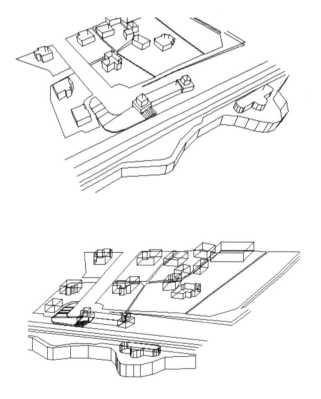

Figure 15   To study of the relation of the project in its surroundings the students   preferred a traditional representation

Conclusions

One result of the application of CAAD to the teaching of architecture is that we diminished the importance of the graphical sign on paper, thus obliging a more intense concentration on architectural content rather than on the formal aspects of representation. Also, we compelled the students to conceive the building object in three dimensions, reducing their tendency to confuse the spatial object with its representation in two dimensions.

Fundamental to the acquisition of CAAD techniques is the interest in them shown by the students. Interest is a key learning factor in all fields, but it is especially important with computers, since the computer is able to amplify the defects or skills of the users. This is one of the reasons many architects, especially those who minimize design time to the detriment of quality, find CAAD unattractive. CAAD apparently affected students on three levels.

First, designers who had no interest in, or did not trust, new possibilities used the software for two-dimensional drawing (mainly of the pictorial type) only, and then only after the design had been decided with a pencil alone; for them, verifying the design by computer was not even considered. It is true that the lack of suitable facilities, and thus lack of computer time for the students, resulted in most of the design work being done without the aid of CAAD, but it is also true that we requested only a part of the students' final presentation on the machine, as long as the portion of the project was interesting and complete. In fact, the use of the Macintosh for the whole design process has been possible only at the level of theses done on computers reserved for this purpose.

Second, students who were more interested in the possibilities of CAAD used the machine in a way that was more in keeping with our design philosophy. They used the computer for parts of the design in three dimensions, even though problems of time and software limited study to the relationships between the external masses or, less frequently, between the internal details.

Third, the enthusiasts responded with passion, devotion, and curiosity. In particular, they became curious about the three-dimensional world. It is important to note that young people in 1989 are much more familiar with the world of computers than are members of our professional world. Even if they have never used computers, they take them for granted and are not afraid of them.

Finally, we reached the comforting conclusion that the quality of the work produced on a computer in the architectural field, in terms of both graphics and design, remains directly linked to the professional skill of the architect who uses it.

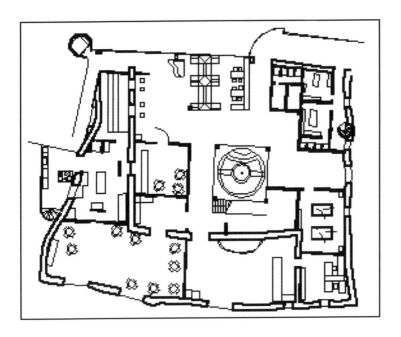

Figure 16   With just some willingness and knowledge of the program one is not limited in use of shapes. Plan of a 3D model drawn by means of Space Edit.

References

A.A.V.V., 1986. *eCAADe Pre-proceedings,* .

De Fusco R. 1983. *Il progetto di architettura [Architectural design].* Bari: Ed. Laterza e Figli.

Mitchell, W. J. 1977. *Computer-aided Architectural Design.* New York: Van Nostrand Reinhold,

Morasso D., and V. Tagliasco. 1985. *Eidologia informatica [Computer-graphic science].* Urbino: Arti Grafiche Ed. srl.

Quaroni L. 1977. *Progettare un edificio. Otto lezioni di architettura [Designing a building. Eight lessons of architecture].* Milano: Ed. Mazzotta

Radford, A., and G. Stevens. 1987. *CADD Made Easy.* New York and Sydney: McGraw Hill.

Rossi G. 1979. " Metodo e sperimentazione nell'industrial design. Modello, verifiche e rappresentazioni nello studio per una barca a vela" [Method and experimentation in industrial design. Model, verifications and representation in the study of a sailboat]. Genoa, Graduation Thesis.

Notes

1.   From the experience of architecture academies to the teaching of Ecoles Polytechniques.

2.   As teaching the use of CAAD and not teaching through the use of CAAD.

3.   Using in particular the Yamaguchi spline interpolation algorithm and several algorithms for the removal of the hidden lines.

4.   We may in fact try to describe architectural design (*composizione* in Italian) not as a technical, specialized discipline, with its own rules for achieving precise objectives, but as a process, open to creativity, with multiple aims in different fields (therefore with considerable interdisciplinary characteristics) and with many different ways to compose into the design the requirements and the contradictions of the problem.

5.

Meaningful space: the architecture that speaks.

Dimensioning the space: the measure of architecture.

Delimiting the space: the boundaries of architecture.

Moving through the space: to approach, to orientate oneself, to perceive architecture.

Sound, light, matter: substance of architecture.

The space continues: architecture does not live alone.

Meaningful space: the architecture that speaks, again.

6.   The students of the course do not usually have access to these machines,.

25

Irises in a Landscape: An Experiment in Dynamic Interaction and Teaching Design Studio

John W. Danahy

Centre for Landscape Research
School of Architecture and Landscape Architecture
University of Toronto

The capacity of most computer-aided design systems is inadequate to represent landscape architectural ideas and compute landscape scenes quickly. As part of our teaching agenda, we decided to write software for the Silicon Graphics Iris workstations to tackle this problem directly. This paper begins with a discussion of our concerns about the use of CAD tools in the representation of landscape architectural space. Secondly, we discuss the approach that Toronto takes to computing and teaching with particular emphasis on the use of computers to support an integrated representational work environment. Finally, a fourth-year design studio that used our software is reviewed. Static illustrations of the system are presented here, although there is a videotape that demonstrates the dynamic nature of the system.

Landscape Architectural Representation

Concerns about the deficiencies of commercial CAD and solid-modeling systems for three-dimensional architectural representation and design have been discussed in the literature.[1] Significant research into much more subtle, semantically correct approaches to operating on architectural models has been started at a number of architecture schools, such as Ohio State, SUNY Buffalo, Harvard, UCLA, Carnegie Mellon, and Michigan. But no such first tier of research has been devoted to the issues of modeling *landscape* architectural form. The effort reported here is to build tools and methods that are relevant to the issues raised in landscape architectural studios. The first issue of concern to us is the representation of landscape form and space.

Landscape architects make extensive use of traditional geometric conventions for the conceptualization of built form and can benefit from advances in architectural modeling. But geometric form is only one of at least three major categories of space and form that a landscape architect must be concerned with to have an adequate palette to represent a landscape. An elementary palette that we have found most useful is one consisting of terrain, built form, and vegetation. A useful system must support at least these three basic types of form.[2]

Most architectural modeling systems are useful for the construction of building form. But there are few useful tools for the modeling of terrain and vegetation at a variety of levels of abstraction or detail. Available tools can seldom respond efficiently and flexibly to issues of landscape design such as vegetation growth. Our experience in building models with full terrain and species-specific vegetative representations shows a three to ten fold increase in crafting time over that required to produce an "equivalent" model assuming a flat empty site.

Another serious issue in the practical use of existing CAD systems arises when one tries to model the complexity of landscape scenes. The computational and concomitant data storage problems that develop when representing landscapes overwhelm systems that are adequate for the representation of buildings at equivalent levels of abstraction. Images of landscapes that yield significantly more information than manually crafted sketches take far too long to generate on most microcomputers to be useful. The microcomputers capable of providing fast three-dimensional architectural information useful in the design process become unacceptably slow if image complexity is pushed to the levels that we have found necessary in professional landscape architectural work.[3] Dynamic feedback and the opportunity to cycle through iteratations in design development are all but lost under such conditions.

Toronto's Approach to Computing and Teaching
We place a strong emphasis on visual representation and simulation media in the Landscape Architectural Programme and the Centre for Landscape Research. We are very interested in the development of tools and strategies to improve students' and professionals' visual thinking and decision-making skills. We have found that the computer makes complex spatial configurations more visually accessible through an array of sophisticated visualization tools available to us for several years through our links with the Dynamic Graphics Project of the Computer Systems Research Institute at the University of Toronto. These general-purpose representation tools have been used by us on a series of professional projects and studios in which we focused our creative attention on the definition of adequate design vocabulary and procedure. That

experience has served as the basis for our recent efforts in software development.[4]

We try to teach students to examine issues of information organization, classification, interrelation, and substitution. For now, most of this must be handled in the brain of the computer operator and, for the most part, our use of computers has been task oriented. Until very recently, sophisticated computer rendering tools have been extremely primitive from the standpoint of knowledge structure and dynamic interaction with design information. As a result, the onus for the organization and creation of information has been the responsibility of the user.

Evolution of Our Computing Tools
The first studio we attempted (four years ago) used terminals connected to a Vax computer over telephone lines. We have used a variety of tools for creating polygon models of landscape. AutoCAD has been extensively as a digitizing and polygon-modeling tool. This has been accomplished with a completely customized AutoLISP interface. The process of constructing models this way is laborious and demands of the user a massive commitment to maintain a cognitive map of the intended shape or space while operating the tools.

A range of traditional image-processing and rendering software is currently available to students on Irises, Macs, and IBM-ATs; however, the students prefer to focus their use on two new programs under development in the research lab. These programs are referred to as TRIM (Toolkit for Representation & Modeling) and Polyed (a polygon modeler with some specialized functions for landscape architects not found in traditional modeling packages).[5]

In the spring of 1989, the Landscape Architecture Programme had a unique opportunity to run a studio using our new software, specifically designed for use by a landscape architect working on an IRIS computer. The eight students in the fourth year were able to use four Silicon Graphics Iris computers, three Mac II micro-computers, and an IBM-AT running AutoCAD with a Targa framebuffer and an E size digitizer. The Macs were connected to the Irises on 19.2 baud serial communication lines. The Irises and the AT were connected by Ethernet.

The software utilized was TRIM. This is a software package being written at the Centre for Landscape Research as a prototypical work environment for environmental designers. The specific orientation of the system is toward the support of work on urban design and landscape architectural problems.

The title, TRIM, stands for the four major conceptual areas of design process that we support.

Toolkit : a general means of operating on and communicating information
Representation: a means of articulating ideas
Interaction: a means of instructing and manipulating data representations
Modelling: a means of creating a representation of an idea

TRIM allows students to load polygon files of site models and move about the models as if walking or flying through the model in perspective (see figures 1 and 3). The Irises are capable of generating shaded perspectives quickly enough to permit a freewheeling approach to the exploration of the data. TRIM also permits the user to pick a parametric object or file and perform cloning, scaling, translation, and rotation operations by opening up a dialog box for the object. Parametric objects also permit one to undertake a variety of parametric operations related to shape, costing, and density calculations for buildings. (Figure 3 shows a tower block being illustrated using these functions).

Polyed (figure 2) has been developed as an interim replacement for the polygon modeling tools we have been using for some time on AutoCAD, and to provide parametric assembly programs in UNIX using the Makefile facility. The previous studios we ran relied on an extensively customized version of AutoCAD using AutoLISP to craft and digitize three-dimensional polygon models of buildings, terrain, and vegetation. The resulting DXF files were transferred to the Irises, where a "C" program scanned the DXF files and converted them into our laboratory's ASCII polygon format. (Figures 14, 15, and 16 are examples of a model produced this way.)

For the first time, in this studio, students were able to freely move about an arbitrarily-defined polygon data base, with a shaded-lighting model running in real time. Previously, on the older Iris 3000 series machine, they could examine a model in wireframe (with no hidden surfaces) in real time. If they wanted to test the model with hidden surfaces or lighting, they had to run one of our conventional cpu-based, general-purpose rendering packages. This process would require a minimum of several minutes to invoke. The system used in this studio permits students to dynamically manipulate the geometry or placement of objects while viewing the model in perspective with a shaded-lighting model. They can do more work directly on the computer, without resorting to sketching at every turn in order to adequately represent and understand a design idea.

We are interested in studying the degree to which the real-time shaded graphics and ten million instructions per second computing speed of the 4D-20 and 70/GT Iris computers can adequately deal with the complexity of landscape representations.

In our CAD teaching, one issue is how to make the best use of existing computer-aided design tools through the careful organization and management of design knowledge. In our case it is done the traditional way—in the mind of the student. For the most part, organizing and experimenting with the classification, structure, and hierarchy of the information in the machine is the user's responsibility. We believe that it is premature to try to use highly structured knowledge base systems on complex problems in the landscape architectural design studio.

We foresee the use of didactic systems for introducing new areas of knowledge to students so that they can learn very specific lessons. The computer would be used to eliminate "wasted" time in crafting models and to direct the students' intellectual attention to the specific principle or theory behind the exercise. We use this approach to introduce students to the fundamental spatial concepts and semantics of urban design with our TUMMS software on the Iris computers (see figure 4).[6] However, at the advanced levels of studio teaching we believe that we must emphasize the development of experience with the formulation of personal design- thinking methods.

To support this notion, we believe the computing environment should be configured by the user to suit his or her interpretation of issues and of subsequent relevance of specific forms of information representation. Therefore, our focus is on the development and use of computers to support intuitively driven and structured design processes. The didactic nature of a future system could result from the user's knowledge, the professor's, or some normative professional knowledge base such as those typically associated with traditional models of expert systems. In the meantime, until good theory and organizational methods are available in landscape architecture, we are not making extensive use of sophisticated knowledge base software.

Using the Computer in a Fourth-Year Studio

Course Objectives

Our specific educational objectives in the studio were:

—to understand the importance of perceived details, dimension, and time in the realization of design concepts;
—to develop better visual analysis and design skills through the use of computers and traditional visual design media;
—to learn the appropriate use of the computer as a means of testing the translation of two-dimensional ideas into three-dimensional form and experience in time.

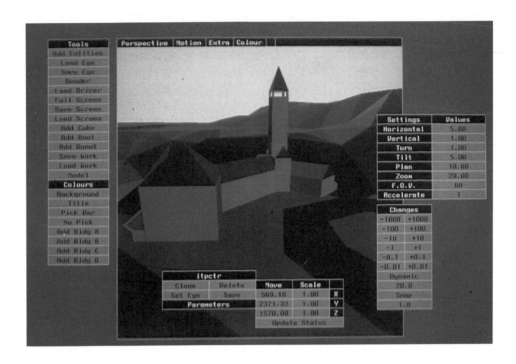

Figure 1 TRIM

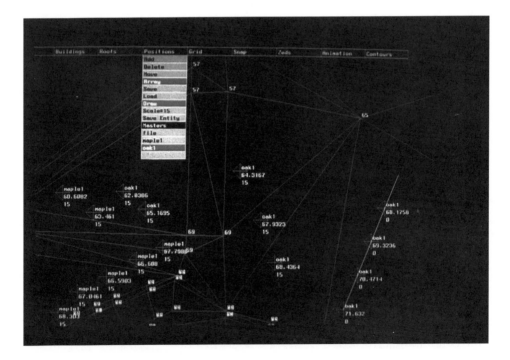

Figure 2 Polyed modeler

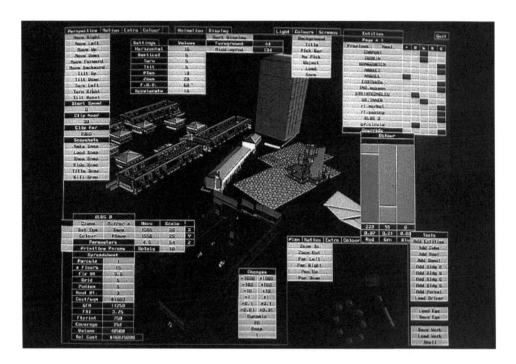

Figure 3   Parametric modeling

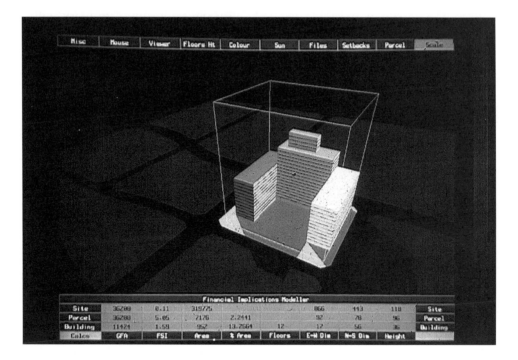

Figure 4   TUUMS modeler

In this studio the computer was introduced to students in a way that did not require them to understand a programming language. It was expected that they would know how to operate a text-editing program and a "paint" program and that they could undertake simple system operations on the Macintosh. Exercises began with operations that took no more than a couple of pages and a fifteen- to twenty-minute tutorial to describe. These exercises were used to gradually introduce students to the other equipment and software available in the course.

A great deal of the preparation and drafting of base material that is normally associated with a studio project was eliminated from these exercises. The base mapping and three-dimensional computer model of the sites under study were prepared ahead of time and were available on the computers' data library. A preliminary symbol library of urban design and landscape elements,such as tree symbols, was also ready for use. Students were able to start on the Iris computers the first day and test some preliminary design ideas.

The Studio Projects

Part 1: Translation and Representation
The first two exercises of the studio were intended to be used as an introduction to the computer tools and as a look at normative visual design composition issues. The computer provided students with the opportunity to work with perspective composition from the standpoint of perceived eye-level experience of the user. The goal was for the student to gain a better intuitive understanding of the translation of two-dimensional symbolic representation of spatial ideas into perceived form. These two exercises ran concurrently during the first two weeks of the term. Students worked in groups of two on both exercises.

Exercise 1: Exploring Archetypal Space and Learning the CAD Tools.
In this exercise students were asked to go through the assigned readings and "experience" or view the diagrams from the course readings that were on the Iris computers. They viewed these archetypal spatial arrangements using the TRIM program. The assignment was to generate three unique, interpretive views of a series of diagrams (contained in the course readings) on the Macintosh computer. The images explored were submitted as diagrams in the text of a Word document that explained what each image portrayed   (see figure 5).

Exercise 2: Framing the Pavilion in the Landscape.
In this exercise, students were instructed to interpret the landscape of the Parliamentary Precinct in Ottawa from the standpoint of the "roving eye." They were to find a path in space that created an interpretive trail through

the Capital. In this first stage of the exercise, they identified and composed three eye-level views along the trail. The Iris computers were used to traverse the site and locate the three vantage points. (Figure 6 is an example of the Parliamentary Precinct data base with which students worked). The students then generated and saved the images on the Macintosh computers using a paint program. The paint program was then used to develop and present a set of potential viewing masks or frames to visually structure or enhance each scene. The images were submitted as diagrams in the text of a Word document that explained what each image portrayed. Stages of the second exercise were:

1. composition of a landscape scene;
2. enhancement of a scene with a two-dimensional frame;
3. translation of a two-dimensional frame into three-dimensional form;
4. interpretation of the Precinct with a moving eye.

Part II: Major Project —Community Design

The major project in this computer-aided design studio spanned eight weeks and dealt with concepts of neighborhood open space and housing design. A variety of approaches to design typology were explored. The typological approach provided students with a conceptual framework that they applied using the forms of computer representation and modeling tools available to the studio. Students evaluated a variety of typological strategies for the formation of neighborhood open space. The design strategies were examined using a range of forms of representation to develop, test, and communicate understanding of the typologies proposed. Projects were evaluated from both the standpoint of a user at eye level and as abstract relationships in a scheme.

The students were presented with several authors' ideas about typology. The authors obviously held contradictory views of the "correct" way to use typology, which each student had to resolve and incorporate into his or her design thinking. The goal was to have students develop their own design vocabulary. In this studio they were asked to organize their definitions of urban landscape space into patterns and units that facilitate design, analysis, implementation, maintenance, and behavioral use. The units they define form a typology that was to respond to the requirements of each individual design program. Stages of the major project were:

1. Site analysis
2. Search for housing precedents
3. Sketch problem of College Street infill project
4. Formation of a computable working design vocabulary for community design (Reading week)

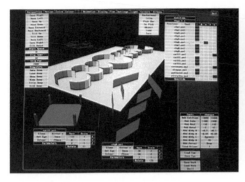

Figure 5 Experiencing a diagram
from class readings

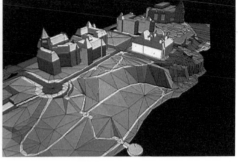

Figure 6 Parliamentary precinct:
data given to students

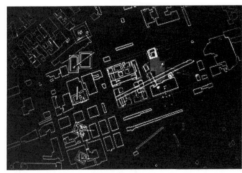

Figure 7 Student Project

Figure 8 Student Project

Figure 9 Student project

Figure 10 Student project

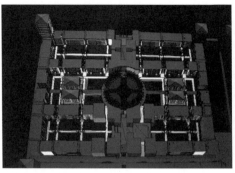

Figure 11 Student project

Figure 12 Student project

Figure 13 Student project

Figure 14 Student project

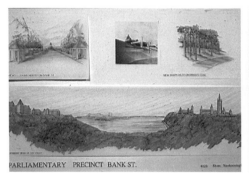

Figure 15 Student project

Figure 16 Student project

5. Morphology of neighborhood: community open-space structure proposals
6. Housing project: program and space-planning concept specification
7. Preliminary design development
8. Design development
9. Revisions and documentation
10. Final presentations

Documentation/Submission

Submissions for the project were made digitally, on video, and on paper. Presentations in studio (both formal and desk critiques) took place directly on the Iris computers. Also required is a videotape of three to five minutes in length that overviewed the project. The paper submitted for the major project consisted of an 11 by 17 inch newspaper-like report given to all critics. All text and titles were to be computer-generated fonts. The document was to be developed and presented at each formal stage of review and revised for the final submission. (Selected images generated by students for the major project appear in figures 7–16.)

Conclusions: Realization of Intentions for the Studio

Preliminary results indicate that a number of our intentions for the course are being realized and that some unforeseen issues are arising. In the Iris-based studio all of the students were able to generate more complex models and more imagery during the first three to four weeks of the term than most of the previous year's studio members were able to accomplish during the whole term. We saw students test a greater number of ideas in more depth. Instead of taking hours and days to test schemes, the students actually responded to criticism during studio critiques. For the first time, we saw students model and test ideas about terrain and detailed landscape elements, but we are not yet satisfied with the sophistication of these representations. We need a more careful presentation of methodological strategies to the students and further development of efficient software.

A great surprise to us has been the desire on the part of many of the students to work almost exclusively on the computer to develop conceptual ideas and test them. (In past studios we generated two or three times as much manual drawing in perspective as a traditional studio.) We are not yet sure if this is a positive development. However, a number of the students are beginning to design primarily in perspective.

Acknowledgments

The author would like to acknowledge the contributions of Shannon McKenzie, Rodney Hoinkes, Steven Ginsberg, and Robert Wright to the development and operation of our system. We would also like to thank the Dynamic Graphics Project of the Computer Systems Research Institute for their assistance in the development of software used in these projects. Student work illustrated was produced by Eckhard Pastrik, Ann Cheung, Dennis Lago, Werner Schwar, and Sham Nankoosingh.

Major funding for the activities of the lab has been provided by Alias Research Inc., Silicon Graphics, Inc., the University Research Incentive Fund of the Province of Ontario, The Natural Sciences and Engineering Research Council of Canada, Apple Computer, Inc., and Autodesk, Inc. Databases used by the students have been created in professional association with the National Capital Commission, Ottawa, the City of Ottawa, and the City of Toronto.

Notes

1. Chris Yessios. 1986."What Has Yet To Be CAD." *ACADIA Proceedings '86.*. Houston.

2. Mark Lindhult. "The Road Beyond CAD." *Landscape Architecture* (Magazine of the American Society of Landscape Architects) (July–August 1988).

3. John Danahy. 1988. "Engaging Intuitive Visual Thinking in Urban Design Modelling: A Real-Time Hypothesis." *ACADIA Proceedings 88* . Ann Arbor.

4. Detailed descriptions of the techniques. projects. and impact on decision-making of our previous work can be found in the following papers:

John Danahy. 1987. "Sophisticated Image Rendering in Environmental Design Review. Human Factors in Computing Systems and Graphics Interface." pp. 211–218. *CHI + GI Conference Proceedings.*

John Danahy. 1987. "The Parliamentary Precinct Study: Visual Simulation in Urban Design Decision-Making and The Need for GIS-CAD Linkages." *GIS' 87* (San Francisco Second Annual International Conference Exhibits and Workshops on Geographic Information Systems). Post Conference Proceedings. Volume 111.

5. We tested several Macintosh 3D-CAD programs but found no way to extract their three-dimensional databases for use on the Irises. These programs appeared extremely efficient in crafting conventional hardline geometric form. However, they were extremely limited in their capacity to represent terrain and vegetation in a manner acceptable for an advanced landscape architectural studio. One could not adequately shape and interactively change the form of exterior spaces using these packages. Finally, databases that provide any significant level of detail become laboriously slow on Mac IIs or 386 machines, let alone the IBM-AT machine we had been using. We also discovered that a fully configured 386 PC or Mac II with advanced graphics and software was costing us in the neighborhood of $15,000 to $20,000 (CDN). That is the price of Silicon Graphics Personal Irises. As a result, we decided to write our own modeling software and use Silicon Graphics computers.

6. John Danahy, "Engaging Intuitive Visual Thinking in Urban Design Modelling." Unpublished paper.

26
Integrating Computing into an
Architectural Undergraduate Program

C. William Fox

Division of Architecture
Temple University

This paper will discuss the process of integrating computing into the undergraduate architectural program at Temple University. It will address the selection and use of hardware and software consistent with the issues and concerns of introducing a new tool to expand the repertoire of skills available to students for use in the design process.

History of Computing in the College

The Department of Architecture, along with the College of Engineering at Temple University, was founded in 1969. Prior to that, the college was a two-year technical institute. In 1978 accreditation was granted for a professional Bachelor of Architecture degree. In 1986 Computer Information Science was moved from the Business College into the College of Engineering and Architecture, and the name was changed to the College of Engineering, Computer Science and Architecture, CECSA. The college presently has four divisions, including the Division of Architecture. The division has approximately 350 full-time students and graduates about fifty students each year with a Bachelor of Architecture degree.

In 1982 a committee of college faculty was formed to research and select appropriate computer hardware and software for teaching computer graphics to engineering and architecture students. At this point, few in the college had any experience in computer graphics. The only required computer course involved very basic programming for word processing and spreadsheet applications. The committee sought to select a system with sufficient capacity for engineering analysis and 3D viewing capability. Choosing the appropriate hardware, software, and peripherals from a myriad of vendors was confusing and compatibility of items was unclear. In 1983 the committee decided to request proposals from several turnkey vendors. The primary justification for this was sole-source responsibility for installation, operation, support, and training. In the spring of 1983 a decision was made to purchase software, hardware, and peripherals from Autotrol Technology. The initial system included a network of four monochrome Apollo workstations, a dot matrix printer, and an HP plotter.

Training was offered with the purchase of the system, and several of us volunteered. Initially frustration was high, for at this point the software had no menus, only keyboard commands, and still contained some errors. With our inexperience, it was difficult to determine when a problem was the result of incorrect input or deficient software.

One year later, in the spring of 1984, the first course was offered to the architectural students, using Series 5000 software developed by Autotrol Technology. On reflection, this course was quite elementary because of our limited experience with the software. The course focused mainly on learning very basic geometric constructions. With additional experience and more confidence, we were able to see the creative opportunities that computers can bring to the design process. In following semesters, the course content has been revised to focus more on modeling, shading, rendering, and 3D drawing (axonometric and perspective). Working with this software is analogous to constructing form with planes, much like a deck of cards or, in conventional terms, like building a model in chipboard.

In 1986, after attending a session at the Graduate School of Design at Harvard, my focus shifted to solids modeling. The opportunity to sculpt, join, and erode blocks to make space offered additional unique alternatives to surface modeling. Inquiry and research led to the selection of I-DEAS, a solid-modeling system developed by Structural Dynamics Research Corp. (SDRC), for automotive and aeronautical engineering design. The college subsequently joined the SDRC University Consortium. In 1987 a new course in solids modeling was offered.

Course Evolution/Development

Students are required to take a computer programming and application course in their second year. The course content and outline are based on the book *The Art of Computer Graphics Programming: A Structured Introduction for Architects and Designers* by Mitchell, Liggett, and Kvan, and the course is intended as an introduction to graphic programming and computing. It is taught by faculty from the Division of Computer Sciences. No additional computing courses are required for graduation; however, two courses, one in surface modeling and one in solids modeling, are offered. The purpose of these courses is to provide students interested in acquiring new tools for design with a theoretical and practical introduction to two alternative methods of graphic computing. These two courses are an introduction to the fundamentals of surface and solids modeling. Both are structured around weekly lectures and supporting exercises. The courses are conducted in a classroom, lecture/lab, and hands-on environment. The lectures and exercises examine the principles and concepts of the respective modeling methods. A final project for each course requires the student to select a small building of architectural merit and make a critical analysis of the project. Either course is required for students desiring to participate in a computing design studio. If a student is interested in acquiring more in-depth programming skills, he/she is encouraged to take courses offered in the Division of Computer Sciences.

Surface Modeling
Arch 190 is generally the first course taken by interested students. Approximately 15 percent of the students in the program take this course. Figures 1 and 2 illustrate representative exercises for learning the fundamentals of generating patterns with lines, geometric constructions, and painted surfaces. In these exercises a simple element is constructed and painted. Generally, these elements are then manipulated into more complex compositions through scaling, rotation, and translation. These exercises build over several sessions and become the vehicle for introducing groups of new commands. Reiterations of these patterns are then examined and scrutinized for visual ramifications in color, texture, and surface characteristics. Initially the exercises are 2D and deal with only the X and Y coordinates; eventually the Z axis is introduced and 3D wire-frame constructions are generated. Figure 3 shows an exploded view of a small church by Schinkel. This wire frame is more complex than an introductory exercise, but it demonstrates the spatial relationships of planes and edges and permits simultaneous viewing of the regulating lines in plan and section. Figures 4 and 5 show examples of a final project. Figure 6 is an example of an abstract design problem which involves manipulating and duplicating two forms to show movement and a hierarchy of spaces.

Solids Modeling
Arch 192, a true solids-modeling course, was first offered in the fall of 1987. Although this course has been offered for only two semesters, the contrast solids modeling offers to surface modeling and the capability of the software have intrigued and interested many students. Figure 7 shows several objects

Figure 1   Polar point construction using translation, and rotation

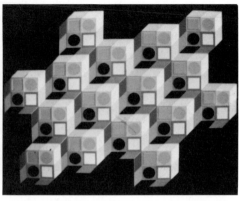

Figure 2   Painting by V. Vasarely, replicated, by using scaling, duplication and translation

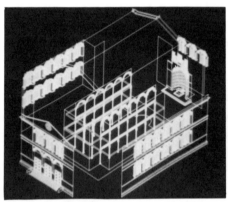

Figure 3   Church by Schinkel, wire-frame exploded view, modeled by D. Gehron

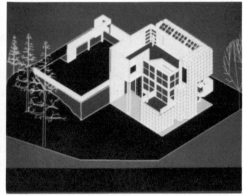

Figure 4   House by R. Meier, painted-surface model by D. Van Horn

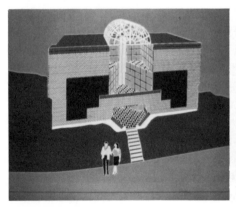

Figure 5   House by M. Botta, painted surface by R. Darus

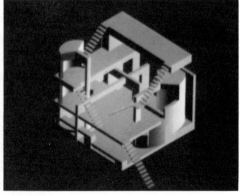

Figure 6   Abstract spatial composition drawn by M. Hollenbach

(primitives) constructed as 3D blocks with the solids software. This is perhaps most similar to building models in clay. Other more complex forms can also be constructed by combining forms with Boolean operations (join, intercept, and cut). This software also allows very sculptural forms to be constructed by making a profile and extruding, revolving, and skinning (stretching a surface over a group of profiles). Figure 8 shows a profile revolved 360 degrees to construct an example of a column used by Frank Lloyd Wright in the Johnson Wax Headquarters building. Figures 7 and 8 are representative of the exercises in this course. Other important options include multiple light sources and surface characteristics, as well as system assembly, and use of a hierarchical data structure. In figures 9 through 14, the individual elements were constructed, and in system assembly instances or clones were created and duplicated into subsystems. In figure 9 the data base subsystems are viewed as a build up or layering of systems, with repetitive elements abstracted. The column shafts in figure 10 were constructed by skinning, and the capitals by revolution. By replacing one element in figure 9 with the more detailed element in figure 10, all the columns in figure 9 could be replaced with the more detailed column. Figures 11 and 12 show examples of how conceptual elements can be constructed, composed, and then later refined, expanded, and exploded in the X, Y, and Z axis into a hierarchical display of the systems. Figures 9 through 12 are all examples of the final projects in the solids modeling course.

General Observations

Most students can learn the fundamentals of surface or solids modeling within one semester. The examples show they can interact with the computer and generate a real architectural building project, inclusive of building components and material detail. New releases of software have become more powerful but still are friendly enough to allow users to learn to manipulate sequences of commands within a semester of work. Generally, the more facile students spend more time at the workstation and tend to experiment with the power and potential of this new tool. Use of the software in these courses is factual and analytical, much like building a model of an existing building in chipboard or clay to study its topology and anatomy.

Computer Design Studio

In the spring semester, a vertical studio, Arch 137/139, is offered to students in the third and fourth year. Within this framework, a design studio, utilizing the computer as the primary tool, is offered for ten to fifteen students. These students must have completed the programming course and at least one of the other computer graphics courses. To date, the computer studio has been offered three times. Each time new areas of computing have been explored and

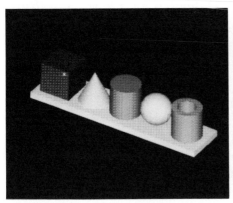

Figure 7 Primitive solid blocks
on plank

Figure 8 Profile revolved translated resting
360 degrees, columns from Frank Lloyd
Wright's Johnson Wax Headquarters

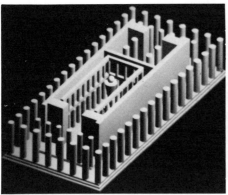

Figure 9 Parthenon,
constructed in system assembly
by G. Volk

Figure 10 Parthenon,
column detail constructed in skinning
by G. Volk

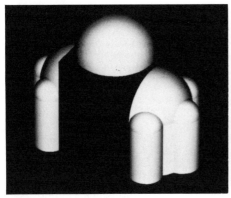

Figure 11 Hagia Sophia,
constructed in system assembly
by R. Darus

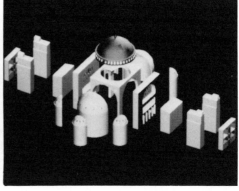

Figure 12 Hagia Sophia,
exploded view, system assembly
by R. Darus

discoveries made. Both the surface modeling and solid modeling software are used. Comparisons are made and examined to study the different influences on the design project.

The studio experiments with alternative ways of using computing in the design process. Although plan and section remain important, 3D views are extremely revealing and helpful in evaluating the form, space, and detail. Reviews tend to focus more on simulating the what and the how of an experience within the space, rather than on the formal relationships of plan and section.

The use of alternative media throughout the semester is encouraged, but emphasis is given to experimenting with computing. Design crits frequently take place in front of the monitor at the workstation. The media used for reviews and presentations include prints, plots, and slides. Prints and plots are frequently overlaid with soft pencil and/or colored pencil or magic marker. The prints are important for reference work away from the workstation. These sketches serve the same purpose as the conventional yellow sketch paper. Often this information is fed back into the data base and tested as the work is refined. Experimentation of this nature is encouraged to test alternative ways of using the computer as a tool to facilitate a more comprehensive design process. Figures 13 and 14 are views of an abstract spatial composition using two contrasting forms, one rectilinear and one curvilinear. These were then manipulated to form one large space and three smaller spaces. The intent was to take some risks and explore space that would be difficult to explore using conventional tools. Figures 15 through 18 are examples of modeling fragments of existing buildings to show architectural detail.

The shading, light sources, and 3D viewing (perspectives) all allow more extensive evaluations of a design, as the designer can view the form and space as the user will actually experience it. Use of this powerful tool, through the design process, appears to place less emphasis on the formal relationships and more on the evaluation and analysis of the actual spatial experience.

Evaluation of the Past and a Look into the Future at Temple

Looking back over the past five years, I sometimes feel that we have accomplished a great deal, but in that same period of time the software and hardware have changed so rapidly that there is still a great deal to explore. From a more pragmatic point of view, there are some fundamental issues that need to be addressed for computing to be more fully embraced within the Division of Architecture.

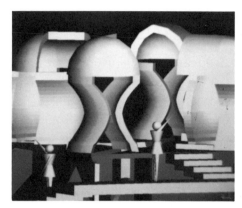

Figure 13   Spatial design problem, design studio,   by G. Volk

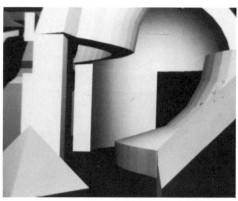

Figure 14   Detail, spatial design, design studio, by G. Volk

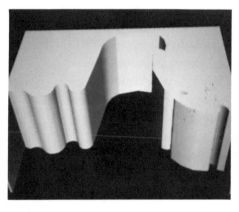

Figure 15   Church by Utzon, model of roof by R. Rozman

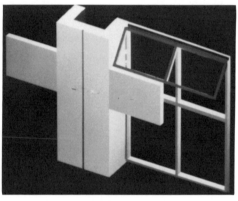

Figure 16   Office building, M/G model of facade repetitive element

Figure 17   Building by A. Rossi, model of facade by G. Volk

Figure 18   Building by M. Botta model of facade by S. Bwint

The computers are currently in a "computer lab" five floors from the studio. This means a real effort must be made to use the facilities. This set up may work for a graphics course, but is totally inappropriate for encouraging spontaneous studio use. This fall, to ease this condition, we are installing a Macintosh lab adjacent to the studio spaces. This will permit students to move freely between their drafting boards and the workstations. We hope eventually to locate workstations within the studio.

The department has no intention of offering any more than a limited programming course to the architectural students. If a student is interested in programming, courses are available through other departments. The real question is how many different types of hardware platforms and what software applications should be made available, and how they should be introduced in the program.

The computer graphics studio is only in its infancy at Temple. This past semester was the first time related design issues of program, conceptual development, and architectural detail were dealt with in a comprehensive way. The process of design development is still fragmented and sometimes short circuited. Crits are often consumed with the technical process of constructing the database. Key to this is understanding the development of appropriate databases, their size, and the required generation time. Perhaps this is a temporary condition until more powerful workstations are available at affordable prices. In the meantime, alternative methods of utilizing the computer and a more flexible interchange with conventional tools all need to be tried and tested. The power and capability of the tool cannot be denied, and the studio is the best location for integrating its use and exploring its potential. More effort by everyone needs to be applied to the integration and mainstreaming of its use.

File storage is of key concern. As the projects become more ambitious and data bases increase in size, more disk storage is needed. Although we have approximately one gigabyte of storage in the network, this was filled two weeks before semester projects were due. During the last two weeks rigorous management of files was necessary by the systems manager. Lack of adequate storage limited development of projects, and subsequent crashes often involved loss of important files. This could be alleviated with more disk storage space. As the workstations and the software become more powerful, it is inevitable that projects will become more complex and that there will be a greater need for more storage. What is enough storage?

How would we like to expand the computing equipment? Always by more than the budget allows. We currently have fourteen Apollo workstations on two separate networks: the original network, which at this point seems antiquated (five years old), and a new network of eight more powerful Apollo workstations (DN3000s to DN4500s), an ink-jet printer, and a pen plotter. Only these eight are used for studio work. They are in high demand by both architects and engineers. Students must sign up for two to four hour blocks of time, and frequently the lab is open twenty-four hours a day when projects are due. Obviously more workstations would alleviate this condition, and as funds become available workstations will be added. In addition to more workstations, we would like to purchase a scanner for photographs and slides, photographic equipment that captures an image through the workstation ,and a paint package for touch-up work in image processing.

At Temple through telephone connectivity, all students and faculty can access the library stacks and, with an account number, the Vax mainframe. This coming year the various networks within each college will be connected to the larger university-wide network, allowing files to be shared between many workstations on the campus. This will also allow movement of files between the Macintosh lab in the Division of Architecture and the Apollo lab in the college.

In an article about the scholar's workstation of the 1990s in the October 1988 issue of *Academic Computing*, R. Weissman predicted more powerful work-stations with up to 100 MIPS, 130+ MB of memory, and a gigabyte of local storage. Predictions also indicate that future networking and file exchange may be comparable to today's Fax communication via the telephone. With this capability, many of the technical concerns I have cited above will disappear. Then, perhaps, we can really explore the creative potential of computers in design.

## 27

The Organization of CAD Teaching in Design Schools

Robert S. Frew

Yale University School of Architecture

Introduction
This paper is the result of a survey of European CAD teaching that was conducted in 1987 and 1988. It makes comparisons with teaching at the Yale School of Architecture, and goes on to analyze the issues that should be addressed in a CAD program in a school of architecture.

Development of CAD Teaching
In the United States in 1965 CAD teaching options were very limited. If you had a Fortran compiler with graphic extensions, you were able to teach the introduction to CAD as an introductory graphics class. Often you had to introduce the student to programming in a separate class and then introduce graphics. Recently, this first class has become unnecessary because of the ease of using graphics with a high-level language. About five years ago the wave of CAD systems teaching hit the schools and in many cases programming was not offered. The exclusion of programming cuts out the important connection between language and product, which should be addressed in the future, when programming will be used as a general tool to introduce problem-solving skills into the curriculum.

Current CAD Teaching at Yale
At Yale we now have the following optional courses:

Introduction to CAD—word processing, spreadsheets, and CAD with a little programming in graphics

Advanced CAD—a continuation of CAD with graphics 3D wireframe and 3D surface modelling

Management and Computing—a new course that gives the student the basics of project management using spreadsheets and a project management system

Energy, Lighting, and Computing—a new course not yet offered that will give the student design-oriented lighting software and an introduction to energy systems and design

Outside Project—Students in the outside building project that is part of the first year studio should produce the documents, including the cost estimates, schedule, and drawings, using the computer. This is done as a group project, and the students who have taken the CAD course do most of the computer work.

During this past year a faculty task force on computing has recommended that the introductory computer class be required in the professional program.

The Relationship between CAD Teaching and Research

In all the schools I visited in Europe where there were people working on research, and there was a clear increase in the CAD activities and equipment within the professional program, even though research and teaching activities were separated both organizationally and physically. At Sheffield and Cambridge a system that was originally developed in the academic environment has been moved to an independent "for profit" company. Strathclyde intends in the next year to establish a company that is a part of the university but whose purpose is to do business in the professional community. At Edinburgh the graduate students are doing quite abstract work on data structures for geometric models, while the undergraduates have, as at most schools, a lab with low-level CAD systems.   In all of the above cases the impact of the research activity on the professional program is quite positive.

In Britain, as in the United States, the individual researcher applies for funding from central agencies. In France, however, the central government has determined that there will be three CAD research centers—at Paris, Marseille, and Nantes—and researchers are naturally attracted to those schools. The work being done is quite interesting. It is executed primarily on the MAC platform and is the responsibility of one principal researcher at each location.   In each institution there is a small group of graduate research students and staff. There is no need for this group to teach in the school of architecture and consequently the amount of research work done is substantial.

If one accepts that research and teaching are mutually beneficial, then one can focus on the way the relationship is organized. Some kind of research and development arm might, for example, be established. One of the first design schools to establish an outside practice within the school was the Ulm School of Design in Germany. Associated with the school was an Institute of Design that was responsible for many important design products, the Braun product line being one example. This model was later copied at the University of Waterloo in Canada in the 1960s, where a number of the more innovative buildings for Expo '67 were designed. The important issue at Waterloo was shared facilities and personnel; that is, by putting all of the academic and professional personnel in one place, there could be a real interchange of ideas. In addition, the school could also justify more equipment, since much of it would come from the income of the institute. One issue that was very carefully dealt with was the position of the student. A student could be either a student or a professional in the institute, but not both at the same time. When the student was a professional, he or she was paid more than the normal professional scale, which further emphasized the difference.

It is important to consider the basic objectives of university-run practices. In the past they were merely a way for professors to extend their work into the community, and they reflected the university's inability to provide the opportunity. In return the staff were well paid and profits were typically distributed to the staff. In the Waterloo model the excess money was used for scholarships and equipment, and only those who worked in the institute had the right to determine the distribution. In general the objective should be to make the subject of CAD more accessible to students and to provide the students with the best equipment possible.

At Yale research is centered on the interest of the individual faculty member and student. Either one can develop a project and can arrange for assistance to complete the work. The role of the CAD faculty is to review and assist the assessment of time and technical knowledge needed to complete the work and to monitor progress. At present there is one major project and there are two smaller ones, which together do not present sufficient demands to justify a separate organizational structure.

Methods of CAD Teaching

Should computer-aided design be taught more as a design course than a computer course, or should it be formally taught at all? The primary objective of the student taking a course is to learn how to use CAD systems as design tools, which normally means that the theory behind the systems is taught after the student learns how to use them.

One of the best examples of teaching CAD that I found in Europe was at the Open University. In general the Open University is organized as a TV-Video University; in CAD that means that 200 students per term sign up for the course and in return they are given videos, a workbook, a tutor, and a computer with a CAD system that they rent for the term. It is then up to the students to fulfill the assignments, to meet with the advisor in their particular city, and to pace their way through the course. There is presently a waiting list of 400 for the course, which is some indication of the need for general CAD teaching. The method of teaching at the Open University is as follows. The student learns how to use the system at his or her own speed through the videos and workbooks. Then the theoretical basis of the system can be taught in a traditional lecture format. [1].

Design faculties are divided about whether the CAD course should be required. At Aberdeen each student is required to take a computer course; that they have only one AutoCAD workstation and about twenty general workstations makes one concerned about the content of the course. At the Mackintosh School of Architecture in Glasgow there is no requirement for a computer course, but there is an active CAD group that serves as a resource center for students in general. The work began with the desktop publishing programs that the students use for various publications, and they have AutoCAD as their CAD system. Only the students who want to work on the machines are there, and the environment is very positive. The equipment can be more specialized in this school, as the objective is not to provide a large number of workstations for a class but to provide a quality graphic product that is then used in the design studio.

At Yale we use the analogy of the library to explain our activity in the computer lab. The staffing of the lab is a reflection of this. There is one overall coordinator, as is the case in all the curriculum sections, and there is a staff person in each of the subject areas, which are structures, energy, lighting, management, and design. The responsibility of the staff is to review the current software available and to encourage teachers to use the CAD software in their courses. One might think that this is easy; but the most obvious areas are often the most difficult. Although problems exist in the implementation of the library concept at this time, it appears to have the most merit.

CAD and the Theory of Design

Any theory or analysis of design can eventually lead to computer-aided design. In the same way, any development of the graphic capability of the computer can lead to an impact on computer-aided design. The gap between theory and practice is getting smaller, and student interest is increasing. The attitude to CAD that seems to be least threatening to the design faculty is that the computer is like a car that they should learn how to drive, and that the computer is here to stay and they should know how to use it. What the curriculum usually requires is that the student learn how to create a building database and how to draw a perspective. It is an unfortunately limited view of the role of CAD.

The analysis of form and problem-solving are basic subjects that should be incorporated into the architecture curriculum. Problem-solving can be taught in a CAD course, through the introduction to Pascal or C programming. The analysis of form has been introduced by a number of "theorists," but it is not generally taught as a separate course. Some of the information can be taught in a geometry course, but the real need is to offer a design course that deals with the analysis of the plan by abstracting and generalizing the plan types that can be used in buildings.

CAD and Architectural Technology

A computer is used in a design problem because it either gives greater accuracy, does it faster, or gives the designer greater analytical power to deal with the problem. Early programs for problem structuring and space allocation did not give the designer more but rather presented a number of alternate ways to think about design. The first major impact of the computer was at the time of the energy crisis, when it became necessary to use the computer to analyze the effect of passive solar strategies. The long-range outcome was the production of a number of books that gave the results of the computer analysis; it did not result in significant use of computer methods in design. The development of CAD systems has resulted instead from the need for drafting, and the systems are increasingly used for design and rendering.

One technique that may well change designers' attitudes toward the computer is lighting simulation. A system developed at Lawrence Berkeley Laboratories can produce a fully rendered view of a space with the simulated effect of the lighting design. The visual effect in combination with the extensive mathematical model that calculates the distribution of light gets at the qualitative aspects of the design. This system is important because designers do not have a good alternative. Existing methods of calculation by producing light contours and using physical models have major scale problems. The problems with the existing methods are significant enough that designers do not use them. In general, the computer models that will find success in architecture are those that give the designer the ability to design the 3D form with the technical calculations embedded in the program.

Note

1 From this program, see: Joe Rooney and Philip Steadman, Principles of Computer-Adied Design. 1987. London: Pitman/ The Open University.

28
Case Studies in Moviemaking and Computer-Aided Design

Earl Mark

Department of Architecture
Massachusetts Institute of Technology

A movie which is developed from site location video, sync sound, and computer graphics animation can provide a highly convincing simulation of reality. A movie that conveys a sense of the space, materials and juxtaposition of objects of a proposed architectural design provides a special kind of realism, where the representation may be of a proposed building that exists only within the mind of an architect. For an experienced architect, however, the movie may not provide a good surrogate experience for what it feels like to actually be within the architectural space.

In these case studies, a few projects that combine moviemaking and computer-aided design technologies are examined. These projects were completed using a combination of resources at the MIT School of Architecture and Planning and the Harvard Graduate School of Design. The integrated use of these media is presented as conceptualized with the Electronic Design Studio, a research project that has been supported over the past five years by Project Athena at MIT. The impact of movies and computer-aided design on the perception of architectural space is also reported—based on a pilot study of twenty architectural students.

Introduction

The quest for realism in computer graphics is reflected in efforts to simulate real—time movement through three-dimensional space. Yet, the perception of three-dimensional space acquired from computer animation may be fragmented and illusory. Moviemaking is based on the illusion of taking still images and flipping between them more rapidly than is apparent to the human eye (i.e., typically at greater than 1/18th of a second). We may take it for granted that greater realism is obtained in movies, and forget that watching a movie is technically a process of watching a sequence of still pictures [1]

Nevertheless, in some architectural offices, moviemaking has become a routine part of professional practice. For example, at The Architect's Collaborative (TAC), the architect may develop a shotboard, a scriptwriter and narrator are hired, and a videotape is carefully produced to convey the issues and key features of a proposed architectural design [2] Although such a production may serve to reach an audience that is unaccustomed to interpreting more traditional paper based presentations, it may not prepare viewers to critically sort out the key elements of a proposed design. In particular, the audience of such a presentation may not have a clear understanding of the scale of an architectural space, the boundaries of an architectural space, the identification of objects within the architectural space, and the juxtaposition of objects to one another.

For a naive member of the audience, motion pictures may convey three-dimensional space with a degree of realism that is not provided by static drawings. For example, during a screening of one of the first of silent films, members of the audience became so frightened by the motion picture images of an oncoming train that they sought to move out of its pathway [3]. In the case of architectural space, however, the apparent realism of a motion picture may lead to the false presumption that it is more informative than non-animated drawings. In particular, a person may face some cognitive hurdles in attempting to study an architectural space through the use of an animated visual medium. For example, there is a limited opportunity for the sustained observation of objects within the viewing frame of a motion picture as compared with the prolonged opportunity to observe objects within the still frame of a traditional plan, section or elevational drawing. Understanding the shot-to-shot partition of an architectural space in a movie may also require a highly literate orientation to the medium. Rudolf Arnheim claims of some of the more successful film directors that "their imagination and keen observation could hardly bear such remarkable fruit were it not for the erudition and the sense of quality acquired" during years of scholastic preparation [4].

The break-up of a motion pictures into sequences of shots and the organization of those shots into a coherent framework is what Eisenstein referred to as the *mise-en-scène* [5]. In the case of a simulated walk through of an architectural space, the moviemaker may decide to take specific liberties with the *mise-en-scène*. In particular, the moviemaker may juxtapose sequences in order to make building components seem to fit together . For example, in the making of the film "Beauty and the Beast", Jean Cocteau constructed a single architectural space from a series of shots recorded at separate site locations [6]:

"One of the advantages of making films is that you can mix, muddle up and reconstruct your place of action just as it suits you. This cresting of wall will become a ramp, this ramp will end in the balustrades which go round the chateau moat."

A person viewing the movie may interpret the montage of shots as representing a single architectural space. As evidenced in some of the case studies below, however, each person may reconstruct the architectural space in a different manner.

Moviemaking and its Relationship to the Electronic Design Studio

The initial concept for the Electronic Design Studio was based on a role for electronic media, including motion pictures, that would mirror the role of traditional drawing media as diagrammed in figure 1. The Electronic Design Studio is an Athena funded research project within the School of Architecture and Planning at MIT. Within this environment, (1A) CAD drafting and solid modeling tools are mirrored by (1B) paper based drawing, and clay or cardboard modeling tools. The (2A) role played by experts within a traditional design studio is mirrored by the (2B) the role of knowledge based or expert systems as an on-line computer resource. Finally, the role of (3A) still and motion picture visual information systems, such as provided by videodisc technology, is mirrored by the role of (3B) visual references, such as slides and archive drawings. These components have been linked within the Electronic Design Studio, as documented elsewhere [7].

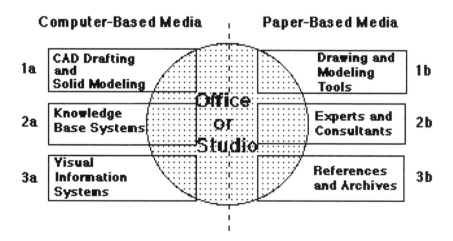

Figure 1

The use of visual information systems as diagrammed in figure 1 presently involves the retrieval of archive movies over both computer and cable television networks from both local and remote videodisc sources. This includes access to slides stored on videodisc at Rotch Visual Collections at MIT. Access to these remote resources has become more convenient than would be possible without the network, but the visual information system does not provide for applications beyond the traditional role of reference material in the design studio. With regard to the role of motion picture production as a potential design medium, however, there is no precedent in the traditional paper-based studio. Nevertheless, it is speculated that moviemaking can work as a design tool in a manner similar to the use of thumbnail sketches.

An architect will make and study a series of thumbnail sketches when contemplating a particular design proposal. Similarly, it is speculated that an architect can also make and study a sequence of motion picture images in the creative design process. As provided by the case studies cited below, an architect may study (1) the movement of an observation point through an architectural space, (2) the movement of people through a proposed architectural space, or (3) the dynamic conditions of light and sound within an architectural space. In general, the movie may represent some key features of a proposed building in a way that will influence an architect's development of a particular design proposal. For example, in response to an animated walk-through, the architect may make make some modifications to a given layout of spaces that removes impediments to the circulation of people or which provides greater aesthetic coherence to the sequencing of views.

Yet, a number of major obstacles are still apparent. A first major obstacle is that, while ideas may be captured in the fleeting moments of a rapid thumbnail sketch on the back of paper envelope, moviemaking is a relatively protracted, carefully planned and not spontaneous process. (The techniques of cinema verité break many conventions of traditional moviemaking, and offer some hope for a sketchbook like and spontaneous production process. But the turn-around time from image making to image viewing may still be a problem. This discussion is beyond the scope of this paper). A second major obstacle is that it is difficult for the moviemaker to gain control over the animation of many images in the same manner as an architect can control the content of a single image. A fear is that the overwhelming number of animated pictures may "control the architect"[8]. A third major obstacle is that merging animated computer graphics with site location video, which has only been partially addressed in the work referenced below, is a cumbersome undertaking and not without technical limitations. Finally, the illusory power of this simulated movement may not be satisfying to an experienced architect, such as Steen Eiler Rasmussen.

It is not enough to see architecture, you must experience it. You must observe how it was designed for a special purpose and how it was attuned to the entire concept and rhythm of a specific era. You must dwell in the rooms, feel how they close about you, observe how you are naturally led from one to the other." [9]

Three types of movies were experimented with by architecture students of mine in the 1989 Spring semester at MIT [10]. They were

1. A computer graphics/site location videotape of moving figures as viewed from a still frame of reference.

2. A computer graphics/site location videotape of moving images as viewed from a moving frame of reference

3. A cinema verité movie using time lapse film and documentary video of an architectural space.

Project One: A Computer Graphics/Site Location Videotape of Moving Figures as Viewed From a Still Frame of Reference

The production process involved the use of a VHS Video Camera, a Computervision CADDS4X CAD system running on a Sun 68020 Workstation, the Artisan Paint Package running on a Sun 386i "Roadrunner" Workstation, an IBM PC-AT based TARGA Board with a chroma key and patched to a video editing production suite. This project concerned the description of a proposed architectural design for residential housing located in the South End of Boston. The basic steps in putting together the production were (see figure 3):

(a) Documentary video footage of the site location was recorded from a steady camera held on a tripod. This included an aerial view from nearby Hancock Tower as well as street level views. Four cardinal views of the site were selected.

(b) Still video frames from the four cardinal views were grabbed by means of the Targa Board attached to a VHS video player. Next, a Targa format bit map file of these still images was produced on the Targa Board system. The format file was then transferred to the Artisan Paint Program running on the Sun 386i "Roadrunner" Workstation.

(c) A three-dimensional surfaced and shaded model of the proposed residential housing was developed on the Computervision CADDS4X Workstation. Perspectives of the model were generated (using software written by the author when he was employed by Computervision). Bit mapped images of these perspectives were then transferred to the Artisan Paint System.

(d) On the Artisan Paint System, the still video frames from site (step a and step b) and the CAD perspective renderings (step c) were merged. Step c

Figure 2 Stills from movie 1

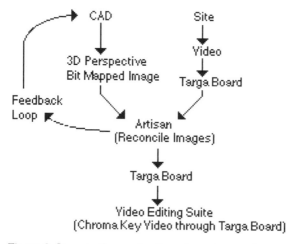

Figure 3 Steps in the production of movie type 1

was repeated until there was a good correspondence between (1) the perspectives generated on the CAD system and (2) the video images from the site location footage.

(e) Once the proper CAD perspective images were obtained, they were prepared for final merging with the motion picture images from the site location video. Each CAD perspective image was transformed on the Artisan system so that the parts of the computer graphics model that would appear in the final movie were isolated. Other parts were painted out with a blue color that could later be used for chroma key mixing (see step f). The resultant painted images was transferred from the Artisan to the Targa Board.

(f) The videotape of the site location was played through the Targa board and then chroma keyed to the blue color that was painted during step (e) onto the CAD generated perspective images.

Project Two: A Computer Graphics/Site Location Videotape of Moving Images as Viewed from a Moving Frame of Reference

The production process involved the use of a VHS Video Camera , a Computervision CADDS4X CAD system running on a Sun 68020 Workstation, the Starbase

Figure 4 Stills from movie 2

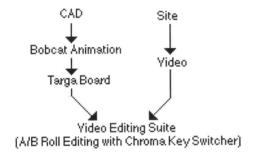

Figure 5 Steps in the production of movie type 2

Graphics Package running on a Hewlett-Packard Bobcat Workstation, a broadcast quality 3/4 inch video camera, a VHS video camera, a video editing suite with a/b roll editing and a chroma key switcher. This project was the description of a proposed architectural design for residential housing located in Charlestown, Massachusetts. The basic steps in putting together the production were (see figure 4):

(a) A 3-D computer graphics CAD model of the proposed design was created on the Computervision CADDS4X Workstation .

(b) The 3-D database from the CAD model was then translated to the Starbase Graphics Package. A translator was developed for the purpose of transferring the data.

(c) An animation package was developed on top of the Starbase package with several optional methods of moving about the architectural space in real time [11]. The animation package allows a user to script an animation sequence and specify the camera position and angle. A front end to the animation package provides for the interpolation of camera movement and angle between explicitly defined camera positions. Two sequences of movement through the architectural space were generated on the animation system, and this movement was then recorded on videotape. Most importantly, the movements include views out of some windows. While looking out one particular window, the camera panned from left to right. The area within the window was filled with a solid shade of blue. These video sequences constitute videotape a.

(d)   On-location video documentary footage was recorded of exterior views similar to those that might be observed by looking out the windows of the proposed architectural design. Within one particular sequence, the camera panned from *right to left*. These video sequences constituted videotape b.

(e)   Videotape a and videotape b were synchronized within an a/b roll video editing suite. The exterior views recorded in videotape b where chroma keyed over the color of the windows recorded in videotape a. The camera movement from *right to left* in videotape a was synchronized with the panning shot from *left to right* in video to b. The result of this synchronization is the apparent effect of looking from right to left out of the window, and the exterior scenery seeming to change naturally from left to right. The synchronization of these two sequences required a computer video editing capability, and still was lacking in precision.

Project Three: A Cinema Verité Movie Using Time Lapse Film and Documentary Video of an Architectural Space.

This was a less technically ambitious movie that combined time-lapse photography with video documentary footage. The movie included sync and non-sync sound. The purpose of the project was to capture the qualities of the architectural space as reflected in the cycle of its daily use.

The merger of the video and computer graphics in these efforts was achieved with considerable effort. The spontaneous qualities of working with a sketchbook was not achieved. The feedback to the designer was to suggest how the building might appear within the context of dynamic conditions at its site location. As it turns out, the movement of people and traffic are quite distracting in the videotapes, minimizing the attention given to the proposed building. A design which responds more clearly to the movement and the environment might have provided a more significant focus for the case studies. In the aforementioned projects, however, this was not the most obvious concern of the proposed design, and so the purposefulness of using the moviemaking technology was not very clear. Only in the case of the third project, where camera movement was completely unrestricted, was there a more complete sense of the building within the context of moving people and changing shadows in the environment.

Certain design issues may shift closer to the foreground in moviemaking than they they do in other media—such as the movement of people, and light and shade at the site location. Further study seems necessary, however, before it is evident which issues are raised in a manner which is meaningful to architectural design.

Some of the technology used to create the animations described here is becoming commercially available on personal computer platforms. In particular, it is not difficult to move from a 3-D CAD model to a computer animation tool within a single PC platform [12]. On the other hand, the mixing of computer graphics and video requires the use of more extensive video editing facilities than might be typically found within a School of Architecture and Planning. In particular, a video editing suite with so-called a/b roll editing and a good chroma key switcher is needed for more advanced merging of video and computer graphics. The cognitive and purposeful architectural content of these productions, however, is perhaps less certain than the technology. Therefore, a scheme was piloted for measuring the perception of architectural space arrived at through viewing a movie.

A Pilot Study of Twenty Architectural Students:

A central issue of this study is the role of media as a vehicle for an architect to work with in terms of developing abstractions of a particular design concept. There are many particular applications of moviemaking which seem sufficiently distinct to warrant separate studies. In each case, it would be useful to examine how an abstraction contributes to an architect's understanding of his or her work. This study, however, examined the abstractions available through a single instance of moviemaking in a specific instance of architectural design. This study, although it was focused on one application of moviemaking, was difficult to constrain. It was greatly complicated by consideration of different techniques for making the movie and different levels of audience sophistication. In the process of narrowing down the cognitive study, it was discovered that a seemingly focused testing scenario had to be further constrained in order to capture meaningful results.

A preliminary test was not that very useful. Its purpose was to record students' perceptions of an architectural space that resulted from listening to the sound track of a sequence within the movie "The Third Man." The sequence takes place within an underground sewer where one character is being chased by a group of pursuers. The long reverberating sync sound of the characters moving within the sewer seem revealing of the architectural space. The architectural critic Steen Eiler Rasmussen wrote of this sequence within the movie that :

"The characteristic sounds which tunnels produce are clearly heard in the splashing of the water and the echoes of the men hunting the third man. Here, architecture is certainly heard. Your ear receives the impact of both the length and the cylindrical form of the tunnel." [13]

Eighteen architecture graduate students all had similar responses to hearing the sound track of the sequence within the movie described by Steen Eiler Rasmussen (figure 6a-d). They were asked to produce drawings and give verbal descriptions of the architectural space that conveyed their impression of listening to the sound track. Their drawings are surprisingly consistent. They describe an underground passageway that is partially flooded by water.

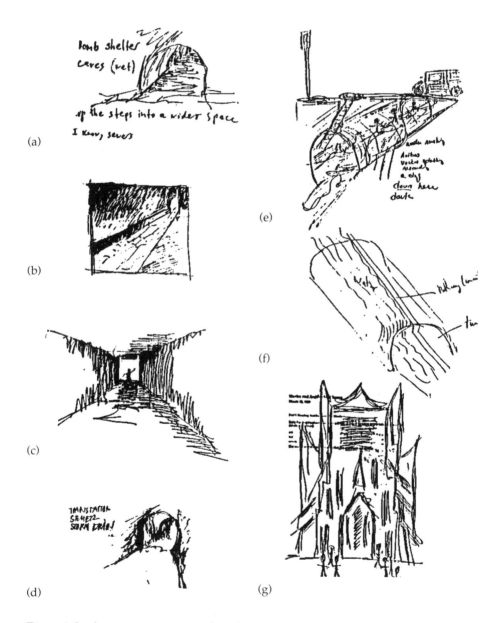

Figure 6 Student responses to sound track

The same test was also given to a similarly sized group of non-architecture graduate students. The drawings produced by these students were not as consistent with one another as those produced by the architecture graduate students nor as focused on the spatial attributes depicted within the movie (figure 6e-g). The persons listening to the sound track from the movie may have been attending to entirely different aspects of it. One person may be thinking about the architectural space whereas a second person may be interested in the narrative. Therefore, in a revised testing scenario, subjects were examined for how well they could reproduce specific characteristics of a given architectural space.

The revised testing scenario compared the responses of two groups of architecture students. The first group of students, Group A, viewed a videotape of an architectural space. The second group of students, Group B, viewed a plan of the same architectural space. Both groups of students were then required to draw a plan of the architectural space. The intent of this comparison was to uncover differences that exposure to each medium had in terms of how the two groups reproduced (1) the boundaries of an architectural space, (2) the identification of objects in the architectural space, and (3) the juxtaposition of objects within the architectural space. The three steps of the testing scenario were:

Step 1:
   A—The architectural space was recorded within a two minute videotape:
The two-minute videotape consists of two major sequences and a minor sequence. Each major sequence consists of a combined series of pans that provides a continuous 360 view of the architectural space. The minor sequence consists of a series of still close-up shots of objects in the room. Clearly, the videotaping technique had an impact on what was recorded. For example, the identification of objects in the space might be enhanced by special use of spot and fill lighting. Tracking equipment could have provided smoother continuity between shots. A wider angle lens might have taken in more information. The results of this study, therefore, are only relative to the particular techniques employed in making the movie, and the skills of the moviemaker.
   B—A measured plan drawing of the architectural space was also made.
The measured plan was a conventional plan drawing that incorporated standard notations for doors, windows, and other objects.

Step 2: The two groups of architecture students were tested.
Each group consisted of ten graduate and upper level undergraduate students. Each student was tested separately and then interviewed. Each student from

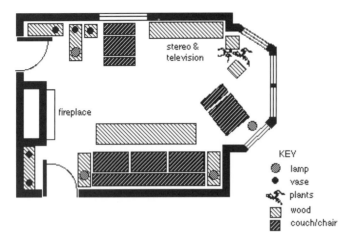

Figure 7 Measured Plan

Group A viewed the videotape once for its two-minute duration, and then was not permitted to see it again. Each student from Group B viewed the plan, also once for two minutes, and then was not permitted to see it again. After viewing the videotape or the plan for two minutes, each student was asked to draw a plan of the architectural space. The plan drawing was to include all of the objects that could be recalled from the within the architectural space.

Step 3: The student's plan drawings were scored:
Each student's plan reproduction of the architectural space was scored according to the following system (ideal scores in each category of performance are shown in bold face):

* number of non-wall furniture objects found: 24
* number of non-wall furniture objects invented: 0
* number of wall objects found: 8
* number of wall objects correctly placed: 8
* number of wall objects invented: 0
* correct order of walls: (1 to 4) 4
* correct proportions/delineation of walls
(rated on a scale of 1 to 5): 5

Within this scoring scheme, a "non-wall" object is any material item which may be seen within the room, such as a vase, a lamp, or a table which is not physically built into the wall. A "wall" object is any material item which is incorporated into a wall, such as a door, a window, or a fireplace. Also within this scheme, the order of the four walls in the architectural space is scored as correct if the walls are accurately positioned relative to one another. Finally, the walls are judged to be correctly delineated if they correspond to the actual layout of the four walls in the room enough that there is a faithful representation of the dimensions, symmetry, angles, little nooks, etc. . .

The plan drawings of students in Group A, the Videotape Group, and of Group B, the Plan Group, are shown in figures 9 and 10. Each of the plan drawings within these figures has been reduced from an original size of approximately 8 1/2 by 11 inches. In all categories, the average scores of students within Group A were lower than the average scores of students in Group B.

The test had an obvious asymmetry. On the one hand, one group of students, Group B, saw a plan of the architectural space and were then ask to reproduce it in plan. On the other hand, the other group of students, Group A, saw the videotape of the architectural space and where then asked to switch media and reproduce it in plan. Therefore, the test did not fully measure a student's recollection of architectural space from plan versus a student's recollection from videotape, but rather, the test only measured what could be reproduced in plan. Yet, it may be advantageous to examine how the impressions from both mediums could be conveyed in a context that is limited to a "plan" drawing. For example, if the boundaries of a space are accurately recorded by both groups of students within their plan drawings, then it is an indication that the videotape communicates to one group of students, Group A, the same information about boundaries of an architectural space that was communicated by the initial plan drawing to the other group, Group B. In the same way, it could also be determined how similar was the information perceived about the identification and the juxtaposition of objects within the architectural space. Still, a key disadvantage due to the asymmetry of this approach is that it was not possible to learn about what information was conveyed in the videotape that could not be reproduced in plan. This is a key limitation in that the particularly unique contribution made by moviemaking to the perception of architectural space is not isolated.

The evaluation of each student's performance in reproducing the plan of the architectural space was measured in terms of three areas:

1)   the number of objects that were recalled;
2)   the correct placement of objects;
3)   the correct proportions/delineations of walls.

In general, Group A did worse in that fewer objects were recalled, more objects were invented, the order of the walls was not always correctly perceived, and the proportioning and layout of the walls was least faithful to the actual

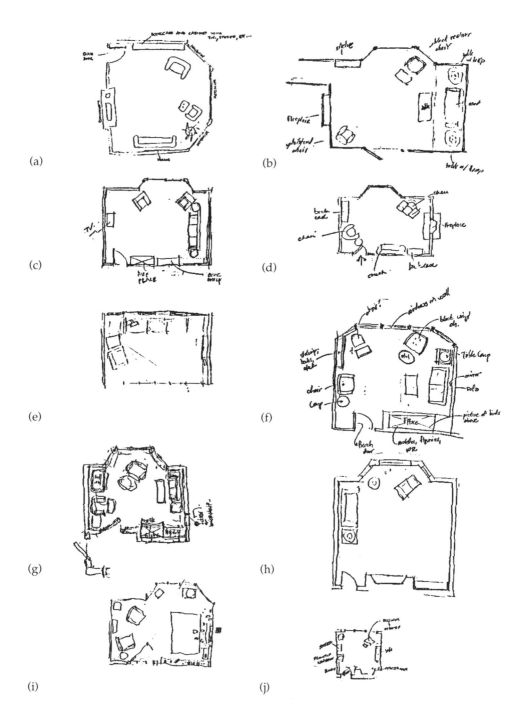

Figure 9 Recollection of architectural space from *videotape*. Responses ordered from top to bottom of page in terms of least experienced to most experienced architectural students. The most experienced students include practicing architects.

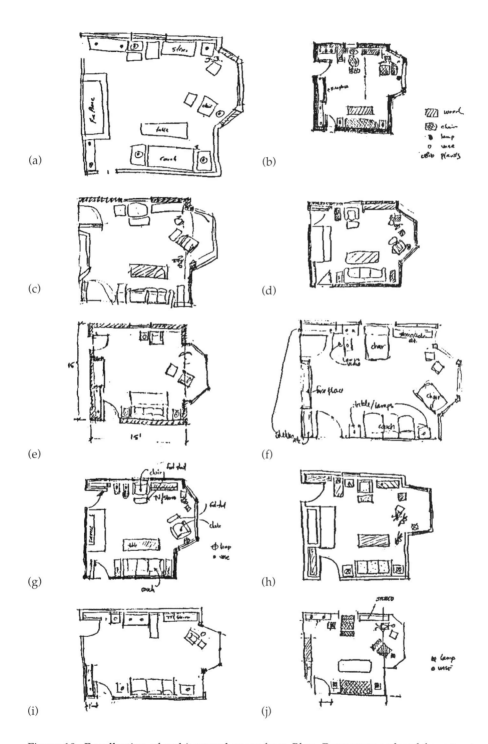

Figure 10 Recollection of architectural space from *Plan*. Responses ordered from top to bottom of page in terms of least experienced to most experienced architectural students. The most experienced students include practicing architects.

Average Results of "Videotape" Group A: Average Results of "Plan" Group B:

* number of non-wall furniture objects found: 7.4   * number of non-wall furniture objects found: 18.7

* number of non-wall furniture objects invented: 1.4 * number of non-wall furniture objects invented: .9

* number of wall objects found: 5.5   * number of wall objects found: 7.2

* number of wall objects correctly placed: 4.1   * number of wall objects correctly placed: 6.9

* number of wall objects invented: .7   * number of wall objects invented: .3

* correct order of walls: (1 to 4) 3.4   * correct order of walls: (1 to 4) 4

* correct proportions/delineation of walls   * correct proportions/delineation of walls

    rated on scale of 1 to 5): 2.6   rated on scale of 1 to 5): 4.5

Figure 11   Average results of Group A and Group B

layout of the architectural space (figure 11). The Videotape group was less accurate on (1) the number of objects in the space, (2) the juxtaposition of objects in the space, and (3) the boundaries of the space. They were more likely to (4) draw plans which included organizational symmetries not present in the architectural space. It also appears that the more experienced students had more accurate recall. On the other hand, in the Plan group, (5) the accuracy of the recall was independent of the level of the student.

Most striking is the lack of consistency of the drawings of students in Group A versus the consistency of the drawings in Group B. The degree of distortion of some students in Group A (figure 9a-e) compares with the relatively faithful reproductions of other students in Group A, such as 9f and especially 9g. In the case of figure 9g, the student did better job at some aspects of proportioning and delineating the room than some students in Group B. It is also indicated in figure 9g that the student included a door which could be glimpsed outside of the room (at lower left of drawing). Without the inclusion of this exceptional drawing, however, the results would suggest that there was not enough information within the movie to convey a faithful representation of the architectural space. With this exceptional drawing, it is speculated that the information was available, but that most students in Group A were not able to perceive it.

Insights Gained from the three Case Studies

The results of these case studies suggest that movies may not have the capacity to convey the precise arrangement of objects within a scene. As suggested by the student responses to the movie "The Third Man", a videotape may also communicate distinct impressions that are highly dependent upon the disposition and sensitivities of the viewer. On the whole, it is necessary to better identify the particular abstraction which moviemaking does provide and to clarify what it informs us about architectural design that other media do not.

On the one hand, the use of a medium in a particular area of design problem solving may be constrained by its capacity to abstract information. For example, a motion picture abstraction may be useful in helping to characterize the aesthetic qualities of some vases in the room, but not useful in describing the locations of the vases. Similarly, a plan drawing may help to locate the vases in an architectural space, but not convey their color, texture and sculptural qualities. The combined use of both videotape and plan representations, however, may provide a more complete representation of an architectural space. For example, to more thoroughly understand the Taj Mahal, it may be useful to view a videotape of it, and to see it drawn in plan, section and elevation.

An expert movie goer or critic may be more sensitive to the way in which a particular editing sequence is used, and because of his or her familiarity with the pattern of editing, could be more receptive to the structure that joins together different sequences within the movie. As a result of understanding the structure of the movie better, such an expert may be in a better position to find a scheme by which different objects within the movie of an architectural space could be related into a coherent whole. This is related to De Groot's expert chess player study [14]. In De Groot's study, the ability of a chess master to recall the locations of chess pieces more easily than a novice was only evident when the chess pieces were in legal positions (as might be experienced in tournament play). It was speculated by De Groot that the masters were able to recall more pieces because they were located in patterns that were meaningful to an expert.

Similarly, the better performance in reproducing a floor plan of the architectural space by the student in Group A who completed plan 9g may have resulted from his greater expertise in movies. In a separate questioning of his interests, he indicated that he had a strong interest in the use moviemaking "to experiment with modes of expression" of architectural concepts. Yet, the impact that a person's expertise may have had in viewing the movie is only speculated upon here. Therefore, any conclusions from the evidence gained must be cautiously considered with regard to both the nature of the movie made and the varying levels of expertise of the participants within the study.

Conclusion

In the first case study of moviemaking cited in this paper, the position of the observer was fixed, whereas people and cars moved through the scene. In the second case study, the position of the observer could move, but only where the movement of the camera recording the computer graphics was coordinated with the movement of the camera which was used to record the site. The next technical leap forward is perhaps to provide complete freedom of movement of the viewing position in real time. The Aspen Colorado Videodisc Project completed at the Architecture Machine Group at MIT in the early 1980's simulated such freedom of movement of the observation point, although it was restricted to predefined images stored on a videodisc. More recently, Professor Patrick Purcell at the Media Lab transferred a CAD model of Frank Lloyd Wright's Robie House to a Trillium real time animation computer. In attempting to provide an environment in which the camera can move about unrestricted, he was unable to completely merge the 3D coordinate systems of both a video recording and a 3D CAD model. The result was that if you moved the observation point around the scene, the Robie house would occasionally "take off like a Harrier Jump jet " [15].

The quest for realism may be relatively unimportant in moviemaking and computer aided design. Technical advances should perhaps not strive to provide greater proximity to the perceptual experience of being within an architectural space, but rather provide the visual abstractions that better take into account the cognitive styles of architects engaged in design. In all potential scenarios, architects will need to be trained in the use of the media technology, and will need to incorporate it purposefully into their cognitive processes. On the one hand, the use of such tools may burn "new brain cells" in the mind's of the architect, and identify unprecedented aesthetic domains and design methods [16]. On the other hand, architects may always need traditional plan, section and elevation drawings to be certain about such important considerations as: (1) the boundaries and scale of architectural space; (2) the identification of objects within architectural space; (3) and the relationship of objects within architectural space. In some incompletely understood cases, moviemaking and real time animation may make a contribution to the cognitive process of architectural design.

Notes and References

[1] The term movie is used to avoid making the distinction between motion picture film, video production, and computer animation.

[2] Downs, Gregory, Presentation at Harvard University, Graduate School of Design on the use of video at The Architect's Collaborative, March 1982.

[3] Strickland, Rachel, Lecture at M.I.T. Film/Video Section, October 1981.

[4] Arnheim. Rudolf. 1957. *Film As Art.* Los Angeles: University of California Press. p. 7.

[5] Nizhny. Valdimir. 1979. *Lessons With Eisenstein.* New York: Da Capo Press. pp. 19-62.

[6] Cocteau. Jean. 1972. *Beauty and the Beast: Diary of A Film.* New York: Dover Publications. p. 47.

[7] Mark. Earl and Frank Miller. 1988. "Report to Project Athena: The Electronic Design Studio Project". Presented at Computers in Design Research Symposium. Chicago. Illinois. May 3.

[8] Professor Morris Smith, School of Architecture and Planning, M.I.T., expressed his reservations about moviemaking as a design medium because he felt it may overwhelm and control the aesthetic decisions of the designer. His remarks were expressed to me in informal conversation during a faculty meeting in May 1989.

[9] Rasmussen. Steen Eiler. 1959. *Experiencing Architecture.* Cambridge: M.I.T. Press. pp. 33 - 34.

[10] The computer animation/video work referenced here was performed with the considerable efforts of Branko Kolarevic on the South End Project, and Pegor Papazian and Iffat Mai on the Charlestown project. The cinema verité movie was completed by Aniruddha Das Gupta, Geno Fruet, Anurudha Joshi, Lei Xi and Jian Zhao. There were a total of eighteen students enrolled in the subject.

[11] This animation package was principally developed by undergraduate student Bob Sabiston. A front end to the animation package was developed by undergraduate student Chris Thorman working in consultation with graduate student Brian Press.

[12] For a recent description of PC based CAD and Animation tools, see the June 1989 edition of MACWORLD, Volume 6, Number 6, Published by IDG Communications, Inc., San Francisco, California. This issue is devoted to use of the MacIntosh computer in film and video animation.

13   Rasmussen, Op. Cit., p. 224.

14   Anderson. John. 1985. *Cognitive Psychology and Its Implications.* New York: W.H. Freeman. pp. 243 - 244..

15   Purcell. Patrick. October 1987. Lecture to a Computers & Architecture subject at M.I.T.

16   Hubert Lundqvist, The National College of Arts and Design, Stockholm, Sweden, used the term "burn new brain cells" with respect to discovering computer aided design methods at a Seminar on "What Would The Architect Gaudi Have Created With A Computer", May 30 - June 6, 1985, Barcelona, Spain, Sponsored by the Swedish National Board of Universities and Colleges.

29
Low-Threshold Modeling

Malcolm McCullough

Harvard University Graduate School of Design

This is a case study of teaching at the University of Texas at Austin. It is about using an electronic design studio to provide architecture students with their first exposure to computing. It suggests that, despite the limitations of present technology, there is reason to lower the thresholds to computer-aided design. The study presents a studio which attempted such by allowing students to find their own level of commitment to use of electronic media for geometric modeling. More generally, the paper aims to document issues presently facing the many professional schools not having substantial traditions in computer-aided design education.

Response

Fascinated with our creation, we think ourselves dependent upon computing:

> *The computer was not a prerequisite to the survival of modern society; its enthusiastic, uncritical embrace. . . quickly made it essential to society's survival* in the form *that the computer itself had been instrumental in shaping.* [1]

Wanting it to usable by all, we have learned to cover up its inelegant insides with convenient interfaces:

> *"Paradoxically, by virtue of digital computers, mankind may soon ignore the numbers."* [2]

Even in a discipline as small and conservative as architecture, we feel great practical and intellectual pressure to respond to the possibilities of computing. In contrast to the few who have researched and developed systems for computer-aided design, there will now be the many who actually use the stuff.

While the computer, (whether in its current data structures or in its very essence), may be inadequate for the work of speculative design conception that so preoccupies architects, it is already very good for the work of structuring, developing, and presenting, which design professionals really spend most of their time doing. While CAD researchers may still work on methods which do not generalize well to complex, useful problems, and CAD users may have done work without subtlety just for the sake of having it on the machine, computing today is in a position to help us *make beautiful things*.

Education

Schools hope to change their ways in order to provide general and critical introductions to computing for everyone [3]. Computer-aided design education must now speak not only to a technical cadre but to the the best and busiest of mainstream designers. Geometric modeling, which is easier than ever [4], makes computing both attractive to designers and teachable in a studio setting.

Most design schools, including the one discussed in this study, have recently become involved in such work, but few have an orientation toward research and development [5]. Instead, they focus on professional education, where an immediate response to computing is in demand. Whether or not by choice, they use commercial technology, "shrinkwrapped" CAD systems, which have power, ease, documentation, reliability, and support to make them more useful than in-house systems, but which also have their costs: using precise, production-oriented programs for ambiguous, conceptual designing requires great care. Technology-driven teaching can be academically impure [6]. Work of this nature often has none of the image of scientific legitimacy so often sought after by researchers, and may have yet to develop any of the image of artistic legitimacy which presently motivates most architecture students and teachers.

It may be in the artistic realm that the design schools will more strongly influence good use of computing in architecture. These could be the places to disrupt the architect's perception of the computer as a necessary evil, useful solely for documentation, (and therefore to be avoided by the aspiring). This perception, which holds partly as a matter of computing's weaknesses mentioned above, and because of cost, owes also to habit: within the design education studio, the sense is that method was found wanting some time ago [7], and at the moment, for better or worse, improvisation dominates. To date, computing has mostly opposed this habit; it would do better to alter it, or if not that, then to serve. CAD must be accessible, intellectually, physically, and socially.

This is a case study of a studio that allowed students having no prior experience to seek their own level of commitment to use of computer-aided design. Hence the title: Low Threshold Modeling. This sort of studio was able to educate students who would never before have been interested. In comparison to its more specialized (and albeit less well equipped) predecessors, it was the most successful yet conducted in its school.

Conditions for the Lower Threshold

There are many necessary components to low threshold modeling. Some of these have only recently become available; this case study describes the first studio in its school to reach many of them [figure 1].

To begin with the technical conditions, which are more explicit: sufficient hardware is whatever will keep most students challenged with things other than compensation for machine performance. Given just about any current cpu power, sufficiency is then in fact more likely to be distinguished by peripherals. Adequate color is especially important. Display list processing (e.g. hardware zoom) helps. Laser printing (and not mechanical pen plotting), is a necessity not just for transfer to manual media, but for purposes of daily criticism.

With respect to software, this paper and its topic are made possible by affordable three dimensional modeling. On specific issues: software must be reliable, easy enough to use fruitfully in the first month, capable of delineation in any plane, and capable of rendering. It must allow rewarding returns on a wide range of time investments. In addition, software users must have adequate operating systems support [8]. The costs of working without any of these should be self-evident. Beyond these necessities, particular advantages follow from integration of modeling with image processing techniques, and availability of an environment having sufficient stability over time to allow cumulative learning.

In communications, the value of a network differs from that in professional situations; users here do not continuously share files. A network does offer easier sharing of peripheral devices and better control over software dissemination, but its greater value here is allowing use of many applications per project. In this way, the network serves to educate about the increasingly incremental and multi-media nature of computing environments.

The main social components of the lower threshold are access and with it relaxation. These can be a matter of logistics (dedicated machines, preferably almost one per student, and around-the-clock availability) or of atmosphere (correct lighting, artsy clutter, proximity to the traditional studio). They are realizable today. The idea is to minimize departure from the attitudes that motivate the studio.

Less obviously, accessibility can also take the form of ready conversion between manual and electronic media. The ability to fall back on manual methods can make it easier to try the electronic ones.

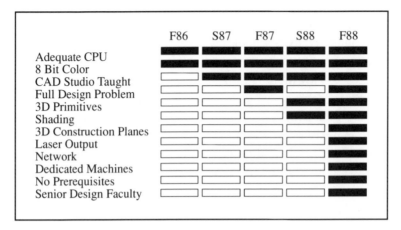

Figure 1 Arrival at CAD Studio Conditions

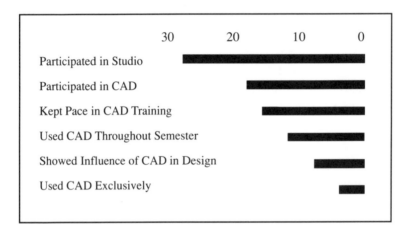

Figure 2 Students Using Computer-Aided Design in the Studio

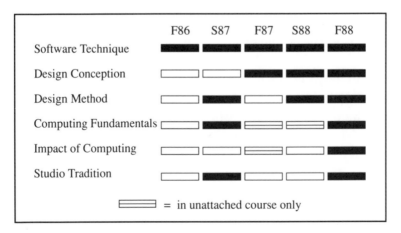

Figure 3 Topics of Investigation in CAD Studios

Access is also very much a matter of curriculum. If qualification for a CAD studio requires a lot of foresightful preparation within already overloaded student careers, most people will never have it. If the studio is perceived as a haven for those somehow deficient in conventional abilities, or as primarily a celebration of technical mastery, the busier designers are often the ones least likely to participate.

On the other hand, if the electronic design studio is presented as an imaginative way to develop what has become necessary knowledge, then CAD can become more attractive. If an established designer participates in teaching, perhaps to assess computing himself or herself, the students will follow.

In summary, sufficient access depends upon the possibility to investigate computing without much prior preparation, on a full time basis, in a relaxed setting, without having to abandon manual methods. What must then occur to maintain rigor has to be very intensive.

Studio Format

The studio described in this case study took place in the fall of 1988 at the School of Architecture of the University of Texas at Austin. Co-teaching with the author was senior design faculty member Lance Tatum. The thirty participants were fourth- and fifth-year undergraduates and third-year graduate students [9]. The majority had never used a computer before. Two thirds of the students were concurrently enrolled in a support course on computing, and had the option to apply CAD to any extent in their work [figure 2]. These students were also enrolled in a support course which, when combined with the studio, allowed for almost undivided attention. The remaining third of the people planned to work manually the whole time.

The studio began with a two week site analysis from an urban design perspective, followed by an intensive three week software training period, and finished with a nine-week investigation of a design problem on the analyzed site.

The systems used included twelve dedicated PC/AT workstations equipped with expanded memory and eight bit color (PGA), and the Autocad release 10 and Autoshade software packages [10].

The main design problem was chosen on the basis of having a strong context, the textures and planning of which would minimize the tendency with the computer to treat projects as isolated formal constructions, a simple program, clear hierarchy and modularity of which encouraged logic and inflection in the schemes, and arts-oriented clients, who could appreciate the innovative look at their buildings that the studio would provide.

The review format emphasized the combination of manual and electronic work and encouraged comparison between projects developed using the computer to varying degrees.

While the studio demanded mastery of software, the support course encouraged understanding of the conceptual basis of computers and subjective consideration of the impact of technology.

The studio built upon experience from efforts in its three predecessors [figures 3 and 4] and took advantage of always-better technology. The three earlier studios included a computer-only workshop doing two-dimensional problems, a mixed media studio using 2 1/2 D and manual methods on a straightforward building design, and a computer-only studio using three-dimensional modeling through macros to do pavilion studies [11].

This studio's format was innovative in this school in many respects. It was the first to integrate computer-aided design for use on an optional basis by a subset of its participants. It was the first to use off-the-shelf three-dimensional modeling software. It was also the first computer studio to be co-taught by a senior faculty member having no experience with CAD. Finally, it was the first computer studio without any prerequisite software course.

Teaching the Low Threshold Studio

Teaching computer-aided design to neophytes at the same time as using it to resolve a substantial design problem is the essential problem raised by the low threshold strategy. Such a challenge is not ideal, but is forced by the already overwhelming amount of subject matter that young architects face in a few short years in school. Few of today's risk-averse students are ready to give up a valuable studio to one in which portfolio quality results are less guaranteed, and fewer still are willing to work hard on anything other than the studio, so the computer-literate design instructor is lucky to get exactly one semester with most of them. During this time, there are several teaching priorities that come into play [figure 3]. Here are a few that we faced:

Technique—Skills, which still come first, can come fast. In three weeks, the studio moved through two-dimensional measured drawing of a neoclassical facade, two-dimensional logic manipulations on a motif and variations, and three-dimensional construction planes followed by surface construction and shading for a simple pavilion [figure 5].

Conception—The computer was presented as a means of structuring and resolving, as opposed to fully conceiving or merely documenting design. Its use called attention to the influence of any representation, including the pencil, on the issues considered. Its externalizations were predicted never to become a substitute for imagination [12]. Its limitations as a medium were presented as the source of strength for design [13]. In the long run, it was asked not to disrupt the

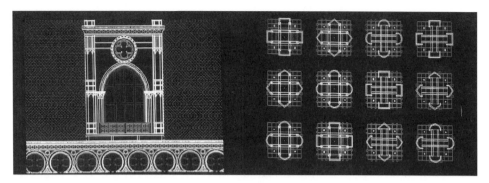

(a) two dimensional delineation, historical work (Andrew Kjellberg)

(b) two dimensional cycle of variations (Eric Kotila)

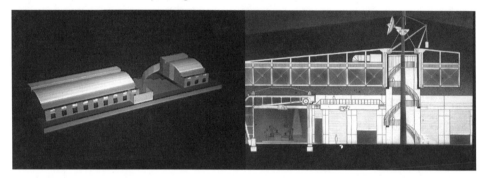

(c) first 3D work (Kirk Ellis)

(d) mixed media: airbrushed plot of a section (Demetrio Jimenez)

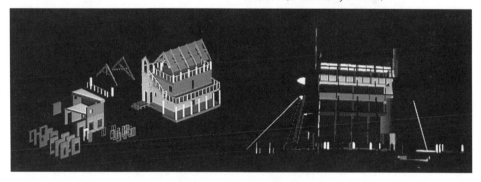

(e) pavilion parts study (David Nobles)

(f) pavilion lighting study (Ron Bateman)

Figure 4   Some work from the three preceding studios

importance of the reflective process or the unconscious content of expertise[14], but nevertheless was presented as capable of strongly influencing design thinking.

Method: While there was no attempt to alter any current pattern of improvisation, the studio did guide the students through a kit-of-parts approach to geometric modeling and a combination of analytic and experiential presentations of resulting designs. Attention was to design logic or construction and not to numerical description. Computer is the wrong name for the systems we used; ordinateur is closer.

Technology: It was presented that comprehension of the basis of the underlying technology improves the chances for best use of CAD. Lectures outlined fundamentals of hardware, software, and data structure in the most general terms possible. An exam helped students to distinguish concepts and identify trends in the technology. Students were to have a detailed idea of what happened "under the hood" when they drew a line.

Interpretation: While applying computers in the studio, the students also read from selections intended to show contrasting expectations of computing in the longer term. Much to contrary to habit, they then formulated their own positions in responding papers.

Social Conditions: Students rapidly identified preconceptions by writing short papers in the first week. They learned software technique fast and hard before the studio chemistry was set. They made the mood of their work area more relaxed by means mentioned earlier.

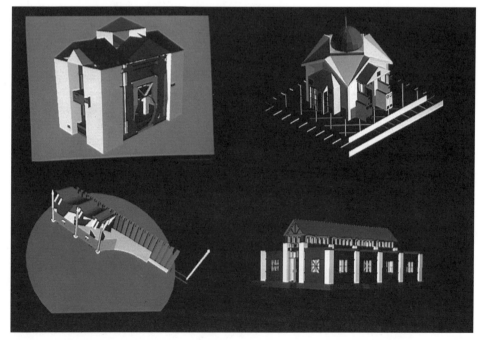

Figure 5   First exercises in modeling
(Tracey Denison, Pat Tangen, Mercedes de la Garza, Michael Mauldin)

Knowledge—Presented as a justification for current inconveniences was the eventual possibility that computing could make it possible to restate the principles of architecture more eloquently.

Observations and Consequences

The primary advantage of this studio was the opportunity to reach busier and better students; the primary disadvantage was the tendency to overwhelm weaker ones. It is the opinion of the author that for the first time at UT Austin, a representative sample of the most talented and creative students enrolled in an electronic design studio [15]. Such a trend has important implications for eventual improvements of computer-aided architectural design media, for it will bring new input to the debate on better data structure. Here in the short term are some observations on progress toward artistic legitimacy:

—The best-received designs were more dependent upon the capacity of the students than on the choice of the medium. Juries inexperienced in critiquing computer graphics had no trouble identifying well conceived projects.

—Several of the projects showed distinct influence of the computer upon their content. Some were designed expressly for the experience of walking through, (which could now be represented more easily than on paper [figure 6]). Several showed a clear hierarchy of components [figure 7]. Fewer showed the stylistic clichés that were currently fashionable in the school. On the other hand, fewer showed attention to material and texture, which were all but impossible to represent on the software at hand, and fewer were as completely resolved as those done with familiar media.

—The least-resolved designs were those of students for whom the computer amplified any lack of confidence. Faced with designing a building, and learning to model, the weaker students did neither. They did imitate manual methods and got locked into flawed schemes, insignificant aspects of which they resolved in great detail.

—Concentration upon three-dimensional modeling reduced the tendency to treat the software as a drafting system. The experience of genuinely drawing in three dimensions was enough to disrupt many habits.

—The computer interfered with criticism. It disrupted the conventions of formal juries, and particularly discouraged overviews in individual consultations.

Figure 6 Walk-through (David Wolff)

Figure 7 Kit of parts (Peter Funk)

Figure 8 Use of context (Peter Funk)

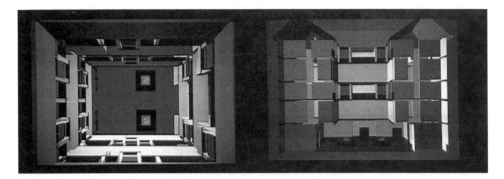

Figure 9   Interior modeling (Tracey Denison)

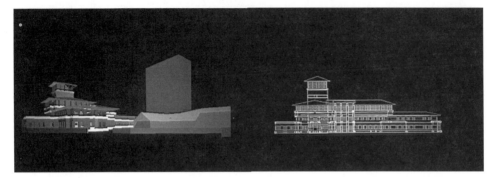

Figure 10 Combination of modeling with conventional drafting (Michael Mauldin)

There were several concerns with logistics:

—Those who gave up on the computer did so quickly. The early conceptual stages of the project, during which the system's precision was most spurious, coincided with the early stages of learning technique, which are the most difficult.

—Overall, the output of the studio was hurt by the computer. Everyone spent a lot of time waiting through view regenerations.

—The main cost of the studio was in design education lost by those overwhelmed by the new medium. Working well with the structured models of current commercial CAD systems had a higher threshold in design ability than in technical facility; in particular it required much more specific knowledge and images of what was being designed. Many of the students needed confidence as designers first.

The main advantage of the studio was the chance for most of the students to develop a strong sense of the capabilities of CAD through intensive use of and critical choice over its applications. Use of a new medium offered fresh angles on fundamental issues in design. The wide range of levels of use of computing coupled with the lectures and readings allowed many students to go away with a sense of perspective on the technology. That several people suggested improvements that are viable or in progress today illustrates that expectations were neither too high nor bound by the media at hand. Among the improvements requested were: faster hardware, good color hard copy, the ability to express texture, the ability to represent simple formal relations without having to express them in cartesian coordinates, allowance for painting and sketching over vector and polygon images, easier data management interfaces, and the ability to draw more with operations on shapes.

Recommendations

Testing the premise of low-threshold modeling has resulted in these reinforcements of or contributions to our knowledge of computer aided design eduction:

—Low threshold modeling is a reality. Current possibilities include conducting a meaningful studio using off-the-shelf technology, for the successive stages of learning to model to be stimulating enough to motivate the students to proceed to further ones, for students to go from no experience to proficiency in geometric modeling in a few weeks, (provided that is about all they are doing), and for students to alter their commitment to use of the computer during the course of a design project. It is also possible, if the necessary conditions described earlier are not met, for none of the above to occur.

—There are unresolved difficulties in both criticizing and altering designs represented exclusively on the computer. Not only because people lose time learning the new medium, this kind of studio will produce less work than a conventional one.

—The real threshold to computer-aided design education is design ability, whose presence or absence CAD amplifies [16]. The low (social) threshold should include a high-pass (design) filter.

—Theoretical supplement to the studio is important. Presentations of the fundamentals of computing help to maintain rigor in a situation where concessions to expediency in confronting a design problem might not. Discussions foster a critical attitude instead of blind acceptance.

—The studio can be the correct place to introduce the computer in design education. Nowhere else is there enough time for simulataneous development of both intuition and technique. Within the studio, daily use of the current technology produces genuine interest in any accompanying explanations of computing theory. Also, the studio's prevailing conventions and biases fall under study in the presence of new media.

—Making computer-aided design with all its current shortcomings accessible to talented and influential members of the design community promotes a useful debate which benefits all.

The conditions which make computing more accessible without sacrifice of clarity or capacity are becoming easier to achieve. By lowering the threshold to computer-aided design education it is possible to reach a wider range of students. It is possible to improve the quality of the application and criticism of the CAD medium, to raise the extent to which the design community becomes aware of computing's implications, and to encourage students to actually use the computer to learn about design.

Acknowledgments

This work was made possible by the teaching skill and experience of Lance Tatum, by hardware furnished by IBM through Project Quest, and by software testing conditions arranged by Autodesk, Inc.

References

Bruegmann, Robert. 1989. "The Pencil and The Electronic Sketchboard: Architectural Representation and the Computer", in Eve Blau and Edward Kaufman, (eds.) , *Architecture and Its Image*, Montreal: Canadian Center for Architecture, and Cambridge: The MIT Press.

Davis, Philip, and Reuben Hersh. 1987. *Descartes' Dream—the World According to Mathemetics*. Boston: Houghton Mifflin.

Dreyfus, Hubert and Stuart Dreyfus. 1986. *Mind over Machine*. Berkeley: Free Press.

Gombrich, E.H. 1956. *Art and Illusion*. Washington: Pantheon.

McCullough, Malcolm, 1988. "Representation in the Computer Aided Design Studio". In Pamela Bancroft (ed.), *ACADIA '88 Proceedings*.

Meurant, Robert. 1988. "Some Metaphysical Concerns Raised by the Computer Generated Electronic Environment". In Pamela Bancroft (ed.), *ACADIA '88 Proceedings*.

Solomon, Jacob. 1988. "ACSA Computer Survey". Washington: ACSA.

Weizenbaum, Joseph. 1976. *Computer Power and Human Reason*. New York: W.H. Freeman.

Notes

1   [Weizenbaum]

2   [Davis & Hersh]

3   For a normative position on this issue, see an editorial by 1987 AIA president Donald Hackl, in *Design Graphics World*, Feb. 1987.

4   Thanks, for example to 3D in standard AutoCAD, easy and innovative modelers on the Macintosh, and affordable, appealing, links to painting and image processing.

5   [Solomon] notes 57% of ACSA member schools using computers in the studio in 1988. A few years earlier, *Pioneers of CAD in Architecture*, Kemper (ed.) 1985., accounts for only ten schools. But studio case studies aside, the present volume cites present research in only seven American archiecture schools.

6   On such sophistry: "They. . . do in fact teach nothing but the opinion of the many. . . might compare them to a man who should study the tempers and desires of a mighty strong beast who is fed by him—he should learn how to approach and handle him. . . you may suppose that when he has become perfect in all this, he calls his knowledge wisdom, and makes of it a system or an art, which he proceeds to teach, although he has no real notion of what he means by the principles or passions of which he is speaking. " Plato, *The Republic*, Book VI.

7   As this generalization relates the computer, see [Bruegmann]

8   Mastery of data management remains a crucial factor in achievement of successful projects done mostly or entirely on the computer.

9   Much of the didactic nature of the teaching described here is based on the undergraduate audience; teaching postprofessional students would be another matter.

10   AutoCAD has an undo trail which is indispensible in lowering thresholds and powerful user coordinate systems for disrupting old drawing habits.

11   [McCullough]

12   It is sad that this even has to be said. See [Meurant] .

13   [Gombrich]

14   [Dreyfus]

15   Despite the efforts of the registrar to reduce all students to numbers, documentation of this occurrence would be very difficult.

16   This is interesting in juxtaposition with the fact that many professional firms cite reluctance to enlarge as one incentive for automation. The thresholds to becoming an architect may be increasing.

30
The Thousand-Acre Sketch Problem

John McIntosh

School of Architecture

Madis Pihlak

Department of Planning

College of Architecture and Environmental Design
Arizona State University

Introduction

An unusually large sketch problem in urban design was given to an undergraduate studio class to introduce visualization techniques and to explore fundamental urban design principles. This *thousand-acre sketch problem* was distributed to students on a floppy disk as a three-dimensional computer model. The availability of a large number of Macintosh IIs and access to a pre-release version of the three-dimensional modeling program ModelShop™ allowed us to conduct this prototype *electronic studio*.

This paper looks at the productivity gains experienced by our students during this project and discusses the increased level of understanding witnessed in student performance. More importantly, this sketch problem is examined as a philosophical parable for several pedagogical issues of design education in the microcomputer age.

The Debate on Design Pedagogy

The authors of this paper have an ongoing debate about design pedagogy, which we are arguing directly in the context of the design studio. In this debate, McIntosh is the Devil's advocate. He holds that design education is an oxymoron. We do not instruct students how to design, so much as we contrive exercises by which their more-or-less innate talents will be revealed. The students have a learning experience to be sure, but there is no pedagogy employed here that is worthy of the name.

Pihlak takes on the role of Dan'l Webster, arguing for Jabez Stone's soul, as it were (Benét, 1937). He holds that there is a process of design that can be taught, although the instruction is by example rather than by explication. It is an evolutionary process in which students watch design taking place; they mimic, they modify, and they personalize. In this way, students evolve a richer personal design process than could possibly be developed by imitating any one style or person. By the Socratic method of question and criticism, students develop the ability to self-criticize and the ability to iteratively develop design solutions. Design is both a process and a product that is never truly complete. There can certainly be relatively or acceptably complete designs; however, design is a perfectionist's profession, an orientation that maintains there can always be improvement or another alternative.

The Devil knows that there is not time in this life for such accidental discovery. Dan'l Webster pleads that the art of design cannot, or at least should not, be taught as a science in which there is only one correct, optimum solution. Design can certainly benefit from a strong leavening of rational thinking and a demystifying of the process. But there will always be competing theories of design, and technology has simply accelerated the process by which theories of design are born, mature, and decline.

To simplify the positions, the Devil asserts that chimpanzees could be taught to produce *competently* designed artifacts on a computer, in whatever style current taste decrees to be fashionable. At the other extreme, Dan'l Webster maintains that only careful nurturing of sensitive, dedicated people will produce *great* design, which speaks to a timeless aesthetic.

The Dilemma of Design Educators

As design educators, we receive into our charge young, immature students with very little experience of the world. We have five or six years in which both to determine whether or not they have the ability and commitment to become designers and to inculcate a set of cultural values that will stay with them throughout their lives. We spend a great deal of time subtly indoctrinating students, particularly with that set of cultural values peculiar to design. Much of this is carried out formally in history courses and study-abroad programs.

Traditionally, we also spend a great deal of time training students in what are essentially craft skills, mainly drawing. But our drawing style is very abstract: it is a notation shorthand that only other designers really comprehend. Now we have the computer, and a pedagogical alternative. From three-dimensional computer models we can quickly and easily produce geometrically precise perspective views of design proposals. By electronically rendering these perspectives, we can also create very realistic, high-resolution color visual simulations.

When animated, these simulations are accurate in reproducing the experiential effects of moving through the real world (Craik, 1971). This was demonstrated with large physical models by Donald Appleyard and Kenneth Craik at the Berkeley Environmental Simulation Laboratory (1978) in work carried on today by Peter Bosselmann. Computer simulations are becoming at least as good as film taken of a physical model; moreover, the computer technology is cheap, readily available, and very easy to use.

So, as design educators, we are now faced with a dilemma. Do we spend our limited time with students teaching them traditional manual drawing techniques, or do we spend it teaching them computer simulation techniques? To semantically load the question: Do we spent our time teaching students how to vaguely communicate with other designers, or do we teach them how to communicate unambiguously with the general public? Developers realize the persuasive powers of an *artist's conception* to project the best image of their proposals. But the general public now has a healthy distrust of architectural renderings because of the *lies* that have been told with these stylized drawings (Appleyard, 1977).

The computer allows the designer to once again become *"the honest broker of information"* (Bosselman, 1989). Computer-generated visual simulations allow the general public to see proposed developments accurately, to say nothing of allowing designers understanding their own creations. The designer can escape the oversimplification of plan, section, and elevation when an endless number of accurate perspectives can be quickly and inexpensively produced on the microcomputer (Sheppard, 1986).

The Undergraduate Experience at ASU

Within the College of Architecture and Environmental Design at Arizona State University, there are three departments: Architecture, Design, and Planning. Within these three departments are five programs, which deal with designed artifacts of progressively larger physical size: industrial design, interior design, architecture, landscape architecture, and planning/urban design. The national renown of these programs, with respect to each other, is probably ranked in that order also: industrial design is very well respected, and planning is too new to even be accredited yet.

The Devil argues that the academic success of these programs is in direct proportion to the degree to which students can simulate, and thus understand, their design artifacts: industrial design students usually build full-scale models, often working prototypes, of their designs; interior design students construct mockups; architecture students sometimes build large-scale models; landscape architecture students create large-scale drawings; and planning students draw oversimplified diagrams of cities.

The first two undergraduate years at ASU are traditional environmental design: basic sciences, a heavy emphasis on drawing, and elementary design courses—very much a craft approach. The first formal computer course comes in the third year; it concentrates on word processing, data base systems, paint programs, and simple computer-aided drafting.

Once accepted into the upper division, students encounter their first design studio, which in the Planning Department is a site-planning studio. It introduces the mainstream ideas of landscape architecture and physical planning to undergraduates. Their second studio introduces urban design; it is the subject of this paper.

In the past ASU might have been charitably described as a good regional school, whose graduates had excellent drawing skills. We were (and still are) known as a *desert school*, whose students had some sensitivity to energy issues in a hot/arid climate and had some understanding of passive solar design strategies. At present, we are in rapid transition, with a predominantly new faculty, a new dean, a new building, and a lot of new technology. In the future, a lively debate is promised between the Devil and Dan'l Webster; between a design position that is analytic, quantitative, realistically simulated, and computer based and another position that is cerebral, symbolic, largely conceptual, and rhetoric based.

There is also the *Raising Arizona* phenomenon at ASU (from the movie of the same name), from which even the Devil shrinks in terror. Students do a lot of simply growing up during their undergraduate years here.

With occasional exceptions, we get *average* students at ASU. We draw from an eclectic talent pool: these students may have relatively poor professional design skills but at the same time a surprising aptitude for spatial manipulation. Some of our undergraduate students do go on to the Ivy League graduate schools of design, and many find employment in the computer-aided design section of major design firms.

The Urban Design Studio

Planning students' first exposure to urban design occurs during their Spring Junior Semester of their four-year undergraduate program. This joint landscape architecture and urban planning studio is organized around three projects: the first develops basic urban design visualization techniques, the second examines theory and the application of urban design principles through guidelines, and the third is a design project within the Phoenix metropolitan area. In this last project-scale design, the students are expected to illustrate their grasp of urban design theory and practice.

Four traditional, basic urban design visualization techniques are taught in this studio and are usually introduced in the following order:

1.   The *figure/ground* drawing is used first to introduce students to large-scale analytical techniques. This two-dimensional technique allows quick visualization of urban patterns, density, pedestrian connectivity, and the general scale of development. It is a very easy technique to master.

2.   The *illustrative master plan* is another two-dimensional technique that is relatively quick and thus allows the student to simulate a number of alternative designs. It is a diagramming technique.

3.   The *axonometric* is the simplest three-dimensional drawing technique. It allows the student to begin to visualize the form of various urban design proposals.

4.   The *aerial perspective* is a true visualization of three-dimensional reality. The big disadvantage of this powerful technique is the time it takes to produce this image manually. Usually only one or two accurate aerial perspectives are produced for large urban design projects.

We had a pre-release version of ModelShop™ written by Mark Van Norman, formerly of Harvard and then of ParaComp. We also had a three-dimensional ModelShop model of the Arizona State University campus and a contiguous area of *Old Town Tempe*, which had been built previously by a senior undergraduate landscape architecture student in an independent study course with Pihlak. Thus, we could give each student this thousand-acre site on one floppy disk, which he/she could modify in any way. An urban design project of this scale would be very difficult using manual techniques, but a thousand acres is quite a doable proposition on a computer.

So, on this project we worked backward. Instead of a base map, we gave the students a three-dimensional model from which aerial perspectives (figure 1) could be produced in unlimited numbers, at no cost in terms of time. Axonometrics (figure 2) could also be derived from the computer model by a simple menu selection. The illustrative master plan, which is much simpler with respect to information content, is actually more complicated and clumsy on the computer than with manual techniques. Consequently, the students produced far fewer illustrative plans and far more three-dimensional views— the exact opposite of the usual undergraduate studio. The figure/ground technique (figure 3) was also difficult because the plan view of the computer model had to be cut from one program and pasted in another. It was the least well completed portion of the assignment; many students *cheated* by completing their figure/ground diagrams manually.

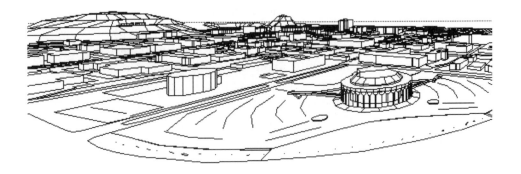

Figure 1   Aerial Perspective

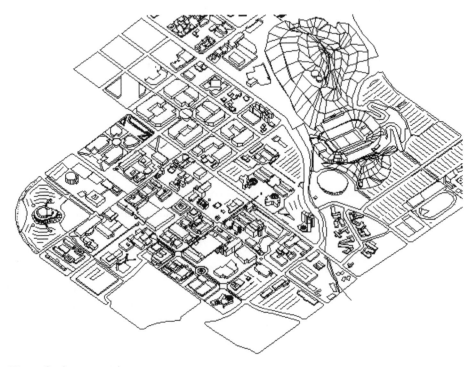

Figure 2   Axonometric

The Case for Using Computers

Productivity gain was the primary reason for introducing microcomputer tools into this urban design course. We did see more deliverable product from the students; moreover, their product was of a higher overall quality than manually produced material.

We also hoped to see evidence of improved understanding on the part of students. They were able to copy and paste large chunks of the thousand-acre sketch problem site, although undergraduates do not have the visual finesse that comes with experience and with travel. The students were able to make conceptual design proposals and then to quickly produce three-dimensional images that exactly illustrated the consequences of their decisions. Many desk critiques occurred around the computer monitor. The students were not always proficient enough to alter their design proposal in the presence of the instructor, but by the next studio period they were usually able to bring an entirely different design proposal forward for critique. The iterative process of design was greatly accelerated. Each of the two-member groups was able to produce alternatives (figure 4).

We hoped that the students would acquire a better grasp of urban design theory, as evidenced by their directly applying theory to design. Whether the students did or did not grasp the theory remains moot. As instructors, we have a very strong bias about what is *good* urban design: it is pedestrian oriented, has street-wall buildings, continuous pedestrian realms, and figural space. But these students are predominantly children of the suburbs, *car kids* for whom these ideas remained very abstract, even after our field trip to San Francisco, the urban Disneyland. Urban design is a difficult proposition to study within the Phoenix metropolitan region: the automobile-oriented fabric of *The Valley of the Sun* does not lend itself to an understanding of good city form. The notion of buildings relating to the pedestrian realm, and to other buildings off-site, is a radical concept, both to our students and to the practicing profession.

Introducing computers into this course was also timely. There is a major university computer site in the architecture building, so we are not being held back by the unavailability of resources. We also had permission from ParaComp to use the pre-release version of ModelShop for instruction. And we have a new building coming online that is programmed around this concept of the *electronic studio*, so it was appropriate to work up another prototype course.

There was a final case-making argument for using computers, which the Devil terms the *Urgency Argument*. The Phoenix metropolitan area is growing out of control: we are at a population of 2.2 million now and predicted to go to 5 million by the year 2012. Many of our graduates will be immediately employed in the creation of this city, a process in which there is little time for abstract

Figure 3   Figure/ground

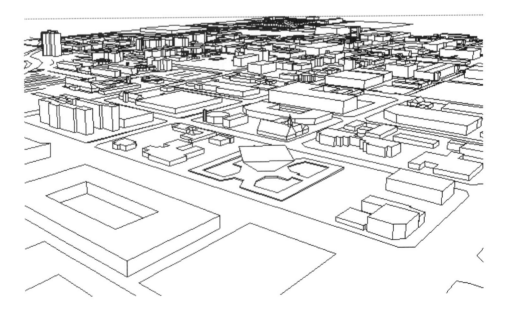

Figure 4   Alternate perspective

intellectual debate, which would be mostly lost on the Philistines anyway. We both think the only design arguments persuasive enough to carry the day with the now very-distrustful public will be built around these experiential visual simulations. Familiarizing our students with state-of-the-art computer technology might create a sort of fifth column within the design establishment. The students might become the advocates for this medium that they take for granted in school.

The Measurable Improvements

We raised the lowest-common-denominator for minimum acceptable quantity and quality of work expected of students. We saw the limits of students' abilities stretched, as evidenced by their ability to accurately simulate change. All but one group of students, who essentially did not take part in the project, received an *A* grade.

While raising the overall level of students' skills, the computer also proved to be a great equalizer, for anyone can produce reasonably presentable graphics with a computer. We saw two patterns that tended to level-out the quality of work. Those students with superior manual skills tended to disbelieve that a computer would improve their work; consequently, they tended to stick with their high-quality but low-volume manual techniques. On the other hand, those students with relatively inferior manual skills wholeheartedly embraced the computer because it allowed them to quickly do what was nearly impossible for them before. There is an inversion of values here, with manual craftsmanship becoming severely devalued and traditional techniques, such as hand lettering, severely undermined. The extreme example of this was our star student, who modeled on the computer with great skill, even though he has a learning disability.

The craftsmanship issue is central to the debate about how far the computer should be integrated into the design studio. There is no doubt that a better overall design artifact is produced by using three-dimensional design software. Contrary to the notion that computers erode studio craft values, the computer produces a quantum leap of craft quality. Central to design is three-dimensional thinking, mental agility, and visual acuity, all of which are accelerated with the computer. The metaphor of a *model shop* holds: skill and resourcefulness are also necessary to build computer models.

What has taken place is simply a change of medium, from foamcore and exacto knife to color monitor and mouse. As with any shift of media in a profession, there are early adopters and there are traditionalists fighting rear-guard actions. Many practicing landscape architects hold dearly to the traditional craft values of the hand-lettered board presentation.

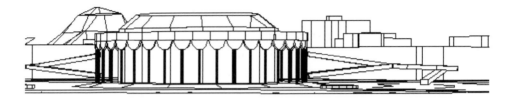

Figure 5   Eye-level perspective

The sheer size of this sketch project, a thousand acres, normally would never be considered at the third-year level, and rarely at the graduate level. We stretched students' abilities simply by dealing with a problem of this scale. Several accurate aerial perspectives were produced by even the weakest student team. All of them were able to easily develop new conceptual designs for the urban area immediately surrounding the campus. They were also able to propose major spatial changes within the rapidly expanding ASU main campus (figure 5).

In design, where the ability to visualize is so closely tied to the ability to understand, the rapid creation of images on the computer allowed students to test their ideas quickly. For example, computer-generated perspectives allowed students to understand open space in the project site and to test their ideas for improved visual quality, both from an aerial view and a ground-level view.

So, using the computer inverts the studio problem for the students. Perfect perspective views of the project are extremely easy to produce, while traditional two-dimensional paraline drafted diagrams are time-consuming. The finesse of a good hand is devalued, or at least transformed. Before the course began, we were worried about asking too much of the students; as it transpired, we set them up for success!

The Expectations of the Profession

Many practicing professionals have discovered how the computer can be used to communicate designs to their clients. Stories such as the following abound in the popular press:

"But on a computer, clients can see a multitude of solutions and contribute to the refinement of the design. The process allows us to investigate many more options. . .which means sometimes we stumble on creative ideas that we just would not have had time to pursue with pencil and paper"   (New York Times, 1989).

In the architecture profession, a good number of the students find their computer-aided design experience to be a highly marketable skill. Many design firms hire our students specifically to bring such skills into the firm.

On the other extreme, there are many Luddites in the landscape architecture profession who resist computers while believing that using them is merely button-pushing and not in the least creative. The Phoenix landscape architecture community is conservative; many firms do not use computers, nor are they terribly interested in hiring students who use computers. And they have one very legitimate complaint; there is not yet any software for realistic-looking planting design.

With respect to landscape architecture, we find academia leading the profession. The students are instantly marketable with yesterday's craft skills, but their computer visualization skills may make the students uninteresting to the old-guard firms. The trade-off is that their education will have a much longer shelf life. Within the next few years, this issue will disappear as some of the smaller, more innovative firms discover their competitive edge (Mitchell, 1988).

The Closing Arguments

Putting a computer at every undergraduate student's workstation is something we can do, and undoubtedly will do, if for no other reason than it is technically possible and economically feasible. Access to the technology is no longer an issue. The fundamental shift of the professional design culture as computer literacy among design students becomes universal is the interesting matter. Computers are liberating our undergraduate students from the tedium of being *drafting drones*, thus freeing them to develop higher-level skills.

This does raise the issue of manual drawing competence: what it is, and whether it is needed. The increasing sophistication of three-dimensional *design* software, as opposed to relatively simple *drafting* software, allows the personal microcomputer to become a true design tool. The proverbial back-of-the-envelope sketch can now be done in 3D digitally. The Devil will trade this magic pencil for your creative soul. Dan'l Webster still values the traditional techniques and evocatively describes the joy of laying graphite down on the tooth of good paper.

The great advantage of the computer that cannot be matched with manual techniques is its recording ability. One studio can create a data base of digital information, upon which a subsequent studio class can build. This cumulative impact is especially important for large, complex urban design problems, which typically require decades to be implemented. Cumulative knowledge could transform the design studio from an anachronism into the core of the applied research arena. The Devil will give you this knowledge; Dan'l Webster argues the cost.

Dealing with complexity is another advantage of using the computer; many urban scale problems are otherwise intractable. Digital simulation is the only way to deal with them effectively. A five-hundred-acre campus and its urban context, or the downtown core of a major city, are impossible to deal with manually. Along with better working models and graphics, the urban designer can also unambiguously communicate these proposals to the general public. The Devil will allow you to peer into the future; Dan'l Webster waxes poetic on the pastoral life.

In Phoenix, the automobile-oriented boom town, there is little coherence in the relentless suburban landscape. Run-of-the-mill architectural practices produce *object buildings*, sculptures in the landscape that have so little to do with the surrounding context that even the building entrance from the street has been eliminated in favor of a single parking structure entrance. The urgency of this out-of-control growth makes a deal with the Devil attractive, versus Dan'l Webster's high-minded design abstractions.

The Verdict
Our initial anxiety about demanding too much of the students caused a tentativeness about introducing this computer technology. We took a hands-off approach, while hoping that students would be attracted to the technology, which they were. And we hedged our bets by selecting fairly conventional projects, albeit outsized ones. Without being directed to it, some students chose to develop their computer skills, while others reverted to conventional manual media.

Succumbing to the urgency argument, we are adopting a proactive, advocacy position with respect to using computers within this urban design studio. In the coming semester, we will introduce urban gaming software, new three-dimensional software, and true-color computer visualization. The authors have agreed that there is such a great need for spatially literate stewards of the built environment that it is now worth the risk of abandoning some traditional pedagogy.

The debate between the Devil and Dan'l Webster goes on, but the authors have negotiated a compromise: the mortgage on Jabez Stone's soul is extended another year. The jury is still out.

Epilogue

The great benefit of publicly presenting one's ideas is the comment of colleagues, both old and new-found. Three points that are softly made in this paper crystallized after we presented it at CAAD Futures '89. First, the studio course described here is not a special computer-aided design studio; that is, the subject is urban design theory, not data base theory and computer graphics. The curriculum and the agenda were set by Pihlak, the instructor of record; McIntosh acted only in a supporting role, albeit with his own hidden agenda. Second, our students will be employed in creating this vast city in the desert, no matter how well or how poorly we equip them, because the growth of Phoenix is so fast and so relentless. Rising to this opportunity for excellence is our greatest challenge. Finally, there was an ironic twist in Benét's short story that had an initially unrecognized parallel in the authors' debate on design education. The Devil was not really after the soul of the hapless New Hampshire farmer, Jabez Stone—the students in our parable. The Devil was after the soul of Dan'l Webster himself.

Acknowledgments

The authors gratefully acknowledge the contribution of the students registered in PLA 362A/B Joint Landscape Architecture/Urban Planning Studio in the Spring semester of 1989, and especially that of Greg Rossel, the student who built the base computer model.

References

Appleyard, D. 1977. *Understanding Professional Media: Issues, Theory and a Research Agenda*. Human Behavior and Environment. Eds. I. Altman and J. F. Wohlwill. New York: Plenum.

Appleyard, D., and Craik, K. H. 1978. "The Berkeley Environmental Simulation Laboratory and Its Research Program." *International Review of Applied Psychology* 27:53–55.

Benét, S. V. 1937. *The Devil and Daniel Webster*. New York: Farrar & Rinehart.

Bosslemann, P. 1989. "Design Communication." Lecture at Arizona State University.

Craik, K .H. 1971. *The Assessment of Places*. Advances in Psychological Assessment. Ed. P. McReynold. Palo Alto: Science and Behavior Books.

Mitchell, W. J. 1988. "Online Design: The accessibility and inevitability of computer-aided design in architecture." *Inland Architect* (November–December):46–51.

New York Times. 1989. "Architects Create 3-Dimensional Graphic Models." (May 30).

Sheppard, S. R. J. 1986. *Simulating Changes in the Landscape*. Foundations for Visual Project Analysis. Ed. R. C. Smardon. New York: John Wiley and Sons.

31
Form Processing Workshop:
Architectural Design and Solid Modeling at MIT

Frank C. Miller

Department of Architecture
School of Architecture and Planning
Massachusetts Institute of Technology

Introduction

Computing impacts the preliminary architectural design process as a tool for observation and analysis, as a formal prototyping tool, and as a vehicle to generate variations of objects and assemblies. Through the use of both traditional and computing tools, the Form Processing Workshop examines the relationship between design decisions and design tools. The Workshop utilizes several software applications, with emphasis on the use of a solid modeler. This curriculum was developed with the support of MIT's Project Athena.

Observation, Documentation, and Analysis of References

"When one. . . works with visual things—architecture, painting or sculpture—one uses one's eyes and draws, so as to fix deep down in one's experience what has been seen. Once the impression has been recorded by the pencil, it stays for good, entered, registered, inscribed. . . To draw oneself, to trace the lines, to handle the volumes, organize the surfaces. . . all this means first to look, and then to observe, and finally perhaps to discover. . . and it is then that inspiration may come."   Le Corbusier

The Discipline of Seeing

Design learning is importantly linked to developing new ways of perceiving and describing the built world. The computer has joined the pencil as a significant tool in this documentary process. The Form Processing Workshop includes a series of exercises intended to sharpen students' analytic capabilities and explore the role of the computer in architectural observation. This project also serves to introduce students to the concepts and functionality of the CAD solid modeler used during the subject.

Students are asked to select a significant work of architecture and adopt one of several points of view as a perceptual framework within which to observe and describe the project. The solid modeler is used as the primary tool with which to build a three-dimensional model of the building.

During the past several years this process has produced a growing number of documented buildings which are available to students for analysis. This collection of architectural references represents the reincarnation of an old institution in the MIT Department of Architecture. Up until the 1960's, there existed a collection of scale models of classical architecture which was referred to unofficially as the Model Morgue. These models were loaned out to studios for the analysis of organization, construction, and various formal characteristics. It is the intention of this new collection of digital models to reestablish this idea and extend it to studios by incorporating the use of computer modeling.

The sources of information from which to build digital models of existing buildings can be found in published books, journals, site measurements, working drawings and photographs. The strategies for constructing these models reflect the available documentation of the building, the structure of the building, and the design issues being explored by the student. These strategiesinclude assembly of parts, subdivision from whole objects, and different techniques for aggregation of assemblies. Some of the design issues which have been explored include:

Primary/Secondary Structure
Dimensional/Modular Studies
Form of the Primary Access
Relations of Public/Private
Light/Shadow Studies

The digital models have also been utilized to generate previously unpublished projections and to animate sequences of views.

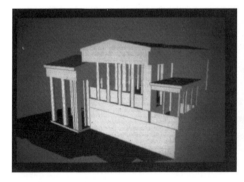
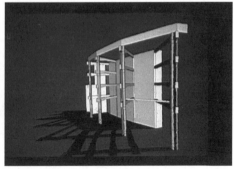

Erectheum, Athens   Boston Five Cent Bank

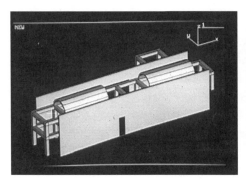

Residence, T.Ando

Residence, T.Ando

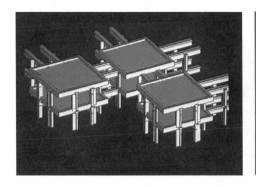

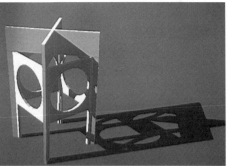

Centraal Beheer, H. Hertzberger

Exeter LIbrary, L. Kahn

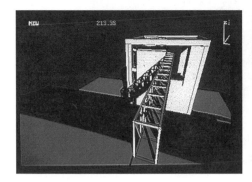

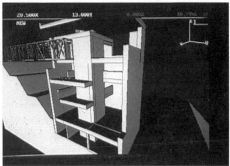

Residence, M. Botta

Section through solid model

Forms of Documentation

In analyzing architectural references, students commonly use many tools in addition to 3D models. These include drawings, diagrams, photographs, text, audio and even motion pictures. The management of this diverse information during the design process in the typical studio is often achieved with the display technology of homosote tack boards and file folders of potentially relevant images. Typically, standard-sized boards serve to group images and permit associations between them. The strategies for organizing the individual images and groups of images vary widely, and reflect the particular design method being explored.

While these references play a crucial role in establishing critical positions and in analysis of precedent, there exist few if any interactive links between CAD application software and these extended collections of reference material. Utilizing Project Athena workstations, we have built a prototype system for collecting, storing, managing and displaying these reference resources. Images can be captured from hardcopy, slides, video and computer screens and stored in either an analogue video format or a digital bit-mapped format. Access to these collections is facilitated

Design Reference Management System. For the key image at right center, the supporting resources include a relational database record at upper left, a quote by the architect about the image, and at bottom, a set of images with which the key image has been associated.

by means of either a relational database (Ingres) or a rule-based shell application (Knowledge Engineering System). While development of this prototype system falls outside the scope of the Workshop, it has proceeded in parallel and has benefited from the image collections and explorations of the problems of using references encountered during the Workshop. One of the primary problems in the effective use of these references is establishing the categories for collecting, grouping, and retrieving images.

The Problem of Classification

"The world was made before the English language and seemingly on a different design."   Robert Louis Stevenson

The classification of books and periodicals is standardized through the Library of Congress system. Images, audio and motion picture have no parallel classification system, and library collections of audio-visual material have had to improvise their own schemes. Typically, they make use primarily of simplified but generally useful categories, and to a lesser extent respond to the local description priorities of departmental teaching and research. The classification needs of studios are usually derived from the design methods used, and therefore vary widely among studios. This situation challenges the capabilities of a computerized reference management system, in that the database tables and relations that describe images suitably for the slide library may be of marginal use to a studio, and a scheme which suits that studio may be of little use to another studio.

The problem of architectural classification is intimately linked to the way in which one structures and represents design knowledge. During the Workshop, this relationship is discussed in an effort to more clearly articulate and elaborate the descriptions essential to the design methods at hand. This problem is explored in greater depth through the parallel research seminar.

Prototyping Artifacts and Formal Organizations

Another primary design issue in the Form Processing Workshop is that of architectural prototyping. While this subject has wide interpretation, our emphasis has been on methods of prototyping structural elements and on the formal organization of the public access in a building. CAD modelers are acknowledged as powerful tools for generating variations of objects, yet we have found that the geometric primitives created with CAD modelers tend to have little intrinsic formal complexity or associative connection to external ordering systems. CAD modelers lack some of the basic constraints found with physical models such as gravity, mass and connection. Exercises which

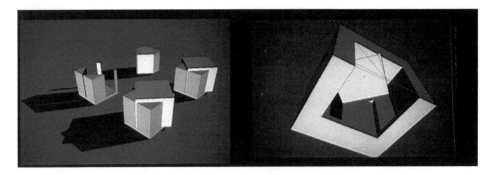

Solid modeling boolean operations: The double cube solid converted
left, difference; rear, intersection;   to a void and placed within a
right, union.   larger cube to create a space

introduce external constraints into the prototyping process have been developed. The goal of these is to encourage use of source objects with origins in structural vocabularies, construction processes, or formal/organizational types.

The spatial notions utilized in generating these source primitives include solids, voids and territories. Solids are described as the positive physical objects and elements of enclosures which are deployed to divide or enclose space. Inversely, voids are the negative spatial shapes which are defined by their own boundaries independent of the objects placed in or around them. Designers commonly manipulate both of these, alternately defining the elements of physical enclosure and shaping the spaces contained within and between these physical artifacts.

The relationship between these these opposing space defining principles of solids and voids has a long history, and is vital to the contemporary aesthetics of architectural placemaking. Fifteen hundred years ago, the Taoist tradition emphasized the primacy of space:

"We make doors and windows for a room. But it is these empty spaces that makes a room livable".

This position reveals a bias in favor of the contained, the space within. The belief that the nonexistent is essential, that it is made tangible by the material form, established the understanding that the true potential of architecture lay within the intangible.

Plato held that space wa composed of air, a *tangible* substance distinct from the other elements. During the Renaissance, Neoplatonists defined the proportions of buildings bythe subdivision of finite tangible forms.

The third notionused in the workshop's design method can be identifiedas 'territory' or 'place', and adds the crucial consideration of perception and inhabitation to the objective geometric representations of solid and void. This notion has origins in Aristotle's theory of place as being distinct from either formor material:

". . . yet form and place do not delimit the same thing: form is the limit of the thing circumscribed; place is the limit of the circumscribed body. . . Thus the place of anything is the first unmoved boundary of what surrounds it."

Descartes extended this understanding with the important idea that spatiality is identical with the extension of matter. If you take away the matter, their exists no space as an independent entity; there is not anything left at all. Therein lay the unity of the historically opposing principles of matter and space, and set the stage for Einstein's proposition that reality consists of neither space nor matter, but rather of the sum of various fields of force.

"This total field [is] the only means of description of the real world. The space aspect of real things is then completely represented by a field, which depends on four coordinate parameters; it is a quality of this field. If we think of this field as being removed, there is no 'space' which remains, since space does not have an independent existence."

This provides a relevant metaphor for the notion of territory as neither solid or void, but rather as the region of optional use which is enabled by the formal and geometric relationship between artifacts and their associated spatial regions.

Out of this perception has come the description of architectural ordering systems based on the continuity of change and the possibilities inherent in a situation. Use, in this context, can be defined as the stream of situations in a setting rather than some mechanistic reference to singular, discrete functions. The involvement inhabitants have with a building is, like history, always richer in content, more varied, more spontaneous, lively and subtle than even the best designers (or historians) can imagine. Inhabitation, like history, is full of curious accidents and juxtapositions of events, revealing the complexity of human interaction, change and association. In this sense, 'territories' can be described as the sum of the possible events which might occur in relation to architectural interventions.

In response to this architectural agenda in the Form Processing Workshop, how do CAD systems enable or constrain the ways by which designers perceive their work? How do CAD systems tend to limit the design concepts which architects employ?

Most CAD systems provide the capability of creating and editing geometry which is composed simply of lines. Some systems include the description of surfaces, or polygons. In contrast, solid modelers, based on constructive solid geometry, are able to represent both solids and voids and often also provide options for editing both lines and surfaces. While solid modelers most closely match the representational needs described above, none of the available CAD applications packages has the ability to recognize or instantiate territories providing options for current or potential use by people. These considerations are therefore pursued though discussion, annotation, arm waving, and sketching, and emerge as a description of the relations between form and use.

Strategies for Prototyping

During the Workshop, three primary strategies are employed in the process of prototyping artifacts. One of these strategies incorporates reference to the constraints and possibilities of processes used in building construction. Secondly, an attempt is made to create the best fit possible between the stated goal of the design and the tools to be used. Thirdly, the artifact being prototyped is evaluated through successive representation in different modeling and drawing media. These are described below.

One of the archetypal form-making methods in building construction involves casting materials into molds. The primary constraints of this process include preventing the mold from leaking the casting material, providing for the removal of the mold from the casting, and securing the structural integrity of the mold during casting. Through the use of plaster casting by students in the workshop, these considerations are used to steer the prototyping process. Students are given blocks of rigid foam measuring four inches square and two inches thick. Using a hot wire cutting table, they are asked to cut the block into two pieces, to be displaced from one another creating a void into which to pour plaster. The exercise is repeated with two cuts, resulting in three pieces of foam with which to build the formwork.

In an effort to evaluate and extend these results, students replicate this process with the solid modeler by making the same cuts to a solid in the software, and using the Boolean operations to make a "cast" of the mold. The resulting object is essentially identical to the piece cast in plaster.

The next step was to instantiate variations of the object in the solid modeler, simply through controlling XYZ proportions of the original. These variations are evaluated with respect to their architectural potential, and the most promising ones are incorporated into a vocabulary of structural elements to be used in assembling a building.

Sometimes, the limitations of the original casting are addressed by altering the foam cutting exercise and cycling through the entire process. In fact, some of the foam cuts yield no possible mold options, and in other cases the cast object seems barren with respect to its architectural potential. In a few cases, castings cannot be removed from the mold, and others leak or explode. In any case, the constraints of casting establish a conceptual frame work within which the form making process occurs, and lends to the CAD models a sense of association and reference to a clear external ordering system.

The one-cut exercise. After the foam block is cut once with a hot wire cutter, the two pieces are displayed to create a formwork void for casting the prototype element in plaster.

Furthermore, moving the object between physical and digital modeling media provides a broader range of context and precedent for the evaluation of design decisions.

Variations of Artifacts and Formal Organizations

The third major focus of the Form Processing Workshop is ondesign procedures which generate variations of prototype artifacts by selectively altering proportional, dimensional and positional relationships. This activity of exploration and optimization is a standard part of design practice, and has traditionally been practiced by hand using drawing and models. The computer offers a powerful new capability in this regard, through its use of digital media and a model structure which distinguishes between the visual three dimensional model and the corresponding abstract representation in the database. By manipulating relations in the database, variations of the original object can quickly be generated through what is commonly referred to as parametric instantiation.

With respect to manipulating the database of the geometric model, several design topics are emphasized in the workshop. The first of these is controlling the size and scale of the architectural elements. This is achieved by altering the

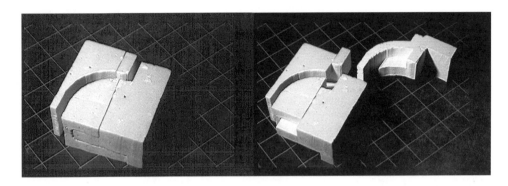

a)   b)

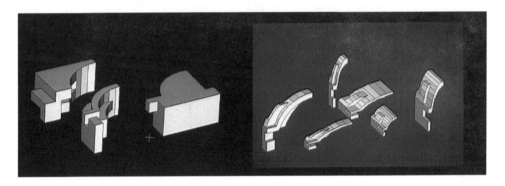

c)   d)

e)   f)

The two-cut exercise:
a) The foam block cut in two directions
b) the displaced foam pieces and the resulting prototype plaster casting
c) the analagous process of cutting and casting with the solid modeler
d) parameteric variations of the prototype element created with the solild modeler
e) and f) parametric elements aggregated into building assemblies

size of an artifact or opening by changing its dimensions while preserving its proportional relationships. In addition to controlling the size, any combination of the X, Y, and Z proportions of the object may be altered.

The second topic focuses on methods for making quick studies comparing alternative instantiations of sets of objects in a model such as columns, windows, or furniture. Through redefining the identity of these objects in the database, previously created variations of them may be swappped in and out of the building design.

The third topic is related to the above two, and addresses the need to manage the level of displayed detail needed for editing the model and making design decisions. The primary strategy is to match the level of abstraction of the model to the kinds of design issues being considered. For example, site design needs only a highly abstracted massing model of the building, while the layout of circulation in a space requires a higher level of detail in the nearby surrounding area, but only an approximate representations of the rest of the building. This serves to focus the designer's attention on the most relevant features of the building, thereby sharpening the inquiry and highlighting the crucial design priorities. With traditional media, greater abstraction is achieved with study models and diagrams, while detailed drawings and models address more focused and precise considerations. No available CAD system directly or adequately addresses this familiar aspect of designing, so specific methodologies must be used to solve these problems.

Another reason to minimize the level of detail in a CAD model is in order to maximize the processing speed of the computer during editing and visualization processes. Regardless of the processing speed of the system, students consistently increase the level of detail in the model to the point where they can't stand to wait the several seconds or minutes it takes to complete editing commands.

Instantiation vs Diagnosis

In addition to controlling the XYZ sizes of an object, the relations between elements of an assembly can be controlled through procedures describing the constraints and rules for assembly. Such procedures model the process of assembly which generated the design rather than merely modeling the current geometry of displayed elements, and may be used for either generating design solutions or for diagnosing problems with an existing design. While the bulk of the work in this area occurs in the associated research seminar, the discussions in the Form Processing Workshop serve as a source of constraints and rules related to design case studies.

Most design decisions are made in relation to the constraints and options of an existing site or physical setting. The exceptions to this include generative formal techniques which instantiate building organizations based on a grammar of spatial elements. These procedures, typically referred to as parametric design, are most useful in making preliminary building schemes which will be subsequently modified in response to site conditions.

Parametric design processes were first developed for mechanical design problems, and later extended to the automation of repetitive components of architectural construction drawings such as fire stairs. In the realm of preliminary design, the effectiveness of parametric instantiation has been seriously limited by several factors. First, even simple design problems may contain a large number of rules and relationships, and the designer is forced to become a programmer in order to get beyond trivial design problems and overly simplistic representations. Secondly, parametric instantiation is useful only for creating variations of isolated objects or assemblies, for these procedures are unable to recognize the constraints or opportunities of the setting in which the designer is working. Architectural decisions made in the absence of context are the legacy of the worst of the modern movement, and designers do not need tools which encourage them in these bad habits. Thirdly, the options for representing design knowledge in these procedures is typically limited to rules, or conditional logic. The scope of architectural knowledge which can be coded in this form is very limited; additional representational schemes such as frames, semantic nets and neural networks provide the means to represent more complex design problems. Fourth, these procedures are only useful for generating variations on a theme or type which have been previously defined. The process of prototyping is often under-emphasized, and left to other means.

Design Themes
Central to the working method described above is the process of observation, creating prototypes and exploring variations. Utilizing this method, several design themes are explored in the workshop.

One of these themes focuses on strategies for aggregation and hierarchical ordering. Within the CAD environment, these issues have relevance to both the architectural scheme and to the options for manipulating the underlying database. While the hierarchical paradigms of top-down or bottom-up tend to dominate architectural discussion, the subject of aggregation serves to draw attention to the middle-up and middle-down options. Designers are continually grouping and regrouping elements, and creating overlapping hierarchies in the process. The grouping of elements into sub-assemblies, and subsequent creation of larger assemblies, stands in

Prototype elements cast by students with plaster and subsequently modeled with the solid modeler.

a)   b)

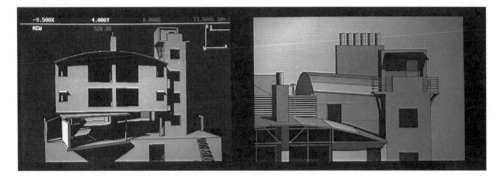

c)   d)

Studio project for an Urban Inn by graduate student David McCulloch; a) CAD solid model using Solid Vision, b) physical model, c) CAD solid model, d) multi-media drawing based on a plotted view of the CAD model

contrast to methods which begin with an overall order and subsequently resolve the details. In order to accommodate growth and change, the relationship between the primary/permanent structure and the secondary/changeable infill raises issues of hierarchy. Also, the role of natural light is studied for its role in clarifying the organization of the public and private realms of the building.

Making interventions into existing settings is another design theme—emphasizing the techniques for understanding the physical, social and institutional context of a project. The CAD modeler is used to help generate and evaluate design decisions. Gaining new perceptions of a site is often aided by multiple representations of it through plans, photographs, sections, and physical models. The addition of a CAD solid model of the site permits a broader set of studies to be made, particularly with respect to visualization, walk throughs, and shadow studies.

Exploring Modeling and Drawing Tools

Design methods incorporate intentions, procedures, media and tools. Graphite on paper, modeling clay, foamcore and plaster are commonly used media, and are associated with such tools as lead holders, knives, glue and casting formwork. Digital computing represents the newest media platform on which CAD software tools are being developed. These media/tool combinations can be summarized into the following five categories:

> Drawing Techniques (pencils, paint, etc.)
> Additive Models (sticks, foamcore)
> Subtractive Models (carved clay or styrofoam)
> Cast Models (plaster, concrete)
> Digital Models (CAD)

The form processing workshop takes the position that the relationship between design ideas and tools used to represent them is symbiotic, and that the designer must establish a critical stance toward them. In addition to the top-down and bottom-up tendencies of these different media/tools, there is an advantage to using combinations which are analogous to the real-world materials and properties which are being proposed. This strategy runs counter to the approach which seeks to constrain the design process to a single medium (e.g., CAD). This latter approach is oriented more to exploring the representational constraints of CAD, as opposed to the workshop's intention of exploring the role which CAD might play in relation to other media during the design process.

One important advantage of combining CAD with other media is related to the nature of the review process and the composition of the review audience. A mixed media presentation is able to engage a broader range of reviewers, and and the discussions tend to be more about architecture, and less about computers. In addition, the review is more interactive as a result of the increased accessibility provided by the range of drawings, physical models, and CAD image sequences.

Conclusions

While the design studio continues to provide a viable approach to learning architectural design, new computing tools still do not easily integrate with the concepts and methods being explored in that context. These tools need to be employed side by side with traditional tools—encouraging students to develop a critical stance toward them. It is only through such a critical approach that we may feel confident that the new design tools are being used in the service of architecture, and not vice-versa.

32
A Primitive-Instancing Interactive 3-D Modeling System for Spatial Design Studies

Mitsuo Morozumi
Hirofumi Nakamura
Yasufumi Kijima

Department of Architecture
Faculty of Engineering
Kumamoto University

The authors have developed a basic, interactive, primitive-instancing 3-D modeling system (CAADF), which is based on a high-speed 3-D color graphic workstation, and have tested its potential ability to support spatial design studies in an architectural design studio. After a review of work performed by a student with the system, this paper concludes that this system provides an attractive environment for spatial design studies which conventional CAD systems have not achieved. The interactive process of 3-D modeling in perspective or isometric view images and the dynamic viewing utility are the most successful features of the system. In contrast to those advantages, the resolution of color graphic display is a limitation of the system. The authors conclude that if sufficiently many appropriate 3-D geometric primitives are supported by a CAD system, a primitive instancing method can significantly reduce the work entailed in object modeling .

Background

With all the anticipation that computer graphics technology would provide new dimensions of visual experience in the field of architectural design, how many CAD systems have really surpassed conventional drafting tools as a tool in spatial design studies, and especially in architectural design education? How many of them can really be used as an effective tool for visual thinking in the 3-D world, which is indispensable in a design studio? Though it is true that most CAD systems have allowed us to present perspective or isometric images of 3-D objects with colorful shading, we still feel irritated and reluctant when we have to work with them.

Most CAD systems, which were developed originally as drafting systems and are based on 2-D graphic display terminals, have provided a poor environment for visual thinking and object modeling in the 3-D world:

1. They usually require users to model 3-D objects using 2-D drawings, such as plans or sections. Even when the systems allow users to model objects in isometric or perspective images, users still cannot change their viewpoints and view directions as freely as their imaginations might desire. In those systems, modeling, viewing parameter setting, and shaded image generation are arranged as separate steps of an operation. As a result, they inevitably impose on users a long interruption of visual thinking, before regenerating shaded images of designed objects. As long as a CAD system impedes the user from continuing visual thinking in a fixed view, it will never be able to stimulate a better image of 3-D objects than a drafting board does.

2. In addition, in spite of the fact that most of the work done in architectural studios is schematic design, most CAD systems require explicit and meticulous definitions of 3-D objects. As many authors have pointed out (Brown and Novitski, 1988; McCullough, 1988; Mitchell, Liggett, and Kvan, 1987), the laborious process of object modeling will not only discourage image generation, but will also reduce the number of heuristic processes in design development.

Objectives and Method of Study

The essential task for making CAD systems a real tool for spatial design studies is achieving dynamic viewing capability and interactive modeling. The recent development of 3-D color graphic workstations with special processors to accelerate shaded image generation and local viewing operations suggests a way to accomplish such a task, if convenient 3-D modeling software can be provided.

The authors have developed a basic interactive 3-D modeling system (CAADF), based on a high-speed 3-D color graphic workstation, and have tested its potential ability to support spatial design studies in an architectural design studio. It is our objective to show such as system, even though it has only simple and basic utilities, provides an attractive environment for spatial design studies that designers cannot find in conventional CAD .

This paper first discusses the functional framework of the developed system, CAADF, and then examines the impact of the use of CAADF on spatial design studies through an analysis of a student's work in a design studio. The speed of design development and the student's consideration of spaces in his design are used as indicators for evaluating the effectiveness of the system as compared to the conventional drafting system.

Environment for the System Development

Hardware included the Tektronix 4336 color graphic workstation and the Tektronix 4693D color image printer. Software included the Unix OS, Fortran77, and Plot-10 STI. The important functional features of the Tektronix 4336 workstation that are related to the development of CAADF are the following:

—The Tektronix 4336 workstation provides a 3-D surface modeling environment. Once the user defines location and surface conditions of 3-D objects as a *segment*, using 3-D graphic elements such as lines and facets, the workstation, with its hardware function, automatically displays perspective/orthographic images of the modeled object. The user is required to define, for each segment, a segment label and status parameters, such as color, surface attributes, location of pivot point, visibility status, etc.

—The user can select a visualizing model from the following list: wire frame, wire frame with hidden surface removal, color surface shading, color surface shading with wire frame.

—As the system furnishes hardware local viewing functions, the user can easily control view motions, such as panning, zooming, or rotation, using the cursor pad, valuator dials, or other such mechanical input devices.

—Since the workstation has high-speed 3-D image generation and display functions (340,000 3-D vectors/sec., 20,000 3-D polygons/sec.), it is possible to refresh shaded perspective images of complicated 3-D objects, which have nearly ten megabytes of graphic data, in one or two seconds.

—By calling segment edit system commands with a segment name, it is possible to translate and rotate a defined object by segment as well as to change visibility or surface conditions. The user can also copy existing segments by defining a new segment that quotes existing segment names.

—Plot-10 STI provides subroutine packages, callable from the Fortran program. It also generate command codes to control the graphic display terminal or to manipulate segments.

Functional Framework of the Interactive 3-D Modeling System (CAADF)

—*Intercative 3D modeling*: Because the system applies the primitive instancing method, the user defines 3-D objects with simple interactive operations such as insert, delete, edit 3-D geometric primitives predefined in the system (table 1). The user also uses formal operation

Commands and Parameters	Comments
[COMMANDS FOR SEGMENT EDITTING]	
edit3 *ix, iy, iz*	Setting pivot point at coordinate *ix, iy, iz* .
opsg *segment-name*	Open segment under the name of *segment-name* .
osfc *i*	Set facet color code to *i*.
lset *i1,i2*	Set line type and line color respectively to *i1, i2*.
insg *segment-name*	Copy facets from the segment *segment-name* to the segment currently opened.
clsg	Close segment.
opfl *file-name*	Input command lines recorded in the file *file-name* and execute commands described in the command lines.
tns3 *segment-name,ix,iy,iz*	Translate the segment *segment-name* so that its pivot point will be located at point *ix, iy, iz*.
dlsg *segment-name*	Delete the segment *segment-name*
rotx *segment-name,deg,i*	Rotate the segment *segment-name* at *deg* degrees around the x/y/z axis.
roty *segment-name,deg,i*	*i*=0 : rotate from the initial position.
rotz *segment-name,deg,i*	*i*=1 : rotate from the current position.
scal *segment-name, i1, i2*	Enlarge or reduce the segment *segment-name* at the rate of *i1*% around the pivot point. *i2*=0 : scale against to initial size, *i2*=1 : scale against to current size.
aftx *deg,i*	Rotate local x/y/z/ axis for segments which will be defined
afty *deg,i*	after this command *deg* degree around x/y/z axis of world coordinates.
aftz *deg,i*	*i*=0 : rotate from initial position , *i*=1 : rotate from current position.
stylx *segment-name, i1, i2*	Stretch the segment *segment-name* i1 % along the X/Y/Z axis.
styly *segment-name, i1, i2*	*i2*=0: i1% of the initial size.
stylz *segment-name, i1, i2*	*i2*=1: i1% of the current size.
visg *segment-name,i*	Change visibility of the segment *segment-name* . *i*=0: make visible, *i*=1: make invisible
vihn *i*	Change handle visibility: *i*=0: make visible, *i*=1: make invisible.
pvnf *i*	Change pivot point visibility: *i*=0: make visible, *i*=1: make.invisible.
mesh *i*	Change mesh visibility: *i*=0: make visible, *i*=1: make invisible.
lsts	List segment names.
hisg *segment-name,i*	Highlight the segments: *i*=0 : highlighting *i*=1 : stop highlighting.
[COMMANDS FOR THE TERMINAL CONTROL]	
para	Select orthographic view transformation.
pers	Select perspective view transformation.
cadf	Activate CADF.
end	Stop the system.
isom	Select isometric view transformation.
zoom	Zoom up or down the objects.
[COMMANDS FOR GENERATING PRIMITIVES]	
cube *ix, iy, iz, xl, yl, zl*	Draw cube: *ix,iy,iz* define the position of the base vertex, *xl,yl,zl* define the length of the edges.
vault *ix,iy,iz,r1,r2,high,angle*	Draw vault: *ix,iy,iz* define the position of the origin which is set on one side of the vault. *r1,r2* define outer and inner radius. *high* defines the length of the vault, and *angle* angle of the sector.
dome *ix, iy, iz, r*	Draw dome: *ix,iy,iz* define the position of the origin, *r* defines the radius.
sphere *ix, iy,iz,r*	Draw sphere: *ix,iy,iz* define the position of the center of the sphere, and *r* defines the radius.
clmn *ix, iy, iz,r,high*	Draw cylinder: *ix,iy,iz* define the position of the origin of the bottom circle *r* defines the radius. *high* defines the length of the cylinder.
line *ix1, iy1, iz1,.ix2, iy2, iz2*	Draw line: *ix1,iy1,iz1* define the position of origin. *ix2,iy2,iz2* define the position of end point.

Table 1 List of commands used in the CAADF

commands to support modeling operations. There are commands to translate, rotate, copy, scale, or repetitively generate design elements (such as segment or a group of segments).

—*3D visual thinking*: The user defines 3-D objects (locations, shapes, and other surface attributes of 3-D objects) step by step, directly in a perspective or isometric view on a display which presents a shaded image of objects defined in the previous steps . Such an input procedure allows the user to test quite easily the visual effects of each design experiment.

—*Dynamic viewing*: The user can freely zoom, pan, or rotate the displayed image to select the best viewing condition for design study by just touching the cursor pad or rotating the valuator dials. This means that the user can even obtain an interior view of designed objects for use in designing interior parts.

—*Recording utility of design process*: The system has a utility for recording automatically the total process of object modeling. Therefore, the user can trace the process of design development as well as use it as a base for modeling studies in the next stage. The system also allows for editing of the record of the modeling process.

Technical Considerations in Developing the CAADF Modeling Software

As the objective of this study is to test the concept of a 3-D interactive modeling system, CAADF has relatively a simple structure with minimum utilities. It consists of independent subprograms that generate various system commands required to control graphic images and a main program that controls the execution of those subprograms. All programs are written in Fortran77 language and use Plot-10 STI subroutine libraries.

After starting the main program, simply typing in the command name and necessary parameters will activate the corresponding subprogram. Once the activated subprogram is executed, the main program is recalled automatically so that the system waits for the next command line. We designed a utility in the main program to file every command line as a character string that can be used to regenerate designed objects or to trace a process of design development. There are three groups of subprograms as listed in table 1:

—Subprograms for defining geometric primitives analyzing parameter values and generate a list of system commands to define geometric primitives having specified size and location in the 3-D world.

—Subprograms for segment editing analyzing parameter values and generate a list of system commands to edit and manipulate segments in the 3-D world. There is a command which calls the command lines recorded in a file and then defines segments following that record.

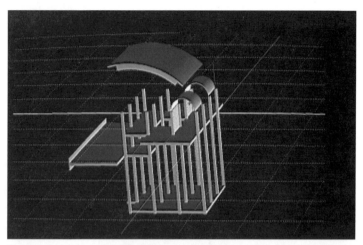

Figure 1 Structural image of the basic unit

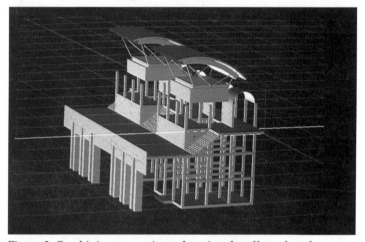

Figure 2 Combining two units and testing the effect of roof

Figure 3 Combining several units to form building complex

—Subprograms for terminal control send out a list of system commands to activate/terminate the modeling system as well as to control viewing conditions.

Table 2 presents a sample list of command lines typed in by a user to model the rotunda illustrated in figure 4. Sixty-five lines of commands and parameters are used. Each photograph shows the graphic display image generated during the process of modeling. The step numbers correspond to those shown in table 2. To illustrate the design development process, in this command list all heuristic processes have been eliminated after the work. Although the view direction was changed during the work, local viewing operations are not indicated in table 2 either, because the system cannot record such operations.

Analysis of Students' Studio Work

Conditions of Test Use and Outline of Students' Work
We tested the use of the system in the architectural design studio, in which senior students work on their own graduation projects. As we have only one 3-D graphic workstation, we selected one student for the test from a group of students who seemed to have good design ability and who wished to work with a CAD system. We asked the student to begin his design studies with the system and to start conventional drawing only after he had to some extent finished modeling the object.

Figure 4 shows aerial views of his project, Commercial Building Complex at a River Boat Terminal, from various view angles. The project site was a 250 meter x 80 meter belt along the Shira River next to the downtown area of Kumamoto City. The student designed a bridge with an outdoor exhibition deck, a shopping center, theater, open-air theater, boat terminal, waterfront plaza with giant steps, and watchtowers within the complex.

Stages of Work
The student took approximately ten weeks to complete his project. He had no previous experience on any CAD systems beyond watching other students working with them; thus we needed to train him on both AutoCAD and CAADF during that period. The schedule he followed can be summarized as below:

1st-3rd week: image sketch on tracing paper, Auto-CAD training, (two half-days on-site teaching and seven days self-study)
4th week: image sketch on tracing paper, CAADF training, (half-day on-site teaching and two half-days self-study).
5th week: spatial design studies with CAADF, (model of parts of the building complex)

COMMAND LINES	COMMENTS	COMMAND LINES	COMMENTS
01) s4336> cadf input work file name	Start CADF.	31) opsg gate1	Open segment 'gate1'.
		32) insg clmn01	Copy segments form 'clmn01'.
		33) insg clmn02	Copy segments from 'clmn02'.
02) rotund.wf	Open work list file 'rotund.wf'.	34) insg valt0	Copy segments from 'valt0'.
03) opsg parts1	Open segment 'parts1'.	35) clsg	Close segment 'gate1'.
04) osfc 6	Set surface color as orange.	36) opsg gate2	Open segment 'gate2'.
05) clmn 0,0,0 ,500,6000	Draw round column: position , X=0,Y=0,Z=0,radius=500 height=6000.	37) insg gate1	Copy segments from 'gate1'.
		38) clsg	Close segment 'gate2'

06) dome 0,0,0
   ,700
	Draw dome: position X=0, Y=0, Z=0,radius=700.	39).rotz gate2
		   ,45,1
			Rotate segment 'gate2' 45 degreeds around the Z-axis from the current position.

07) cube 700,700
   ,6300,1400
   ,1400,700
	Draw cube: position X=700, Y=700,Z=6300,width=1400, depth=1400, height=700.	40) opsg gate3	Open segment 'gate3'.

		41) insg gate1	Copy segments from 'gate1'.
		42) insg gate2	Copy segments from 'gate2'.
08) clsg	Close segment 'parts1'.	43) clsg	Close segment 'gate3'.
09) aftx 180,0	Rotate the local X-axis 180 degrees around the X axis.	44) rotz gate3 ,90,1	Rotate segment 'gate3' 90 degrees around the Z-axis from the current position.
10) opsg parts2	Open segment 'parts2'.		
11) dome 0,0 ,-6300,550	Draw dome: position X=0,Y=0, Z=-6300, radius=550.	45) opsg gate4	Open segment 'gate4'.
		46) insg gate1	Copy segments from 'gate1'.
12) clsg	Close segment 'parts2'.	47) insg gate2	Copy segments from 'gate2'.
13) aftx 0,0	Reset the local X-axis to the initial direction.	48) insg gate3	Copy segments from 'gate3'.
		49) clsg	Close segment 'gate4'.
14) opsg clmn01	Open segment 'clmn01'.	50) rotz gate4 ,180,1	Rotate segment 'gate4' 180 deg. around the Z-axis from the current position.
15) insg parts1	Copy segment from 'parts1'.		
16) insg parts2	Copy segment from 'parts2'.		
17) clsg	Close segment 'clmn01'.	51) opsg beam0	Open segment 'beam0'.

18) visg parts1,0	Make segment 'parts1' invisible.	52) valt 0,0
		   ,9000,8300
		   ,7500,1000.
			Draw vault: position X=0,Y=0, Z=9000,outer radius=8300, inner radius=7500, height=1000.

19) visg parts2,0	Make segment 'parts2' invisible.		

20) opsg clmn02	Open segment 'clmn02'.	53) valt 0,0
		   ,8500,8000
		   ,7000,2000.
			Draw vault: position X=0,Y=0, Z=8500,outer radius=8000, inner radius=7000, height=2000.

21) insg clmn01	Copy segments from 'clmn01'.		
22) clsg	Close segment 'clmn02'.		
23) opsg valt0	Open segment 'valt0'.	54) clsg	Close segment 'beam0'.

24) valt 0,0,0
   ,2500,1500
   ,1000
	Draw vault: position X=0,Y=0, Z=0,outer radius=2500,inner radius=1500, height=1000.	55) opsg beam1	Open segment 'beam1'.

		56) insg beam0	Copy segments from 'beam0'.
		57) clsg	Close segment 'beam1'.
25) clsg	Close segment 'valt0'.	58) rotz beam1 ,180,0	Rotate segment 'beam1' 180 deg. around the Z-axis from the current position.
26) rotx valt0 ,90,0	Rotate segment 'valt0' 90 degreeds around the X-axis from the current position.		
		59) opsg roof	Open segment 'roof'.

27) rotz valt0,
   ,-90,1
	Rotate segment 'valt0' -90 degreeds around the Z-axis from the current position.	60) dome 0,0,
		   10000,7500
			Draw dome: position X=0,Y=0, Z=10000, radius=7500.

		61) clsg	Close segment 'roof'.

28) tns3 valt0
   ,8500,0
   ,7000
	Move segment 'valt0' so that its handle is located at the position X=8500,Y=0,Z=7000.		

29) tns3 clmn01
   ,8000,
   ,-2000,0
	Move segment 'clmn01' so that its handle is located at the position X=8000,Y=-2000, Z=0.	62) mesh 0	Make mesh invisible.

		63) vihn 0	Make handles of segments invisible.
		64) pvnf 0	Make pivot point invisible.

30) tns3 clmn02
   ,8000
   ,2000,0
	Move segment 'clmn02' so that its handle is located at the position X=8000,Y=2000,Z=0.	65) end	End of work. Stop the system.

		66) s4336>	

Notes: Underline indicates a comment line generated by the system.
       The numbers with single parentheses indicate the order of command lines.

Table 2 Listing of command sequence used to design rotunda

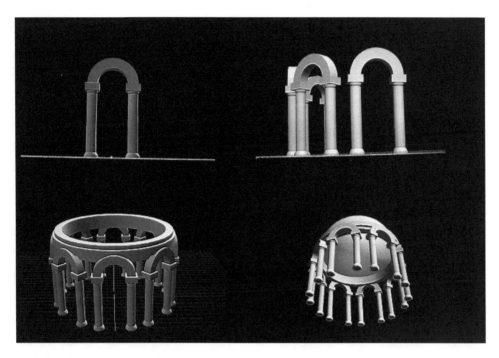

Figure 4 Perspective images generated in the process of designing rotunda

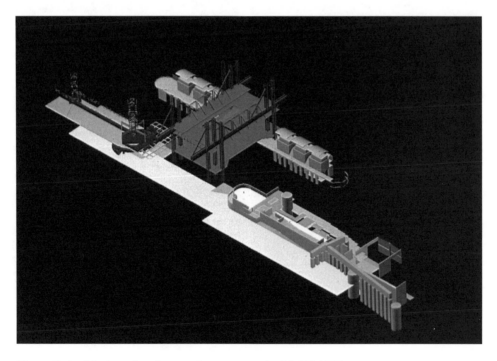

Figure 5 Aerial viewof student project generated with CAADF

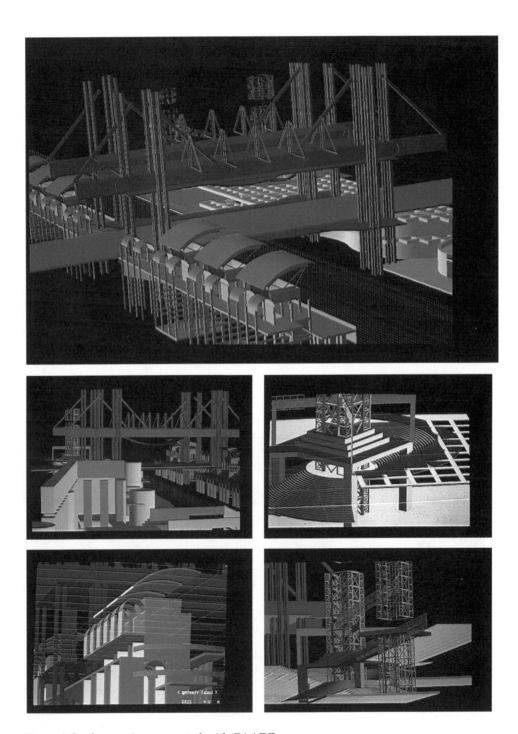

Figure 6 Student project generated with CAADF

6th week: drawing work with AutoCAD, functional check on the graphic documents, spatial design studies with CAADF , (assembly of building parts)
7th-8th week : drawing work with AutoCAD, functional check on the graphic documents, building of styrene board model for presentation
9th-10th week: drawing work with AutoCAD, building of styrene board model for presentation, finishing of presentation documents

Role of CAADF in the Design Process
During the course of his project, the student used four different media for different purposes. He began with tracing paper and pencils to design the schematic or conceptual framework of his project. He used CAADF, in the second stage, for about two weeks, mainly to design the spatial and structural image of his project. From the sixth week he started functional checks of his design with the drawing output from the AutoCAD system. In the final stage, he used styrene board models to present his project image in an urban context.

Though he used CAADF for only two weeks, it still played a very important role in the development of his design. As the photographs of his project (figures 5 and 6) show, he succeeded in designing quite dynamic spaces and complex structures that would have been very difficult to study in 2-D drawings. He also succeeded in testing various alternatives in a short period because the primitive instancing method as well as segment edit commands of CAADF allowed him to quickly model and revise. The fact that he could complete most of his complicated spatial design studies in such a short period cannot be overemphasized.

After finishing his project, the student commented that the interactive 3-D modeling in a perspective image and the local viewing utility of the workstation were quite helpful in designing complicated spaces and structures that were extended three dimensionally because he could visually test his image quite easily in the vest viewing position.

We did, however, notice a single limitation of the system, the resolution of the graphic display. Though CAADF uses a 1280 x 1080 high-resolution color graphic display, it is not still enough to present a large-scale building complex. If we want to display an image of large-scale building whose length exceeds 100 meters, each pixel must correspond to 10 centimeters. This means that if we want to display a graphic image of a large-scale building, small elements cannot be presented properly. Comparison of figures 5 and 6 shows that the total view of the student's work gives us a relatively weak impression, in spite of the energetic dynamism of his work as shown in the close- up view. It is because of this resolution problem that he used styrene board models rather than CAADF to explain his project image in the urban context.

Conclusion

In reviewing one student's work in a studio, we have discussed the advantages and disadvantages of CAADF as a tool for spatial design studies. Although the first version of CAADF has only basic object-modeling utilities, we feel confident that the system has succeeded in providing an attractive environment for spatial design studies, which is something that conventional CAD systems have not achieved. The interactive process of 3-D modeling in perspective or isometric view images and the dynamic viewing utility are the most important features of the CAADF system provides for such studies. In contrast to those advantages, we noticed a single limitation of the system: the resolution of color graphic display. The study also suggests that if sufficiently many appropriate 3-D geometric primitives are supported by the system, the primitive instancing method can significantly reduce the work entailed in object modeling.

In the future, it will be necessary to conduct studies on how to integrate the 3-D modeling system and conventional drawing utilities and how to improve the user interface of the modeling system so that the user can use graphic images on the graphic display as a guide for defining graphic primitives.

Acknowledgments

This study was supported by the Grant-in-Aid for Scientific Research from the Ministry of Education, Culture and Science: Project number 62850109.

References

Brown, G. Z., and Barbra-Jo Novitski. 1988. "A Macintosh Design Studio." *ACADIA Workshop Proceedings*, pp. 151–162.

McCullough, Malcolm. 1988. "Representation in the Computer Aided Design Studio." *ACADIA Workshop Proceedings*, pp. 163–174.

Mitchell, J. William, Robin S. Liggett, and Thomas Kvan. 1987. *The Art of Computer Graphics Programming*. New York: Van Nostrand Reinhold.

Morozumi, Mitsuo, Hirofumi Nakamura, and Yasufumi Kijima. 1989. "3-D Modeling of the Parthenon Temple." *Research Report of AIJ* (Kyuushu Branch), 31, pp. 253–256.

Nakamae, Eihachiro, and T. Nishida. 1986. *Three-Dimensional Computer Graphics*. Shoukoudou.

Tohyama, Shigeki. 1988. *Introduction to Intelligent Solid Modeling*. Ohomu-sha Co.

## 33

Color Contrast and CAAD:
The Seven Color Contrasts of Johannes Itten

Richard B. Norman

Clemson University

Computer-aided architectural design is design with color—the monitor of a CAAD system is a display of color, a place where images are produced by color manipulation. The success of these images can be judged by the ability of the colors selected to communicate graphic ideas and to convey graphic information.

Color as a visual phenomena intrigued the impressionist painters at the end of the nineteenth century; it was the focus of much attention at the Bauhaus in Weimar Germany. When Johannes Itten was appointed as a Master of Form at the Bauhaus in 1919, he developed "an aesthetic color theory originating in the experience and intuition of a painter" (Itten, 1973, 11). In his definitive work, Itten postulates seven ways to communicate visual information with color. "Each is unique in character and artistic value, in visual, expressive and symbolic effect, and together they constitute the fundamental resource of color design" (Itten, 1973, 36).

These seven contrasts provide a lexicon of the methods by which computer images convey graphic information. The colors which form a computer image can be simply manipulated to illustrate these contrasts; today's computers make color manipulation a very simple matter. This paper is composed of short essays about each of these contrasts and how they can guide the selection of appropriate colors to convey visual intent on a picture tube. Considered together the contrasts of Itten provide a fundamental resource for electronic graphic communication.

Contrast of Value

Contrast of black and white—of lightness and darkness—is the most fundamental of the visual contrasts. We have no trouble understanding the meaning of a black-and-white picture. We know that technicolor has added considerable appeal to the movies and that color in television has added appreciably to the enjoyment of home entertainment systems, but it would be difficult to argue that the introduction of color has increased the understanding of content in either film or television, more than did the simple value contrasts of their black-and-white predecessors.

What would television be if these early black-and-white images had been reduced to line drawings, to wire-frame images? Would line drawings have found the acceptance that greeted the early black-and-white pictures? If today's computer images were built with the contrasting grays of black-and-white imagery, rather than with the stick figures of wire-frame construction, they would find greater acceptance among skeptics in the world of art and architecture. The reduction of a color picture to its component areas of contrasting value is an abstraction that we are readily able to accept.

Contrast of value is fundamentally the contrast between black and white; more specifically, it is a series of contrasts between the stages of gray. While it is possible to imagine the scale of grays as an infinite series of colors, in fact the eye can discern only twenty steps with ease, perhaps forty steps with young eyes and a good visual education. These forty grays comprise the palette of all black-and-white presentations; they are a graphic language which we understand.

A scale of grays in twenty parts, perhaps more, perhaps less, can be achieved on the computer. To be useful in graphics these gray values should contain equal visual steps between each color—there should be no perceived line between two color samples where the eye moves quickly from light to dark. One should experience the visual continuum from white to black. Through Itten's careful instruction at the Bauhaus, his students cultivated an ability to write "music" with the gray scales. It takes only four or five colors. Most of us could play Beethoven's "Fifth" on a piano with only four strokes of a finger, or "Mary Had a Little Lamb" with seven. How many colors are needed on the computer to play a song on the gray scale?

Graphic images depend on the contrast of black and white in order to communicate. Compositions need not be drawn in black and white, nor with shades of gray, for the value differences that are to be found within a particular hue can be equally effective in conveying a graphic message. Yet the essential contrast, the communication of content that any composition offers, is achieved through the contrast of value.

Explorations in the use of contrasting value are an excellent introduction to computer color. Such drawings need not be dependent on extensive color capabilities, as ways can be found to draw a scale of grays on even the simplest of computers. Ideas can be communicated using solid areas of color with a strength that is difficult to achieve in line drawing, even if those colors are but shades of gray. Technically, no more is involved than turning on or off the phosphors that illuminate the screen.

Contrast of Hue

The idea of "color" is usually associated with the "hue" of an object. A color's hue is the quality that distinguishes one color from another, that distinguishes redness from blueness or yellowness from greenness. To the artist, hue is the pure substance of a pigment; science defines hue as light of a particular wavelength, a part of the visible spectrum.

Changes of hue add diversity to the world, contributing to its richness and to the uniqueness of every object in it. In its simplest form the contrast of hue is a self-evident concept; we drive or stop our cars based on the contrast of red and green. As black and white are the extremes in value contrast, so red and green represent extremes in the contrast of hue.

When we select a color to identify the different pipes in a boiler room, we would not use values—they are too relative. Instead we use hues; hot water pipes are red and cold water pipes blue. This is a comprehensible code within our culture that needs no guidebook or comparison. It draws strength from the unique qualities of red or of blue to distinguish one item from another.

Contrast of hue is the simplest of contrasts to comprehend, a fact which probably accounts for its frequent and recurring use in primitive art. In Itten's words: "The undiluted primaries and secondaries always have a character of aboriginal cosmic splendor as well as of concrete actuality. Therefore they serve equally well to portray a celestial coronation or a mundane still life" (Itten, 1973, 37).

On a simple color monitor contrast of hue may be the only option available to a designer; the colors of a rudimentary electronic palette allow few choices. These limited colors can be used to improve the business graphics that such computer equipment is designed to produce. A well-colored graph can convey several levels of meaning beyond the raw data it illustrates. Appropriate hues can be selected and combined in ways that are appealing, or perhaps upsetting, if that is the intent of the graph. Meaning can be suggested by hue selection; we all know the meaning of "red ink." Hues can be manipulated to suggest a great variety of moods.

The extraordinary palette of color available today provides an ample opportunity to contrast hues in both art and architecture. The circuit of hues is a key to forming color compositions, a chart from which to select colors according to our mood and purpose. With these colors we can form the most elementary of compositions.

Contrast of Saturation

A color is fully saturated when it is at its maximum brilliance. Though often confused with value, saturation is a very different quality of color and its use as a contrasting element produces a very different effect. Any color, that is to say any hue, has a low saturation when it approaches gray in color. Conversely, saturation is high when the coloring element is most pure. In dealing with pigment, color can be lightened or darkened to produce a change in value by mixing it with other colors. Color may also be reduced in saturation through mixing, bringing it closer to a neutral gray, but the mixing process never increases saturation—the mixture of two colors is always lower in saturation than either of its sources. Fully saturated color is an intense, vivid color that should be used sparingly.

The saturated hues are seldom seen in nature. They appear most often as the blooms of flowers or the colors of the rainbow. Maximum saturation can be found in either pure paint pigment or the phosphors that produce the colored light in a computer terminal.

The phenomena of saturation contrast and value contrast are not easily separated. Yellow, fully saturated yellow, is a very light hue; it is a brilliant color which we often think of as representing light. It cannot be made darker without desaturating the color. There is no "brilliant" dark yellow. Likewise a fully saturated blue is by nature a very dark value. It cannot be lightened without loosing its saturation. Each hue has a value at which its most saturated form is displayed. This is immutable; it is an ingrained quality of the particular hue, a part of the nature of the color.

In developing a graphic composition, or in resolving architectural colors, the control of both value and saturation is paramount to a successful coloration. A room or a building or a painting may be colored in blue or red or green; the ultimate selection of hue is largely an issue of taste, fashion, and psychology. But the selection of both value and of saturation determine readability and establish mood.

Saturation on the computer is achieved directly from red, green, and blue, the colors that form the image and therefore display the highest saturation level; mixing them can only reduce their intensity. If we want a fully saturated yellow, we form this on the computer screen by displaying red and green phosphors at the same time. The result is a brilliant yellow of the maximum achievable saturation. As a mixture it will have a lightness that surpasses either red or green; but its saturation level will be less than that of either parent color. Any color wheel drawn on the computer will show its greatest level of saturation at the color sources. Occasionally it is necessary to gray the hues of the source so that they may be equal in saturation to their adjacent hues.

The subtle as well as the obvious points of difference between value and saturation are not easily demonstrated using paints. On a computer screen these differences can be seen quickly and dramatically by adjusting the percentages of each factor. Comparative colorations of the same composition, drawn at different levels of saturation, provide an easy lesson in saturation contrast.

In articulating the contrasts of value, hue, and saturation, Johannes Itten has defined the three basic color elements that are at the foundation of human color perception. To complete his image of the nature of perception, four additional contrasts should be explored.

Cold–Warm Contrast

You have a good understanding of cold–warm contrast if you enjoy swimming. A lake can feel very cold in the heat of the day; but if you return at midnight when the air has chilled, the same water will feel much warmer. There is a warmth to this midnight water that could not be found because the heat of the sun. We are constantly exposed to the contrast of cold and warmth as we move from heated to cooled and then to natural environments. It is always a relative experience; one place is always colder, or warmer, than another.

This same contrast can be found in color, for every color is perceived as having a temperature. It is no accident that the hot pipes in a plumbing installation are colored red and cold pipes are colored blue. Red is warmer than blue. It has been proven that a room painted red feels warmer than a room painted blue. But color temperature, like water temperature, is relative. One color may be warm in contrast to another, but cool in contrast to a third.

On the computer, cold–warm contrast provides a good graphic method for indicating depth in an illustration. The color of a surface in sunlight appears warmer than the same surface color in shade. The layering of sunlight and shade, of warm and cool, can create steps in the field of vision which are perceived as depth. A scenario can be built into a graphic composition by looking through a dark frame into a field of sunlight, and then into the shadows beyond.

In the design of buildings, architects can lead people through a series of spaces that derive their qualities from their spatial contrasts—low spaces contrast with high ones, big spaces with small ones. As the coloration is developed for architectural spaces, they too can distinguish themselves by their color temperature. It is always a pleasure to move from a cool hallway into a room filled with sun. One must be careful to discern between cold–warm contrast and contrast of value, for while they often go hand-in-hand, both emotionally and physically they are quite different.

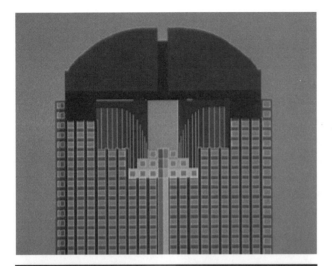

Figure 1
Contrast of Value.
graphic design by
Steven Blisnuk

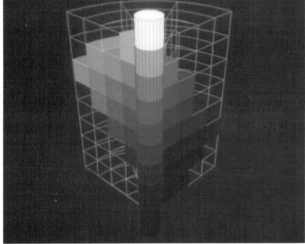

Figure 2
Color Space
graphic design by
John M. Young, Jr.

Figure 3
Contrast of Saturation
graphic design by
Paul Meyer

Complementary Contrast

Complementary colors appear on opposite sides of the color wheel. They are contrasting hues; often one is cool and the other is warm. There are an infinite number of complementary pairs arranged around the wheel.

If the colors are true complements, truly opposite colors, then they combine to neutralize each other and form a middle gray. This can be proven using the computer to draw a simple checkerboard of color. If the colors are complements, pure red and pure cyan for example, they will be seen as gray. If the scale of the checkerboard is sufficiently small, this gray will be apparent at arm's length; if the board is sized for a game of checkers, then you may have to back up across the room for this to happen. But when the scale of the color mixture becomes small enough so that it is seen as one color, the perception of the mixture is gray. On a computer this provides a good test of whether two colors are actually complementary.

The definition of two colors as complements and the visual effect achieved by their contrast are entirely different from that of a cold–warm contrast. When the scale of mixture is sufficiently small, the colors cancel each other; but when the scale is adequate, then the colors intensify each other to their greatest brilliance. As Itten describes them: "Two such colors make a strange pair. They are opposite, they require each other. They incite each other to maximum vividness when adjacent; and they annihilate each other, to gray-black, when mixed—like fire and water" (Itten, 1973, 78).

The eye seems to require a balance of complements, and it is probably the best understood of all color principles. It is a common method of color harmony in interior design; and when faced with a problem in color selection, architects are well advised to begin the search for harmony by turning to complementary contrast, though many a freshman color scheme has been devastated by an overdose of fully saturated complements. Well used, the demand of one color for another can be a forceful design tool.

Simultaneous Contrast

Sometimes the complement for a color is not to be found in a composition, in which case the stage is set for that most mysterious of color phenomena, simultaneous contrast. The psychological demand for the complementary color, like the demand for balance in all composition, is compulsive—it seems to be a rule of vision that the eye, seeing one color, will demand its complement. If it is not there the mind will generate the color spontaneously. "The simultaneously generated complementary occurs as a sensation in the eye of the beholder, and is not objectively present. It cannot be photographed" (Itten, 1973, 87).

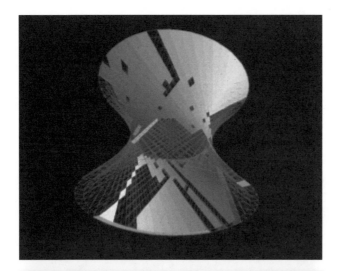

Figure 4
Parabolic Villa
graphic design by
Steven Blisnuk

Figure 5
Simultaneous Contrast
graphic design by
John L. Ciccarelli Jr.

The spontaneous generation of color is explained by your eye's ability to develop and retain afterimages. If you look intensely at an area of color, a portion of the receivers in your eye will become fatigued, and you will temporarily lose the ability to see that particular hue. If you then change your gaze to a white surface, the image you have been looking at will appear, ghosted, in its complementary color. This is called an afterimage; it results because you can no longer see the original color. The white surface, robbed by your eye of this one hue, appears for a while as the remaining hues—the complement of the original color.

This phenomena occurs when you look at any drawing; the colors that you experience quickly fatigue portions of your eye. Afterimages appear that change the way you see the other colors in the composition. Computer images, because of their intensity, form afterimages very quickly.

Simultaneous contrast is generated in a drawing by using two major hues that are not complements and do not create balance by the rule of complements. Each color will cause an afterimage, generating its complement. The interaction between the afterimage and the opposite color produces a vibrancy in the eye— a color tension that comes from the simultaneous generation of a complement. The colors seem to dance with activity as each is intensified by the absence of the other.

These simultaneous contrasts can draw attention to compositions, or to portions of compositions. They can either damage or enhance the message a picture conveys. By understanding the mechanism of simultaneous contrast, it is possible to select colors that anticipate its effect.

Contrast of Size

There is one more contrast in this long list—the contrast of size, or in Itten's words, "contrast of extension. . .the contrast between much and little, or great and small" (Itten, 1973, 104). It is the architect's greatest friend, for it applies as much to the design of space as to the selection of color. The facade of Chartres Cathedral is often cited for the contrast of its two towers, one big and transparent, the other smaller and more solid.

Contrast of size has been essential to several of the contrasts already mentioned, for no composition can be called balanced without a consideration of the size of its elements. One could develop a general rule calling for a small amount of strong color to balance a larger quantity of weak color, defining "strong" and "weak" as contrast of either value, hue, or saturation. Coupled with simultaneous contrast, a contrast of size can effectively give emphasis to a particular color. Likewise a large, cold space can contain a small area of warmth, all achieved with color.

It could be concluded that the contrasts of Johannes Itten seldom stand alone; in virtually every example there are elements of another. But in color design as in any art there is a focus, a theme, to every composition. In teaching the art of computation, the seven contrasts can provide that color theme. Simple exercises can be structured that focus on design basics and are expressed electronically with color. To attempt an isolated example of each contrast, as a learning experience, is a task that can be achieved relatively quickly using the computer. It is an excellent way both to develop a color vocabulary and to learn the fundamentals of design.

The unique advantage of achieving color studies with CAAD is the comparative methodology that the computer provides. Iteration of a design is a simple task, and the colors of copies can be quickly changed. Comparative color study is made easy and accessible. Both colors and the effects of each color contrast can be tested with an efficiency that makes the procedure feasible.

The successful colorist will understand each of these contrasts, orchestrating them to advantage by occasionally featuring the "flutes," sometimes the "violins," as each is called upon to do what it does best. With the development of color graphic computers, the color tool that was needed by Johannes Itten now exists. Color studies that once took days can now be done in minutes. Itten's theories can now be tested with a persistence that was not feasible before the availability of electronic color. Once these fundamentals of graphic communication are learned, they quickly find their place in the design studio.

References

Itten, Johannes. 1973 [1961]. *The Art of Color: The subjective experience and objective rationale of color*. Tr. Ernst Van. New York: Van Nostrand Reinhold.

Whitford, Frank. 1984. *Bauhaus*. London: Thames and Hudson.

Afterword:
The Design Studio of The Future

William J. Mitchell

Harvard University Graduate School of Design

Then

Things began to change in the mid-1940s, though architects hardly noticed. Scientists and engineers started to speculate that the new electronic technologies which had emerged in the wartime years would profoundly change the character of intellectual work. Vannevar Bush (1945) imagined a device called the *Memex*, which would function as a personal information server (figure 1). By the 1950s computers were becoming a commercial reality, and in 1956 *Fortune* magazine published a remarkably prescient depiction of a machine that we can now recognize as a computer-aided design workstation—complete with graphic input devices and a multi-window display showing different views of a three-dimensional object (figure 2). These wonderful machines were never built, much less put to any practical use, but they established a powerful idea.

In the early 1960s there was sufficient international interest to prompt the question, from Moscow *Pravda* (Sinyakov, 1962), "Can a machine create a design?" As if in reply, Steven Coons (1963) outlined the functions of a CAD system in considerable detail, and working prototypes began to appear. At MIT Ivan Sutherland (1963) built *Sketchpad*, and produced a memorable film sequence showing a designer (himself) manipulating an interactive graphic display with a lightpen. Architects could imagine themselves doing that, and a few became enthralled with the idea. *Sketchpad*-like systems with an architectural flavor were soon developed. At Cambridge University, for example, William Newman (1966) implemented one that allowed an architect to select and assemble elements from an industrialized component building system. Timothy Johnson (1963) extended the *Sketchpad* idea to three dimensions. By the end of the decade there were actually a few computer-aided design systems in practical use in architectural offices (Ray-Jones, 1968)

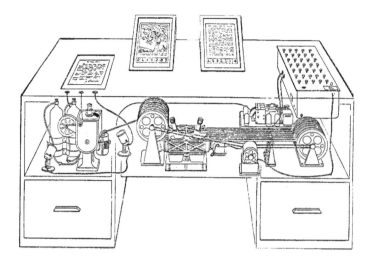

Figure 1   A 1945 artist's conception of a personal information
server. (From *Life* magazine, September 1945)

Figure 2   A 1956 artist's conception of a CAD workstation. (From
Fortune magazine, November 1956)

These first-generation CAD systems were driven by mainframe computers and had refreshed-vector displays—expensive technology by any standards. They were delicate devices that required special air-conditioned environments, represented major capital investments, needed specialized operators, and could only be cost-justified if they were used continuously and very intensively. They did not fit gracefully into design studios, and it is hard to imagine that designers could ever have been very comfortable with them.

A second generation of CAD systems arrived to mark the beginning of the 1970s. Systems of this generation were driven by 16-bit minicomputers (such as the DEC PDP-11) and usually had storage-tube displays. They were more compact, more robust, had a better cost-performance ratio, and provided the vehicle for emergence of the turnkey CAD system industry. Among the first minicomputer turnkey vendors to achieve substantial success with their products were Computervision, Applicon, Autotrol, and Calma. A few of the early products of this industry found their way into large U.S. architectural offices, but their effect on day-to-day design practice was fairly negligible. In Britain, large public-sector construction organizations, with repetitive building programs, provided a context for more effective use of this generation of CAD technology (Mitchell, 1977): among the specialized systems that were developed to serve these organizations were CEDAR (Property Services Agency), HARNESS (Department of Health and Social Security), OXSYS (Oxford Area Health Board), CARBS (Clwyd County Council), and SSHA (Scottish Special Housing Association).

The turnkey CAD system industry began to boom when a third generation of CAD technology appeared at the beginning of the 1980s. New 32-bit supermini computers (such as the DEC Vax), running sophisticated operating systems, replaced the 16-bit minis. As memory costs dropped, high-resolution raster displays replaced storage tubes. CAD system software, in this environment, became extensive and complex—often running to hundreds of thousands of lines of code, and requiring many volumes of technical documentation. Strong men were needed to lift the huge diskpacks on which many of these systems were delivered. The systems were large, impressive-looking, and expensive—typically costing as much per seat per year as the salaries of two or three middle-level employees. This meant that they had to be used very intensively if they were to be profitable investments. Many large architecture and architecture/engineering firms installed them, and used them in multi-shift production drafting applications. Specialist operators were commonly employed, and computer operations were often kept organizationally and physically distinct from the design studios. A few schools of architecture managed to acquire third-generation systems, and pioneered their use in studio teaching—but this was usually regarded as a peripheral and experimental activity, and there was little integration into the general curriculum.

Meanwhile, the first inexpensive personal computers appeared. Eight-bit personal computers first emerged in the mid-1970s, were popularized in the late seventies by vendors such as Apple, Radio Shack, and Commodore, and peaked in popularity in 1981/82. These machines were far too low-powered to perform any useful CAD functions, but they established the idea of personal computing and provided the foundation for growth of a large industry. They were displaced in the mid-1980s by a generation of sixteen-bit machines—most notably the IBM PC and its clones, and the Apple Macintosh—which had more speed and memory, could be equipped with hard disks, and could provide fairly acceptable graphics performance. The Macintosh also introduced to a broad public the mouse-and-windows style of interaction (which had been developed much earlier at the Xerox Palo Alto Research Center).

In everything except cost, early sixteen-bit personal computers were far inferior to 32-bit superminis as environments for implementation of CAD systems. But they *were* affordable by individuals and small organizations—in particular, the thousands of small architecture and engineering consulting firms that exist in the United States. Their success created, for the first time, the possibility of a mass-market for CAD systems. Entrepreneurs were quick to realize this. A fourth generation of simplified CAD systems, offering a subset of the functions of large third-generation systems, and performance limited by the capacities of sixteen-bit, single-user machines, appeared on the market priced in the one thousand to ten thousand dollar range. (By 1989 many capable CAD systems were priced at less than a thousand dollars per copy.) The Autocad system, particularly, gained wide and rapid acceptance: it was first marketed in 1982, and by 1989 more than two hundred thousand copies had been sold. Its use became commonplace in small architectural and engineering firms and in many schools of architecture: for a great many architects, engineers, drafting technicians, and students, it provided a first, relatively easy and inexpensive practical introduction to CAD.

Another effect of fourth-generation, personal computer CAD was to change the pattern of CAD software marketing, training in its use, and technical support. Vendors of earlier generations of systems had usually developed direct sales organizations, and were prepared to put a large amount of effort into discussing a particular client's needs and tailoring a system to suit. They typically provided extensive user training, and sophisticated support to each installation. By contrast, personal computer CAD vendors sold simplified, standardized products through the mail, or through dealer networks, and relied on this simplification and standardization to minimize the need for installation, training, and support services. The software was delivered on floppy disks in small shrink-wrapped packages, and users typically installed it themselves.

The negative effect of fourth-generation CAD was to establish a banal and simplistic conception of CAD functions and style of interaction in the minds of many architects. CAD systems were now seen, by most professionals and teachers of architecture, as the graphic equivalent of word processors—rather simple devices for input, editing, and production of graphic (rather than text) documents. The theoretical foundations of these systems (which had been established a quarter of a century before, and contained much that was problematic) remained mostly unexamined, and the wider possibilities were largely ignored.

As the flood of personal computer CAD software grew, yet another combination of technologies was emerging to provide the foundation for a fifth generation of CAD systems. Powerful graphic workstations that could be combined into networks began to appear. The first of these was the Three Rivers Perq—a sophisticated but expensive machine that came on the market in 1989, but never achieved widespread success. Apollo workstations appeared in 1980, and the first Suns in 1982. The workstation market grew very rapidly through the 80s as performance improved and costs dropped. As the end of the decade approached, the distinction between personal computers and workstations was becoming blurred as costs of some workstations dropped to personal computer levels, and as the speed and sophistication of some personal computers rose into the workstation range.

Networks provide an attractive environment for CAD because they combine the advantages of centralized timesharing systems with the advantages of the personal computer. Like a timesharing system they can provide access to centrally maintained files and software, communication between users, and the possibility of sharing use of expensive pieces of equipment such as large plotters. But, like personal computers, workstations can support a fast and fluid style of graphic interaction.

CAD system vendors from both ends of the industry reacted to the emergence of workstation network technology by adapting their products to it. Many of the large systems that had originally been developed for mainframes or minicomputers were rewritten to run on workstations, with some functions handled locally at the workstation and some at a central server. Some personal computer systems were upgraded to take advantage of the greater speed and capacity, more sophisticated operating systems, communications capabilities, and better graphics that workstations offered. And of course there were some ambitious new systems, such as IBM's AES, designed specifically for workstation networks.

Now (at the GSD)

Since 1987 the Harvard Graduate School of Design has been engaged in incremental development of a CAD network to support teaching and research in architecture, landscape architecture, and urban design and planning. This network is designed to grow over time as CAD becomes increasingly integral to the design professions, to support a heterogeneous mix of technologies and products from different vendors, and to allow for smooth integration of new technologies as these emerge. Its organization and functions will evolve as computer, communications, and media technologies continue to develop, and as we gain experience with its use.

At this stage in the development of CAD technology, specialized CAD laboratories make as little sense as specialized pencil laboratories: it is no longer essential to confine machines to controlled environments, so we can make design tools available in the usual places for doing design work. (We should deliver the technology to designers where they need it, not force designers to go to the technology.) Accordingly, workstations are distributed throughout the GSD. Most of them are in the design studios. We expect gradual evolution of a studio environment in which a computer workstation is as normal a part of a student desk as a parallel rule or a drafting lamp.

Currently (1989) there is a Sun 386i server at the heart of the network, and connection is provided by Ethernet carried on coaxial cable. Workstations and personal computers in the network cover a broad spectrum: a Sun 4, Computervision Suns, Sun 386is, IBM RTs, PS/2s, and PCs, Macintosh IIs, and some older Macintosh Plus machines. The strategy is to provide a large number of inexpensive workstations to perform relatively simple tasks, a smaller number of more sophisticated and expensive workstations to perform more demanding tasks, and where necessary, highly specialized workstations to perform certain specific functions. There is, for example, a Macintosh II configured with a slide scanner, a flatbed scanner, and a digital film recorder, to perform image input and output functions, and there is another configured with devices for input and output of running video.

Our approach to providing application software is guided by the metaphor of the research library and the reading list rather that that of the standardized textbook. We avoid forcing everybody to approach a task in the same way, using the same constructs and techniques. Instead, we attempt to provide ranges of options, to develop in students the capacity to evaluate tools and technologies critically, and to make intelligent choices from among the available possibilities. (The ability to do this is a far more important component of professional competence than skill in application of some particular piece of software that may well be obsolete before the student graduates.)   Students may decide, for example, whether they want to invest substantial time and effort in learning Unix capabilities and commands, or whether they can accomplish what they want within the simpler Macintosh or DOS environments. If they want to manipulate some bitmapped images they may choose to work with a very simple paint system on a Macintosh Plus, intermediate-level systems like Pixelpaint or Photomac on a Macintosh II, or the sophisticated but demanding Artisan system on a Sun 386i. If they want to do some three-dimensional geometric modeling they may choose a simple sketch tool like Modelshop, a widely-used low-end system like Autocad, or a higher-end system like Computervision or AES.

Perhaps even more important than the possibility of choosing among different computer tools to perform the same task is the capability to combine tools freely in order to accomplish results that no single one could provide individually (figure 3). A designer might, for example, begin modeling a building with simple software on an inexpensive workstation, transfer the database to a more sophisticated modeler on a more powerful workstation for more detailed development, transfer again to a specialized rendering system to produce realistic shaded images, move the resulting bitmapped images to a paint and image processing system for retouching and blending with scanned images of the site, and finally send the images to a video

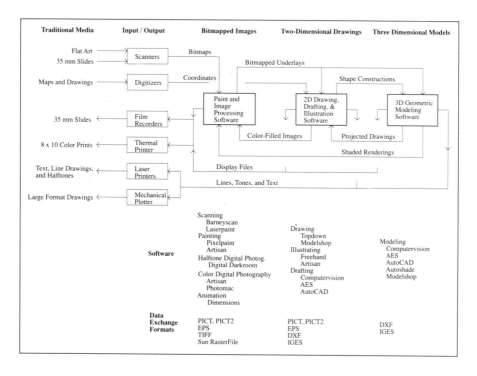

Figure 3   A 1989 conception of a CAD network, as implemented at the Harvard Graduate School of Design.

editing station for integration into a video presentation. Increasingly, software packages provide ranges of import and export formats and device drivers to support this, multi-format graphics translators such as are now available, and there is growing acceptance of standard exchange formats such as IGES, but we have also found that we must often devote extensive effort to writing file translators and device drivers needed to integrate a new device or piece of software into the network.

A complete functional overview of a well-developed network cannot easily be given in a single diagram: the web of interconnections between functional elements become too complex. But slices can be cut through, in various ways, to illustrate different aspects of function. Figure 3, for example, shows how traditional graphic media (drawings, slides, and photographs), bitmapped images, two-dimensional vector drawings, and three-dimensional geometric models are interrelated in the GSD network. The accompanying examples of recent student design work suggest something of what these interconnections mean. Figure 4 shows exploratory sketches made by drawing with pencil and marker on laser prints output from a drafting system. The sectional perspectives in figure 5 were produced by a high-end three-dimensional modeler. The studies of proposals in context shown in figure 6 were made by combining synthesized building images from three-dimensional modelers with scanned images of sites, then using paint and image processing operations to clean up the result. The student who produced the doorway designs shown in figure 7 first modeled basic geometry in Autocad, then performed simple cosine shading with Autoshade, next scanned slides to generate a palette of material textures, and finally used a paint system to make quick sketches of alternatives by brushing lines and textures over shaded images.

Figure 4   Examples of design sketches made over laser prints. (Branko Kolarevic)

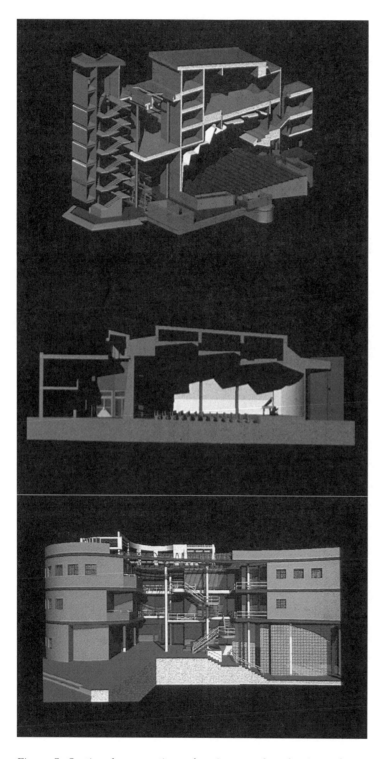

Figure 5. Sectional perspectives of projects produced using a three-dimensional modeler. (Donald C. Cook, Leandro Madrazo, Daniel Tsai)

Figure 6   Studies of projects in context made by blending synthesized images with scanned images. (Daniel Tsai, James Davidson, Nancy Cheng, Doo-Ho Sohn, Branko Kolarevic, Donald C. Cook)

Figure 7   Exploratory sketches made by painting over simple shaded images with a copy brush   (Jerzy Wojtowicz)

Soon

Marvin Minsky (1985) has used the metaphor "society of mind" to suggest ways that complex intellectual processes can be carried out by collections of interacting intelligent agents. More narrowly, we can usefully employ "society of design" as a guiding metaphor for speculation about design environments of the immediate future. With this in view, I shall venture some predictions.

Designers and students of design will soon come to regard computer networks as indispensable utilities, and workstations will be as standard on their desks as telephones. These workstations will provide tools for accessing, manipulating, and disseminating information in a wide variety of forms: text files, numeric databases, geometric models, bitmapped images, sound bites, and video clips: after nearly half a century the *Memex* idea will become reality. Separations between different forms of information will disappear: sound effects might be associated with spaces in a geometric model of a building, sound notes with elements in a drawing, or video clips with technical information in a construction products database.

Modes of interaction will become richer and more various than they are now. Only a few years ago interaction with a CAD system usually meant typing in command lines, in arcane syntax, to laboriously edit static, two-dimensional line drawings on dim storage tube displays. Now it is commonplace to manipulate three-dimensional models, which can be displayed shaded and in color, via much more fluid and intuitive point-and-click interfaces. Real-time movement through complex shaded scenes and real-time parametric variation of complex three-dimensional objects (Danahy, 1989) will soon be standard. Stereoscopic displays and three-dimensional input devices such as the dataglove will allow escape from the picture plane where this seems desirable. (It isn't always: simple, two-dimensional line drawings are often useful to designers precisely because they *are* so abstract and ambiguous.) There will be more input and output channels in simultaneous operation—speech input and output in parallel with graphics and text, for example.

Realistic rendering of details, spaces, and buildings in context will no longer be extremely expensive to generate—as they have been until very recently. Even low-end CAD systems now routinely provide cosine-shaded perspectives. Moderately priced workstations such as the Personal Iris have become sufficiently powerful to produce complex images with texture mapping and global illumination effects (Greenberg, 1989) in acceptable amounts of time for practical design purposes. This will not only enable more effective presentation of designs, but also allow designers to make extensive, routine use of realistic views in the close study of design alternatives.

The databases of architectural modelers will become more sophisticated. Where today's systems represent buildings as collections of lines, surfaces, or closed solids organized into layers, future systems will provide for multiple simultaneous representations of components and subsystems. For example Eastman (1989) has discussed building modelers in which architectural objects have multiple descriptions or views: solid models, default views for plan and section, symbols with centerlines, and so on. As designers become more sophisticated about the organization of design information the simple idea of layering will seem increasingly inadequate: designers will want to associate properties with architectural objects in complex ways, to incorporate procedural elements in designs, to make use of default values and inheritance through use of constructs such as frames and object-oriented programming, and to select and recombine graphic information using relational databases, SQL commands, and so on. Stiny (1989) has suggested a more radical possibility: that multiple design descriptions might be constructed in multiple algebras which are combined in Cartesian products such that linked computations of different aspects of shape information (plan, elevation, section, solid), functional descriptions, assembly instructions, and so on are carried out in parallel.

Specialized network nodes will efficiently provide sophisticated services to large numbers of users. A high-speed graphics processor might, for example, do nothing but produce compute-intensive ray-traced or radiosity renderings from files of geometric data submitted through the network. Another node (like a consulting firm) might deal with structural aspects of designs, another with mechanical aspects, and so on. The different nodes might communicate by simple file transfer, but there are some more interesting possibilities as well. Different nodes might, for example, run different knowledge-based systems that develop different aspects of a design in parallel, using a blackboard system or something similar to receive messages about the evolving work at other nodes and to post requests to other nodes for needed information (Fenves et al, 1988).

Electronic media and information servers integrated into networks will supplant traditional libraries in a broadening range of functions. It is no longer prohibitively expensive, for example, to convert architectural slide libraries to videodisc, and to attach videodisc players to workstations to provide immediate access right in the studio environment (Purcell 1989, Van Bakergem 1989). Video images have quality limitations, but these can be overcome by storing images in digital format in media such as CD ROM. As the technology for handling digital images matures (and it is doing so rapidly) it will be increasingly attractive to replace slide libraries with image servers that maintain image collections and provide access via any of the workstations in the network. (A slide carousel is, after all, just a slow, low-capacity, single-user disk storage system.) In this context there is no need to interpret the idea of an electronic "slide" too narrowly: the collection might include not only bitmapped still images, but also video clips and sound bites.

Electronic "slides" do not just passively provide reference information: they are available for computer manipulation. For example satellite images can be processed to extract site information, videodisc movie-maps of sites can provide frames for combination with synthesized views of design proposals, and history slides can be processed to produce reconstructions (figure 8).

Collections of three-dimensional geometric models are also likely to become increasingly important. These might be disseminated on CD ROM, or from a server through a network—it doesn't much matter. Models that an architect might need include context models of urban environments, precedent models of important buildings, and extensive libraries of construction components and subsystems. A designer might scan these libraries to find interesting pieces, collect a "shopping cart" of them for current use, and instantiate them in a project model as required.

Eventually, networks will serve not only images and models, but also knowledge-bases for selecting pieces and putting them together to generate various types of designs (Eastman, 1989, Geilingh 1988, Mitchell, Liggett, and Tan 1989, Turner 1988). A designer might shop for relevant knowledge-bases—collections of facts and rules that seem to bear on the current situation—as for

Figure 8 Images of Palladio's Loggia del Capitaniato in Vicenza (left) and computer reconstructions (using image processing techniques) of the intended scheme (Branko Kolarevic)

images or models, then use chosen ones as tools to develop the project. Much of the intellectual capital of a design organization may reside in its knowledge bases. Prominent designers may franchise themselves by making available knowledge bases that capture their characteristic ways of doing things. (A system for designing wooden decks has already been franchised to hardware stores, and systems for design of more complex structures cannot be far behind.)

Conclusion

Computer-aided design technology has passed through many metamorphoses in the three decades since it was first imagined, and it will pass through more before the century is out. Early CAD systems, inevitably, automated manual design functions in much the same quaintly literal way that a player piano automated the functions of the pianist's fingers: sketching with a pencil on paper was replaced by sketching with a lightpen on a display surface (to be followed with careful ink drafting by a motor-driven pen). But even the earliest systems contained the seeds of far more radical ideas. Realization of these ideas will fundamentally alter the conditions of production of architecture, standards of architectural discourse and judgement, and approaches to architectural education (Mitchell 1989)

Future CAD environments will bear as little resemblance to the first prototypes as modern music reproduction devices (like the portable CD players favored by joggers) bear to player pianos. As we discover unanticipated new needs and uses for them we will think it just as well—as thoughtful joggers must occasionally be grateful that they don't have player pianos strapped to their backs.

References

Bush, Vannevar. 1945. "As We May Think." *Atlantic Monthly*, July: 101-108.

Coons, Steven A. 1963. "An Outline of the Requirements for a Computer-Aided Design System." In *Proceedings of the 1963 Spring Joint Computer Conference*. Baltimore, Maryland: Spartan Books.

Danahy, John. 1989. "Irises in a Landscape." This volume.

Eastman, Charles. 1989. "Why Are We Here and Where Are We Going: The Evolution of CAD." In Chris Yessios (ed.), *New Ideas and Directions for the 1990s: Proceedings of the 9th Annual Conference of the Association for Computer-Aided Design in Architecture*. Gainsville, Florida.

Fenves, S., U. Flemming, C. Hendrickson, M. L. Maher, and G. Schmitt. 1988. "An Integrated Software Environment for Building Design and Construction." In *Proceedings of the Fifth Conference on Computing in Civil Engineering.* American Society of Civil Engineers.

Geilingh, Wim. 1988. *General AEC Reference Model (GARM).* ISO TC184/SC4 Document 3.2.2.1 (draft). TNO-IBBC.

Greenberg, Donald. 1989. "Light Reflection Models for Computer Graphics." *Science,* 244: 14, pp 166-73.

Johnson, Timothy. 1963. "Sketchpad 3: A Computer Program for Drawing in 3-Dimensions." In *Proceedings of the 1963 Spring Joint Computer Conference.* Baltimore, Maryland: Spartan Books.

Minsky, Marvin. 1985. *The Society of Mind.* New York: Simon and Schuster.

Mitchell, William J. 1977. *Computer-Aided Architectural Design.* New York: Van Nostrand Reinhold.

Mitchell, William J. 1989. "Architecture and the Second Industrial Revolution." *The Harvard Architecture Review,* 7: 166-75.

Mitchell, William, Robin S. Liggett, and Milton Tan. 1989. "Top-down Knowledge-based Design." This volume.

Newman, William M. 1966. "An Experimental Program for Architectural Design." *Computer Journal* 9: 21-26.

Purcell, Patrick. 1989. "LIght Table: An Interface to Visual Information Systems ." This volume.

Ray-Jones, A. 1968. "Computer Development in West Sussex." *Architect's Journal,* 12 February: 42.

Sinyakov, Y. 1962. "Can a Machine Create a Design?" *Moskovskaya Pravda,* 5 July 1962.

Stiny, George. 1989. "What Is a Design?" In Chris Yessios (ed.), *New Ideas and Directions for the 1990s: Proceedings of the 9th Annual Conference of the Association for Computer-Aided Design in Architecture.* Gainsville, Florida.

Sutherland, Ivan E. 1963. "Sketchpad: A Man-Machine Graphical Communication System." In *Proceedings of the 1963 Spring Joint Computer Conference.* Baltimore, Maryland: Spartan Books.

Turner, J. A. 1988. "A Systems Approach to the Conceptual Modeling of Buildings." In Per Christensen (ed.), *CIB Conference on CAD.* TC 5.2 and 7.8. Lund, Sweden.

Van Bakergem, Dave. 1989. "Image Collections for the Design Studio." This volume.

Index

Abdul Aziz, Azizan, 316

Abstraction, 335-336, 451

Accuracy, levels of, 221

Adelson, R.P., cit, 182, 190

Adey, R., cit, 53

Akin, Ömer, 301-316

Akscyn, Robert, cit, 285, 286, 293, 295, 297

Albarn, K, cit, 107

Alexander, C. , cit, 107, 108, 113

Alias Research, Inc., 375

Allegro Object Lisp, 119

Altman, Henry, 316

Alves, M., cit, 130

Ambiguity, 1, 5, 10, 18-20, 26-27, 64, 153

Analysis procedure, 11

Anderson, John, cit, 409

Ando, T., 443

Animation, 239, 241, 393, see also *Movies*

Apple Computer, Inc., 120, 375

Applebaum, Dan, 229-238

Appleyard, Donald, 429, cit, 107

Archer, L.B. , cit, 108

Architectural design, uniqueness, 216-217

Architecture
  infill, 43-44
  layered, 41-42
  mass, 38-39
  panel, 39-40
  wall, 34

Architekturabteilung, ETH Zurich, 77

Argumentation, 247-248, 252-254

Aristotle, 446

Arizona State University, College of Architecture and Environmental Design, 427, 429

Arnheim, Rudolf, cit, 108, 205, 394

Athena, Project, 230-231

Atkinson, Bill, 285

Attributes, 100

Australian Research Grants Scheme, 198

AutoCAD, 2, 73, 80, 88, 246, 353, 365-366, 390, 417, 482, 485

Autodesk, Inc., 375, 425

Autolisp, 88-89, 365-366

Automation, as strategic investment, 328

Autotrol Technology, 378

Baker, G.H., cit, 174

Baldenegro, Maria, 340

Bateman, Ron, 419

Begeman, Michael, 251

Behavior, 50, 128-129

Benet, S.V., cit, 427-439

Berkeley Environmental Simulation Laboratory, 429

Birkeland, Hal, 238

Bitmapped graphics, 64

Blisnuk, Steven, 474, 476

Bongard, A. , cit, 107

Borges, Jorge Luis, 334

Borkin, Harold, cit, 13

Borning, A.H., cit, 126

Bosselmann, Peter, 429

Boston Project, 231,237

Botta, M., 380, 384, 443

Boutin, Paul, 238

Brewer, Ron, cit, 284

Brown, Peter J., 285

Bruegmann, R., cit, 417

Bush, Vannevar, 479

Bwint, S., 384

CAAD Education, see *Education*

CAD
  and studio environment, 483
  future, 485-487
  history, 50, 479-482
  systems, integration with Topdown, 146
  see also *Drafting Systems* and *Modeling*

California, University of, Los Angeles, Graduate School of Architecture and Urban Planning, 17, 137, 139, 363

Calvino, Italo, cit, 335, 337, 345

Cambridge University, 479

Campi, Mario, 88

DATE DUE

5/12/91 IL: 744572		
AUG - 6 1991		
DEC 20 1991		
APR - 5 1992		
DEC 21 1992		
FEB ? 6 1994		
May 25		
MAY 4 1995		
DEC 1 6 2005		
GAYLORD		PRINTED IN U.S.A.